# THE GREENWOOD COMPANION TO

# Shakespeare

## THE GREENWOOD COMPANION TO

# Shakespeare

## A COMPREHENSIVE GUIDE FOR STUDENTS

### Volume III

The Tragedies

### EDITED BY
### JOSEPH ROSENBLUM

GREENWOOD PRESS
Westport, Connecticut • London

**Library of Congress Cataloging-in-Publication Data**

The Greenwood companion to Shakespeare : a comprehensive guide for students / edited by Joseph Rosenblum.

    p.   cm.

    Includes bibliographical references and index.

    ISBN 0–313–32779–3 (set : alk. paper)—ISBN 0–313–32780–7 (v. 1 : alk. paper)—
ISBN 0–313–32781–5 (v. 2 : alk. paper)—ISBN 0–313–32782–3 (v. 3 : alk. paper)—
ISBN 0–313–32788–2 (v. 4 : alk. paper)   1. Shakespeare, William, 1564–1616—Criticism and interpretation—Handbooks, manuals, etc.   2. Shakespeare, William, 1564–1616—Examinations—Study guides.   I. Rosenblum, Joseph.

    PR2976.G739   2005

    822.3′3—dc22      2004028690

British Library Cataloguing in Publication Data is available.

Library of Congress Catalog Card Number: 2004028690
ISBN: 0–313–32779–3 (set)
      0–313–32780–7 (vol. I)
      0–313–32781–5 (vol. II)
      0–313–32782–3 (vol. III)
      0–313–32788–2 (vol. IV)

First published in 2005

Greenwood Press, 88 Post Road West, Westport, CT 06881
An imprint of Greenwood Publishing Group, Inc.
www.greenwood.com

Printed in the United States of America

The paper used in this book complies with the Permanent Paper Standard issued by the National Information Standards Organization (Z39.48–1984).

10  9 8 7 6 5 4 3 2 1

To Ida

Thou art the nonpareil

# Contents

## VOLUME I
## OVERVIEWS AND THE HISTORY PLAYS

### OVERVIEWS

### THE HISTORY PLAYS

## VOLUME II
## THE COMEDIES

# VOLUME III

# THE TRAGEDIES

# VOLUME IV

# THE ROMANCES AND POETRY

## THE ROMANCE PLAYS

## THE SONNETS

## THE LONG POEMS

# Alphabetical List of Plays and Poems

## The Plays

# A Preface for Users

O for a Muse of fire, that would ascend
The brightest heaven of invention!

*(Henry V*, Prologue, 1–2)

In the latter half of the seventeenth century, John Dryden revised William Shakespeare's *Troilus and Cressida*. Explaining why he tampered with the text of the man he had called "divine," Dryden wrote,

> It must be allowed to the present age, that the tongue in general is so much refined since Shakespeare's time, that many of his words, and more of his phrases, are scarce intelligible. And of those which are understood, some are ungrammatical, others coarse; and his whole style is so pestered with figurative expressions, that it is as affected as it is obscure.

The twenty-first-century student of Shakespeare will likely concur with Dryden's judgment. Shakespeare is hard. Even seasoned scholars differ on subjects ranging from the meaning of individual words to the implications of entire plays. No wonder, then, if high school students, undergraduates, and general readers are sometimes puzzled as they read one of Shakespeare's works or watch one of his plays. Literally thousands of studies of Shakespeare are published each year and recorded in the annual *World Shakespeare Bibliography*, which is updated annually and printed in the *Shakespeare Quarterly*, but this thicket of scholarship often renders Shakespeare more forbidding to students rather than less.

Throughout, *The Greenwood Companion to Shakespeare: A Comprehensive Guide for Students* aims to demystify Shakespeare so that students and general readers will be encouraged to appreciate the artistry of the writing and will come to a fuller appreciation of Shakespeare's genius. Students will find here what his works mean, how they came to be, how they make meaning, and how critics and directors have interpreted them over the centuries. No reference work can include all that is known or thought about Shakespeare, but the editor, contributors, and publisher have sought to make this *Companion* the best place to begin a study of this great writer. We hope that you will find the contents both useful and enjoyable.

## CONTENT AND ARRANGEMENT

The four-volume *Greenwood Companion to Shakespeare* includes seventy-seven essays offering a guide to the perplexed. All of these essays have been written expressly for this work by dedicated scholars commissioned because of their scholarship and teaching skills.

The first three volumes are devoted to the plays as follows:

- Volume I is divided into two sections: first, a series of essays about Shakespeare's age, his life, the theater of the time, the texts of his work, and the English language of his era—all of which will deepen the reader's understanding of the works; second, essays that focus on the history plays.

- Volume II explores the comedies.

- Volume III presents the tragedies.

- Volume IV begins with essays on the late plays called romances; the remainder of the volume discusses William Shakespeare's poetry, beginning with an overview of the sonnets. Thirty-one essays examine selected individual or paired sonnets, including full texts of each sonnet reviewed. Compared with the rest of Shakespeare's poetry, these sonnets are the most studied and reveal the widest range of subjects and attitudes. The other essays in this volume discuss the long narrative poems: *A Lover's Complaint*—that fascinating envoi to the sonnet cycle—immediately follows the sonnets, as it did when originally published with those poems; then, in chronological order, *Venus and Adonis*, *The Rape of Lucrece*, and *The Phoenix and Turtle*; *The Passionate Pilgrim* (in which two of Shakespeare's sonnets to the mysterious Dark Lady were first printed) has been placed last because most of the poems contained therein are not by Shakespeare.

The essays are arranged chronologically within genre. To further assist readers in finding essays on particular plays or poems, an alphabetical list of the works studied in this *Companion* follows immediately after the table of contents.

### Other Features

"A Shakespeare Chronology," preceding the overview essays in volume I, shows when William Shakespeare's works were written and published and provides basic facts about his life. An annotated bibliography accompanies each essay. At the end of volume IV, an appendix offers a selected, annotated list of Web sites about William Shakespeare and his work. Following that list is a selected bibliography. A subject index and an index of key passages concludes the work.

## THE ESSAYS

Forty scholars contributed essays to this *Companion*. Their writings add substantially to Shakespeare scholarship. These essays range in length from some 2,500 words for articles on particular sonnets to 26,000 words on *King Lear*. The articles dealing with the plays, subdivided into eleven sections for easy access, provide the following information to readers:

1. A scene-by-scene plot summary to help students understand what is happening on the stage/page.

2. A discussion of the play's publication history and, when relevant, its historical background context.

3. Sources for the play(s), including a discussion of controversies and recent findings.

4. A brief overview of how the play is put together in terms of structure and plotting.

5. The main characters, their actions, and their purposes within the play.

6. Devices and techniques (such as imagery) that Shakespeare used in the plays.

7. Themes and meanings of the play, citing opinions of various scholars.

8. A look at past and current critical discourse on the work to help students understand the issues that have engaged scholarly attention and to show that in many areas there is no single "correct" interpretation of these complex works. Students seeking topics to explore for their own papers may find this section especially helpful.

9. Production history, surveying the play's key theatrical and cinematic representation.

10. An explication of key passages, helping readers to understand sections of the play that are considered to be the most important.

11. An annotated bibliography for further study. This selection of sources will help students choose the most accessible works from the hundreds included in the *World Shakespeare Bibliography* or the dozens listed in bibliographical guides. The books and articles noted here include classic studies but concentrate on recent writing.

## The Essays on the Sonnets and Long Poems

The essays in volume IV discuss the poems. Compared with the essays on the plays they are briefer and contain fewer sections. For the sonnets, the essays provide the following key elements:

1. The sonnet itself, from *The Oxford Shakespeare*, edited by W. J. Craig and published in 1914 by Oxford University Press.

2. A prose paraphrase to explain the content of the work under discussion.

3. A discussion that situates the poem within the sonnet cycle.

4. An exploration of devices and techniques, and themes and meanings.

5. A description of the relationship of the sonnet to Shakespeare's other works, particularly the plays.

6. An annotated bibliography.

In the essays on the long poems the reader will also find discussions of publication history and sources (treated in the overview essay on the sonnets for those poems). All of the essays on the long poems conclude with annotated bibliographies.

## ISSUES IN THE SHAKESPEARE CANON

One poem that readers will not find in this volume is *A Funeral Elegy*. This 578-line poem was first printed by George Eld and published by Thomas Thorpe in 1612. Eld had printed and Thorpe had published Shakespeare's sonnets three years earlier. According to the title page, *A Funeral Elegy* was the work of "W. S." The identity of this W. S. has inspired some recent controversy. In 1989 Donald W. Foster published *Elegy by W. S.* (Newark: U of Delaware P), in which he discussed the question of attribution without reaching any conclusion. However, in the October 1996 issue of *PMLA* Foster argued that the poem was by Shakespeare. Because Foster had successfully identified the author of the "anonymous" novel *Primary Colors* (1996) as Joe Klein, Foster's view was credible enough for the editors of the revised Riverside edition of Shakespeare's works (Boston: Houghton Mifflin, 1997) to include the *Elegy*; they also included, however, something of a disclaimer by J.J.M. Tobin (pp. 1893–1895). In 2002 Foster recanted, arguing that the most likely author of the *Elegy* was John Ford.

This controversy reflects the unsettled state of the Shakespeare canon, which grows and shrinks. Brian Vickers's *Shakespeare, Co-Author* (Oxford: Oxford UP, 2002) assigns joint responsibility to five of Shakespeare's plays: *Titus Andronicus* (with George Peele), *Timon of Athens* (with Thomas Middleton), *Pericles* (with George Wilkins), and *Henry VIII* and *The Two Noble Kinsmen* (both with John Fletcher). Seeking to expand the canon, Eric Sams has argued that *Edward III* is an early work by Shakespeare (see *"Edward III": An Early Play Restored to the Canon* (New Haven: Yale UP, 1996).

On one point scholars agree: the William Shakespeare who wrote the plays and poems discussed in this companion was the son of John and Mary Shakespeare, was born in Stratford-upon-Avon in 1564, and died there fifty-two years later. Since the nineteenth century, various nonscholars have proposed dozens of alternative authors, including Francis Bacon, Queen Elizabeth, and Edward de Vere, seventeenth Earl of Oxford. Those readers curious about the authorship question may consult Samuel Schoenbaum's *Shakespeare's Lives*, new edition (Oxford: Clarendon P, 1991), section VI, which is aptly titled "Deviations." Arguments about the authorship of Shakespeare's works belong to the realm of abnormal psychology rather than literary criticism.

# A Shakespeare Chronology

*Note*: Titles in **bold** are discussed in this four-volume set. Dates for the plays (e.g., 1593 for ***Richard III*** and ***The Comedy of Errors***) indicate probable year of first performance.

| | |
|---|---|
| 1558 | Elizabeth I becomes queen of England. |
| 1564 | William Shakespeare born (ca. April 23). |
| 1576 | The Theatre (Shoreditch), built by James Burbage, opens. The Theatre is regarded as the first true London playhouse. |
| 1582 | Shakespeare marries Anne Hathaway (ca. December 1). |
| 1583 | Shakespeare's elder daughter, Susannah, born (ca. May 23). |
| 1585 | Shakespeare's fraternal twins, Judith and Hamnet/Hamlet, born (ca. January 31). |
| 1588 | Defeat of the Spanish Armada (July 31–August 8). |
| 1589 | Shakespeare probably in London, begins writing ***1 Henry VI*** (published in 1623). |
| 1590–1591 | ***2, 3 Henry VI*** written. The former first published as *The First Part of the Contention betwixt the Two Famous Houses of York and Lancaster* (1594), the latter as *The True Tragedy of Richard Duke of York* (1595). |
| 1592 | Robert Greene attacks Shakespeare in *A Groatsworth of Witte*. This is the first printed reference to Shakespeare as dramatist. |
| 1593 | ***Richard III*** (first published in 1597). |
| | ***Venus and Adonis*** published. |
| | ***The Comedy of Errors*** (first published in 1623). |
| | Shakespeare begins writing his **sonnets**. |
| 1594 | ***The Rape of Lucrece*** published. |
| | ***Titus Andronicus*** (first published in 1594). |
| | ***The Taming of the Shrew*** (first published in 1623). |
| | ***The Two Gentlemen of Verona*** (first published in 1623). |

*Love's Labor's Lost* (first published in 1598).

Lord Chamberlain's Men established.

1595    *King John* (first published in 1623).

*Richard II* (first published in 1597).

*Romeo and Juliet* (first published in 1597).

*A Midsummer Night's Dream* (first published in 1600).

1596    *The Merchant of Venice* (first published in 1600).

Hamnet/Hamlet Shakespeare dies, age 11 (ca. August 9).

1597    *1 Henry IV* (first published in 1598).

*The Merry Wives of Windsor* (first published in 1602).

Shakespeare purchases New Place, Stratford.

1598    *2 Henry IV* (first published in 1600).

*Much Ado about Nothing* (first published in 1600).

Francis Meres's *Palladis Tamia* lists a dozen plays by Shakespeare and praises him highly.

1599    The Globe Theater opens.

*Henry V* (first published in 1600).

*Julius Caesar* (first published in 1623).

*The Passionate Pilgrim* includes two of Shakespeare's sonnets (138, 144).

1600    *As You Like It* (first published in 1623).

*Hamlet* (first published in 1603).

1601    *Richard II* performed at the Globe (February 7) at urging of supporters of the Earl of Essex one day before his ill-fated rebellion.

*The Phoenix and Turtle* appears in Robert Chester's *Love's Martyr*.

John Shakespeare dies (ca. September 6).

1602    *Twelfth Night* (first published in 1623).

*Troilus and Cressida* (first published in 1609).

1603    Queen Elizabeth dies. James VI of Scotland becomes James I of England. James licenses the Lord Chamberlain's Men as the King's Men.

*All's Well That Ends Well* (first published in 1623).

1604    *Measure for Measure* (first published in 1623).

*Othello* (first published in 1622).

1605    *King Lear* (first published in 1608).

1606    *Macbeth* (first published in 1623).

1607    *Antony and Cleopatra* (first published in 1623).

Susannah Shakespeare marries John Hall (June 5).

Shakespeare's brother Edmund dies (ca. December 29).

1608    Elizabeth Hall, Shakespeare's only granddaughter, born (ca. February 18).

Shakespeare's mother dies (ca. September 7).

*Coriolanus* (first published in 1623).

*Timon of Athens* (first published in 1623).

*Pericles* (first published in 1609).

1609    Shakespeare's *Sonnets* published, with *A Lover's Complaint*.

*Cymbeline* (first published in 1623).

The King's Men begin using the Blackfriars as an indoor theater.

1610    *The Winter's Tale* (first published in 1623).

1611    *The Tempest* (first published in 1623).

1612    *Henry VIII* (with John Fletcher; first published in 1623).

1613    Globe Theater burns down during production of *Henry VIII*.

*Cardenio* (with John Fletcher; lost).

*The Two Noble Kinsmen* (with John Fletcher; first published in 1634).

1614    Second Globe opens on site of first Globe.

1616    Judith Shakespeare marries Thomas Quiney (February 10).

Shakespeare makes his will (March 25) and dies on April 23.

1619    Thomas Pavier attempts a collected (pirated) edition of Shakespeare. He publishes ten plays in quarto, some with false dates to conceal the piracy, before he is forced to abandon the project.

1623    The First Folio, the first collected edition of Shakespeare's plays, is published. It contains thirty-six plays, half of them printed for the first time.

# THE TRAGEDIES

# Titus Andronicus

## Deborah Willis

### PLOT SUMMARY

**1.1.** Saturninus and Bassianus, sons to the late Emperor of Rome, clash with each other over who is most fit to succeed their father. The people of Rome, however, led by the tribune Marcus Andronicus, want Marcus's brother, the general Titus Andronicus, to become emperor instead. Their deliberations are interrupted by the return of Titus and his army from war with the Goths. With them they bring Tamora, Queen of the Goths, her sons (Alarbus, Demetrius, and Chiron), and Aaron the Moor (Tamora's lover) as prisoners of war. Though victorious, Titus and his followers are also in mourning for Titus's twenty-one sons who have been killed in battle. To appease their ghosts, Titus and one of his four surviving sons, Lucius, claim the right to sacrifice Alarbus, the oldest of Tamora's sons. Though she makes a moving appeal for his life, Titus and Lucius proceed with the sacrifice, hewing his limbs and burning his flesh. They then bury Titus's sons in the family tomb. Marcus renews his efforts to make Titus emperor of Rome, but Titus declines the position and endorses Saturninus instead. The people agree to accept Saturninus as their new ruler.

Saturninus asks Titus for his daughter Lavinia's hand in marriage, but though Titus consents, Bassianus challenges the marriage, saying he and Lavinia are already betrothed. With the help of several of Titus's sons, Bassianus takes Lavinia from Saturninus by force. In the ensuing fight, Titus kills one of his own sons, Mutius, in a rage at his disobedience. Despite the fact that Titus tries to stop Bassianus, Saturninus blames Titus for this very public humiliation and decides to take Tamora as his bride. Tamora encourages Saturninus to pardon Titus for the time being, while in an aside she promises to destroy Titus and his family once Saturninus is more securely established as ruler of Rome. Saturninus publicly forgives Titus and his sons, and they all agree to go on a hunt together the next day.

**2.1.** Aaron the Moor, in a soliloquy, celebrates Tamora's unexpected rise to power, which also benefits him since he is her lover. Tamora's sons, Chiron and

Demetrius, enter, quarreling over Lavinia, whom each would like to woo. Aaron persuades them that they can both be satisfied if they rape her instead.

**2.2.** Titus and his sons meet with Saturninus's party and embark upon the hunt.

**2.3.** Aaron and Tamora meet in the woods. After they exchange amorous words, Aaron explains his plot to have her sons rape Lavinia and kill Bassianus. Tamora agrees to help. She and her sons confront Lavinia and Bassianus by a pit in the woods, and Bassianus is killed. Chiron and Demetrius drag Lavinia off to be raped, with their mother's blessing. Aaron lures Titus's sons Quintus and Martius into the pit, setting them up to be blamed for the murder of Bassianus. He then brings Saturninus and his party to the site, where Tamora gives the emperor a forged letter implicating Titus's sons in the murder. The sons are taken prisoner, while Titus protests.

**2.4.** Demetrius and Chiron abandon Lavinia in the woods after raping her and cutting off her tongue and hands. She is found by Marcus.

**3.1.** Titus appeals for his sons' lives, but their judges pass him by in silence, much as he himself had ignored Tamora's appeal for her son Alarbus's life. Lucius finds him lamenting to the stones and complaining that Rome has become a wilderness of tigers that prey on his family. Marcus enters with Lavinia, increasing their woe. Titus tries futilely to comfort Lavinia. Aaron enters and tells Titus that the emperor will spare his sons if he chops off one of his hands and sends it to him. Titus lets Aaron cut off his hand, despite the protests of Lucius and Marcus. Shortly thereafter, a messenger returns with Titus's hand and also with the two heads of his sons, who have been executed after all. Saturninus has sent his hand back to him for sport. Titus's grief now takes the form of mad laughter as he, Marcus, and Lucius plan to take action against Rome. Lucius leaves to raise an army of the Goths.

**3.2.** Titus's talk turns increasingly wild as he, Lavinia, and Marcus continue to grieve over their losses. When Marcus kills a fly, Titus denounces him as a murderer. After Marcus points out that the fly was black like Aaron, Titus apologizes and asks for a knife in order to stab the fly for its coal-black appearance.

**4.1.** Lucius's son, young Lucius, is frightened by Lavinia, who is chasing him because he is carrying a volume of Ovid's *Metamorphoses*. When he drops it, she manages to open the book to the story of Philomel. Titus and Marcus guess that she is trying to tell them about her rape in the forest. Titus shows her how to use a staff to write the names of her rapists in the dirt. She spells out the names of Chiron and Demetrius. Titus, in Latin, asks why the gods are so slow to see these crimes, and Marcus and Lucius talk of revenge.

**4.2.** Young Lucius gives Tamora's sons a bundle of arrows wrapped with a quotation from Horace: *Integer vitae, scelerisque purus, / Non egat Mauri jaculis, nec arcu* (The man who leads an upright life free from crime requires neither the Moor's arrows nor his bow. *Odes* 1.22.1–2). Aaron understands that Titus now knows of the guilt of Chiron and Demetrius. A nurse enters with Tamora's newly delivered son, who is black like Aaron. Chiron and Demetrius call Aaron a villain for this disgrace to their mother and want to kill the baby. Aaron, delighted with the baby, rescues him, kills the nurse, and tells Chiron and Demetrius to procure a newly born white child to give to their mother, saving her reputation and leading Saturninus to think it his own. Chiron and Demetrius are appeased by this idea. Aaron leaves with the baby to raise it among the Goths.

**4.3.** Titus and young Lucius shoot arrows with messages into Saturninus's court, as Titus comments that Justice has left the earth and he must seek for help from Pluto's underworld. A Clown enters with a basket of pigeons. Titus asks him to take a message to Saturninus along with the birds.

**4.4.** Saturninus complains to Tamora about Titus's seemingly mad actions, which he correctly interprets as attempts to expose the injustice of his rule. The Clown enters with Titus's message and Saturninus has him hanged once he reads it. A messenger enters with news that Lucius is leading an army of the Goths against Rome. Tamora reassures Saturninus that she can handle the mad Titus and will head off this threat.

**5.1.** Lucius, leading an army of Goths, is met by another Goth who has captured Aaron and his baby. Lucius wants to kill the child and hang Aaron, but Aaron pleads for the life of his child in exchange for his testimony about Tamora's many crimes against the Andronici. He makes Lucius swear to the gods that his child will not be killed, and Lucius unwillingly does so. A messenger from Saturninus enters, asking Lucius to meet for a parley, and Lucius agrees.

**5.2.** Tamora and her sons, disguised as allegorical figures of Revenge, Rape, and Murder, go to Titus's house, hoping to trick Titus into turning over Lucius and dispersing the Goth army. Titus sees through their disguise but plays along, agreeing to host a feast at which Saturninus and Tamora can meet peacefully with the Andronici and discuss their grievances. Titus persuades Tamora to leave her disguised sons behind. After she departs, Titus has them bound and gagged, and with the assistance of Lavinia, slits their throats. Lavinia collects their blood in a basin as Titus explains that he will grind their bones into a paste and bake them in a pie to be served to their mother at the feast.

**5.3.** Lucius and the Goth army arrive at Titus's house with Aaron as prisoner. Aaron has been kept alive to give evidence against Tamora. Saturninus and Tamora arrive with their attendants and various Roman tribunes and senators. They sit down for the feast. Titus enters, dressed as a cook, and places dishes on the table, accompanied by Lavinia, who is wearing a veil. As they are eating, Titus surprises everyone by killing his daughter in front of them. He explains to the shocked guests that he has done this because she was raped by Chiron and Demetrius. He reveals that the pie Tamora has just eaten was made from the flesh of her sons, and stabs her to death. Saturninus then kills Titus, and Lucius kills Saturninus. A general fight breaks out. Lucius and Marcus, with a few other members of their family, escape to a balcony, from which they address the crowd. Lucius explains that Chiron and Demetrius raped Lavinia and were the cause of his brothers' execution. Marcus then points to an attendant who is holding Aaron's child and reveals that this is the illegitimate son of their empress, Tamora, begotten on her by Aaron, the chief architect of the injuries the Andronici have suffered. Marcus asks the crowd whether they now think the Andronici have done anything wrong. The Roman nobleman Aemillius declares that Lucius should be the new emperor, and the crowd agrees. Lucius promises to rule graciously and to heal Rome's wounds. Marcus, Lucius, and his son shed tears over Titus's body, as Aaron is brought in to receive his sentence. Lucius commands that he be buried breast-deep in the earth and left to starve to death. Aaron remains defiant, stating he wishes he had done ten thousand worse evils and repenting of any good deed. Lucius also announces that the bodies of Titus and Lavinia will be taken to the family tomb, while Tamora's body will be left to be eaten by birds and beasts of prey.

## PUBLICATION HISTORY

*Titus Andronicus* was Shakespeare's first experiment in tragedy, written sometime prior to 1594. Philip Henslowe's *Diary*, an account book kept by the proprietor of the Rose Theatre, contains the first record of a performance, giving the date of January 23, 1594, for a "ne" play called "Titus & Andronicus" by the Earl of Sussex's Men (*Henslowe's Diary*, ed. R. A. Foakes and R. T. Rickert [Cambridge: Cambridge UP, 1961], 21). Scholars have suggested that "ne" could mean "new," "newly acquired," "newly revised," or even "Newington"—the location of a theater in a village outside London where plays were sometimes performed when London theaters were unavailable. Henslowe's entry leaves open the possibility of earlier performances, and scholars have noted that some plays and nondramatic works dating from the 1591–1592 period contain parallels to passages in *Titus Andronicus*. (For a summary of such parallels, see "Introduction," *Titus Andronicus*, ed. Alan Hughes [Cambridge: Cambridge UP, 1994], 3–6.) Did these works echo a play already in existence, or was *Titus Andronicus* echoing them? It is impossible to say with certainty. The actual date of composition remains a matter of conjecture. Recent scholars and editors have suggested dates ranging from 1588 to 1593, with several favoring the idea that the play was written before 1592 and substantially revised late in 1593.

The publication history of the play is much clearer than the composition date. Shortly after the performances recorded by Henslowe, the play appeared in a quarto edition (Q1), under the title of *The Most Lamentable Romaine Tragedie of Titus Andronicus*. Very likely the publisher of Q1 was anxious to capitalize on the play's popularity. Only one copy of this quarto is known, and it was not discovered until 1904. It is now housed in the Folger Shakespeare Library, Washington, D.C. Q1 was followed by Q2 in 1600 and Q3 in 1611; these later quartos differ only in small ways from the first one. However, Q2 was printed from a defective copy of Q1. The last three leaves of the printer's copy of Q1 were damaged, so he supplied the missing words with his own inventions. The version included in the First Folio (1623), put together after Shakespeare's death by his friends and fellow actors John Heminge and Henry Condell, was based closely on Q3, though it also adds a new scene (3.2).

Most modern editors have taken Q1 as the basis for the text of the play we use today, with a few minor emendations based on Q2, and the addition of scene 3.2 and some stage directions from the First Folio. Q1 is assumed to be based on Shakespeare's foul papers (that is, the rough draft written in the author's own hand) because it lacks stage directions and includes irregularities characteristic of a working draft. The compositor for the First Folio, in contrast, probably had access to playhouse promptbooks as well as Q3, since the Folio text includes stage directions, act divisions, and other features important in performance. (For a succinct overview of textual issues, see "Introduction," *Titus Andronicus*, ed. Eugene M. Waith [Oxford: Clarendon P, 1984], 39–42). It is unclear why 3.2 did not appear in any of the quarto editions. But based on internal evidence that links this scene to Shakespeare's other work in the mid-1590s, scholars have generally concluded that 3.2 was added to the play early in its performance history. Most likely, the revision was made after the publication of the first quarto but never was included in the later quarto editions, each of which was reprinted from its predecessor. The prompt-books, however, would have included the new scene.

*Titus Andronicus* does not appear to have been inspired by any particular historical event. But revenge was certainly a topic with a great deal of currency in the Elizabethan Age. State authorities and popular reformers throughout this period stressed the need to seek redress for injuries through the legal system and denounced the "private" revenges undertaken by some members of the nobility as well as brawling at all social levels. Elizabethan writers such as Francis Bacon explored the problems associated with revenge. Bacon considered revenge to be a form of "wild justice"; its lawlessness promoted social disorder and should be discouraged. However, he also noted that sometimes the law did not provide a remedy for serious wrongs, making it necessary for people to take the law into their own hands ("Of Revenge," in *The Essays*, ed. John Pitcher [New York: Penguin, 1985], 73). Bacon's ambivalence was shared by many of his contemporaries, including many dramatists. They called into question the emphasis on state-centered justice, often portraying central authorities as too weak, corrupt, or partisan to provide just solutions to quarrels. At the same time, they brought out the innocent suffering and civil unrest wrought by honor-driven feuds and factional violence, which often had revenge as a motive. (For an overview of Elizabethan views of revenge, see Harry Keyishian, *The Shapes of Revenge: Victimization, Vengeance, and Vindictiveness in Shakespeare* [Atlantic Highlands, NJ: Humanities Press, 1995], 1–25.) Many plays of the late 1580s and early 1590s have revenge as a theme and explore its tensions, including Thomas Kyd's *Spanish Tragedy*, Christopher Marlowe's *Jew of Malta*, and Shakespeare's *Titus Andronicus*. Shakespeare also explored revenge in many of his history plays of this period, such as *Henry VI, Parts 1, 2, and 3*, and it is of course the central concern of the slightly later *Hamlet*.

## SOURCES FOR THE PLAY

Unlike Shakespeare's other Roman plays, *Titus Andronicus* is not based on Roman history. Instead, the story is entirely fictional, and the character of Titus Andronicus is not based on an actual historical personage. Most scholars think that Shakespeare did not invent the story but adapted it from a preexisting work, possibly a prose narrative titled *The History of Titus Andronicus, The Renowned Roman General*. This narrative, however, survives only in an eighteenth-century chapbook. It may be that both the play and the prose narrative are based on an earlier source, perhaps an Italian novella translated into English (Hughes, p. 10; Metz, pp. 150–156). A few recent scholars, such as Jonathan Bate, editor of the Arden Shakespeare edition of *Titus Andronicus*, believe that the prose narrative came after the play and was based on a ballad published in 1620. Indeed, Bate argues that Shakespeare invented the Titus Andronicus story himself ("Introduction," *Titus Andronicus* [London: Routledge, 1995], 83–85).

Another theory holds that Shakespeare may have adapted the story from an earlier play. Henslowe entered a play titled "titus & vespacia" in his *Diary* in 1592, and it has recently been argued that this play is the basis for a German play about Titus Andronicus published in 1620 and performed by English actors. It includes a son of Titus named Vespasian, whose role has some parallels with that of Lucius. If such a play was in existence by 1592, it is possible that Shakespeare could have adapted this earlier work (June Schlueter, "Reading the Peacham Drawing," *Shakespeare Quarterly* 50 [Summer 1999]: 173, 178).

Though the origins of the Titus story remain obscure, scholars agree that an important source for the rape of Lavinia is the story of Philomel from Ovid's *Metamorphoses*, book 6. In it, Philomel is raped by her sister's husband, Tereus, who cuts out her tongue to keep her from revealing his crime. Philomel manages to communicate with her sister, Procne, by weaving a picture of her rape into a tapestry. Together the sisters take revenge by killing the son of Tereus and Procne and serving his roasted flesh to Tereus at a private banquet. Tereus, in a fit of fury and grief, draws his sword upon the sisters when they reveal to him what he has just eaten, but all three are transformed into birds before he can kill them. In 4.1 of *Titus*, the similarly tongueless Lavinia brings a copy of Ovid's *Metamorphoses* to her father and uncle, opening it to the story of Philomel in order to reveal her rape to them. The play also refers to the story at several other points (such as 2.3.43, 2.4.26, 38, and 5.2.194–195). Seneca's play *Thyestes* is another probable source, especially for the climactic feast in 5.3. Indeed, the details of the revenge that Titus carries out seem more closely modeled on Seneca's play than on Ovid. Atreus kills two sons of his brother Thyestes (because Thyestes has committed adultery with Atreus's wife, Aerope), has them baked into a meat pie, and serves them to his brother at a very public feast.

Less directly, Shakespeare drew upon many classical sources to convey the Roman identities of his characters. In the first act, for example, Titus is presented as an exemplar of Roman piety and military courage; his values resemble those of Aeneas in Vergil's *Aeneid*. The brief 2.2 recalls Dido and Aeneas's hunt in book 4 of the *Aeneid*, and both excursions lead to tragedy. Titus's speech about the ghosts of his sons (1.1.86–88) echoes Vergil's description of the underworld in book 6 of the *Aeneid*. The name Lavinia also has Vergilian overtones, Lavinia being the cause of civil war in the latter half of Vergil's epic. Later in the play, however, Shakespeare turns to Ovid to expose the underlying instability of Roman values. As the critic Heather James has suggested, though "Shakespeare first invokes the *Aeneid* as the epic of empire-building, order, and *pietas*," he then "allows Ovid's *Metamorphoses* to invade, interpreting the fundamental impulses of Vergil's poem as chaotic, even apocalyptic. Simply put, the founding acts of Empire turn out to contain the seeds of its destruction" ("Cultural Disintegration in *Titus Andronicus*: Mutilating Titus, Vergil, and Rome," in *"Titus Andronicus": Critical Essays*, ed. Philip Kolin [New York: Garland, 1995], 287). Ovid's treatment of Philomel's story presents a world in moral collapse; similarly, Lavinia's rape initiates us into a world that has become a "wilderness of tigers" (3.1.54).

*Titus Andronicus* was also influenced by other dramatic and cultural traditions. Scholars consider the Vice character of morality plays to be an important source for Aaron the Moor. Like the Vice, Aaron delights in deceiving others and doing evil for the pure sport of it, and he possesses a flamboyant bravado that does not falter even in defeat (Bernard Spivack, *Shakespeare and the Allegory of Evil* [New York: Columbia University Press, 1958], 379–386). Shakespeare combined the Vice with Renaissance stereotypes of Moors that demonized them as "other" and made black skin color the sign of a villainous nature; Aaron declares that he "will have his soul black like his face" (3.1.205). Aaron also resembles another notorious villain popular on the stage at this time, Barabas the Jew in Christopher Marlowe's

*The Jew of Malta*; and *Titus Andronicus* as a whole shares with many of Marlowe's plays a taste for highly theatrical scenes of violence. Finally, Thomas Kyd's *Spanish Tragedy* provided a precedent for coupling the display of classical learning with an intricate revenge plot, helping to establish conventions that would shape the genre of revenge tragedy for decades to come. Like Titus, Kyd's Hieronimo cannot obtain justice for a murdered son and is driven first to the edge of madness and then to revenge. The play climaxes with an elaborately orchestrated bloodbath. As the critic Eugene Waith has put it, like *The Spanish Tragedy*, *Titus Andronicus* is "sensational, serious, learned, and spectacular" (Waith, p. 38).

## STRUCTURE AND PLOTTING

*Titus Andronicus* is a revenge tragedy, and revenge drives the plot. One way to think of the plot is as an escalating series of retaliatory responses to traumatic events. Revenge, on the one hand, is a way of easing grief, restoring honor, and getting "satisfaction" after the violent death of family members; on the other hand, its excesses cause new destruction and suffering. The first traumatic event, the death of Titus's sons on the battlefield, happens before the start of the play, but its devastating effect upon Titus's family is made clear in the opening scene when they enter the city carrying coffins and burdened by grief. Mere victory in battle is not enough to compensate for the loss of these sons; grief can only be eased through the ritual sacrifice of Alarbus. That sacrifice, however, precipitates a new trauma for Tamora's family, who view the sacrifice as a "cruel, irreligious," even "barbarous" act (1.1.130–131). Significantly, Shakespeare presents the events that set the play in motion as a culture clash: the Goths do not accept this supposedly pious Roman custom as a legitimate practice. To them it is a brutal murder that, according to the honor code both Goths and Romans share, must be avenged. The revenge of Tamora and her sons culminates in the rape and mutilation of Titus's daughter, Lavinia, along with the death of her husband, Bassianus, and the execution of two of her brothers. These events, in turn, precipitate the revenge of Titus and the surviving members of his family, culminating in the bloodbath of 5.3, during which Titus slaughters Tamora's sons, tricks her into eating them in a pie, and then kills her. Titus also kills his daughter, Lavinia, and dies himself in the ensuing melee. Each act of revenge is more horrific than the one that precedes it, as the injured parties attempt to "o'er reach" each other "in their own devices" (5.2.143). Because Titus's revenge on Tamora and her family also leads to the murder of the emperor Saturninus, it brings Rome to the brink of civil war. But this nearly complete collapse of order is averted by Lucius and Marcus, who persuade the people of Rome that the revenge of the Andronici has been justified. Lucius is elected emperor, and the impulse for further violence is vented instead on the bodies of Tamora and Aaron, the foreign "others."

As revenge escalates, the play moves from city and court to the "green" world of the forest, following a structural pattern familiar in pastoral tradition and in many of Shakespeare's later comedies. Here, however, the sylvan scene of 2.2 is quickly transformed into the "barren detested vale" and "abhorred" pit of 2.3.93, 98; the festive hunt meant to celebrate royal marriage is replaced by the savage pursuit of human prey. By act 3, Titus and his family have returned to the city but find that Rome has become "a wilderness of tigers" (3.1.54) when Titus's pleas for justice go unheard. Rome itself is now as savage as the forest that surrounds it. The movement from city to forest to "wilderness of tigers" parallels the collapse of Roman values and of stable distinctions between such binary opposites as civilization/barbarism, Roman/Goth, piety/irreligion, good/evil. Only in the final scene is a semblance of order restored, once the devouring energies of revenge have run their course.

## MAIN CHARACTERS

### Titus Andronicus

Titus Andronicus, the title character, is clearly the play's pivotal figure, a commanding presence who appears in most scenes and is given the lion's share of the lines. Yet to some critics he is almost too flawed to be considered a tragic hero. In the opening scene he embodies classic Roman virtues of patriotism, military courage, honor, and piety. He is a loyal servant of Rome and an astonishingly prolific father who has sired twenty-five sons and raised them all to be soldiers. By the time the play starts he has lost twenty-one of them in wars with the Goths. But very quickly our view of him is complicated by his faulty judgment, lack of compassion, and rigid view of honor. His refusal to be swayed by Tamora's moving appeal to spare her son shows dedication but also cruelty. In choosing Saturninus to be emperor instead of his younger but worthier brother, Titus adheres blindly to the right of the eldest son to succeed his father. He is inflexibly patriarchal, insisting on his right to marry off his daughter to Saturninus despite her preexisting betrothal to Bassianus, and expecting absolute loyalty and obedience from his sons. When he kills his son Mutius and refuses to bury him in the family tomb, he twists the notion of honor into something even his brother Marcus views as "impiety" and "barbarous" behavior (1.1.355, 378). Titus's own actions are what first bring barbarity into Rome and set the revenge plot in motion.

Titus becomes more sympathetic once he becomes a victim. His despair is palpable as he talks to the stones at the beginning of act 3; we realize he is an old man, startled by his sudden powerlessness, facing devastating losses. The middle of the play powerfully dramatizes the problem of the "private man" who cannot find justice from the state or the gods. While Titus never recognizes or takes responsibility for his past errors, he does grow beyond what the critics C. L. Barber and Richard P. Wheeler have called the "paternal egotism" he displays in the first act ("*Titus Andronicus*: Abortive Domestic Tragedy," in *Shakespeare's Early Tragedies: A Collection of Essays*, ed. Mark Rose [Englewood Cliffs, NJ: Prentice Hall, 1995], 81). His response to Lavinia after her rape is emotional and consoling. As his grief descends into mad laughter and seemingly erratic behavior, he also becomes a slyly subversive figure, compulsively authoring coded messages that critique Saturninus's rule, chastise the gods, and unsettle his adversaries. His madness is part real, part stratagem. By the end of the play he has regained the upper hand, overcoming his enemies by stage managing the climactic, cannibalistic feast, degrading his enemies in a spectacular fashion as he destroys them. His vengeance, however, also shocks the audience, particularly when he kills Lavinia, and his own death, though it comes at Saturninus's hands, is in effect a suicidal act. The tensions in his character persist until the end.

## Lavinia

As a character, Titus is reasonably complex, and critics have considered him a precursor to Shakespeare's King Lear, another difficult father whose fall is accompanied by great suffering. Others in the play are types more than fully realized characters. Titus's daughter, Lavinia, is at first not much more than the embodiment of the ideal Roman daughter: chaste, virtuous, beautiful, and obedient. After being raped, she becomes a personification of suffering. The play provides us with little direct access to her thoughts and feelings, and her choices are sharply circumscribed by Rome's patriarchal codes. In act 1, she is treated as a trophy bride, to be given or withheld as her father determines, with no regard for her own desires. To her father's enemies, she is a symbol of his family's honor, to be violated and despoiled as a way of getting back at him. In later acts, she becomes a more powerfully moving character, if not more multidimensional. Ironically, we come to know her better when she no longer is able to speak. Without a tongue or hands, she struggles to communicate through bodily gestures and the written word, finally writing out the names of her rapists in the dirt and assisting her father in butchering them. As the critic Mary Laughlin Fawcett has shown, in acts 3 and 4 father and daughter collaborate in making meaning and become increasingly inseparable ("Arms/ Words/Tears: Language and the Body in *Titus Andronicus*," *ELH* 50 [1983]: 261–277). Hence her death at her father's hand in 5.3 can seem particularly shocking. Yet Titus appeals to the tradition of honor killing in part to provoke and entrap Saturninus, and it is possible to see death as something that Lavinia herself seeks at this point. Killing her may be a merciful act of assisted suicide. It may also be viewed as an example of Titus's madness, a way of underscoring the grotesque extremes to which honor and revenge can lead.

## Tamora

The play clearly polarizes women's roles. While Lavinia is virtuous, chaste, and obedient, Tamora is at the opposite extreme: lustful, villainous, and outside the control of the Roman males. Though at the beginning of the play she claims our sympathies as a prisoner of war and as a mother who movingly appeals for her son's life, after his sacrifice her villainy is unleashed. She quickly becomes a stark embodiment of misogynist stereotypes about women, as her desire for revenge takes hold and her amorous attachment to Aaron the Moor becomes apparent. A Goth outsider who marries the Roman Emperor Saturninus while keeping Aaron as her lover, she has been linked to such exotic, sexualized, and treacherous figures as Semiramis and to the stereotype of the "lusty widow" (Sara Hanna, "Tamora's Rome: Raising Babel and Inferno in *Titus Andronicus*," *Shakespeare Yearbook* 3 [1992]: 11–29; Dorothea Kehler, " 'That Ravenous Tiger Tamora': *Titus Andronicus*'s Lusty Widow, Wife, and M/other," in Kolin, ed., pp. 317–332). Tamora's volatile combination of eroticism and aggression comes to seem almost a family trait when, under Aaron's influence, she coaxes her sons into becoming rapists and murderers. By the end of the play she is punished not only for her vengeful excesses but also for her ungovernable sexuality, which has produced such offspring as Chiron and Demetrius: Titus wants to make "that strumpet," that "unhallowed dam / Like to the earth swallow her own increase" (5.2.190–191).

### Aaron

Aaron is in some respects the most vital and captivating character in the play, while surpassing even Tamora in villainy. Indeed, for some critics, Aaron steals the show (Hughes, 38–39). He is ruled by Saturn, as he tells us; blood and vengeance hammer in his head (2.3.31, 39), and Bassianus and Lavinia are his first targets, though they have given him no direct offense. His revenge seems curiously unmotivated, though his situation as a prisoner of war and as a black man in a white world gives him ample reason for resentment. As the play progresses his evil becomes increasingly multidimensional, and he moves beyond the stereotypes in his background. As Philip Kolin has summed up, Aaron's "many accomplished roles" include "Machiavellian plotter, lusty paramour, glib-tongued rhetor [orator], notorious outlaw, morality-play Vice, misleader of Youth—yet a loving father" (*"Titus Andronicus* and the Critical Legacy," in Kolin, ed., p. 31). Aaron's tender concern for his infant son, dramatized powerfully in 4.2, stands out in a play where the supposedly "good" characters kill their own children. He also forcefully counters the racial views of other characters: "Zounds, ye whore, is black so base a hue?" he retorts when Tamora's nurse brands his child a "dismal, black, and sorrowful issue" (4.2.71, 66). Aaron's commitment to evil never wavers; at the end of the play he defiantly refuses to repent and is sorry only that he could not perform worse deeds (5.3.185–190). His open, unapologetic embrace of evil is refreshing when compared to characters who commit acts of violence in the name of honor or piety. Nevertheless, as the critic Emily Bartels has pointed out in her essay "Making More of the Moor," ultimately Aaron remains irreducibly "other" in a world where distinctions between Romans and Goths have blurred: "The capture and containment of Aaron provides the one sure sign that at least some wrongs have been righted and some order restored" (272).

## DEVICES AND TECHNIQUES

*Titus Andronicus* is a play famous for its extreme violence. Multiple acts of mutilation, murder, and rape build to a cannibalistic climax. One critic sums up: "14 killings, 9 of them on stage, 6 severed members, 1 rape (or 2 or 3, depending on how you count), 1 live burial, 1 case of insanity and 1 of cannibalism—an average of 5.2 atrocities per act, or one for every 97 lines"; another critic calls it "the daddy of all horror plays" (quoted in Kolin, ed., p. 6). Shakespeare uses a number of devices and techniques to convey the meaning of these violent acts and, at times, to maximize their shock value. In act 1, the tomb of the Andronici dominates the stage, a potent symbol of family honor. The tomb is a monument to the accumulated military achievements of Titus's ancestors and his sons, "sumptuously re-edified" to withstand the ravages of time and spread their fame (1.1.351). But it is also a reminder of the abiding presence of death and the high cost of the honor that Titus prizes so greatly. In act 2, the "abhorred pit" (2.3.98) becomes central; in contrast to the tomb, it brings dishonor, shame, and violation as well as death. The imagery used to describe the pit by Titus's sons when they fall into it emphasizes its horrors and also links it to the female body: it is an "unhallow'd and blood-stained hole," a "detested, dark, blood-drinking pit," a "fell devouring receptacle," a "swallowing womb" (2.3.210, 224, 235, 239). The pit acts as a reminder of the offstage rape of

Lavinia and gestures toward the destructiveness associated with Tamora's womb, now that she is revealed as the monstrous mother of rapist sons. Act 2 also introduces the use of animal and hunting imagery to suggest that revenge turns humans into beasts: Lavinia has become a "dainty doe" (2.2.26) to be hunted down by predatory animals, such as tigers (2.3.142).

The idea that Rome has become a "wilderness of tigers" (3.1.54) devouring Titus's family is brought out through numerous images of mutilation and dismemberment. First Lavinia appears, "*her hands cut off, and her tongue cut out, and ravish'd,*" as the stage directions tell us (2.4), to be followed by the chopping off of Titus's hand and the return of his sons' severed heads (3.1). Such visual and verbal images take us into a frightening realm of fragmentation and cruel irony. Other images drive home the overwhelming grief produced by these atrocities, as tears are compared to a flood and turn a fountain into a brine-pit (3.1.122–129). A few passages later, Titus imagines Lavinia as the "weeping welkin" [that is, the sky] (3.1.226) and himself the earth:

> Then must my sea be moved with her sighs;
> Then must my earth with her continual tears
> Become a deluge, overflow'd and drown'd. (3.1.227–229)

Such grief, these images suggest, engulfs father and daughter and almost dissolves boundaries between them.

Shakespeare also makes use of techniques that heighten our sense of incongruity. Drawing upon the declamatory style of Senecan revenge tragedies, he gives Marcus a peculiarly artificial speech after his first encounter with the raped and mutilated Lavinia (2.4). The speech is full of elaborate comparisons and classical allusions, as when he describes Lavinia's bleeding mouth:

> Alas, a crimson river of warm blood,
> Like to a bubbling fountain stirr'd with wind,
> Doth rise and fall between thy rosed lips,
> Coming and going with thy honey breath. (2.4.22–25)

Such poetic declamations (which also occur elsewhere in the play) are at odds with modern notions of psychological realism; it can be difficult for twenty-first-century readers to accept that Lavinia's uncle, upon first beholding her terrible injuries, would spend more than forty lines weaving elaborate poetic conceits about them. Such a technique may simply illustrate the different tastes of audiences in different centuries. Yet some critics, such as Albert H. Tricomi, believe an important purpose is served by this type of incongruity: the contrast between Lavinia's mutilated body and Marcus's poetic language brings home the inability of language to respond adequately to such a painful reality, and may be seen as part of the play's investigation of "the chasm between the spoken word and the actual fact" ("The Aesthetics of Mutilation in *Titus Andronicus*," *Shakespeare Survey* 27 [1974]: 13). Marcus's speech may have, after all, a psychological aptness, suggesting his need to distance himself from Lavinia's pain by making her body into an aesthetic object. To others it underscores the gap between "Lavinia's experience and the possibilities of communication" in a culture that here has quite literally rendered a woman speechless

(Cynthia Marshall, " 'I can interpret all her martyr'd signs': *Titus Andronicus*, Feminism, and the Limits of Interpretation," in *Sexuality and Politics in Renaissance Drama*, ed. Carole Levin and Karen Robertson [Lewiston, NY: Edwin Mellen P, 1991], 200).

Another type of incongruity is evident when the play combines comic effects with tragedy. This first happens when Titus responds with laughter when the messenger from Saturninus returns with his sons' severed heads (3.1.264–266). In 3.2, Titus and Marcus obsessively make punning references to hands, and Titus's encounter with the Clown (4.3–4) also has a wacky humor. Such effects culminate with the cannibalistic feast in the final scene (5.3), when Titus appears dressed as a cook and feeds Tamora her chopped-up sons in a pie. While some critics have found the grotesque comedy of these scenes to be inappropriately farcical, others view it as crucial to the play's purpose. Titus, comments one, "resorts to laughter . . . when his ability to express emotion in language is stretched to the breaking point" (Bate, ed., p. 29). The farcical effects also disrupt the audience's stock responses. As distinctions between civilization and barbarism collapse, we enter the realm of the absurd (James Hirsh, "Laughter at *Titus Andronicus*," *Essays in Theatre* 7 [November 1988]: 59–74).

The sly wit displayed by Titus in the play's final scenes underscores the fact that his revenge seeks to humiliate as well as punish: the cannibalistic feast is a way of getting the "last laugh." At the same time, it shows the perverse extremes to which revenge can lead. Scenes 5.2 and 5.3 include images that recall the "blood-drinking . . . devouring" pit of 2.3.210, 235: the basin that Lavinia uses to collect the blood after Titus has slit Tamora's sons' throats; the frequent references to eating and drinking and mouths and stomachs; the hole in the ground in which Aaron is half-buried; the birds of prey that will feed on Tamora's body. Such imagery suggests that a substratum of barbarism and savagery still persists in Rome even as we move toward a restoration of order. But as the escalating cycle of revenge finally comes to an end and Lucius takes over as emperor, Shakespeare also invokes the language of healing and restored wholeness: Marcus, speaking to the Roman crowd after the bloodbath of 5.3, says: "O, let me teach you how to knit again / This scattered corn into one mutual sheaf, / These broken limbs again into one body" (70–72), while Lucius, accepting his new position as Emperor, promises to "heal Rome's harms, and wipe away her woe!" (147). Rome, though its order is still precarious, has a chance for a fresh start.

## THEMES AND MEANINGS

Given that *Titus Andronicus* is a revenge tragedy, it is no surprise that revenge is a major theme. Revenge tragedies typically focus on the dilemma of the private man who has been greatly wronged but cannot find justice through established institutions. As a result, the avenger must take matters into his own hands. As he does so, however, he comes into conflict with the rule of law and with key moral teachings. His revenge becomes excessive, and the lines between himself and his enemies blur. Though his actions help to restore order in a world that has lost its moral center, they also produce injustices of their own. The avenger dies in the act of achieving his revenge, in part because his own guilt requires it.

*Titus Andronicus* shares these basic features. Revenge in the play is both a problem and a solution, destabilizing distinctions between civilization and barbarism yet also helping to reestablish them. Titus restores justice, but he becomes an agent of hell in the process. Though Tamora, her sons, Saturninus, and Aaron clearly deserved to be punished for their crimes, the death of the Clown, the killing of Lavinia, and the cannibalism forced upon Tamora all testify to an excess in Titus's methods. For Roman justice to be restored, Titus himself must die as part of the climactic bloodbath.

Titus, however, is not the play's only avenger. Tamora, her sons, Aaron, Saturninus, Marcus, Lucius, and Lavinia—all become avengers before the play is over. Shakespeare is interested in the dynamics that draw families, clans, and even whole cultures into an escalating revenge cycle. In that regard, it resembles the history plays Shakespeare was writing around this time, *Henry VI, Parts 1, 2, and 3*. A few years later, in *Romeo and Juliet*, Shakespeare will set his tragedy of lovers against a similar backdrop. Romans and Goths, individuals and families, males and females, turn to revenge when they feel their honor has been injured.

Thus, closely related to the theme of revenge is that of honor. Shakespeare in this play is especially interested in the ways that honor can be taken to an extreme. For some characters, honor shades into false pride and manifests itself as an oversensitivity to insult. It is understandable when Chiron and Demetrius want revenge for the death of their brother Alarbus, or when the Andronici want to avenge the rape of Lavinia and the unjust execution of her brothers. But it is more problematic, when, in the name of honor, Titus kills his son Mutius for publicly disobeying him and wants to refuse him burial in the family tomb (1.1.340, 345). Similarly, it is unjust for Saturninus to seek revenge on Titus for the "dishonor" of Bassianus's abduction of Lavinia, when clearly Titus had no part in it (1.1.303, 332–333). Honor is a civilized value that can sometimes lead to barbaric actions.

Shakespeare also explores the effects of the powerful emotions generated when family members are injured, killed, and dishonored. Characters struggle with overwhelming grief and rage in the aftermath of the traumatic events that have affected their families, and as these emotions intensify they transform humans in strange, even grotesque ways. As Eugene Waith has put it, Shakespeare portrays "the extraordinary pitch of emotion to which a person may be raised by the most violent outrage." That violence becomes "both agent and emblem of a metamorphosis of character which takes place before our eyes. Character in the usual sense of the word disintegrates completely" (109). Revenge functions as a perverse therapy for the effects of trauma; it brings "ease" to the "gnawing vulture of [the] mind" (5.2.31). Both Tamora and Titus struggle not only with grief but also with a powerful sense of humiliation, leading to the desire not to be even with but to outdo their enemies with ever more spectacular revenges (Deborah Willis, " 'The Gnawing Vulture': Revenge, Trauma Theory, and *Titus Andronicus*," *Shakespeare Quarterly* 53 [Spring 2003]: 21–52).

Another theme in the play concerns what it means to be a Roman. In act 1 Shakespeare draws eclectically on many classical sources to associate Rome with a variety of "civilized" values, especially piety, patriotism, and military courage. As Robert Miola has written in his study *Shakespeare's Rome*, "Titus embodies *Romanitas*, here defined as a military code of honor that encompasses the virtues of pride, courage, constancy, integrity, discipline, service, and self-sacrifice" (198). To be Roman is, above all, not to be "barbarous," as Marcus insists (1.1.378). Being Roman is also closely associated with a gender ideology and a patriarchal social order, as Coppélia Kahn in *Roman Shakespeare* dissects in detail. Women must be chaste wives in order to produce legitimate sons, and their wombs are an important signifier of family honor. It is therefore necessary to protect those wombs from violation by rape or by illicit sexual relations; Roman order breaks down if either one occurs. Through the "good" female, Lavinia, the play explores the horrific consequences of rape not only for herself but also for Titus and the other Andronici: violating Lavinia violates the whole family and, in a sense, Rome itself. Through the "bad" female, Tamora, the play explores the effects of illicit female sexuality. Tamora, as a woman who strays from chastity, profoundly threatens the system through her liaison with Aaron, Rome's enemy, as well as by cuckolding Saturninus and producing an illegitimate child.

As we have seen, the play profoundly questions basic distinctions between civilized Romans and barbarous Goths. The Roman practice of human sacrifice is presented as a savage custom, and Roman honor leads to barbarous acts. Titus, the Roman general, is responsible for bringing the Goth Queen, her sons, and Aaron, inside Roman walls, and Saturninus, the Roman Emperor, by marrying her, is responsible for raising her to great power. As she herself proudly announces, "I am incorporate in Rome, / A Roman now adopted happily" (1.1.462–463). What it means to be a Roman has, by this time, been thoroughly confounded and confused. Yet, though many aspects of what it means to be Roman are rendered suspect, woman's place in Roman culture is not. The womb remains a frightening locus of vulnerability or a dangerous locus of destructive power throughout the play. Both threaten patriarchal Rome: it is sadly appropriate that Titus is responsible for the deaths of both the "good" and the "bad" woman.

## CRITICAL CONTROVERSIES

The first of many controversies about *Titus Andronicus* concerns the play's authorship. Though Shakespeare's name does not appear on any of the earliest published versions of the play (Q1, 2, and 3), he was credited with authorship of the play by a contemporary, Francis Meres, in 1598, and the play's inclusion in the First Folio (1623) by Shakespeare's close friends Heminge and Condell strongly supports this claim. As far as we know, the play was accepted as Shakespeare's work in his own time. As G. Harold Metz shows in *Shakespeare's Earliest Tragedy*, doubts surfaced by the end of the seventeenth century, when Edward Ravenscroft reported that he had been told by "some anciently conversant with the Stage" that Shakespeare only gave a few "Master-Touches" to a text written primarily by another, unnamed "private Author." This rumor, he felt, was rendered credible by his own judgment that the play was "the most incorrect and indigested piece in all [Shakespeare's] Works," its structure a "heap of Rubbish" (quoted in Metz, p. 18–19). Though others immediately disputed the rumor, many critics throughout the eighteenth and nineteenth centuries shared Ravenscroft's evaluation of the play and welcomed an excuse to believe that it was written by someone else. The content was too horrific, too violent, too extreme, to fit their conception of "gentle" Shakespeare. Others based their belief on a more thoughtful evaluation of stylistic evidence, pointing to features of versification and word choice that seemed inconsistent with Shakespeare's practice in his other plays and closer to that of certain contemporaries. One early argument of this kind was made by T. M. Parrott, who in 1919 suggested that George Peele, a "university wit" and author of several plays with classical themes, was the probable author of *Titus*. Parrott based his view on a careful analysis of the use of feminine endings—lines of blank verse that include an additional unstressed syllable at the end. Shakespeare often used them, whereas Peele seldom did. *Titus*, at least in some scenes, is characterized by a heavy use of masculine endings.

By the mid-twentieth century, evaluation of the play had taken a more positive turn, and for some this meant embracing the idea that the play was entirely by Shakespeare. Earlier doubts about Shakespeare's authorship were dismissed as too strongly motivated by simple dislike of the play. Inconsistencies of style could be accounted for by the fact that it was an early work; writers often try out different styles and imitate others when they are first learning their craft. Most late-twentieth-century editors of the play followed the First Folio and attributed *Titus Andronicus* wholly to Shakespeare. Yet the debate over authorship is far from settled. A powerful argument has recently been advanced by Brian Vickers reviving and adding support to T. M. Parrott's argument that George Peele wrote at least part of the play (*Shakespeare as Co-Author: A Historical Study of Five Collaborative Plays* [Oxford: Oxford UP, 2002], 148–243). Based on a variety of stylistic tests, Vickers argues that all of act 1, the first two scenes of act 2, and the first scene of act 4 were Peele's work. If Vickers is right, it is very likely that Shakespeare took over the writing of a play that Peele had started but was unable to finish. This still leaves the play mostly by Shakespeare. Even in the scenes probably by Peele, Shakespeare very likely made editorial changes and worked to integrate them into his own overall conception of character and action.

Clearly, the debate over the play's authorship has been closely related to the question of the play's overall value. Whether it was written by Shakespeare or not, the overwhelming majority of critics from the seventeenth century through the middle of the twentieth century held it to be an inferior work. Such critics argued, among other things, that the play is full of bad poetry, its characters are too flat, its structure is incoherent, and its style is unsuitable for its content. But the principal complaint has centered on the play's over-the-top violence. The famous eighteenth-century critic and man of letters Samuel Johnson, for example, deplored the "barbarity of the spectacles" and thought them "scarcely . . . tolerable to any audience" (quoted in Kolin, ed., p. 4). The poet Samuel Taylor Coleridge, writing in the next century, thought that the play was "obviously intended to excite vulgar audiences by its scenes of blood and horror—to our ears shocking and disgusting" (quoted in Kolin, ed., p. 99). T. S. Eliot, writing in the early twentieth century, famously denounced it as "one of the stupidest and most uninspired plays ever written," and he complained especially about "the wantonness, the irrelevance" of the onstage violence (Metz, p. 47). Two rather different threads can be detected in these complaints. One is that the violence in the play is there to pander to "vulgar" (that is, lower class and uneducated) tastes and serves no other purpose; the other is that the violence is simply something no civilized person wants to watch.

Since the mid-twentieth century, however, critics have increasingly disputed both points. Many now see the play as a much more serious exploration of the causes and effects of violence and believe its apparent incongruities of style and content serve subtle artistic goals. As mentioned in "Themes and Meanings," above, the critic Eugene Waith, writing in 1957, thought the play's style effectively evoked the tragic metamorphosis of characters under pressure from extreme emotion. Albert Tricomi in 1976 argued that the play's figurative language, "far from being divorced from the action . . . points continually toward the lurid events that govern the tragedy" ("Aesthetics," p. 11; see "Devices and Techniques," above). Shortly thereafter, Richard T. Brucher in " 'Tragedy, Laugh On': Comic Violence in *Titus Andronicus*," argued that the play's dislocating mixture of violence and black comedy was a successful way to engage the audience in "a sense of the chaos afflicting the characters onstage," ultimately revealing "painful truths about the world" and undermining "cherished notions about human values and conduct" (91). Though the ultimate meaning of the play's representation of violence continues to be a matter of debate, few now view the violence to be gratuitous or too offensive for audience sensibilities.

Indeed, the play's violence does not seem particularly extreme in the context of late-twentieth- and early-twenty-first-century popular culture: contemporary films, videos, graphic novels, computer games, and media representations have normalized violent images. Moreover, the atrocities enacted in *Titus* have a grim topicality in our increasingly globalized world. As Philip Kolin has pointed out, brutal crimes are a regular feature of today's news reporting, as has been the political violence of fascist and totalitarian regimes since World War II and Hitler (283). News of rape as a weapon of war in places such as Bosnia and Kosovo, followed by the rejection and even murder of raped women by their families, gives the story of Lavinia a harrowing currency.

Given such a backdrop, how then should we read the play's representation of Lavinia's rape and, more broadly, its depiction of women's roles and other gender issues? Is the play endorsing or critiquing Titus's murder of Lavinia? Such questions have been a topic of debate in many recent discussions of the play, especially in feminist work. For some critics, such as Catherine Stimpson, the play is notable for its sympathetic treatment of a rape victim: "Shakespeare never falters, never hedges, as he shows how defenseless women are before sexual violence and the large destructiveness it entails" ("Shakespeare and the Soil of Rape," in Rose, ed., p. 60). They have also appreciated the way Lavinia is eventually able to communicate despite the attempts to silence her and is given an active role in hunting down the perpetrators of the rape.

Other feminists, however, have criticized the play for not going far enough in a critique of patriarchy. Some argue that Lavinia's male relatives treat her insensitively and are more interested in their own pain than in her suffering. They silence her figuratively after her literal silencing by Chiron and Demetrius. (For an example of this line of argument, see Derek Cohen, *Shakespeare's Culture of Violence* [New York: St. Martin's P, 1993], 79–93.) Others are deeply appalled by Titus's murder of Lavinia at the end of the play (for example, Bernice Harris, "Sexuality as a Signifier for Power Relations: Using Lavinia, of Shakespeare's *Titus Andronicus*," *Criticism* 38 (1996): 383–406). Even Stimpson notes that "Shakespeare deplores warped patterns of patriarchy but not the patterns themselves" (63). Shakespeare represents Rome as a deeply patriarchal culture and in so doing provides a shrewd and detailed analysis of patriarchal attitudes. But though the play questions other Roman values, it does not particularly question its gender ideology.

Tamora's role has also been controversial. Some feminists have focused on the way Tamora's character is built out of misogynist stereotypes and criticize its demonization of female sexuality (see, for example, the articles by Hanna and Kehler mentioned in "Devices and Techniques," above). For others, such as Stimpson, the play importantly shows how even women can become complicit with patriarchal violence. Still others have stressed that it is important not to forget that males are also victims of violence in the play. Sons as well as daughters are mutilated, degraded, and killed, and the play shows vividly the way a whole family can be damaged and traumatized in the aftermath of a rape (Willis, pp. 22, 42–46).

As with so many of Shakespeare's plays, just about all of its central characters, themes, and techniques have given rise to questions and disagreements. Titus's character in particular has a long history of controversy. Is he too flawed for a tragic hero? What are we to think of his many acts of bad judgment in act 1? How "mad" does he become in the last half of the play? How does his revenge compare with that of Tamora and Aaron? Is there ultimately any meaningful moral distinction to be drawn between Titus and his enemies? A few critics think that Titus changes places with Aaron by the end of the play. Aaron protects his child, while Titus destroys his own offspring as well as that of others. After act 3, the critic Nicholas Brooke suggests, "Titus deteriorates into a mad beast, while Aaron displays a kind of nobility: the issues of right and wrong are indeed confounded" (quoted in Kolin, ed., p. 18). Most, however, think that though Titus remains a problematic figure, his actions are not as wicked as those of Aaron and Tamora. Titus's killing of Alarbus, Mutius, and Lavinia reveals a barbaric side to Roman honor and piety, but his killing of Tamora and her sons is justified. He targets the actual perpetrators of the wrongs against his family, whereas Tamora and Aaron's vengeance targets Lavinia, her husband, and two of her brothers, none of whom had anything to do with the sacrifice of Alarbus.

How far, then, does the play's interrogation of Roman "barbarism" ultimately go? What are we to think about the restoration of order at the end of the play? These, too, have been much-debated questions. Our answers depend on how we see the character of Lucius, who becomes the new emperor. Some critics see Lucius primarily in heroic terms. (See Kolin, ed., pp. 34–41, for a survey of perspectives on Lucius.) He embodies the best traits of his father, such as his military heroism and his respect for the dead, and his reign brings hope of Rome's spiritual regeneration. But Lucius is also at the center of many of the play's unresolved questions. In act 1, he is deeply involved in the sacrifice of Alarbus. Whereas his father at least shows some concern for Tamora's feelings ("Patient yourself, madam, and pardon me" [1.1.121]), Lucius calls for the sacrifice in the most bloodthirsty terms (1.1.96–101, 143–144). He reacts to Lavinia after the rape more with horror ("This object kills me!" [3.1.64]) than with sympathy. He is ready to murder Aaron's infant son for his father's crimes and makes blatantly racist comments about them both (5.1.40–52). He kills Saturninus, Rome's lawful emperor, and however understandable this act is at the time, it is still an act of regicide. When the Roman people decide to forgive his actions and take him as their new emperor, the play seems to be endorsing the idea that vengeance on behalf of a blood-relative is an acceptable motive for killing a ruler—a rather surprising moral in light of Renaissance views about the divine right of kings.

Or is the play instead inviting us to see the persistence of barbarism in Rome? Lucius's rule could be seen as a coup d'état, assisted by Rome's former enemies, the Goths, one that simply reinstates an order in which family honor and piety sanction vigilante violence, torture, and mutilation. It is difficult to say. The last act of the play seems to "forget" the problems made visible in act 1, especially the sacrifice of Alarbus. The final speeches of Marcus and Aemilius locate the source of all Rome's troubles not in its own internal divisions, but in Tamora and Aaron, the non-Roman "others," who are implicitly compared to the Trojan horse ("Tell us what Sinon hath bewitch'd our ears, / Or who hath brought the fatal engine in / That gives our Troy, our Rome, the civil wound" [5.3.85–87]). Though Tamora and Aaron are rightly punished for their crimes, Rome's participation in its own undoing is not acknowledged.

Such questions are unlikely to be resolved any time soon. But one thing is clear: the play is no longer being dismissed as a "heap of Rubbish." Though it is an early (and perhaps collaborative) work, without the depth and complexity of Shakespeare's later tragedies, most critics would now agree that the play has an important place in the Shakespearean canon and is worthy of serious study. The play raises significant questions about revenge and justice, civilization and barbarism, violence and human suffering, and its style and content are now generally seen to be guided by a coherent, if not always effective, artistic vision. The proliferation of critical studies of the play since the late 1950s testifies to the play's profound hold on the modern imagination and its continuing relevance to contemporary concerns.

## PRODUCTION HISTORY

*Titus Andronicus* was very popular in Shakespeare's time. The title pages of all three of the published quarto versions of the play refer to recent performances, and other records support the claim that it was indeed performed "sundry times" in the 1590s and early 1600s. A drawing, believed to be made by a man named Henry Peacham in 1595 and commonly referred to as the Longleat manuscript, shows what is generally believed to be a scene from an early production of *Titus Andronicus*. In it, Tamora kneels before Titus, presumably appealing for Alarbus's life. To the right her sons also kneel, and Aaron is pictured holding a sword and pointing to its tip. To the left, behind Titus, are two soldiers in Elizabethan dress. Titus himself wears a Roman toga and a wreath. The drawing shows what is thought to be a common Elizabethan stage practice: costumes eclectically mingle styles from different historical periods, as some modern productions do.

Henslowe's *Diary* records a number of performances that yielded a high profit, and a record exists of a privately commissioned performance. By 1614, however, it appears that *Titus Andronicus* had come to seem old-fashioned; Ben Jonson's Induction to his play *Bartholomew Fair* attests to the play's popularity but mocks it as an old warhorse, beloved only by backward-thinking, cruder sorts. Though the play continued to be sporadically performed throughout the seventeenth century and was adapted for the Restoration stage, it soon fell completely out of favor. Only a handful of productions were mounted during the eighteenth and nineteenth centuries, and in the twentieth century the play did not begin to be frequently performed until Peter Brook's 1955 production at Stratford-upon-Avon, with Laurence Olivier as Titus, Anthony Quayle as Aaron, and Vivien Leigh as Lavinia. This production was so strikingly successful that it changed the way both theatergoers and literary critics perceived this supposedly "bad" play. Much-praised performances by Olivier and the other actors were part of the reason, but so was Brook's stripped-down, stylized approach to the play's violence. Brook believed the play to be "about the most modern of emotions—about violence, hatred, cruelty, pain," but he also thought that the best way to represent violence and pain on the stage was by non-literal means (Dessen, p. 15). Thus, when Lavinia appeared after the rape, crimson scarves, symbolizing blood, fluttered from her sleeves. Brook believed that the effects of violence needed to be shown in a form that was "*unrealistic*" and "*quite abstract*" in order to be "*totally real.*" He also made cuts in the text to reduce the likelihood of what he viewed as inappropriate laughter. Titus was presented, according to one reviewer, "not as a beaming hero, but as a battered veteran, stubborn and shambling, long past caring about the people's cheers." Another wrote that "a hundred campaigns have tanned his heart to leather." But Lavinia's rape tapped into a deep vulnerability, and once touched, Titus "suffered on a superhuman scale." (All of the preceding reviews are quoted in Hughes, p. 41.) The overall effect of the production was somber, solemn, and brutally tragic.

Brook's production struck a deep chord in the post–World War II era; its horrors seemed all too contemporary. It also inspired many other theater companies to stage productions of *Titus Andronicus*. (Alan C. Dessen's *Shakespeare in Performance: "Titus Andronicus"* provides an excellent survey of productions of the play in the twentieth century.) Many post-Brook productions made the parallels to modern-day atrocities more explicit, drawing connections between Rome and the age of Hitler and Stalin through fascist or other totalitarian imagery or costume. Others have made connections to revenge killings among urban gangs or the Mafia. (Philip Kolin discusses such productions in detail in " 'Come Down and Welcome Me to this World's Light': *Titus Andronicus* and the Canons of Contemporary Violence," in Kolin, ed., pp. 305–316.) Still others have eschewed any overt reference to a particular time and place. One particularly notable production of this kind was Deborah Warner's 1987 Royal Shakespeare Company production, with Brian Cox in the title role. Unlike Brook, Warner made few cuts in the text; and instead of attempting to limit laughter, she made use of it in order to show that "laughter and horror . . . [were] inseparable" (Dessen, p. 62). Titus himself was shown to be a master of black comedy. The play's violence was also represented more realistically, employing blood on white linen at key moments and emphasizing Lavinia's disfigurement along with her traumatized state of mind. While Brook had cut Marcus's long speech in which he responds to Lavinia's mutilation with elaborate poetic images, Warner retained it to show Marcus's "deeply moving attempt to master the facts, and thus to overcome the emotional shock, of a previously unimagined horror" (Dessen, p. 59). "Trust in the script" was the byword of Warner's production, and judging from this production's very favorable reception, it was an extremely effective approach.

Two recent productions are now available on video. Jane Howell's version for the British Broadcasting Company's Shakespeare series is memorable for the way it uses the part of young Lucius, the grandson of Titus. Howell directs attention to the young boy as a deeply affected observer, trying to make sense of the violence committed by the grown-ups of his world. The play's end is a dark one, strongly suggesting that Rome will continue to be a brutal regime. When Aaron and his child are brought out at the end of 5.3, we see, through young Lucius's eyes, that Aaron's son has been killed and is in a coffin—the promise Lucius made to Aaron to care for the infant has been brutally broken. Similarly, Julie Taymor's film *Titus*, first released in the year 1999, uses young Lucius as a key figure. She gives the film a frame story, in which the boy is seen in a modern kitchen playing with action figures on a kitchen table. His play gets increasingly aggressive until he steps back, as if suddenly frightened by his own capacity for violence. An adult-sized living version of one of the action figures bursts through the window and carries the boy off—into the story of *Titus*. As if combining Brook's and Warner's approaches, Taymor's visually stunning production alternates between intense realism and highly stylized effects. Taymor's Rome is a quasi-fascist, militarized world, with an effete Saturninus presiding over a decadent court. Titus, played by Anthony Hopkins, is a steely, violent general who becomes increasingly malevolent and deranged. His performance has more than a few overtones of his famous role as Hannibal Lector in *Silence of the Lambs*; indeed, we glimpse him apparently chewing a bit of the pie he has baked for Tamora. There are no "good guys" in this production, and the film as a whole emphasizes the dehumanizing, destructive aspects of retaliatory violence. Yet the end offers hope: the film's last images show young Lucius taking Aaron's infant son into his arms, then escaping the nightmare world of Rome into a new one in which the sun is rising.

## EXPLICATION OF KEY PASSAGES

**1.1.104–141. "Stay, Roman brethren! . . . upon her foes."** In this important passage, Tamora asks Titus to spare her son, Alarbus, appealing to a common humanity that transcends national boundaries in an attempt to sway him to feel pity for her as a mother. She speaks passionately, yet logically, and makes the following five significant points:

1. Because Titus is himself a parent, he should understand how "dear" her son is to her.
2. Titus should be satisfied with the fact that he has already defeated the Goths, taken their queen and her sons captive, and paraded them through the streets.
3. Her sons do not deserve to be degraded by a humiliating death when they have fought valiantly for their country just as Titus's sons have.
4. It cannot be piety to stain his family tomb with blood from a murder.
5. Showing mercy is a quality that will make Titus godlike and demonstrate his true nobility.

Tamora tries to make the Roman custom of human sacrifice look narrowly provincial, unfair, unfeeling, and unbecoming to a man of Titus's high station. Despite the persuasiveness of her argument, Titus refuses to give in. To him, the sacrifice is a religious duty that must be carried out in order to appease the ghosts of the Roman sons who have died in battle. Interestingly, the ritual is presented as something especially important to Titus's sons; they are owed it for their own sacrifices on the battlefield. The brotherhood of man that might transcend national ties is not as im-

Anthony Hopkins (right) as Titus Andronicus and Alan Cumming (center) as Saturninus in Julie Taymor's 1999 film *Titus*. Courtesy of Photofest.

portant as the literal brotherhood of blood relatives or the brotherhood of comrades-in-arms. Moreover, whatever identification Titus might feel with Tamora as a parent, it is outweighed by his duty to his own sons. Titus's decision shows the great importance he attaches not only to Roman piety but also to family ties.

So far the exchange between Titus and Tamora enacts a clash of cultures and of two different "goods"; out of this clash the play's revenge plot will unfold. The speeches that follow, however, tilt the balance in favor of the Goth perspective. While Titus addresses Tamora politely and implies that the sacrifice is a sad necessity, Lucius strikes a more disturbingly bloodthirsty note in his call to hew Alarbus's limbs and burn his flesh (1.1.126–128). To Tamora's sons, Chiron and Demetrius, the idea that human sacrifice can be thought of as religious is a contradiction in terms ("cruel, irreligious piety," Tamora calls it [1.1.130]); such a practice makes Rome more barbarous than the central Asian country of Scythia, notorious for its savage peoples. Demetrius calls for revenge and draws a parallel between Tamora and Hecuba, the Trojan queen; the gods who allowed Hecuba to get revenge on the "Thracian tyrant" (1.1.138) who killed her son may eventually help Tamora to do this, too. Significantly, he draws upon classical precedent, appealing to a story from epic tradition that Romans would hold dear; Rome was supposedly founded by the Trojan hero Aeneas, a nephew of Hecuba. Demetrius's speech points to a common cultural legacy: the honor code that requires family members to avenge the death of blood-relatives is shared by both Romans and Goths. Overall, this passage not only sets the revenge plot in motion but also begins the play's questioning of Roman values and its confounding of distinctions between so-called civilization and supposed barbarism.

**3.1.219–233. "If there were reason . . . bitter tongues."** In this passage, Titus expresses his feeling that he and his daughter, Lavinia, have entered into an uncannily symbiotic relationship, due to their common experience of profound grief. He has now been mutilated like Lavinia, having just lost one of his hands in a futile attempt to stop the execution of his sons, and they are both attempting to console each other and to wrest pity from the heavens through their prayers. Marcus tries to get Titus to restrain himself, urging him to "let reason govern [his] lament" (218). But Titus insists that since his grief is so overwhelming, it requires the kind of extravagant language he uses in this speech. He goes on to compare grief to a storm that floods the earth and stirs up the ocean. Grief is like a force of nature, unstoppable and engulfing, and it binds Titus and Lavinia together. She is the "weeping welkin" (that is, the storm-filled sky from which rain is falling, 3.1.226) and he is the earth and its seas, which must necessarily react to the storm. Lavinia's sighs and tears are equated with the wind and the rain; together they turn Titus's ocean into a flood that overflows and drowns the earth (that is, Titus himself). At this point Titus shifts to body imagery to make his comparison; his "ocean" is now equated with the "bowels" (3.1.230) in the body's inner cavities. Just as Titus's "ocean" could not contain his daughter's tears, so also his body cannot contain her woe, but only "vomit" (3.1.231) it back up again. Titus's flood imagery suggests the way powerful grief can lead to the dissolution of individual identity; father and daughter seem almost to merge together. At the same time, his body imagery suggests the way grief can lead to a disturbing loss of physical and mental control. The passage foreshadows Titus's descent into madness (his "sea wax[es] mad," 3.1.222), which begins later in this scene, and it underscores the growing intimacy he feels with his daughter, which he earlier called a "sympathy of woe" (148). The passage also brings out Titus's sense of confidence in the power of language to represent, and therefore to ease, grief by the use of excessive images. That confidence, however, will shortly be destroyed. Once the messenger brings news of his sons' execution, Titus will renounce tears and lamentations, exchanging them for mad laughter and revenge (3.1.263–270).

## Annotated Bibliography

Bartels, Emily. "Making More of the Moor: Aaron, Othello, and Renaissance Refashionings of Race." In *"Titus Andronicus": Critical Essays*. Ed. Philip C. Kolin. New York: Garland, 1995. 265–284. An important essay on Aaron's role and race issues in *Titus Andronicus*.

Brucher, Richard T. " 'Tragedy, Laugh On': Comic Violence in *Titus Andronicus*." *Renaissance Drama* 10 (1979): 71–91. Shows that black comedy is an important part of the play's design and is used to suggest the collapse of moral order in Titus's Rome.

Dessen, Alan C. *Shakespeare in Performance: "Titus Andronicus."* Manchester, Eng.: Manchester UP, 1989. A succinct overview of theater productions and performance issues.

Kahn, Coppélia. *Roman Shakespeare: Warriors, Wounds, and Women*. London: Routledge, 1997. A thoughtful study of gender issues in Shakespeare's Roman plays, including a substantial section on *Titus Andronicus*.

Kolin, Philip C., ed. *"Titus Andronicus": Critical Essays*. New York: Garland, 1995. An excellent anthology of major critical essays and theater reviews of *Titus Andronicus* from diverse perspectives. The editor's introductory chapter provides a detailed overview and extensive bibliography of twentieth-century criticism on the play.

Metz, G. Harold. *Shakespeare's Earliest Tragedy: Studies in "Titus Andronicus."* Madison, NJ: Fairleigh Dickinson UP, 1996. An extended study of the play, emphasizing questions of authorship, sources, dating, and text. Also provides an overview of twentieth-century criticism and stage history since 1970.

Miola, Robert S. *Shakespeare's Rome*. Cambridge: Cambridge UP, 1983. A study of Shakespeare's Roman plays, with attention to Shakespeare's probing of Roman values and family issues, along with his use of classical sources.

Rose, Mark, ed. *Shakespeare's Early Tragedies: A Collection of Critical Essays*. Englewood Cliffs, NJ: Prentice Hall, 1995. Includes six important critical essays on *Titus Andronicus*.

Waith, Eugene M. "The Metamorphosis of Violence in *Titus Andronicus*." In *"Titus Andronicus": Critical Essays*. Ed. Philip C. Kolin. New York: Garland, 1995. 99–114. An influential essay first published in 1957 that explores the play's relationship to Ovid's *Metamorphoses* and examines the effects of violence on character.

# Romeo and Juliet

## Michelle M. Sauer

### PLOT SUMMARY

**Prologue.** The Chorus provides a brief overview of all the events that will take place within the play, setting up the feud between the two noble houses of Verona, the Montagues and the Capulets, as well as foretelling the fate of the "pair of star-cross'd lovers" (l. 6).

**1.1.** Samson and Gregory, two Capulet servants, enter and begin to make a series of threats against the House of Montague. Abram and Balthasar, two Montague servants, soon enter, and the four exchange heated words. Before they exchange blows, they are joined by Benvolio, Lord Montague's nephew, who attempts to make peace by drawing his own rapier and beating down the servants' swords. Soon, Tybalt, Lady Capulet's nephew, arrives, and he challenges Benvolio to a duel. The two begin to fight. Citizens decry both houses.

In the meantime, Lord Capulet and Lord Montague, along with their wives, arrive, and they, too, attempt to fight with each other. Prince Escalus enters and orders the houses to find a solution to their problem, declaring that any member of either family found fighting in the future will be executed. The Montagues stay behind to speak to Benvolio about their son, Romeo. They are concerned about him because he appears to be in a black humor. Benvolio assures them that he will discover the cause. Soon after this, Romeo arrives. He announces that his melancholy results from his being in love with Rosaline, who has declared her intent to remain chaste. Benvolio scorns Romeo's declarations of love.

**1.2.** Lord Capulet is speaking with County Paris, a nobleman related to the Prince, about his reluctance to end the age-old feud. Paris listens politely, but continues to press his request upon Lord Capulet: he seeks permission to woo Lord Capulet's daughter, Juliet. Though Capulet grants his permission, he also warns Paris that Juliet is too young to take marriage seriously. Furthermore, Capulet insists that Juliet's consent to the match is as necessary as his own. As the men leave, Capulet orders his servant to go around town issuing invitations to a masked ball to everyone on the guest list. As the servant is walking about, he encounters Romeo and Benvolio. The illiterate servant asks for help reading the guest list. After the servant departs, Benvolio and Romeo make plans to sneak into the Capulets' costume ball because Rosaline will be attending.

**1.3.** Later that evening, Lady Capulet enters her daughter's rooms to discuss the County Paris. Because of her faithful service, Lady Capulet allows the Nurse to remain. After the Nurse reminisces about her husband, Lady Capulet seizes the opportunity to urge Juliet to consider Paris as a potential suitor. Juliet obediently agrees to study him at the ball that evening.

**1.4.** Wearing masks, Romeo, Benvolio, and Mercutio, the Prince's relative and Romeo's friend, progress toward the party. When Romeo continues to sigh over Rosaline, Mercutio begins to tease him. Mercutio suggests that sexual desire is understandable; love, however, is not. When Romeo says that he had a dream that makes him think he should not attend the Capulet ball, Mercutio launches into a long digression about Queen Mab, "the fairies' midwife" (1.4.54) and deliverer of visions, in an attempt to convince Romeo that dreams mean nothing. Benvolio urges them on, and they continue to the ball.

**1.5.** Servants scurry around completing last-minute preparations. Lord Capulet enters and makes a brief welcoming speech to the revelers. Romeo enters and asks a servant about the identity of a young lady he has seen across the floor. He remarks to himself about her beauty and feels the first stirrings of love. Tybalt, overhearing his comments, storms over to his uncle, Lord Capulet. Tybalt informs Capulet that Romeo, the son of his archenemy, is at the ball. Lord Capulet counsels Tybalt to be patient. He has heard that Romeo is a courteous gentleman and does not want any fighting. In the meantime, Romeo has made his way to Juliet. When he approaches her, she appears to be just as taken by him. The two exchange words and kisses before Juliet is whisked away by her faithful Nurse. Romeo forestalls the Nurse to inquire about Juliet's parentage. She informs him that Juliet is the daughter of Lord and Lady Capulet, and Romeo is devastated. The Nurse catches up to Juliet, who in turn inquires after Romeo's identity. The Nurse informs her that Romeo is the son of Lord Montague, and Juliet is equally distressed. The party ends.

**2.Prologue.** The Chorus again takes the stage to reiterate that love has sprung up between Romeo and Juliet. These feelings will not be denied, and the lovers will contrive ways to meet despite the enmity between their families.

**2.1.** A heavy-hearted Romeo wanders the street thinking about Juliet. He hears his friends Benvolio and Mercutio looking for him, but he hides. Mercutio begins to mock Romeo, jestingly conjuring him by calling upon Rosaline, whom both assume Romeo still loves. Benvolio attempts to quiet Mercutio but is unsuccessful, as is their search for Romeo.

**2.2.** Ignoring his friends, Romeo vaults the Capulets' garden wall and watches Juliet, who is standing on her balcony. He ruminates on his newfound love: "But soft, what light through yonder window breaks? / It is the east, and Juliet is the sun" (2.2.1–2). Juliet, unaware that Romeo is underneath her window, also speaks of her love for the young Montague: "O Romeo, Romeo, wherefore art thou Romeo?" (2.2.33). She laments that he is a Montague, and wishes he could cast off his identity. Seizing the opportunity, Romeo calls out to Juliet, and the two openly declare their love for each other. Romeo attempts to woo Juliet with poetic phrases and flowery promises, but she demands simple reality. He is brought to earth by her requests, and the two exchange sincere promises of love. Juliet is called away by her Nurse, but she returns to say goodnight and to ascertain Romeo's intentions: "If that thy bent of love be honorable, / Thy purpose marriage, send me word to-morrow," (2.2.143–144). Romeo assents, and arrangements are made to meet the next day. Once again Juliet withdraws into her chambers, only to return a moment later to agree upon a time. Romeo resolves to go immediately to see his confessor, Friar Lawrence.

**2.3.** Friar Lawrence is returning to his cell carrying a basket of plants that he has gathered. An expert herbalist, the Friar mutters to himself about the various uses for the plants he carries, remarking on both the helpful and harmful properties "in plants, herbs, stones" (2.3.16). Romeo enters and approaches the Friar, who is startled to see him so early in the morning. Romeo pours out his heart to the Friar, telling him about Juliet; eventually he begs the Friar to marry them later that day. The Friar is taken aback, both by Romeo's sudden shift in affections from Rosaline to Juliet and by the speed of the planned marriage. Romeo is steadfast in his insistence, however, so the Friar agrees to perform the ceremony. Despite his misgivings, Friar Lawrence has hopes for the future, "For this alliance may so happy prove / To turn your households' rancor to pure love" (2.3.91–92), and agrees to marry Romeo and Juliet that same day.

**2.4.** Benvolio and Mercutio stroll through Verona discussing Romeo, who had not returned home all night, and mocking Tybalt. Tybalt, still infuriated about the ball, had sent a letter to the Montague estate in which he challenged Romeo to a duel. Romeo, of course, did not answer the challenge because he did not know about it. Romeo enters, and Mercutio begins to tease him mercilessly. The two exchange barbs until Benvolio attempts to put an end to it. Just then, Juliet's Nurse and her servant, Peter, enter, looking for Romeo. Mercutio intercepts them and teases the Nurse. Though she is insulted, she endures the jests in order to get Romeo's message for Juliet: "Bid her devise / Some means to come to shrift this afternoon, / And there she shall at Friar Lawrence' cell / Be shriv'd and married" (2.4.179–182). He further enjoins the Nurse to wait for his servant, who shall provide a rope ladder, with which Romeo can then climb into Juliet's bedchamber. The Nurse praises Romeo, and agrees to do as he asks.

**2.5.** Juliet is impatiently awaiting the Nurse's return. When the Nurse arrives she keeps Juliet waiting for Romeo's response but eventually tells her to go to Friar Lawrence's cell. "There stays a husband to make you a wife" (2.5.69). Juliet hastens to prepare herself for her wedding, while the Nurse leaves to meet Romeo's servant.

**2.6.** Friar Lawrence and Romeo enter. Though the Friar is still wary about the clandestine marriage, Romeo urges him to forget his fears in the face of all the ensuing happiness. Somewhat mollified, the Friar is still cautionary. Juliet enters. She exchanges pleasantries with the Friar and words of love with Romeo. The Friar leads them away for the ceremony.

**3.1.** Mercutio and Benvolio are once again in the streets of Verona. Just as Benvolio suggests that they retire in order to avoid conflict with the Capulets, Tybalt appears accompanied by a group of friends and servants. Tybalt accuses Mercutio of consorting with Romeo, and heated words are exchanged. Just then, Romeo enters and is challenged by Tybalt. Since Tybalt is now his cousin by marriage, Romeo attempts to elude the challenge and make peace. Tybalt is enraged, and Mercutio, who cannot understand Romeo's actions, draws his own rapier. Romeo attempts to make peace between Tybalt and Mercutio to no effect, and the two begin to fight. Romeo pleads for Benvolio's assistance and, though unarmed, steps between the combatants. Instead of stopping the fight, however, Romeo's action causes Mercutio's death. Tybalt thrusts his rapier under Romeo's arm and into Mercutio. Tybalt and his companions then flee. At first, Mercutio and his friends believe that the wound is a small one, but soon Mercutio realizes that he is mortally injured. The dying Mercutio calls for "A plague a' both houses!" (3.1.91) before he is carried off. Tybalt reappears, and Romeo, furious with grief, attacks and kills him. At Benvolio's urging, Romeo flees. The Prince arrives soon afterward, accompanied by the Capulets and the Montagues. The Prince asks Benvolio to explain the situation. He complies, indicating that Tybalt challenged and killed Mercutio before Romeo challenged and killed Tybalt. Though the hysterical Lady Capulet demands Romeo's execution, the Prince commutes his sentence to immediate banishment in light of Tybalt's actions.

**3.2.** Juliet is pining for her new husband, wishing for night to fall. Her Nurse enters in a state of woe. She mournfully describes a dead body that Juliet believes is Romeo. Juliet finally pries the real story out of the Nurse—Tybalt has been killed by Romeo, and Romeo has been exiled. At first, Juliet denounces Romeo for his apparent falseness, but when the Nurse joins her in denigrating him, Juliet quickly comes to his defense. Juliet recognizes that her love and loyalty belong to her husband. Assuming that Romeo has already departed Verona, Juliet bemoans the loss of her wedding night. The Nurse, however, knows that Romeo is at Friar Lawrence's, and agrees to conduct him to her lady's chamber.

**3.3.** Romeo is at the Friar's cell awaiting news of the Prince's sentence. Friar Lawrence returns and tells Romeo that he has been banished. Though the Friar endeavors to make Romeo understand the mercy the Prince has extended, Romeo is too self-absorbed and too youthful to understand. He believes that banishment—which means separation from Juliet—is the same as death and threatens to commit suicide. The Friar continues, unsuccessfully, to persuade Romeo of his good fortune. A loud knocking is heard at the door, and Romeo is so willing to die that he refuses to hide. The intruder is none other than the Nurse, who has come from Juliet. She sees his pitiful state and proceeds to berate Romeo for Juliet's distress. Romeo recklessly offers to commit suicide by stabbing himself, but the dagger is snatched away by the Nurse. Friar Lawrence upbraids Romeo for his "womanish" tears and "wild acts," (3.3.110) and encourages him to go to Juliet and comfort her. He also suggests that Romeo accept his banishment for the time being until the houses can be reconciled. Brought to his senses by the Friar, Romeo agrees to this plan, and the Nurse hastens back to Juliet with a message to await Romeo's arrival.

**3.4.** Lord Capulet apologizes to Paris for Juliet's absence, explaining that she is upset over Tybalt's death. Paris asks Lady Capulet to pass on his concern to Juliet, and she agrees to do so. Lord Capulet, assuming his daughter "will be rul'd / In all respects by me" (3.4.13–14), suggests that Paris and Juliet be married in three days. Paris eagerly agrees to this plan. Lady Capulet is ordered to tell Juliet the news. All depart for bed.

**3.5.** Romeo and Juliet stand by her window to take leave of each other. Juliet attempts to convince Romeo that it is not yet dawn by insisting that it is a nightingale they hear, not a lark. Romeo reluctantly disagrees with her, knowing that if he remains too long he will be caught and executed. Juliet continues to cling to him, however, and Romeo eventually allows himself to be persuaded. Juliet comes to her senses and urges Romeo to depart before dawn breaks. The Nurse enters and tells

Juliet that her mother is on her way to Juliet's chamber. Romeo descends the rope ladder, says farewell, and departs. Shortly after Romeo leaves, Lady Capulet enters the chamber. Assuming that Juliet is still mourning Tybalt's death, she encourages her daughter to put aside her grief. Lady Capulet suggests that Romeo should have been executed and reveals a plan to send an assassin to Mantua after him. Juliet joins her mother in denouncing Romeo.

Pleased, Lady Capulet reveals the real reason she is visiting Juliet's chamber—arrangements have been made for Juliet to wed Paris in three days. Juliet vehemently refuses to consider Paris's suit. Lord Capulet arrives, and Lady Capulet disgustedly informs him of Juliet's disobedience. Lord Capulet responds by cursing Juliet, threatening to beat and disown her. Both parents storm out. Juliet turns to the Nurse for comfort but finds none. The Nurse has abandoned her and believes that "it [is] best you married with the County. / O he's a lovely gentleman!" (3.5.217–218). Juliet realizes she can no longer trust the Nurse. She sends the Nurse to tell Lady Capulet that she has gone to confession to repent her disobedience. Juliet secretly resolves to seek out Friar Lawrence in hopes that he may provide a solution to her dilemma.

**4.1.** Paris is at Friar Lawrence's cell making wedding arrangements, explaining that the haste is due to Juliet's grief over Tybalt's loss. Juliet enters. She spars with Paris, refusing to grant him her love. After Paris departs, the desperate Juliet expresses her desire to die and suggests that she might stab herself. The Friar begs her to wait and shares with her a risky plan that he has concocted. He will give her a vial of "distilling liquor" (4.1.94), which is an exceptionally strong sleeping draft. Upon drinking it, Juliet will fall into a slumber so deep that she will appear to be dead. Instead of being married in three days, she will be enclosed in the family mausoleum, where she will awake and then be free to join Romeo in exile. The Friar assures her that he will send a letter to Romeo explaining the plan. Juliet joyfully agrees to the plot.

**4.2.** Lord Capulet is busy arranging the wedding feast. Juliet returns home and informs her father that the Friar has instructed her not to disobey her father and to ask for his pardon. She also tells her father that she saw Paris and "gave him what becomed [appropriate] love I might, / Not stepping o'er the bounds of modesty" (4.2.26–27). Lord Capulet extends his forgiveness and, in celebration, makes arrangements for the wedding to take place the next day, Wednesday, instead of Thursday.

**4.3.** Juliet informs Lady Capulet and the Nurse that she would like to be alone on her last night as an unmarried woman. They agree to give her privacy and withdraw. Juliet prepares to drink the potion, vowing to stab herself if it does not work as expected. She expresses her various fears: that the potion is truly poison, that she will awaken too soon and suffocate in the tomb, or that she will go mad because of the ghosts—or because of Tybalt's body. Calling Romeo's name for strength, Juliet drinks the potion and collapses on her bed.

**4.4.** Lady Capulet and the Nurse bustle around finalizing the wedding feast. Lord Capulet enters and watches over the preparations. Servants come and go with wedding goods. Morning breaks, and Paris arrives with musicians. Lord Capulet calls the Nurse and orders her to fetch Juliet. He leaves to greet Paris.

**4.5.** The Nurse enters Juliet's bedroom to wake her but instead discovers her "body." Her shouts bring Lady Capulet hurrying in, and in turn, her cries for help bring Lord Capulet into the chamber. The women tell an unbelieving Capulet that Juliet is dead. Friar Lawrence arrives asking after the bride and is informed of Juliet's death. Paris denounces death, and all mourn Juliet's loss. The Friar attempts to comfort the assembled company with assurances of Juliet's ascendance into heaven. The wedding party becomes a funeral as the Friar leads the way to the Capulet tomb. The musicians attempt to leave but are stopped by Peter, who suggests that they stay and play comforting songs for the mourners.

**5.1.** In Mantua, Romeo is musing upon a dream he had in which Juliet awoke him from the dead by a kiss. His servant, Balthasar, enters and informs him that Juliet has died and is interred in the Capulet monument. He bears no letters from the Friar. Desolate, Romeo vows to join Juliet in death. He recalls seeing an impoverished apothecary, from whom he intends to purchase a lethal poison, and goes to the man's dwelling. At first, the apothecary demurs, since poison has been outlawed in Mantua, but eventually he reluctantly agrees, as he desperately needs the money.

**5.2.** Friar John, the messenger Friar Lawrence had dispatched to Romeo, meets Friar Lawrence in the garden and reveals that he was unable to deliver the letter to Romeo. Mantua was closed to all strangers for fear of the plague, so no messenger got through. Fearing disaster, the Friar makes haste to the Capulet tomb in order to be there when Juliet awakens.

**5.3.** The grief-stricken Paris goes to the Capulet tomb to mourn Juliet's loss. Hearing noises outside the tomb, he retreats into the shadows. Romeo and Balthasar enter carrying tools. Romeo gives Balthasar a letter for his father, Lord Montague, in which he has explained his actions. He then gives Balthasar a sack of gold and tells him to leave and not return. Instead of leaving, Balthasar hides in the shadows and spies upon his master. As Romeo begins to enter the vault, Paris confronts him. Romeo begs him to leave, but Paris persists, and the two fight. Romeo slays Paris and then grants his final wish by dragging him into the tomb where Juliet is interred. Romeo gazes upon his young wife, railing against death, praising her beauty, and proclaiming his eternal love. At last, he feels the moment has come to join her: "Here's to my love! [*Drinks.*] O true apothecary! / Thy drugs are quick. Thus with a kiss I die" (5.3.119–120).

Just after Romeo collapses, Friar Lawrence arrives. After briefly speaking with Balthasar and examining the scene, the Friar enters the tomb. Juliet awakes, asking for Romeo. The Friar sadly informs her that both Paris and Romeo are lying dead beside her and offers to spirit her away to a convent. Juliet refuses and instead flings herself on Romeo's body: "I will kiss thy lips, / Haply some poison yet doth hang on them, / To make me die with a restorative" (5.3.164–166). Not finding any poison, Juliet then seizes Romeo's dagger and stabs herself, falling dead upon his body. Soon, the Prince, the Montagues, and the Capulets, accompanied by the city watch, all arrive at the tomb. Chaos ensues. The Prince confronts Friar Lawrence and demands an explanation, which the Friar provides. The story is confirmed by Balthasar, Paris's page, and by Romeo's letter. The Prince declares that all have suffered from these events and upbraids Lord Montague and Lord Capulet for their continued ill will. The two lords vow to erect monuments in honor of the ill-fated young couple and to cease the feud that has torn them apart for years.

## PUBLICATION HISTORY

*Romeo and Juliet* was written in 1595–1596, around the same time as *Richard II* and *A Midsummer Night's Dream*. This is sometimes referred to as Shakespeare's "lyrical period," for these plays all contain large sections of lyrical lines. The work was first published in 1597 as the "Excellent Conceited Tragedie of Romeo and Juliet." This first quarto (Q1) version, also known as the "bad quarto," has been the focus of much scholarly debate; it is now generally accepted to have been a text reproduced from memory of a stage production, though there have been challenges to that notion. Nonetheless, it is fairly accepted that Q1 is indeed an acting version of the play. Most authorities today believe that the version printed in the second quarto (Q2) in 1599, also known as the "good quarto," is the most "authentic," meaning that it was likely printed from Shakespeare's own manuscript, or, foul papers. Subsequently, the second quarto version was reprinted in the third quarto (Q3; 1609), which led, in turn, to the fourth quarto (Q4; ca. 1622), which contained a number of emendations, and finally to the fifth quarto (Q5; 1637). The First Folio version (1623) was taken directly from Q3.

Comparisons of Q1 and Q2 reveal some overlap, which could be due either to the accuracy of Q1 or to the lack of other sources for Q2. Furthermore, there is evidence that Q2 itself contains a number of erroneous readings, most likely due to the confused corrections on the manuscript itself. For instance, there are vague and inconsistent speech prefixes; awkward but typically Shakespearean spellings; imprecise and random stage directions; and a number of textual revisions in which the original version remains alongside the emendations. This muddle certainly could have led to confusion for the printer of Q2, which, of course, calls some of Q2's authority into question. Thus, most modern editions take all of these factors into consideration, and most use portions of Q1 to reconstruct and/or to situate the Q2 version. For instance, in modern editions 1.2.46–1.3.34 is taken directly from Q1. In addition, Q1 provides some stage directions, as well as lines or partial lines in the following: 1.4.7–8; 2.2.41; 2.2.163; 4.5.127. Since Q3 and Q4 are predominantly based on Q2, they are less valuable in determining the text. Q4 did contain a number of revisions, but the text has virtually no authorial connection.

## SOURCES FOR THE PLAY

Most critics agree that Shakespeare based his play mainly on Arthur Brooke's lengthy poem *The Tragicall Historye of Romeus and Juliet* (1562). In turn, Brooke owed a debt to several other authors who captured the famous love story. One of the early versions was Masuccio of Salerno's *Il Novellino* (1476). The first of these to appear in the sixteenth century was Luigi da Porto's *Historia novellamente ritrovata di due nobili amanti* (ca. 1530). Other versions appear in Matteo Bandello's *Novelle* (1554); Pierre Boaistuau's translation of Bandello (1559); Brooke's verse translation of Boaistuau; and William Painter's prose translation of Boaistuau in *The Palace of Pleasure* (1567). (See Jill Levenson, "Romeo and Juliet before Shakespeare," *Studies in Philology* 81.3 [1984]: 327.) Further sources for Shakespeare's main plotline probably included Thomas Nashe's *Have with You to Saffron Walden* (1596)—probably also a source for *Love's Labor's Lost* (1594–1597; rev. 1597), John Eliot's *Ortho-epia Gallica* (1593), and Samuel Daniel's *Complaint of Rosamund* (1592).

Besides these works, Shakespeare also drew upon dueling books in order to capture the flavor of the fight scenes. Most likely, he relied upon Vincent Saviolo's seminal manual, *Vincentio Saviolo, his Practise* (1595). Prior to *Love's Labor's Lost* and *Romeo and Juliet*, Shakespeare did not include specific fencing terms in his works, and "it is probably not accidental that Shakespeare's introduction of such language into his drama coincides with the publication of Saviolo's volume in 1595" (Joan Ozark Holmer, "Draw If You Be Men," *Shakespeare Quarterly* 45.2 [1994]: 164). This more decisively settles any lingering scholarly debates about the dating of the play, as Shakespeare could not have read Saviolo until 1595. Moreover, Shakespeare's inclusion of the rapier techniques is exclusive to his version. Both Brooke and Boaistuau, for instance, have street brawls.

Interestingly, throughout the many versions of the story of Romeo and Juliet, the basic plot remained unchanged. Even Shakespeare's version followed what Jill Levenson identifies as the "sequence of the Romeo and Juliet narrative" (328). Each event has a distinct cause; each event follows in the order it originally was presented. What changed throughout the versions were details. What remained the same was the overall tone of counsel, rationality, and emotion. Shakespeare uses these same ideals but, as Levenson indicates, transforms them into an irony-producing framework. Thus, for example, Benvolio's calm explanation to the Prince is counterbalanced by the bloody scene behind him.

Minor sources for the play abound. For centuries playwrights had used the sleeping potion device to orchestrate an escape from an undesired marriage. An early example, *Ephesiaca*, was written by the Greek Xenophon in the fourth century B.C. Edmund Spenser's *Faerie Queene* (1590) and Nashe's *Terrors of the Night, or a Discourse of Apparitions* (1594) both contributed to the Queen Mab speech delivered by Mercutio (1.3.54–94). Scholarly study has also indicated that the Montagues and the Capulets may be nicknames of two medieval Italian political factions—the *Montecchi* (from Verona) and the *Cappelletti* (from Cremona), which are both mentioned in Dante's *Purgatorio*. Other critics claim that several Greek myths contributed to the development of Shakespeare's characters. In particular, the myth of Thanatos (Death) and his younger brother Hypnos (Sleep), the sons of Nyx (Night), are thought to have provided background material for the play's obsession with death and the treatment of the overlapping of sleep, dreams, and death.

## STRUCTURE AND PLOTTING

Though *Romeo and Juliet* is most certainly a tragedy, it also has numerous comedic elements. Much scholarly attention has focused on the idea of the play as a "comedy into tragedy." Yet, according to Levenson, this transformation causes no disruption in the play's structure, since "Elizabethan tragedy and comedy share the same 'external structure.' . . . In both types of dramatic representations the narrative advances in three phases whose proportions may vary: exposition and beginning of the action; complication of incidents; and catastrophe or resolution" (Jill Levenson, "Tragical-Comical-Lyrical," *Proceedings of the PMR Conference* 12–13 [1988]: 33). The complication is often referred to as a pivot scene, in which the rest of the play's action is set up for better or for worse. In this work, Shakespeare depends on a pivotal scene near the middle of the play, and on parallel scenes between the first half and the second. The pivotal scene in *Romeo and Juliet* is Mercutio's death, which occurs in the first scene of act 3.

Several critics have commented on the rather abrupt reversal of fortune experienced in *Romeo and Juliet*. Despite the audience's foreknowledge of the resultant tragedy (noted in the prologue to the play), events appear to lend hope that Romeo and Juliet will live, that the feud will be ended, and that all will be well. Yet, almost immediately after the pivotal scene, the play's actions descend rapidly into tragedy. In general, Elizabethan comedies were quick-paced, full of chance occurrences, and organized around the central idea of social unity. This concord was often achieved, or at least symbolized, through one or more marriages at the conclusion of the play. The action before Mercutio's death fits these broad parameters. The impetuous heroes meet through a series of coincidences, fall in love, defy society, arrange a series of go-betweens, and plan marriage. This would not be simply any marriage, either, but rather it would be a marriage that restored social harmony. All of this action unfolds in the span of less than two days. During this time, Mercutio is presented as a witty and lively man, full of jests and puns. When he dies, the riotous spirit leaves the play: "In Mercutio's sudden, violent end, Shakespeare makes the birth of tragedy coincide exactly with the symbolic death of comedy" (Susan Snyder, "*Romeo and Juliet*: Comedy into Tragedy," *Essays in Criticism* 20.4 [1970]: 395). The tragic events so gloomily foretold by the Chorus in the prologue and hinted at by various dreams and allusions now progress unimpeded. Romeo seems to understand this instinctively, as he comments, "This day's black fate on moe days doth depend, / This but begins the woe others must end" (3.1.119–120). Romeo is now fated to kill Tybalt, and Tybalt's death in turn leads to the other tragic events and the downfall of his love. As Snyder points out, this sense of helplessness is a function of the tragic half of *Romeo and Juliet*, and it is a "function of onrushing events" (Snyder, p. 396). What once had at least seemed avoidable is now inevitable. Political law rules where social law had previously prevailed. However, despite these two "halves," *Romeo and Juliet* is still one complete dramatic work. Levenson notes that "*Romeo and Juliet* emphasizes the points of congruence in its strikingly balanced configuration of tragedy and comedy" (Levenson, "Tragical-Comical-Lyrical," p. 33). Just as harbingers of disaster stalked the lovers in the initial "comic" portion of the play, comedic undertones run throughout the final tragic acts. For instance, as Paris's musicians prepare to pack up after Juliet is discovered to be dead, Peter rushes in with a request for "some merry dump [dirge] to comfort me" (4.5.107–108).

E. Pearlman holds that this "comic option" was meant by Shakespeare to "cheer and deceive" his audience ("Shakespeare at Work," *English Literary Renaissance* 24.2 [1994]: 315–342). Despite the prologue's warning, and despite the numerous versions of the story, Shakespeare may have meant for his audience to hope that the lovers would survive. Favorable signs include the opportunities given to forestall the intended marriage between Juliet and Paris, Paris's dying before Romeo (thus removing him from the picture), and Romeo's final dream. Still, the basic storyline was so ingrained in sixteenth-century culture that it would have been difficult for a happy ending to be believable.

The play's language is also worthy of exploration in regard to structure. As Levenson notes, "they [scholars] have identified three genres in a unique arrangement: tragedy, comedy, sonnet sequence" (Levenson, "Tragical-Comical-Lyrical," p. 31). Thus, the sonnets are as integral to the plot structure as are the tragic and comic elements. The play opens with a prologue, spoken by a formal Chorus, in the form of a sonnet. The sonnet form is the English one favored by Shakespeare, which he used in his own sonnet sequence, not the Petrarchan (Italian) form. The English sonnet form consists of three quatrains followed by a couplet [*abab cdcd efef gg*], as opposed to an octet [*abba abba*] followed by a sestet. However, as Jay Halio has pointed out, "Petrarch . . . is otherwise much in evidence, especially in the first half of the play" (*Romeo and Juliet*, p. 47). Like the unattainable Laura, Romeo's Rosaline proves elusive and off-putting, and his responses evoke the typical cruelmistress scenario. Similarly, act 2 opens with a sonnet in English form spoken by the Chorus. These are the only two acts to open in this way. More than that, however, Romeo relies upon Petrarchan language to express himself before he meets Juliet. He overflows with elaborate, tortured references to the pain of love. Once he meets Juliet, however, he gradually withdraws from the overblown Petrarchan speech into the more refined language of the English sonnet.

Shakespeare also relies upon the sonnet as a form of language in the play. As Ralph Berry points out, "The sonnet is the channel through which the play flows" (Berry, p. 37). Many scholars have noted that the first words exchanged by Romeo and Juliet are in sonnet form (1.5.92–107). This "co-created encounter sonnet" is crucial in the establishment of their relationship (Whittier, p. 35). The lovers divide a sonnet between them, linking themselves together linguistically and stylistically as well as emotionally and physically. In fact, this very first exchange of a sonnet ends with the first physical expression of love between Romeo and Juliet—a kiss. And the rest of their conversation is yet another aborted sonnet—the Nurse interrupts the exchange—that also ends with a kiss. Words are mingled as lips meet.

Besides sonnets, Shakespeare employs a variety of poetic forms, "set pieces," within the play's structure, including epithalamium (wedding song), elegy, rhapsody, quatrains, octaves, aubade (poem of lovers' parting at dawn), quartet, sermons, prothalamion (pre-marriage poem), sententiae (pithy sayings), and plain rhyme. Furthermore, iambic pentameter couplets abound, especially in the more comedic first half of the play. Rhyme is the common mode of communication in Verona. Berry notes two distinct schema: the "heavy, jogging rhymes" of the older generation, and the "quicker," flexible rhyme employed by the younger set (Berry, p. 38). Sonnet form becomes a marker of social status, cultural values, and personal disposition, but verse as a whole remains the preferred form of communication. For instance, Romeo and Juliet first speak to each other through the formal language of a sonnet. At their next meeting, they initially rely on standard poetic terminology, until Juliet resorts to plain diction in an attempt to ascertain Romeo's motives. Once they have broken the standard amatory versification, the lovers resort to formality only when presented with a troubling event.

However, the majority of the play is composed in blank verse, just like the majority of Shakespeare's later great tragedies. Even the Nurse speaks in blank verse, which is unusual given her social class. Hers is a unique blank verse, though, that is continually intermingled with colloquialisms, stories, bawdy puns, and bits of memory. The other servants speak in standard Elizabethan prose. Though earthy, the servants' lines serve as excellent foils for the lyrical blank verse spoken by the upper classes. Another character that displays remarkable flexibility of language is Mercutio, who speaks in both verse and prose despite his elevated social status. His prose lines are usually those meant to tease and cajole, as in his first exchanges with Romeo (1.4) or even his last quip, "No, 'tis not so deep as a well, nor so wide as a church-door, but 'tis enough, 'twill serve. Ask for me to-morrow, and you shall find me a grave man" (3.1.96–98).

Such jarring oppositions, or juxtapositions, are an essential part of the structure of *Romeo and Juliet*, as it was for many Elizabethan plays. For instance, in 1.1 the Montagues worry about their son, and in the following scene, Lord Capulet worries aloud about his daughter. Mercutio's vulgar sexual jests open act 2; in the second scene, Romeo and Juliet speak of love without crude lust. Act 2 ends with Friar Lawrence's heavenly invocation for peace, and act 3 opens with Benvolio's warning of impending strife: "the Capels are abroad" (3.1.2). Juxtapositions can also occur within scenes, such as Friar Lawrence's discussion of the helpful and harmful qualities of the same plants, and Juliet's description of a loving Romeo coupled with the Nurse's report of his duel with Tybalt.

Jay Halio suggests that the play can be seen as a series of "movements" that begin or end with dawn (Halio, pp. 22–23). Shakespeare contracts time in his work. The entire play occurs within the compact span of four days, beginning and ending with dawn, as opposed to Brooke's allowance of several months. The characters' relative youth makes the whirlwind of events more believable.

Because of its unusually unified structure, *Romeo and Juliet* does not rely upon subplots to the extent that Shakespeare's other works do. However, Romeo's initial infatuation with Rosaline can be considered a minor subplot. Though nothing ever comes of it, Romeo's initial foray into love is used as a contrast to his real relationship with Juliet throughout the rest of the play. Similarly, the other subplot that can be discerned is Paris's quest to marry Juliet. He is a sincere suitor, well-established, well-connected, and approved by her family. Both subplots involve one-sided love and serve to highlight the true, mutual love experienced by the two heroes.

## MAIN CHARACTERS

Besides the obvious divide between the Montagues and the Capulets, critics often refer to the characters as falling into one of two groups: the older or the younger generation. Yet both families, whichever way they are divided, are victim to the same tragic circumstances, including the inability to give up a blood feud until it is too late.

### Romeo

Several critics have explored the changes Shakespeare made in his version of the story, especially in reference to the title characters. More precisely, many scholars claim that Romeo and Juliet exhibit a more mature love than that found in his sources, particularly Brooke's poem, in which the lovers were more intensely emotional: "The key words, rude and violent, best describe the Romeus and Juliet of Brooke. Shakespeare's hero and heroine, on the other hand, though they surely have deep feelings, express them in a much more temperate manner" (Lanphier, p. 33). Bandello is the first to introduce the lovesick Romeo, casting him in the traditional role of suffering lover, with Boaistuau closely paralleling him. This Romeo is pathetic; he moans, weeps, and pines for Rosaline, who has steadfastly ignored him. Still, this passion is easily quenched after one reasonable conversation with a friend (who will, in Shakespeare, become Benvolio). Levenson points out, "As Boaistuau, Brooke, and Painter corroborate, this Romeo has a disposition to ponder and resolve" (Levenson, "Romeo and Juliet before Shakespeare," p. 333). Beyond this, Brooke's Romeo is more devastatingly handsome than Shakespeare's, and more violently passionate than his novella-producing counterparts. Shakespeare's Romeo, is, however, more loving and less dependent upon pure rationality than are the previous versions.

## Juliet

Juliet's character also undergoes subtle transformations throughout the different versions. Largely, however, she ends up being less rational than Romeo, though not in Shakespeare's play. In Boaistuau, Bandello, and Brooke, Juliet is prone to extended fits of weeping and deep despair. Yet, she is able to overcome these emotions through rational argumentation, usually imposed on her by other characters. In particular, Brooke's Juliet is self-centered, teary, and waspish, where Shakespeare's Juliet is giving, strong, and supportive. Shakespeare's Juliet is also significantly younger than in his sources. Brooke's Juliet is sixteen; in Painter, Bandello, and Boaistuau she is eighteen. Shakespeare's Juliet is not quite fourteen. While she would thus have been quite young to be married, even for the noble class, it would not have been impossible. Emphasizing Romeo and Juliet's relative youth (Shakespeare's Romeo is sixteen) serves not only to explain the sped-up timeline, but also to heighten the tragedy.

## Mercutio

The other character that has received a great deal of critical attention throughout the play's history is Mercutio. Though Mercutio is on the stage fewer times than either the Nurse or Friar Lawrence, his presence is felt throughout the four days. His death is the pivotal scene; his jests are the central theme. Shakespeare's Mercutio is more prominent than in any depiction in his source materials.

Mercutio has fascinated critics and casual readers alike for centuries. He is noble and a kinsman to the Prince. He jests like the common servants, yet he duels like the aristocrats. His sense of honor is as unique as is the rest of his personality. He is fiercely loyal to his friends yet pitilessly skewers them with his pointed barbs. When Tybalt impugns Romeo's name, calling him a coward for not answering the challenge, Mercutio leaps to Romeo's defense, pursuing the insult even after Romeo himself appears and refuses to fight. Joseph A. Porter suggests that Mercutio is aggressive in the way that Romeo is passive. Whereas Romeo waits for events to happen to him (or around him) and then reacts, Mercutio undertakes the actions himself. (See Porter, pp. 102–104.) Some of Mercutio's more forceful words reveal this aggressive quality, often in reference to sexual play; for example: "If love be rough with you, be rough with love; / Prick love for pricking, and you beat love down" (1.4.27–28 ); "Alas, poor Romeo, he is already dead, stabb'd with a white wench's black eye, run through the ear with a love song, the very pin of his heart cleft with the blind bow-boy's butt-shaft" (2.4.13–16). In all of Mercutio's references to Romeo's romantic liaisons, he assumes the woman in question to be Rosaline, for he dies not knowing about Romeo's relationship with Juliet. Thus Mercutio's remarks can all be seen as a commentary upon infatuation instead of true love. Underneath all the jibes, mocking, and lewdness, however, Mercutio is a true friend to Romeo.

### The Nurse

Juliet's nursemaid, who has been with the family for many years, occupies a position somewhere between servant and family member. She openly mourns the loss of her own husband and daughter, yet she readily accepts Juliet as a substitute daughter. The Nurse desperately wants Juliet to be married and considers herself the best judge of character. She begins the play by seemingly supporting Romeo, yet ultimately she urges Juliet to choose Paris. She acts the part of go-between for the young lovers before her change of heart and openly mourns Juliet's "death." Her chief dramatic function is to provide comic relief. Hence, in the latter half of the play, where the tone becomes tragic, her role diminishes, and she is absent from act 5.

### Tybalt

Tybalt, Juliet's hotheaded cousin, is impulsive, violent, and provocative. Always itching for a fight, he sends a challenge to Romeo at the Montague estate. The challenge goes unanswered—not because Romeo is a coward, but because he had spent the night with Juliet. The enraged Tybalt prowls the streets of Verona looking for Romeo but instead provokes a duel with Mercutio. After disreputably killing Mercutio, Tybalt is in turn slain by Romeo. This is the act that leads to Romeo's banishment and is the catalyst for the unfolding tragedy.

### Benvolio

Benvolio, Romeo's cousin, is the peacemaker. Though provoked into a fight by Tybalt early in the play, he refuses, for the most part, to encourage the feud and strives to defuse tense situations. He is a good friend and a good listener who provides solid advice to Romeo despite teasing him. He is also the one who must explain other characters' actions. Because of Benvolio's reputation, his explanations are usually taken at face value, and his truthfulness is questioned only by the hysterical Lady Capulet.

### Paris

Paris is a young nobleman and kinsman to the Prince. He falls in love with Juliet and eagerly seeks her father's permission to woo and win her. Though seemingly concerned for Juliet's welfare, he is willing to take a reluctant bride upon her father's promise. But he truly mourns Juliet, and his death is yet another tragic event in the play. In death he is, in fact, united with her in the tomb of the Capulets.

### Friar Lawrence

The Franciscan Friar Lawrence is confessor to both Romeo and Juliet. Though he has cautioned Romeo about his hasty infatuation with Rosaline, the Friar is willing to accept that a true relationship has begun between Romeo and Juliet. He aids the young lovers, both for the sake of true love and for the opportunity to end the bitter feud between the two noble houses. He wants to do good, but his efforts fail.

Shakespeare treats him more sympathetically than does Brooke, but he emerges in the play as somewhat naive, perhaps even scheming. He never tells the parents about their children's love, and he misjudges Juliet's passion when he tries to take her away from the dead Romeo at the end of the play. He even deserts her when he hears people coming to the tomb and so leaves her alone to kill herself.

## Lord Capulet

Lord Capulet, Juliet's father, is a cordial host and a respected man of the city. He initially seems a considerate father, telling Paris, "My will to her consent is but a part; / And she agreed, within her scope of choice / Lies my consent and fair according voice" (1.2.17–19). When Tybalt objects to Romeo's presence at the Capulet ball, Capulet quiets him. The death of Tybalt changes him, though. In 3.5 he insists that Juliet marry Paris or "hang, beg, starve, die in the streets" (3.5.192). In the end he mourns her death, and he begins to make amends with Montague at the close of the play. His first action will be to raise a gold statue of Romeo as his symbolic payment of Juliet's dowry.

## Lady Capulet

Though Lady Capulet is concerned about the welfare of her husband and daughter, she is also concerned with what is proper. She continually urges Juliet to consider Paris's suit and is stunned by her daughter's refusal to obey. Some directors have interpreted her extreme reaction to Tybalt's death as an indication of her involvement in an affair with the younger Capulet. She seems more belligerent than her husband in pursuing the Capulet-Montague quarrel.

## Lord Montague

Romeo's father, Lord Montague, worries about his son and the ongoing feud. At the end of the drama he matches Capulet's generosity by agreeing to raise a gold statue of Juliet that will remain by Romeo's side. Too late, the older generation makes peace. Romeo's mother appears only briefly but is supportive of her husband and son. At the end of the play, she is reported to have died from grief over Romeo's banishment.

## DEVICES AND TECHNIQUES

Light in its many permutations is a dominant image in *Romeo and Juliet*. Upon first seeing Juliet, Romeo is overcome not only with her beauty but also with her brightness:

> O, she doth teach the torches to burn bright!
> It seems she hangs upon the cheek of night
> As a rich jewel in an Ethiop's ear. (1.5.44–46)

Juliet's beauty is likened to a flame, and for Romeo she burns with the intensity of passion. Metaphorically comparing Juliet to a jewel adds to the overall sense of fire and light. Cut jewels are designed so that their facets catch and reflect light, thus making the jewel sparkle. Juliet's light is further emphasized by her dark background. Literally, the masked ball is in a darkened hall, yet Romeo is able to recognize her beauty. Figuratively, Juliet is a bright jewel against an "Ethiop's" dark skin and a snow-white dove set against a flock of black-feathered crows (1.5.48).

Other light-related images include the heavenly bodies, particularly the sun and the stars. These appear in the first extended meeting between Romeo and Juliet, beginning with the famous lines: "But soft, what light through yonder window breaks? / It is the east, and Juliet is the sun" (2.2.2–3), but the images continue on to include not only stars but also other sources of light and brilliance:

> Two of the fairest stars in all the heaven,
> Having some business, do entreat her eyes
> To twinkle in their spheres till they return.
> What if her eyes were there, they in her head?
> The brightness of her cheek would shame those stars,
> As daylight doth a lamp; her eyes in heaven
> Would through the airy region stream so bright
> That birds would sing and think it were not night. (2.2.15–22)

Juliet is a luminous heavenly object, a "bright angel" as Romeo later calls her (2.2.26). Beyond mere radiance, Juliet is a dazzling force that blocks out every dark concern—infatuation, family feud, murder, exile, even death. As Romeo remarks, even in the tomb Juliet's light cannot be dimmed: "For here lies Juliet, and her beauty makes / This vault a feasting presence full of light" (5.3.85–86).

Juliet applies similar conceits to Romeo, likening him to the stars: "and, when I shall die, / Take him and cut him out in little stars" (3.2.21–22) and to daylight: "Romeo, come, thou day in night, / For thou wilt lie upon the wings of night, / Whiter than new snow upon a raven's back" (3.2.17–19).

Juliet extends the concept of light to the whole experience of love, instead of confining it simply to her husband. In the first garden scene, Juliet, punning on the word "light," which can also mean wanton, asks that Romeo "pardon me, / And not impute this yielding to light love, / Which the dark night hath so discovered" (2.2.104–106). While waiting for the Nurse's news of her impending marriage, Juliet exclaims, "Love's heralds should be thoughts, / Which ten times faster glides than the sun's beams, / Driving back shadows over low'ring hills" (2.5.4–6).

Nature is a source of images, particularly birds, flowers, and the sea. Birds, such as ravens and doves, are often linked to the lovers. In their famous dawn aubade, Juliet attempts to convince Romeo that the lark (symbol of the morning) is really the nightingale (symbol of the evening), so they may spend more time together. In her attempt to convince Juliet to marry Paris, the Nurse compares him to an eagle (4.1.219). Paris is the character most often linked to flowers. Lady Capulet describes the County glowingly, saying "Verona's summer hath not such a flower," to which the Nurse adds, "Nay, he's a flower, in faith, a very flower" (1.3.77–78). The Nurse informs Juliet that Romeo is "not the flower of courtesy" (2.5.43), an opinion she later upholds in her support of Juliet's marriage to Paris. Finally, Paris brings an armload of flowers to Juliet's bier and strews them around in mourning. In death, he lies among the flowers with her.

Sea images are most often connected to Romeo, particularly in regard to sailing. Early on, he invokes fate: "He that hath the steerage of my course / Direct my sail!" (1.4.112–113). He also reassures Juliet that "I am no pilot, yet, wert thou as far / As that vast shore wash'd with the farthest sea, / I should adventure for such merchandise" (2.2.82–84). Sailing also figures into his final journey: "Come, bitter conduct [conductor, guide], come, unsavory guide! / Thou desperate pilot, now at once run on / The dashing rocks thy sea-sick weary bark!" (5.3.116–118).

However, at one point Lord Capulet also associates the stormy sea and Juliet:

> In one little body
> Thou counterfeits a bark, a sea, a wind:
> For still thy eyes, which I may call the sea,
> Do ebb and flow with tears; the bark thy body is,
> Sailing in this salt flood; the winds, thy sighs,
> Who, raging with thy tears, and they with them,
> Without a sudden calm, will overset
> Thy tempest-tossed body. (3.5.130–137)

The difference is subtle but important. Romeo is the "pilot," that is the sea captain, even if he is a poor one, whereas Juliet is the boat and/or the sea itself, to be commanded by the captain.

One of the more prominent literary devices in the play is foreshadowing. Not only does the initial prologue reveal the lovers' fate but there are also many more subtle clues that confirm the fact that Romeo and Juliet will die. For example, even before attending the Capulets' ball, Romeo is stricken with a sense of foreboding: "for my mind misgives / Some consequence yet hanging in the stars / Shall bitterly begin his fearful date / With this night's revels, and expire the term / Of a despised life clos'd in my breast / By some vile forfeit of untimely death" (1.4.106–111). Later, as husband and wife part in the morning, the thought of death once again mars the lovers' happiness: "O God, I have an ill-divining soul! / Methinks I see thee now, thou art so low, / As one dead in the bottom of a tomb." Romeo replies, "And trust me, love, in my eye so do you; / Dry sorrow drinks our blood" (3.5.54–59).

The manner of the suicides is alluded to at several points as well. When Romeo finds out he is banished, he asks the Friar, "Hadst thou no poison mix'd, no sharp-ground knife [?]" (3.3.44), and then attempts to stab himself later in the same scene. Similarly, Juliet informs the Friar, "Do thou but call my resolution wise, / And with this knife I'll help it presently" (4.1.53–54). Later, as she prepares to drink the potion the Friar provided, she worries that it may truly be poison, but she drinks it anyway.

Shakespeare is particularly dependent upon the soliloquy in *Romeo and Juliet*, though not all of these are conventional. At least two speeches intended to be soliloquies are overheard by other characters. The first occurs in 1.5.44–53 when Romeo first sees Juliet. Though he is exclaiming to himself, Romeo is, unfortunately, overheard by—and thus recognized by—Tybalt. The second takes place during Romeo and Juliet's midnight meeting. Juliet has walked onto her balcony and is wondering aloud about her love for Romeo, who stands in the shadows and debates whether or not to reveal himself. Of the true soliloquies, there are powerful examples: Romeo's first glimpse of Juliet on her balcony (2.2.2–23); Friar

Lawrence's description of his herbs (2.3.1–22); Juliet's plea for nightfall to come (3.2.1–31); Juliet's fearful debate about the potion (4.3.14–58); Romeo's resolution to commit suicide (5.1.34–56); and Romeo's final good-bye to Juliet in the tomb (5.3.74–120). These speeches serve the typical function of the soliloquy, to reveal to the audience what a character is thinking. However, in Shakespeare's plays of this period his soliloquies begin to show characters actually discovering their thoughts themselves. They are truly thinking out loud, not just telling the audience what they (the characters) already have decided.

Another literary technique employed in *Romeo and Juliet* is the blazon, or *blason du corps*. A blazoned body is one that is fragmented and eroticized. In traditional poetry, such as the Petrarchan sonnet, the fragmented body is usually female and usually the love object. Thus, one might expect to see Juliet's body blazoned in this play. However, that is not the case. Two bodies in particular are dismembered in this way: Rosaline's and Romeo's. As the ideal yet unattainable mistress, Rosaline is the superlative choice to be subject to the *blason*. Yet, breaking with traditional poetic form, it is not the love-sick author (Romeo) who praises her individual parts; rather, it is his friend, Mercutio, who details her body:

> I conjure thee [Romeo] by Rosaline's bright eyes,
> By her high forehead and her scarlet lip,
> By her fine foot, straight leg, and quivering thigh,
> And the demesnes that there adjacent lie. (2.1.17–20)

The blazon begins conventionally enough, as Rosaline is described in standard terms applied to romance heroines. It takes a decidedly unconventional path with Mercutio's reference to Rosaline's "nether region."

Unlike Rosaline, who never physically appears in the play, Romeo is the subject of a self-blazon. In his final address to his (presumably) dead wife, he fragments his own body into the parts that can best enjoy Juliet:

> Eyes, look your last!
> Arms, take your last embrace! and, lips, O you
> The doors of breath, seal with a righteous kiss
> A dateless bargain to engrossing death! (5.3.112–115)

This is an active blazon, in that Romeo is focusing on the function, not form, of the body parts. Gayle Whittier suggests that Juliet "negatively blazons Romeo in her famous 'What's Montague? It is nor hand nor foot, / Nor arm nor face, nor any other part / Belonging to a man' (2.2.40–42). In dismissing his name, she scatters his body" (Whittier, "The Sonnet's Body," *Shakespeare Quarterly* 40.1 [1989]: 34). Lady Capulet performs a similar function for Paris, Juliet's other suitor. Before the masked ball, Lady Capulet encourages Juliet to "Read o'er the volume of young Paris' face" (1.3.81) and proceeds to single out several of his attributes.

Finally, *Romeo and Juliet*, like many of Shakespeare's other plays, is dependent upon wordplay to reach its fullest dramatic potential. This takes the form of ironic utterances, puns, and bawdy remarks in the form of double entendres among other elements. In *Romeo and Juliet*, wordplay is particularly crucial to the humor of the play, despite its tragic circumstances. Many of the puns revolve around death, such as Mercutio's quip, "Ask for me to-morrow, and you shall find me a grave man"

(3.1.97–98), and Juliet's remark comparing her wedding-bed to a grave (1.5.133–134). Not all puns, however, are so morbid. Mercutio adeptly turns Tybalt's intended insult into a joke simply by choosing another definition of the word in question: [Tybalt] "Mercutio, thou consortest with Romeo," [Mercutio] "Consort? what, does thou make us minstrels?" (3.1.45–46).

Bawdy wordplay abounds in *Romeo and Juliet*, particularly in Mercutio's lines and the servants' sallies. Mercutio's initial comments about Rosaline demonstrate his preference for sex over love: "Now he will sit under a medlar tree, / And wish his mistress were that kind of fruit / As maids call medlars, when they laugh alone. / O, Romeo, that she were, O that she were / An open-arse, thou a pop'rin pear!" (2.1.34–38). These lines suggest a variety of sexual activities. The medlar tree was well known for its "apple-like" fruit that was reminiscent of female genitalia; the pop'rin pear was a Flemish fruit that was phallic in shape. Thus, standard penile-vaginal penetration is suggested in the combination of pear and medlar. That Romeo would sit under the tree implies some sort of oral sex. However, a more literal meaning would suggest that Mercutio is referring to sodomy—at least in addition to, if not in lieu of—penile-vaginal penetration.

Mercutio is more witty than crude in his later exchange with the Nurse. His clever sallies combine references to hare hunting and whoredom through which he mocks the Nurse. The exchange begins with: "A bawd, a bawd, a bawd! So ho!" (2.4.130), which contains a skillful dialectical twist. "So ho," was the traditional cry when hunters spotted a *hare*, and, in turn, *bawd* is slang for *hare*, and *hare* is slang for prostitute. He continues, "No hare, sir, unless a hare, sir, in a lenten pie, that is something stale and hoar ere it be spent" (2.4.132–133). Thus, Mercutio neatly insults the Nurse by simultaneously calling her a prostitute (hare), something illicitly bought on the black market (a meat pie bought during Lent), and a disgusting old woman who is dried up and unappealing (stale, hoar)—and also relying on the double meaning of "spent," as in money used to purchase something (hare pies or a prostitute's favors) and orgasm. The scene continues with further sexual innuendo.

Though the title characters do not engage in as much bawdy talk as the others in the play, their conversations are not devoid of quips. For example, as Romeo prepares to leave the Capulet garden, he asks, "O, wilt thou leave me so unsatisfied?" Juliet demurely replies, "What satisfaction canst thou have to-night?" (2.2.125–126). Despite this modesty, Juliet does indeed eagerly anticipate the consummation of her marriage. Awaiting the return of the Nurse and the rope ladder, Juliet laments: "O, I have bought the mansion of a love, / But not possess'd it, and though I am sold, / Not yet enjoy'd" (3.2.26–28). Now that she is properly married, Juliet cannot wait for satisfaction.

Puns on the word *die* provide another source of bawdy wordplay between the two lovers. In Early Modern society, the verb *die* meant both the end of physical existence and sexual orgasm, which was known as "the little death" (*la petit mort*). It was believed that sexual activity drained away one's vital forces, shortening one's life. Thus, Early Modern writers often relied upon puns about death to allude to sexual situations, further conflating sex/love and death. This metaphor was common enough that it would have been easily understood by the audience.

Both lovers' dying words contain sexual overtones. Upon hearing of Juliet's demise, Romeo resolves: "Well, Juliet, I will lie with thee to-night" (5.1.34), punning on the word lie as a euphemism for sex and as a reference to killing himself in her tomb. As he prepares to commit suicide, Romeo announces, "Thus with a kiss I die" (5.3.120). He has just rhapsodized about Juliet's beauty and her place as Death's paramour—as her husband it would be his place both to lie with her, and to "die" with her. Juliet's final words also contain sexual overtones: "I will kiss thy lips, / Haply some poison yet doth hang on them, / To make me die with a restorative" (5.3.164–166). She, too, will "die," both literally and orgasmically, with a kiss. Her final deed is reminiscent of the sexual act itself: "O happy dagger, [*taking Romeo's dagger*] / This is thy sheath [*stabs herself*]; there rust, and let me die. [*Falls on Romeo's body and dies*]" (5.3.169–170). Juliet appropriates Romeo's dagger, a phallic symbol, penetrates her own body—the word "sheath" is particularly evocative of the vagina—and falls dead upon her husband's body. The blood that seeps from her body onto the funeral shroud is surely reminiscent of the virginal blood she had shed a mere two days before.

## THEMES AND MEANINGS

The mixture of death and love runs throughout the play. In the opening scene, the two servants Samson and Gregory make a series of jokes in which they relate cutting off the heads of the maids with taking "their maidenheads" (1.1.22–23). Next, Romeo must exterminate his infatuation with Rosaline in order to pursue Juliet. Juliet charges her Nurse to "Go ask his [Romeo's] name.—If he be married, / My grave is like to be my wedding-bed" (1.5.134–135). Romeo almost kills his wedding-night plans by killing his wife's cousin. Thinking her newly acquired husband has already fled Verona, Juliet laments, "I'll to my wedding-bed, / And death, not Romeo, take my maidenhead" (3.2.136–137). Lady Capulet, bemoaning Juliet's refusal to marry Paris, cries, "I would the fool were married to her grave!" (3.5.140). The mourning Lord Capulet remarks to Paris, "O son, the night before thy wedding-day / Hath Death lain with thy wife. There she lies, / Flower as she was, deflowered by him" (4.5.35–37). When Romeo hears of Juliet's supposed death, he reacts by declaring, "Well, Juliet, I will lie with thee to-night" (5.1.34) before he goes to the apothecary to purchase poison.

The final scene in the tomb carries even more weighty references to the mixing of death and love, as Romeo proclaims, "Arms, take your last embrace! and, lips, O you / The doors of breath, seal with a righteous kiss / A dateless bargain to engrossing death!" (5.3.113–115). Of the two lovers, Romeo has been the one more prone to hasty death. He willingly braves the Capulet wrath in order to attend the ball. Later, when conversing with Juliet in the garden, he announces, "My life were better ended by their hate, / Than death prorogued [delayed], wanting of thy love" (2.2.77–78). Similarly, after killing Tybalt, Romeo flees to Friar Lawrence's cell, and it is all the Friar and the Nurse can do to prevent him from committing suicide. Yet his haste toward death is equally coupled with his haste toward passion. As he awaits his bride in Friar Lawrence's cell, Romeo remarks, "but come what sorrow can, / It cannot countervail the exchange of joy / That one short minute gives me in her sight" (2.6.3–5). Romeo, it seems, welcomes death and love equally.

Moving beyond the standard pun on "die," Lyndy Abraham calls this combination of love/sex and death "alchemy" (Abraham, p. 305) in the sense that alchemy was a pseudoscience dedicated to creation and reproduction, but in order to create the new substance, the old substance had to be destroyed. Similarly, Romeo and

Juliet's love is predicated upon such exchanges. Abraham further supports her alchemical reading with the swiftness of the love relationship. Unlike their counterparts in Shakespeare's source materials, who are allowed weeks or even months to fall in love, Romeo and Juliet fall deeply and truly in love within the span of a single night. Abraham also contends that the reconciliation between the two great houses of Verona is alchemical in nature as a transformative process.

Whether or not it is alchemical, the theme of reconciliation is another large one in the play. This is a significant departure from the Brooke poem, which dedicates only 5 lines (out of more than 3,000) to the settling of the feud. In Bandello's version, it is Juliet who first sees the possibilities of her romance with Romeo:

> And yet, is it just possible that this union could bring the two families together again in peace and harmony? I have heard it said many times that such marriages have brought about peace. . . . Perhaps I shall be the one to bring peace to these two households by such means. (Bandello, p. 377; in Levenson, "Romeo and Juliet before Shakespeare," p. 335)

Similarly, Shakespeare uses individual characters to further the theme of reconciliation. Benvolio and Prince Escalus are the most obvious choices. Both attempt to make peace between the warring families with words, but when words fail, each is ready to use force. Benvolio duels with Tybalt, and the Prince issues his execution edict. Friar Lawrence is another character that personifies reconciliation. In his first scene with Romeo, he reveals his hopes that a union between Romeo and Rosaline would bring the two houses together. When Romeo announces his newfound love for Juliet, the Friar is certainly taken aback by the quick change of heart; yet he is willing to support Romeo and Juliet and declares, "For this alliance may so happy prove / To turn your households' rancor to pure love" (2.3.91–92). Mercutio also recalls the theme of reconciliation with his dying curse: "A plague a' both your houses! / They have made worms' meat of me" (3.1.106–107). Though his words are harsh, they serve to shock the bystanders into remembering that peace would end all the killing. Despite the drive toward unification, Shakespeare leaves the fate of several characters unresolved; as the play ends, the Friar and Balthasar are still in custody. This is kinder than Brooke's version, however, in which Friar Lawrence and Balthasar are pardoned, the Nurse is banished, and the apothecary is executed. The conciliatory goal is still left incomplete; the Prince, however, provides hope: "A glooming peace this morning with it brings" (5.3.305).

Of course the play also focuses on love and its companion emotion, hate. As Friar Lawrence advises Romeo, "These violent delights have violent ends, / And in their triumph die like fire and powder, / Which as they kiss consume" (2.6.9–11). Love in its various manifestations is the prominent sentiment in the play. Romeo's initial besottedness with Rosaline portrays the heat of infatuation. The crude jests of the servants and even Mercutio's bawdy puns demonstrate lust, which is the love of sexual gratification. Paternal love is shown through the characters of Lord Capulet and Lord Montague, with the former taking a stern stance on duty, and the latter speaking out about his concern. Lady Montague, through her sudden demise due to Romeo's exile, exemplifies maternal love, while Lady Capulet, who viciously turns on her daughter, epitomizes the opposite. Paris and Prince Escalus each embody the love of duty, whereas Tybalt, despite his hotheaded streak, typifies love of honor above all. Romeo and Juliet are the embodiment of true love. Each is willing to die for the other, and both are willing to oppose a long-standing feud in order to be together. Had their marriage succeeded, perhaps the years of hatred would have ended.

Hate, the other strong emotion in the play, is the ultimate catalyst. The bitter enmity between the Montagues and Capulets ends up causing the death of their only children. Just as he represents an overweening love of honor, Tybalt also personifies sheer hatred. He provokes fights where otherwise none may have occurred and goads fighters who may not have fought. In turn, this hatred leaks onto Romeo, who slays Tybalt; and, in return, he earns the wrath of the Prince and the Capulets.

A traditionally held theme of *Romeo and Juliet* is the idea of fate—or, perhaps, of fortune, though philosophically, fate was considered to have authority over fortune. This is a somewhat unusual mechanism in a Shakespearean tragedy, which generally depends upon an internal characteristic, a "fatal flaw," rather than an outside force. In the opening lines of the prologue, Romeo and Juliet are presented as "star-cross'd lovers," who have fate against them (Prologue, 6). Stars that cross paths can never remain together, just as the audience knows that Romeo and Juliet can never remain joined. The characters echo the sense of impending doom, often invoking references to stars, too. Before Romeo enters the Capulet ball, he remarks upon his fear of "Some consequence yet hanging in the stars" (1.4.107). Juliet also makes several references to the heavens, as does the Friar. Attempting to invoke God's approval of the marriage, the Friar remarks, "So smile the heavens upon this holy act, / That after-hours with sorrow chide us not!" (2.6.1–2). And at the close of the play, Prince Escalus admonishes the assembled families: "See what a scourge is laid upon your hate, / That heaven finds means to kill your joys with love" (5.3.292–293). Fate, as a higher authority, has pronounced judgment and levied the fine.

Closely related to the idea of fate is the concept of chance, of which Fortune is the personification. Many of the tragic events that happen throughout the play occur seemingly by accident. Romeo happened to be at the Capulet ball only because the servant could not read the guest list. He then glanced Juliet's way at the same time she saw him, and the two fell in love before discovering they were from opposing families. The list of "accidental" events—the drug, Tybalt's death, the waylaid messenger, and so forth—continues, and often parallels the events discussed earlier as mechanisms of fate. This idea that Romeo and Juliet are merely pawns in Fortune's game is expressed by both of them during the play. After killing Tybalt, Romeo exclaims, "O, I am fortune's fool!" (3.1.136). Later, after Romeo has left for Mantua, Juliet cries, "O Fortune, Fortune, all men call thee fickle; / If thou art fickle, what dost thou with him / That is renown'd for faith? Be fickle, Fortune: / For then I hope thou wilt not keep him long, / But send him back" (3.5.60–64). These closely related concepts, fate and chance, serve to ameliorate the sting of the enormous loss Verona suffers: Lady Montague is dead, both houses have lost their heir, and the Prince has lost a "brace of kinsmen" (5.3.295). If circumstances are being controlled by a higher power, then there must be a purpose behind the inescapable tragic events.

Related to the idea of fate/fortune are the dreams Shakespeare incorporates into his play. These additions are primarily original. Both Romeo and Juliet have dreams (or visions) that are portents of the future, dreams that Romeo firmly believes. Mercutio is set up as the disbeliever in opposition to Romeo. When the latter seems worried about a dream, Mercutio launches into a tirade against dreams in his Queen Mab speech. Romeo, however, is still shaken by his feeling of doom. Mercutio dismisses dreams, airily remarking: "I talk of dreams, / Which are the children of an idle brain, / Begot of nothing but vain fantasy" (1.4.97–99). In fact, Romeo's dream is not a vain fantasy, but a premonition of disaster. This can make him a more likeable character than the dismissive Mercutio. "Romeo's susceptibility to dreams correlates with his temperamental imbalance due to excessive extremes of grief and joy, inviting our sympathy for his plight" (Holmer, "No 'Vain Fantasy,' " p. 55). Shakespeare added Romeo's dark dream to the story. Brooke mentions that Romeus would have been happier with his first love, but there's no ominous dream involved. Brooke's Romeus, however, also spent months wooing Juliet; Shakespeare's spends hours. The addition of the dream messages adds to the overall feeling of haste and inevitability. Romeo also has a positive dream. In Mantua, he muses, "If I can trust the flattering truth of sleep, / My dreams presage some joyful news at hand" (5.1.1–2). He then describes the dream he had about dying and being restored to life by Juliet's kiss. Mercutio is no longer alive to warn Romeo that dreams are merely vain fantasies, however, and Romeo's dream is a harbinger of doom, not of joy. This dream provides the last ray of hope suggesting that the lovers might survive, despite all of the evidence against that outcome.

## CRITICAL CONTROVERSIES

Early scholarship devoted much time and energy to debates over the authenticity of the various quartos, especially the accuracy displayed by the so-called bad quarto (Q1). Though long and bitter debates ensued, it became almost universally accepted that Q1 is a memorial reconstruction based on viewing(s) of the play in performance. By the early 1950s, scholars such as E. K. Chambers and H. R. Hoppe had firmly established the supremacy of Q2, and most of the remaining editorial debates concerned the amount of material to use and/or correlate from each of the various extant quartos. A later exploration of this issue (Random Cloud [Randall McLeod], "The Marriage of Good and Bad Quartos," *Shakespeare Quarterly* 33.4 [1982]: 421–431) discusses the inherent problems with the labels "good" and "bad" for the quartos, as well as the contents therein. The author ends up arguing, in part, for a partial rehabilitation of Q1. However, despite this attempt, established criticism holds with the authority of Q2; virtually all modern editions of the play are based on this quarto, though many contain reference lists illustrating the differences among the various quartos.

Current textual studies center on the partial rehabilitation of Q1 as a tool for reaching a better understanding of Q2, which is still the definitive edition. Toward this end, critics have been going back and forth between Q1 and Q2 in particular to provide the "best" reading of passages. This includes the restoration of words that were excised, phrases that were mangled, and speeches that were reassigned. Pitfalls in these discussions include debates about authorial intent and declarations of what does or does not constitute Shakespearean language, as well as assignment of relative dramatic value. More interesting textual analyses have focused on the stage directions, which were mostly absent in Q2, but present in Q1 and other "corrupted" versions. For instance, if the "balcony scene" did not specifically include an enclosed area, does that change our perception of the lovers' meetings? It is interesting that textual studies of *Romeo and Juliet* retain a greater popularity than do textual studies of many other Shakespeare plays, even some of those that have similarly corrupted quartos. Perhaps popularity is the key here. This play is one of the most popular in the Shakespearean canon, thus spurring the quest for an authoritative version.

Another traditional area of inquiry is the structure of *Romeo and Juliet*. Is the play a comedy, a tragedy, or both? For many years, H. B. Charlton provided the answer: *Romeo and Juliet* is an "experimental tragedy" that never achieves full tragic quality (*Proceedings of the British Academy, 1939* 25 [1940]: 143–185). More modern examinations of the play's structure have focused on the blending of these genres and the inclusion of poetry in the overall structure. In particular, the influence of the sonnet and the esteem with which the sonnet sequence was regarded in Elizabethan society is of special importance to a play that relies on sonnet techniques for many of its major scenes. These analyses are less concerned with how "good" a tragedy *Romeo and Juliet* is than with an holistic examination of the language and structure in order to provide a unified interpretation of the play.

Recent scholarship has also capitalized on the growth of feminist, gender, and queer studies. In particular, these approaches have resulted in analyses of Mercutio's homosocial nature, and in the feminization of various characters, particularly Romeo. Several readings offer not only a homosocial orientation for Mercutio but also an extended relationship between Romeo and Mercutio—which is Shakespeare's own invention, not gleaned from his sources. Where does friendship cross the line? Opponents of such readings argue that Early Modern society was homosocial by definition. Women were not part of the public world; therefore, men would have had to develop intimate friendships with other men. However, proponents of gender analyses point out specifically compelling evidence, particularly Mercutio's phallocentrism. His jests almost all contain penile references. Mercutio's phallic talk is concerned not just with his own "tale" (2.4.95–98), as he terms it, but also with others': love's, noon's, a stranger's, and, significantly, Romeo's. In fact, as Porter argues, Mercutio is perhaps more concerned with Romeo's phallus than his own: "Mercutio here exhibits an attitude toward Romeo's phallus that is at once generous and interested" (Porter, p. 157).

Mercutio is acutely concerned with not only Romeo's desire for women but also his performance with these women. Other critics point to Romeo's refusal to tell Mercutio (and, by default, Benvolio) about Juliet, Mercutio's scatological talk and overt references to sodomy, and Mercutio's apparent jealousy over Romeo's disappearance as more "evidence" that Mercutio is meant to be homosexual. The character has been played in this manner in the two most critically renowned film versions of the play, Franco Zefferelli's and Baz Luhrmann's. In Zefferelli's movie, Mercutio is wildly despairing during his Queen Mab speech, and in Luhrmann's, he is a jealous drag queen. (See "Production History" below for more information about these films.)

Another major area of discussion centers on the nature of Romeo and Juliet's love and the nature of desire. Coppélia Kahn (1980) explores the maturation of the two young lovers. Her essential claim is that the feud is the pervasive tragic force, an embodiment of the patriarchal society that Shakespeare feels must be challenged. Against this backdrop, Romeo and Juliet attempt to create new identities, but they are ultimately unable to overcome the impinging social forces. Not surprisingly, other readings have also focused on the combination of violence and love as a separate issue from death and love. Some scholars claim that the play concludes that the only way to achieve love is through violence. Still other scholars focus on the role that *Romeo and Juliet* plays in the development, and sustaining, of the ideal of romantic love. In her important essay, Dympna Callaghan (2001) studies the play's centrality in the construction of desire. This cultural production was necessary, she says, to sustain the capitalist economy that was developing and to promote the rise of a centralized state. *Romeo and Juliet*, she argues, was produced at a critical moment in history when the ideology of marriage and desire were still in flux, not fully formed. Just like post-Reformation society, and the Elizabethan world that was becoming more influenced by Puritan concepts, *Romeo and Juliet* addresses growing contradictions. For instance, "Romeo and Juliet's love, while it offers resistance to their feudal households, is perfectly compatible with the interests of society as a whole" (Callaghan, p. 86). The problem here is with the production of authority—should it lie with the husband, the father, or the state?

Both feminist and gender studies also examine the representation of femininity and/or masculinity. Several studies explore the notion of Juliet as a desiring subject. Callaghan claims that Puritans allowed women more latitude by reducing their role as vehicles of evil sexuality. Other critics look at Juliet in light of comic heroines, particularly those in citizen comedies, who participate in bawdy banter almost to the degree that male characters do. Many of these explorations focus principally on Juliet's explicit desire for the consummation of her marriage. She, more than Romeo, begs for nightfall, worries about the cord ladder, and makes frank references to losing her maidenhead. Masculinity studies have tended to focus on the connection between masculinity and violence more than sexual desire. In his exploration, Robert Appelbaum argues that the underlying problem is this: to be a man is to not be a woman, and therefore to not be weak, because women are those "weaker vessels . . . thrust to the wall" by men (1.1.16). Codes of violence dictate the codes of masculinity. This is a point acutely felt by Romeo, especially after Mercutio's death: "O sweet Juliet, / Thy beauty hath made me effeminate, / And in my temper soft'ned valor's steel!" (3.1.113–115). The Friar later admonishes Romeo, "Thy tears are womanish . . . / Unseemly woman in a seeming man" (3.3.110, 112). It is his refusal to act violently in the first case that makes Romeo effeminate, but it is improper violence (suicidal thoughts) that makes him thus later. The pressure to perform as a man makes many men, according to Appelbaum, failed subjects.

## PRODUCTION HISTORY

Despite debates among critics and reviewers, *Romeo and Juliet* has always been popular with audiences, and numerous productions on the stage, screen, and television have entertained people for centuries. These productions include both those that are faithful to Shakespeare's "original" and adaptations thereof.

Of its original production, no record remains; however, the evidence points to its popularity even during the Elizabethan era. In Shakespeare's time, it would probably have been performed by the Lord Chamberlain's Men. As such, the most likely candidate for the first Romeo would have been Richard Burbage, who was the company's leading actor. All is speculation until December 12, 1660, when William Davenant was "granted a warrant to act *Romeo and Juliet* along with a number of other Shakespeare plays and several by Shakespeare's contemporaries" and proceeded to "revive the play in March 1662" (Halio, p. 101).

During the 1700s, Shakespeare's plays were not as immensely popular as they had been during his lifetime. Audiences deplored the difficult language and the lack of display. Still, the eighteenth century witnessed several adaptations of Shakespeare's original. Several of these productions alter the tragic ending, allowing for a brief, but glorious, reunion of the parted lovers. In these versions, Juliet awakens just as Romeo is dying, but in time to share his last moments. Romeo then realizes the consequences of his rash act. The first playwright to alter the ending in this manner was Thomas Otway, in his play entitled *The Rise and Fall of Caius Marius*. Otway's rendering was staged in October 1679 and continued to be moderately successful into the beginning of the eighteenth century. Other common changes during this time included the elimination of Lady Montague and Rosaline.

Following Otway's success, other adaptations were penned by aspiring playwrights: for example, Theophilus Cibber, whose 1744 version incorporated both Otway and Shakespeare. Similarly, Thomas Sheridan produced a version in 1746 that proved to be somewhat more successful than Cibber's. However, the most popular rendition of *Romeo and Juliet* in the eighteenth century was written by David Garrick, who became the owner/manager of Drury Lane Theatre in 1747; one year later he staged his version of *Romeo and Juliet*. It was quite successful, and for nearly a hundred years, from 1750 to 1845, Garrick's adaptation was the most frequently performed Shakespearean tragedy. Although his dialogue and variations have not been used since the mid-nineteenth century, many modern productions owe his version a debt. Taking a key from Garrick, some directors have added intensity to the death scene by allowing the audience to see Juliet stirring just as Romeo dies.

Shakespeare's play languished during the nineteenth century until Charlotte Cushman took on the challenge of reviving it in 1845. Cushman restored most of Shakespeare's dialogue and his original staging and structure. She then went on to play the title role of Romeo, and cast her sister, Susan Cushman, as Juliet. The production garnered not only success for the production house but also personal accolades for Charlotte, who was hailed as a genius.

The advent of the motion picture industry allowed for numerous productions of *Romeo and Juliet*. George Cukor's 1936 production (MGM) was lavish and sophisticated. The studio spared no expense and snagged top stars. The lead roles featured Leslie Howard as Romeo and Norma Shearer as Juliet. Other cast members included John Barrymore (Mercutio), Edna May Oliver (Nurse), and Katherine DeMille (Rosaline) among others. Though the lead actors exceeded the characters' ages by many years (Shearer was thirty-four and Howard forty-three), they were still able to capture the desperate passion shared by the lovers. The film was a huge success.

Also in 1936, Sergey Sergeyevich Prokofiev wrote his *Romeo and Juliet* ballet at the behest of the Kirov theater in Leningrad. However, choreographic problems caused the premiere to be delayed until 1938. By 1940, it had become a staple of the Soviet repertoire. A similar popular adaptation was the American musical *West Side Story* (1957). In this version, the setting is updated to 1950s New York City, with rivals from two gangs as the lead characters. The musical score was composed by Leonard Bernstein, and the production was an immediate sensation.

The next famous film version of *Romeo and Juliet* (*Romeo e Giulietta* in Italy) was directed by Franco Zeffirelli and starred Leonard Whiting as Romeo and Olivia

Hussey as Juliet. This 1968 production (Paramount) was modified from Zeffirelli's 1960 British stage production, which starred John Stride as Romeo and Judi Dench as Juliet, and premiered at the Old Vic in London. If Zeffirelli's stage production was a hit, his film was even more so. The biggest criticisms of both his versions targeted his willingness to sacrifice dialogue for visual effects. Zeffirelli's film boasted sprawling sets of a reconstructed Verona, elaborate gardens, and the desolate mausoleum. The film was also quite sensual, focusing as much on the physical attraction between the two young lovers as on their spiritual connection. Reviewers also believed that Zeffirelli managed to capture elements that had been lost from previous productions: youthful passion, aggression versus pacifism, and rebellion against family. Furthermore, his attention to historical accuracy and period authenticity was lauded by all, as reflected by the two Oscars the film garnered (Best Cinematography; Costume Design).

Another version to reach great heights of success and popularity was directed by Baz Luhrmann (1996; Twentieth Century–Fox). Starring Leonardo diCaprio as Romeo and Claire Danes as Juliet, this production brought with it not only star power and audience appeal but also adaptations that reflected its late twentieth-century context. The story is set in Verona Beach, Florida, and within it are the elements of urban legend: drugs, guns, gangs, sexual promiscuity, and violence. Overtones of racial conflict are deliberately added to this dangerous mixture. Both Captain Prince ("Paris," played by Vondie Curtis-Hall) and Mercutio (Harold Perrineau Jr.) are played by African American actors. Further, this Mercutio is more overtly homosexual than previous versions of the character. He wears drag to the Capulet ball and appears possessive—almost jealously so—of Romeo's company. The manipulative Friar Lawrence openly schemes to end the feud by uniting the two lovers, and a TV anchor report structures the telling of the events as a modern parable. Many reviewers complained about one particular change: Mercutio slips Romeo ecstasy during his Queen Mab speech, both of which occur before Romeo and Juliet meet for the first time. Though the drugs certainly fit with the culture portrayed in the film, having Romeo high when he meets Juliet detracts from the true love and emotions. The two lovers almost fade into the vivid events surrounding them until the closing scene. Combining adaptations, Luhrmann's version had Romeo and Juliet remain completely alone in the tomb, and while Juliet wakes up in time to give Romeo a passionate good-bye kiss, her subsequent suicide, accomplished by shooting herself in the head with Romeo's gun, leaves no one there to put an end to the tragedies.

Though not strictly a film version of *Romeo and Juliet*, the 1998 film *Shakespeare in Love* (Miramax) is a twist on the classic love tale. Directed by John Madden and co-written by Marc Norman and Tom Stoppard, the movie is basically the fantasy story of how *Romeo and Juliet* was written. In it, the young Shakespeare (Joseph Fiennes) is experiencing writer's block with his latest play, *Romeo and Ethel, the Sea-Pirate's Daughter*. He is rescued by Viola de Lesseps (Gwyneth Paltrow), who desperately wants to act. Viola masquerades as Thomas and wins the part of Romeo. In the meantime, Shakespeare and Viola become enmeshed in a doomed love affair. The supporting cast is excellent: Geoffrey Rush plays Philip Henslowe, Shakespeare's producer; Rupert Everett plays Christopher Marlowe; and Dame Judi Dench plays Queen Elizabeth I. Even Ben Affleck, who plays Ned Alleyn, a prima donna, acts adequately. Both critics and audiences alike loved the movie, which ultimately ended up winning seven Oscars (Best Picture; Best Actress [Paltrow]; Best

Leonardo DiCaprio as Romeo and Claire Danes as Juliet in Baz Luhrmann's 1996 film *Romeo + Juliet.* Courtesy of Photofest.

Supporting Actress [Dench]; Best Original Screenplay; Art Direction; Score; Costume).

## EXPLICATION OF KEY PASSAGES

**1.4.53–95. "O then I see . . . This is she—[.]"** One of the most famous—and famously debated—passages in *Romeo and Juliet* is Mercutio's Queen Mab speech. Recent scholarship suggests that a likely source, at least for his inspiration, for this address is Thomas Nashe's *The Terrors of the Night, or a Discourse of Apparitions* (1594). Shakespeare takes the basic functions of dream lore from Nashe but turns them into a discussion about love and fate, setting up Romeo as the "dream-believer" and Mercutio as the "dream-mocker" (Holmer, "No 'Vain' Fantasy," p. 50). Romeo believes not only in the veracity of dreams but also in other flights of fancy, such as true love and immediate reconciliation. Mercutio, however, is more jaded and believes not in dreams, but in reality. Nevertheless, he cares about his friend Romeo and attempts to cheer him up while at the same time debunking his belief in fantasy. Porter notes that the speech "is notable as an example of failure to observe several of the conversational maxims that fall under Grice's 'cooperative principle'" (Porter, p. 105). In other words, Mercutio's speech is in poor taste, yet it accomplishes its task: to distract Romeo from his woes. Instead of simply telling Romeo to ignore his dreams, Mercutio illustrates the reason why he should. Dreams, he says, are nothing but fantastical children of an idle brain, delivered by the fairies' midwife. He then proceeds to gather a ridiculous assortment of dreams both for Romeo's pleasure and for his censure. The dreams that Mercutio describes all have materialistic content, in keeping with his rejection of the spiritual.

Many scholars have said that though this speech is somewhat "alien," meaning it is not precisely harmonious with the rest of the play's language, it contains the best imagery found within *Romeo and Juliet*. Still, a common complaint is that its imagery is "too much." It does not draw its ideas from the subject of the play itself (while there are dreams, there are no fairies, for instance). Still others feel that it is out of character for Mercutio. Though Mercutio is mocking, he is rarely as nasty as he is in this speech. His bright, witty poetry and clever prose seem at odds with the persona this speech creates—one that is in love with poetic language and convention, if not with fairies and dreams. Still others point out that while Mercutio is decidedly homosocial, if not homoerotic, he is not a misogynist. These critics and others have pointed out a certain measure of misogyny in the Queen Mab speech. Maids are depicted with "lazy finger[s]" (1.4.69), and ladies with tainted breath and plaguey lips (1.4.75–76); and all have "foul sluttish hairs" (1.4.90). Mab, who began as the fairies midwife, becomes a "hag" (1.4.92). The name Mab itself was common slang for a promiscuous woman, and Queen is most likely a play on the word *quean*, which was another term for "slut."

However, other critics point out that Mercutio is depicted as a misogynist, so the speech is less out of character than some believe. He is cruel to the Nurse and to Rosaline, though she is not around to hear him. He is not cruel to Juliet only because he does not know of her existence. According to these critics, the Mercutio in the Queen Mab speech is the real Mercutio who loathes women.

**1.5.93–106. "If I profane . . . prayer's effect I take."** The first exchange between Romeo and Juliet is in the form of a shared sonnet. The most striking set of metaphors within it are the combinations of the sacred and the profane. By blending earthly with spiritual love, Romeo and Juliet illustrate the true nature of their passion. It merges their entire being on all levels.

Romeo begins the exchange by elevating Juliet to the status of Christian saint. He thus immediately distinguishes her from his former love, Rosaline, whom he had compared to the pagan goddess Diana, who refuses "saint-seducing" gold. (1.1.214). As a Christian saint attracting holy palmers, Juliet is raised above the cold pagan deity who is dedicated only to chastity. Diana, goddess of the hunt, was a virgin goddess. Juliet, as an unmarried noblewoman, would also have been a virgin, but Christian chastity allows sexual activity within marriage.

The sonnet continues with a dexterous combination of traditional courtly love phrases with devotional language. The terms "gentle," "tender," and "mannerly" recall chivalry, and the word "despair" is relevant to both spheres (1.5.94, 96, 98, 104). The Early Moderns were especially concerned with the sin of despair: that is, the feeling that one is unworthy to receive God's forgiveness and thus never asks for it. In courtly love, despair is the result of the lover's being scorned and then feeling too unworthy to continue the pursuit. In both cases, the word is apt. Romeo asks for a prayer/kiss from the saint's mouth, lest he give up and fall into despair. Whether the issue is faith in God or faith in love, despair may follow if requests are never answered.

By casting himself as a pilgrim, Romeo indicates that he has made a journey to reach Juliet, and that this was a journey he needed to undertake. He is guilty of at least the "gentle sin" he mentions. Many editors revise the word sin, choosing *pain* or *fine* as a substitute. Yet sin makes more sense in the overall scheme of the sonnet. People often undertook pilgrimages as a penance for a particular sin. In calling his sin "gentle," Romeo is most likely referring to the sin inherent in the courtly love tradition or, perhaps, the sins to which love can lead. In either case, as pilgrim, he claims the sin; Juliet, as saint, should help him eradicate it. In calling Juliet a saint, Romeo acknowledges not only that she can save him but also that she has the power to decide whether or not to save him. His fate is in her hands. Underlying the notion of pilgrimage and saints' shrines, however, is a darker image. Shrines worthy of pilgrimage would have been those with saints' relics—fragmented body parts. Thus calling Juliet a saint implies a sort of dismemberment (and, by extension, her death). Indeed, the only body parts referred to throughout the exchange are lips and hands; neither speaker is whole.

Traditionally, the sonnet is the poem of love, so it is fitting that Romeo and Juliet first express their feelings in this form. Though the sonnet exchange appears to talk mostly of spiritual love, or at least a purer form of earthly love, there are still hints of bodily awareness. Romeo begins the exchange by immediately requesting a kiss, which Juliet demurely declines when she replies that his touch was not too rough (thus no kiss would be needed). She then offers him a "palm kiss" (1.5.100), a touching of hands, which he considers inadequate. Instead, Romeo continues to press for a "real" kiss. Juliet again demurs, pointing out that saints do not initiate any action themselves ("move," 1.5.105), ostensibly because that is God's province. Romeo seizes the advantage and instructs Juliet to "move not" (1.5.106) while he claims his kiss. Significantly, the stage directions specifically say "kissing her," not "they kiss." Romeo is distinctly the pursuer, and he is interested in physical love as well as spiritual connection. Gayle Whittier points out that "the poetic word deals on behalf of the flesh. Romeo's 'mannerly devotion' hides the English 'manly' and the French word for hand, *la main* [and] it is in her [Juliet's] more material medium, flesh itself, that the sonnet concludes with a pair of kisses" (Whittier, "The Sonnet's Body," *Shakespeare Quarterly* 48.3 [1997]: 35). Voice and flesh reciprocate in this initial sonnet; the carnal is always simmering underneath the spiritual.

Some critics have referred to this merger as a "religion of love." Not all scholars, however, agree that this is positive. John F. Andrews explores the philosophical underpinnings of Romeo and Juliet's attraction, citing St. Augustine's distinction between *caritas* (spiritual love) and *cupiditas* (bodily love). All actions of the soul are dependent upon the will, and the impetus behind the will is love. The type of love propelling the will determines the soul's nature. In this case, then, Romeo and Juliet are subject to a fatal flaw, as they have wrongly raised their profane love to the status of sacred love.

### Annotated Bibliography

Abraham, Lyndy. "The Lovers and the Tomb: Alchemical Emblems in Shakespeare, Donne, and Marvell." *Emblematica* 5.2 (1991): 301–320. Demonstrates, through an examination of contemporary handbooks, how Romeo and Juliet symbolized the Early Modern fascination with alchemy and change.

Andrews, John F. "Falling in Love: The Tragedy of *Romeo and Juliet*." In *Classical, Renaissance, and Postmodern Acts of Imagination*. Ed. Arthur Kinney. Newark: U of Delaware P, 1996. 177–194. Treats Romeo and Juliet's relationship from a philosophical standpoint.

Appelbaum, Robert. " 'Standing to the Wall': The Pressures of Masculinity in *Romeo and Juliet*." *Shakespeare Quarterly* 48.3 (1997): 251–272. Considers the production of a code of masculinity within *Romeo and Juliet* that is directly linked to violence and virtually impossible to uphold consistently. Men are presented as failed subjects.

Berry, Ralph. *The Shakespearean Metaphor*. Totowa, NJ: Rowman & Littlefield, 1978. An in-depth study of Shakespeare's poetic language. Of particular interest are the investigations of sonnets and conceits. Focus is on both imagery and metrics.

Callaghan, Dympna C. "The Ideology of Romantic Love: The Case of *Romeo and Juliet*." In *Romeo and Juliet*. Ed. R. S. White. Houndsmills, Eng.: Palgrave, 2001. 85–115. Examines the cultural construction of desire in relation to the development of a capitalist economy and centralized state. Patriarchal authority in the multiple forms of father, husband, and state is reinforced as long as these institutions are in agreement.

Fein, Susanna Greer. "Verona's Summer Flower: The 'Virtues' of Herb Paris in *Romeo and Juliet*." *American Notes & Queries* 8.4 (1995): 5–9. Discusses the properties of the common plant *Paris quadrifolia*, also known as herb Paris, and suggests a connection between the character Paris and this herb.

Halio, Jay L. *"Romeo and Juliet": A Guide to the Play*. Westport, CT: Greenwood P, 1998. Provides an excellent overview of the play's history, interpretations, and continued impact.

Holmer, Joan Ozark. " 'Draw, if you be Men': Saviolo's Significance for *Romeo and Juliet*." *Shakespeare Quarterly* 45.2 (1994): 163–189. Maintains that Saviolo's fencing manual provided the terminology present in *Romeo and Juliet*. This sets up the idea of the duel as opposed to a brawl and further refines Mercutio's character.

———. "No 'Vain Fantasy': Shakespeare's Refashioning of Nashe for Dreams and Queen Mab." In *Shakespeare's "Romeo and Juliet": Texts, Contexts, and Interpretation*. Ed. Jay L. Halio. London: Associated UP, 1995. 49–82. A study of Nashe's work, which has previously been underrated as a potential source for some of Shakespeare's dream imagery.

Kahn, Coppélia. "Coming of Age in Verona." In *The Woman's Part: Feminist Criticism of Shakespeare*. Urbana: U of Illinois P, 1980. 171–193. An investigation of the impact the aggressive patriarchal society has on the maturation of the young lovers' relationship. The anthology is also a good introduction to early feminist critiques of Shakespeare.

Lanphier, David N. "How Shakespeare Purified and Idealized the Love Story of Romeo and Juliet." *Publications of the Arkansas Philological Association* 23.2 (1997): 29–39. Examines differences between Shakespeare's version of the main storyline and Brooke's version. Particularly interesting because Brooke is Shakespeare's acknowledged main source.

Levenson, Jill L. "*Romeo and Juliet*: Tragical-Comical-Lyrical History." *Proceedings of the Patristic, Medieval, and Renaissance Conference* 12–13 (1988): 31–36. Looks at the merger of comedy and tragedy, but also looks at the inclusion of a third genre, the sonnet. Concludes that Shakespeare uses these different modes of address to better illustrate a "drama of two voices," the public and the private.

———. "Romeo and Juliet before Shakespeare." *Studies in Philology* 81.3 (1984): 325–347. Traces the fundamental story of the two lovers in the sixteenth-century novellas and poems that predated Shakespeare's play. The reader can glean the differences between Shakespeare's story and these stories.

Pearlman, E. "Shakespeare at Work: *Romeo and Juliet*." *English Literary Renaissance* 24.2 (1994): 315–342. Wide-ranging, mostly textual exploration of the play that begins by looking at textual issues between Q1 and Q2, and moves into close readings of several scenes based on textual aberrations. Includes a section on the Queen Mab speech and its place in the textual debate.

Porter, Joseph A. *Shakespeare's Mercutio: His History and Drama*. Chapel Hill: U of North Carolina P, 1988. A thorough background and in-depth analysis of the character Mercutio not only in the text of *Romeo and Juliet* but also in his various representations on the stage and in other adaptations. Relates Mercutio to the god Mercury among other allusions.

Snyder, Susan. "*Romeo and Juliet*: Comedy into Tragedy." *Essays in Criticism* 20.4 (1970): 391–402. Discusses the "two halves" of *Romeo and Juliet*, positing the first half as basically a comedy with undertones of tragedy, and the second half as the full-fledged tragic portion.

Whittier, Gayle. "The Sonnet's Body and the Body Sonnetized in *Romeo and Juliet*." *Shakespeare Quarterly* 40.1 (1989): 27–41. Analyzes the play from the standpoint of the sonnet—its indebtedness to the Elizabethan sonnet sequence, its internal sonnets, and its sonnet conventions and disruptions. Pays careful attention to language and structure. Ultimately explores the poetic word and its implications for "flesh" (that is, the characters' actions and adventures).

# Julius Caesar

### Robert G. Blake

## PLOT SUMMARY

**1.1.** As the play opens, the tribunes (officials chosen by the plebeians to protect their rights against the patricians) Flavius and Murellus berate a group of tradesmen for appearing in public on "a laboring day" (1.1.4) without the signs of their professions but rather dressed in their best attire to watch the triumphal entry of Julius Caesar into Rome in celebration of his defeat of the sons of Pompey the Great some months before. Murellus's exchanges with a cobbler contain various puns that lighten the mood of an otherwise ominous scene. He angrily addresses the plebeians as "You blocks, you stones, you worse than senseless things!" (1.1.35) and recalls their earlier adulation of the late Pompey, whom Caesar defeated at Pharsalia four years earlier. Flavius commands the craftsmen to assemble others of their class and to weep their tears into the Tiber River until it overflows. He then entreats Murellus to join him in removing all accoutrements from the statues of Caesar that had been set up around the city in honor of his impending entry. The scene ends with Flavius's assuring his fellow tribune that "These growing feathers pluck'd from Caesar's wing / Will make him fly an ordinary pitch, / Who else would soar above the view of men, / And keep us all in servile fearfulness" (1.1.72–75).

**1.2.** The time is the Feast of Lupercal, held every February 15 in honor of the god Pan. Part of the festal activities was a race on the Palatine Hill in which the participants carried goat thongs with which they struck those in their path. Anyone so struck was supposed to be cured of sterility. Hence Caesar tells his wife to stand "directly in Antonio's way / When he doth run his course" (1.2.3–4) and instructs Mark Antony to "touch Calpurnia" (1.2.7). The voice of a Soothsayer warns Caesar to "Beware the ides of March," exactly one month in the future (1.2.18), but Caesar dismisses him as a "dreamer" (1.2.24) and goes to watch the race, leaving Cassius and Brutus behind. Proceeding indirectly, Cassius seeks to determine Brutus's feelings about Caesar. Shouts are heard in the background, leading Brutus to say, "I do fear the people / Choose Caesar for their king" (1.2.79–80). That comment causes the envious Cassius to speak openly of his contempt for Caesar. In a long speech he fabricates events in Caesar's life to suggest that Caesar is cowardly, and he appeals to Brutus's vanity by asking him, "Why should that name [Caesar] be sounded more than yours?" (1.2.143). Brutus will not openly commit himself to Cassius's position but agrees to consider his words.

Caesar and his train return from the games, thus interrupting the conversation between Brutus and Cassius. Caesar remarks to Antony regarding Cassius, "Such men as he be never at heart's ease / Whiles they behold a greater than themselves, / And therefore are they very dangerous" (1.2.208–210). He immediately adds, "I rather tell thee what is to be fear'd / Than what I fear; for always I am Caesar. / Come on my right hand, for this ear is deaf, / And tell me truly what thou think'st of him" (1.2.211–214).

Caesar and his followers depart, but Casca is detained to be interrogated by Brutus and Cassius about what has transpired to make Caesar look so disgruntled. The blunt Casca describes the scene of Antony's offering Caesar the crown of kingship three times, Caesar's repeated refusal to accept it because he senses the disapproval of the crowd, Caesar's having an epileptic seizure, and Cicero's words in Greek, which Casca could not understand: "it was Greek to me" (1.2.284). Casca agrees to dine with Cassius the next day and then exits. Brutus, having promised to speak with Cassius the next day, leaves Cassius alone. The scene concludes with a short soliloquy by Cassius. He admits that he acts purely out of self-interest, and he concocts a plan to ensure Brutus's participation in the conspiracy, thereby legitimizing it: "I will this night, / In several hands, in at his windows throw, / As if they came from several citizens, / Writings, all tending to the great opinion / That Rome holds of his name; wherein obscurely / Caesar's ambition shall be glanced at" (1.2.315–320).

**1.3.** This atmospheric scene takes place in the dark of night amidst thunder and lightning. An unnerved Casca with drawn sword encounters Cicero in the street. Cicero asks, "Why are you breathless, and why stare you so?" (1.3.2). Casca replies that he has encountered a number of unnatural events such as a tempest dropping fire, a lion that looked threateningly at him, and a slave whose burning hand was untouched by fire. Such strange phenomena are known as portents, and to Shakespeare's contemporaries as well as to the ancient Romans they foretold a catastrophic disruption in the state. Cicero, an Epicurean rationalist, dismisses these occurrences as being of no consequence. He then asks, "Comes Caesar to the Capitol to-morrow?" (1.3.36). Cicero then goes on his way, and Cassius approaches out of the darkness. He tells Casca that he has walked about the streets inviting lightning to strike him dead and that the prodigious events presage a "monstrous state," as does "A man no mightier than thyself, or me / In personal action, yet prodigious grown, / And fearful, as these strange eruptions are" (1.3.71, 76–78). In the ensuing exchange Cassius enlists Casca in the conspiracy and informs him that he is on his way to "Pompey's Porch," the portico of the Theater of Pompey (1.3.147), to meet with some of "the noblest-minded Romans" (1.3.122) who will take part in the approaching assassination, which he refers to as "an enterprise / Of honorable-dangerous consequence" (1.3.123–124). The scene ends with the entry of Cinna, whom Cassius instructs to put in Brutus's praetor's (that is, judge's) chair and in other places those papers forged in various hands attesting to Brutus's greatness.

**2.1.** In his dark orchard Brutus calls Lucius to bring a candle to his study. Waiting for the candlelight, Brutus soliloquizes that Caesar must be killed, not for what he has done but rather to prevent what he might do if he is crowned king. Lucius informs his master that the taper is lighted and that he found a paper in the study, one of Cassius's missives to win Brutus over to the conspiracy. The burden of the letter is "Speak, strike, redress!" (2.1.47). But Brutus has already decided that Caesar must die. In a second, short soliloquy he says he has not slept since his earlier talk with Cassius and admits to a profound spiritual turmoil.

There is a knock at the door, and Lucius announces, "Sir, 'tis your brother Cassius" (2.1.70). Historically, Brutus and Cassius were brothers-in-law, Cassius having married a sister of Brutus. Before the conspirators enter, Brutus in a brief soliloquy apostrophizes Conspiracy to mask its "monstrous visage" in "smiles and affability" (2.1.81–82). Once the conspirators have gathered in Brutus's study, the details of the assassination are planned, but first Cassius must introduce each of the assassins to Brutus, who welcomes them into his home. Cassius craves a private word with Brutus, and, while they confer, several of the other conspirators make small talk about the direction of the sunrise. The private conversation with his brother-in-law ended, Brutus shakes hands with each conspirator. Then Cassius says, "And let us swear our resolution" (2.1.113). Brutus objects to an oath on the grounds that it would be beneath the dignity of the honor and motivation of their enterprise. All the conspirators acquiesce. Cassius then proposes including Cicero in the conspiracy. Metullus Cimber argues that Cicero by virtue of his age and judiciousness will lend gravitas to the assassination. There is general agreement, with the exception of Brutus, who exclaims that Cicero "will never follow any thing / That other men begin" (2.1.151–152). Again, the others submit to Brutus's judgment. Next, Cassius urges that Mark Antony be killed with Caesar, as he is a "shrewd contriver" (2.1.157). Once more Brutus overrules Cassius. Brutus argues that killing Antony will be too bloody and that Antony is too given "To sports, to wildness, and much company" to pose a threat without Caesar (2.1.189).

The clock strikes three. Cassius wonders whether Caesar will come to the Senate on this day since he has lately become superstitious and might be influenced by the night's portents. Decius Brutus assures his fellow conspirators that he can persuade Caesar to go to the Senate by eight o'clock this very morning. Brutus advises his fellow conspirators as they leave his home to "look fresh and merrily; / Let not our looks put on our purposes" (2.1.224–225). At this point Portia enters and desires to know what has recently been troubling her husband, since he has been preoccupied and out of temper with her. His excuse is that he has been weak in health, but Portia replies: "No, my Brutus, / You have some sick offense within your mind" (2.1.267–268). Portia pleads with Brutus to share with her the source of his inner conflict, but he remains unmoved even after she kneels before him, leaving her to feel that she dwells in the "suburbs" of her husband's "good pleasure" (2.1.285–286).

Their dialogue is interrupted by a knock at the door. Brutus promises to tell Portia the "secrets of his heart" (2.1.306), but now she must leave him immediately. Brutus's servant boy brings in "a sick man that would speak with" Brutus (2.1.310). This is Caius Ligarius, who will renounce his sickness if "Brutus have in hand / Any exploit worthy the name of honor (2.1.316–317). Brutus will explain what he is about as they go to Caesar's house. Ligarius agrees to follow Brutus "To do I know not what; but it sufficeth / That Brutus leads me on" (2.1.333–334). The scene ends with the sound of thunder and Brutus's imperative, "Follow me then" (2.1.334).

**2.2.** This scene takes place in Caesar's house as he prepares to leave for the Capitol amid thunder and lightning. Caesar alone in his nightgown remarks to himself on the tumultuous elements and says that three times Calpurnia screamed out in her sleep, "Help, ho! They murther Caesar!" (2.2.3). Caesar commands his servant to have the priests "do present sacrifice" (2.2.5) and to bring him their report. Calpurnia enters and says that although she has never had faith in omens, there have been so many strange and unnatural events in the night that she is now afraid for her husband's safety. When Caesar insists that he will go to the Capitol, Calpurnia warns, "When beggars die there are no comets seen; / The heavens themselves blaze forth the death of princes" (2.2.30–31). These words do not move Caesar, who replies, "Cowards die many times before their deaths, / The valiant never taste of death but once" (ll. 32–33).

A servant brings word that the priests would not have Caesar leave the house this day because they could find no heart in the sacrificed beast, a bad omen. Caesar remains unimpressed, exclaiming, "Danger knows full well / That Caesar is more dangerous than he" (2.2.44–45). Calpurnia replies, "Your wisdom is consum'd in confidence" (2.2.49) and on her knees implores her husband to stay home. At last Caesar is convinced and will have Antony inform the Senate that he, Caesar, is not well. Decius Brutus enters to escort Caesar to the Senate, only to be told that Caesar will not come today. Caesar tells Decius about Calpurnia's dream that his statue was running blood from "an hundred spouts" (2.2.77), and that the Romans were washing their hands in it. Decius gives an alternate interpretation that appeals to Caesar's vanity: his bleeding statue provides Rome with sustaining life blood. Immediately, Caesar changes his mind and resolves to go to the Senate. He is ashamed that he temporarily yielded to his wife's fears. The other conspirators, led by Brutus, enter to accompany Caesar. As the scene draws to a conclusion Caesar tells Trebonius to "Be near me that I may remember you." Trebonius replies, "Caesar I will; / [*aside*] and so near will I be, / That your best friends shall wish I had been further" (2.2.123–125). Caesar invites all of them to drink some wine and then "we, like friends, will straightway go together" (2.2.127). Brutus has the last word in an aside: "That every like is not the same, O Caesar, / The heart of Brutus earns [grieves] to think upon!" (2.2.128–129). That is, not everyone who seems to be Caesar's friend really is so.

**2.3.** Artemidorus, a teacher of rhetoric, reads a letter that he will give to Caesar as the latter walks to the Capitol. The letter names each of the eight conspirators as an imminent danger and concludes, "If thou beest not immortal, look about you; security gives way to conspiracy. The mighty gods defend thee! Thy lover, Artemidorus" (2.3.6–10). This short scene ends with Artemidorus's words: "If thou read this, O Caesar, thou mayest live; / If not, the Fates with traitors do contrive" (2.3.15–16).

**2.4.** In front of Brutus's home a distraught Portia tells Lucius to hasten to the Senate house without giving him a reason for doing so. She questions why he has not gone immediately, and he is naturally confused: "Madam, what should I do? / Run to the Capitol, and nothing else? / And so return to you, and nothing else?" (2.4.10–12). Portia wants to know whether Brutus looks well—he looked ill as he left his house—what Caesar is doing, and who asks favors of him. She hears a noise coming from the Capitol, but Lucius hears nothing. At this point the Soothsayer of act 1, scene 2, enters and is questioned by Portia. It is nine o'clock, and Caesar has not yet gone to the Capitol. Portia asks the Soothsayer whether he has business with Caesar and whether he knows of any harm intended for him. The Soothsayer replies, "None that I know will be, much that I fear may chance" (2.4.32). He leaves to secure a better vantage point from which to address Caesar on the way to the Capitol. Portia is so filled with anxiety that she grows faint. Still, she instructs Lucius to go to the Senate house, tell Brutus that she is in good spirits, and report back to her what Brutus has to say.

**3.1.** This scene begins in front of the Capitol with Caesar saying to the Soothsayer, "The ides of March are come." The Soothsayer replies, "Ay, Caesar, but not gone" (3.1.1–2). Artemidorus greets Caesar and requests that he read his letter of warning, but Decius intervenes. Caesar ignores Artemidorus's further importuning and, followed by the conspirators, enters the Capitol. Popilius Lena tells Cassius, "I wish your enterprise to-day may thrive" (3.1.13). He ignores Cassius's question of what he is referring to and goes over to speak with Caesar. Cassius and Brutus, observing from a distance, fear the conspiracy is discovered, but Caesar's demeanor does not change. In the orchestrated prelude to the assassination, Trebonius lures Mark Antony away. A kneeling Metullus Cimber beseeches Caesar to recall his brother from banishment, and Brutus adds his voice to beg the repeal of the sentence against Publius Cimber. Cassius is next to ask for mercy for the banished man. Caesar rejects all requests with high hauteur, "I could be well mov'd, if I were as you; / If I could pray to move, prayers would move me; / But I am constant as the northern star" (3.1.58–60). Soon after these words Casca stabs Caesar from behind, and the other conspirators set upon him. Caesar dies with the words, "Et tu, Brute?—Then fall Caesar" (3.1.77). Caesar's death at the foot of the statue of Pompey the Great is followed by a series of staccato remarks on the ensuing general confusion.

Brutus and Casca make cynical remarks about benefiting Caesar by reducing his days of fearing death. Then all the conspirators bathe their hands in Caesar's blood. A servant of Mark Antony arrives to inquire if his master may come into their presence. Brutus guarantees Antony's safety and welcomes him as a friend. Antony enters, apostrophizes the lifeless body of Caesar and offers his own life to the assassins; but he is reassured by Brutus that no harm is meant to him. Cassius promises Antony, "Your voice shall be as strong as any man's / In the disposing of new dignities" (3.1.177–178). Antony shakes the hand of each conspirator in turn and assures them that he loves them all. He then asks permission to carry Caesar's body to the marketplace and to speak at Caesar's funeral. Dismissing Cassius's concern that Antony may move the people against the conspirators, Brutus agrees to let Antony speak, provided Antony speak last and make it clear that he speaks by permission. Everyone leaves except Antony, who prophesizes in soliloquy that "Domestic fury and fierce civil strife / Shall cumber all the parts of Italy" (3.1.263–264). A servant of Octavius enters and informs Antony that Octavius is on his way to Rome. Antony tells the servant that Rome is presently too dangerous and to delay his entry until Antony can determine how the people will react to his funeral oration. They exit with Caesar's body.

**3.2.** At the Forum Brutus speaks to the plebeians. In a classical style of oratory characterized by parallelism and ratiocination Brutus seeks to convince the plebeians that he loved Caesar, but that he loved Rome more and slew Caesar for Caesar's ambition to be absolute ruler of Rome. Brutus's speech persuades the plebeians to support him and, by extension, the other conspirators. Brutus exits, and Mark Antony now addresses the Roman citizens. Antony uses an Asiatic style of oratory characterized by heavy irony and high emotion, and in the course of some twenty-five lines he is able to change the mood of the mob. He refers to the conspirators as "honorable men" (3.2.83 and following) and employs such stage props as Caesar's torn and bloody mantle—"See what a rent the envious Casca made" (3.2.175)—and Caesar's will, which, he eventually discloses, bequeathed to the plebeians "all his walks, / His private arbors and new-planted orchards, / On this side Tiber" (3.2.247–249). By the time Antony has finished speaking, he has stirred the crowd to a brutal frenzy against the conspirators. They leave in a rush. Receiving word from Octavius's servant that Octavius and Lepidus are at Caesar's house, Antony resolves to join them.

**3.3.** In a Roman street, a poet sharing the same name as Cinna the conspirator is pursued by a crowd of plebeians. Four plebeians interrogate him, and when they discover his name they drag him to his death despite his desperate words: "I am Cinna the poet, I am Cinna the poet. . . . I am not Cinna the conspirator" (3.3.29, 32). The scene ends with the mob's vowing to burn down the houses of the conspirators.

**4.1.** The conspirators have all fled for their lives; and Mark Antony, Octavius Caesar, and M. Aemilius Lepidus have established themselves as a triumvirate to rule Rome. In Antony's house they cold-bloodedly make up a list to purge Roman citizens who they believe may pose a threat to their governance. Lepidus consents to his brother's death, "Upon condition Publius shall not live, / Who is your sister's son, Mark Antony" (4.1.4–5). Antony consents to his nephew's demise and sends Lepidus to Caesar's house to bring the will to them so that they may alter it to their benefit. Antony tells Octavius that Lepidus "is a slight unmeritable man, / Meet to be sent on errands" (4.1.12–13). Antony will use Lepidus as a triumvir to ease himself and Octavius "of divers sland'rous loads"; then Lepidus will be dismissed to "graze in commons" as a laboring ass when his work is done (4.1.20, 27). Octavius argues that Lepidus is a "tried and valiant soldier" (4.1.28), but Antony reposts, "So is my horse, Octavius, and for that / I do appoint him store of provender" (4.1.29–30). Antony adjures Octavius to speak of Lepidus only "as a property" (4.1.40). Antony then discusses the dangers posed by Brutus and Cassius, who are mobilizing troops to make war. Antony suggests that they prepare for the coming conflict. Octavius agrees in anachronistic language alluding to Elizabethan bearbaiting: "Let us do so; for we are at the stake, / And bay'd about with many enemies" (4.1.48–49).

**4.2.** Brutus's army is encamped near Sardis. Standing in front of his tent, Brutus asks his ever-faithful servant Lucius whether Cassius is near. Lucius announces the arrival of Pindarus, Cassius's servant. Brutus is irate with Cassius for certain offenses and tells Pindarus of his concern. Brutus asks Lucius how he had been received by Cassius and concludes that Cassius's behavior was that of a "hot friend cooling" and reflects that when "love begins to sicken and decay / It useth an enforced ceremony" (4.2.19–21). Cassius enters with his army, and his first words to Brutus are "Most noble brother, you have done me wrong" (4.2.37). Brutus will not begin a quarrel with his brother-in-law before their armies, and both command their forces to move away. The two leaders agree to discuss their differences in Brutus's guarded tent.

**4.3.** This scene begins with a heated altercation between Brutus and Cassius over various accusations on both sides. Cassius criticizes Brutus for disregarding Cassius's defense of Lucius Pella, whom Brutus had condemned for taking bribes. Brutus, in turn, accuses Cassius of having an "itching palm" (4.3.10), that is, accepting bribes himself. Cassius is beside himself with anger in the ensuing argument, but Brutus remains calm and unmoved: "There is no terror, Cassius, in your threats; / For I am arm'd so strong in honesty / That they pass by me as the idle wind, / Which I respect not" (4.3.66–69). The argument grows heated to the point that Cassius offers his heart for Brutus to stab, an action that brings reconciliation. The end of their dangerous quarrel is immediately interrupted by the intrusion of a Poet, who chides them for arguing and then leaves at the command of Cassius. Brutus tells Cassius that he is "sick of many griefs" (4.3.144). Portia has taken her life by swallowing fire. Cassius is aghast and filled with commiseration but is told by Brutus to speak no more of her, and the two drink wine together.

Titinius and Messala enter with news that Antony and Octavius with a powerful army are moving toward Philippi and that they have had a hundred senators executed. Brutus's information mentioned seventy senators including Cicero. Messala asks whether Brutus has received information about Portia. Strangely, Brutus denies having heard anything concerning her and is informed that she is dead. Brutus's stoic reaction is: "Why, farewell, Portia. We must die, Messala, / With meditating that she must die once, / I have the patience to endure it now" (4.3.190–192). At this point Brutus asks Cassius what he thinks of marching to Philippi immediately to engage the enemy. Cassius thinks their armies should stay put and let the opposing forces wear themselves out in facing them. As always, Brutus overrules Cassius and so relinquishes the strategic high ground to engage the armies of Octavius and Antony at Philippi. It is now late at night. Cassius leaves Brutus's tent. Alone, Brutus asks the sleepy Lucius to bring him his gown, play on the harp, and summon Varrus and Claudio to sleep in his tent in case he has to send for Cassius. After Lucius falls asleep playing on his harp, Brutus is visited by the Ghost of Caesar, who tells Brutus that he will see him at Philippi. As soon as the Ghost disappears, Brutus awakens the others to ask why they cried out in their sleep and whether they saw anything. They all deny being disturbed. The scene ends with Brutus's commanding Varrus and Claudio to tell Cassius to mobilize his troops early in the morning and that Brutus will follow.

**5.1.** Octavius, Antony, and their armies are the first to enter the plains of Philippi. They know the enemy is descending from "the hills and upper regions" (5.1.3). Antony thinks they are merely trying to appear brave and tells Octavius to place his army on the left flank, but Octavius is obstinate and will take the right flank instead.

Brutus, Cassius, and their forces enter and seek parley. Antony and Octavius agree to talk before they fight. A rash of insults ensues. Antony refers to the assassins of Caesar as "villains": "You show'd your teeth like apes, and fawn'd like hounds, / And bow'd like bondmen, kissing Caesar's feet." (5.1.39, 41–42). Cassius contemptuously refers to Octavius and Antony as "A peevish schoolboy, worthless of such honor [that is, being killed by Brutus], / Join'd with a masker and a reveler!" (5.1.61–62). Antony and Octavius withdraw, challenging the enemy to the field when they are brave enough to fight. While Brutus speaks with Lucilius, Cassius tells Messala that it is his birthday, that he has always followed Epicurus's philosophy of reason, but that now he gives some credence to omens. It seems that on the march from Sardis to Philippi two great eagles perched on the conspirators' ensign, but this morning the eagles are gone. Instead, "ravens, crows, and kites / Fly o'er our heads, and downward look on us / As we were sickly prey" (5.1.84–86). Cassius partially believes this is an omen of impending defeat, but he is resolved to fight. He and Brutus speak of what might chance on this fateful day and bid each other farewell, perhaps never to meet again. The scene ends with the words of Brutus, the Stoic: "O that a man might know / The end of this day's business ere it come! / But it sufficeth that the day will end, / And then the end is known" (5.1.122–125).

**5.2.** Brutus sends Messala to give battle plans to the legions on the far side of Octavius's flank, which he sees as vulnerable to a sudden attack: "I perceive / But cold demeanor in Octavio's wing, / And sudden push gives them the overthrow" (5.2.3–5).

**5.3.** Cassius has just slain his own standard bearer for cowardice, and Titinius has observed that Brutus gave the order to attack Octavius prematurely—his soldiers took to looting—and "we by Antony are all enclos'd" (5.3.8). Pindarus enters with a warning for Cassius to pull further back since Mark Antony has taken Cassius's camp. Cassius will not withdraw but sends Titinius to reconnoiter and bring him word whether troops in the distance "are friend or enemy" (5.3.18). He then sends Pindarus to ride higher on the hill and observe Titinius. Pindarus sees that Titinius is surrounded by cavalry and dismounts to a shout of joy. Cassius makes a fatal mistake at this point, thinking Titinius has been captured by the enemy when in fact he had been received by his friends. Thinking that all is lost, Cassius declares Pindarus, a former enemy whose life he had saved with the understanding that he would perform whatever Cassius commanded him in future, a freeman but also orders Pindarus to kill him. Cassius's last words are "Caesar, thou art reveng'd, / Even with the sword that kill'd thee" (5.3.45–46). Pindarus, now free, flees. Titinius and Messala enter and see the body of Cassius. Titinius says, "So in his red blood Cassius' day is set! / The sun of Rome is set. Our day is gone, / Clouds, dews, and dangers come; our deeds are done! / Mistrust of my success hath done this deed" (5.3.62–65). Titinius tells Messala to leave, and he will seek Pindarus. Once he is alone, Titinius is unable to accept the reason for Cassius's death and commits suicide with Cassius's sword. Brutus, accompanied by friends and servants, enters. When told of Cassius's death, he exclaims, "O Julius Caesar, thou art mighty yet! / Thy spirit walks abroad, and turns our swords / In our own proper entrails" (5.3.94–96). Brutus orders Cassius's body to be sent to the nearby island of Thasos to prevent his funeral from lowering morale on the battlefield. It is three o'clock and Brutus will take the field to "try fortune in a second fight" (5.3.110).

**5.4.** Young Cato is slain and Lucilius is captured. Lucilius identifies himself as Brutus, believing that lie will ensure him an immediate and honorable death. Antony enters and sees that Brutus has not been taken prisoner, but ever magnanimous in victory he proclaims that Lucilius is "a prize no less in worth" (5.4.27) and commands that Lucilius be safely guarded and treated kindly.

**5.5.** Brutus knows that all is lost, and he privately asks Clitus, Dardanius, and Volumnius in turn to kill him. Each refuses. An alarm sounds for an imminent attack and all flee except Brutus and Strato. Brutus asks Strato to hold his sword so that he may run upon it. Brutus's last words are "Caesar, now be still, / I kill'd not thee with half so good a will" (5.5.50–51). Octavius, Antony, and their captives Messala and Lucilius enter. They discover the body of Brutus. Strato explains the manner of his death. In a kind of eulogy Antony proclaims that Brutus "was the no-blest Roman of them all" (5.5.68). Octavius will insure that Brutus has a proper burial and says that tonight Brutus's body will repose in Octavius's own tent. Octavius has the last word: "So call the field to rest, and let's away, / To part the glories of this happy day" (5.5.80–81).

## PUBLICATION HISTORY

Although it is not possible to date any of Shakespeare's plays with absolute certainty, there is critical consensus that *Julius Caesar* was written in 1599. The play does not appear in Francis Meres's list of Shakespeare's plays in *Palladis Tamia*, which appeared in September of 1598. This list is not complete, but it is thought that due to its great popularity *Julius Caesar* would have appeared on the list if it had been performed earlier. A European traveler reports seeing in September of 1599 at two o'clock in the afternoon a play about Julius Caesar in a thatched-roof theater on the far side of the Thames—an obvious reference to this play, which would indicate that *Julius Caesar* was one of the first of Shakespeare's plays to be performed in the new Globe Theater (built in 1599). According to David Bevington, *Julius Caesar* is a pivotal play of the 1590s, following the English histories and looking toward the tragedies to come.

*Julius Caesar* first appeared in print in the First Folio (1623) with the title *The Tragedie of Julius Caesar* while in the table of contents it is listed as *The Life and Death of Julius Caesar*, which would suggest a history play. It poses no textual problems of consequence. In fact, it is often regarded as the least corrupted text of the First Folio, suggesting that it was copied directly from Shakespeare's manuscript. The text, known as F1, is so free of errors that it has served as the basis for subsequent editions to the present. Charles Boyce (*Shakespeare A to Z* [New York: Roundtable, 1990]) believes that F1 "had probably been used as or taken from a Prompt-Book, in which the playwright's characteristic mis-spellings and unnecessarily elaborate stage directions had been corrected" (328).

## SOURCES FOR THE PLAY

Shakespeare almost never invented his plots. He used sources, and because he wrote hurriedly under time constraints dictated by the needs of his theatrical company, he generally avoided multiple sources when one would do. When he came to write *Julius Caesar*, Sir Thomas North's English rendering of Jacques Amyot's French translation of Plutarch's *Lives of the Noble Grecians and Romans* (1579, 1595) stood ready to hand. Although various other sources for *Julius Caesar* have been suggested—such as John Higgins's biography of Caesar in *A Mirror for Magistrates* (1559), Thomas Kyd's *Cornelia* (1594), and Cicero's writings—North's translation of Plutarch is the major one.

Because Shakespeare wrote his plays for entertainment and commercial success, he was not interested in fidelity to his sources or historical accuracy. His plays are replete with examples of the sacrifice of historical fact for dramatic effect. For instance, in *Richard II* Shakespeare greatly expands the negligible character of John of Gaunt from his source, making him into a great patriot whose deathbed speech contains one of the best-known descriptions of England in literature. In *1 Henry IV*

Shakespeare makes Hotspur the same age as Prince Hal—when in fact he was older than Hal's father—to create an imaginary but dramatically effective tension between the two. A final example must suffice: Shakespeare transforms the character of Macbeth from a not-entirely evil figure in Raphael Holinshed's *Chronicles* (1577; 2nd ed. 1587) into a monstrous regicide.

Shakespeare's use of North's translation of Plutarch is no less imaginative. He had at his disposal a huge body of material in the lives of Julius Caesar, Marcus Brutus, and Mark Antony; and he had no choice but to ignore most of it. Boyce (328) and Frank Kermode (in *The Riverside Shakespeare*, ed. G. Blakemore Evans with J.J.M. Tobin, 2nd ed. [Boston: Houghton Mifflin, 1997], 1147–1148) provide helpful laundry lists of the changes that Shakespeare made from Plutarch. What he left out is perhaps as significant as what he used. The net effects of Shakespeare's use of Plutarch in writing this play are twofold: a general denigration of the major characters and a telescoping of events from two years to seemingly as many months, the results of this time concentration being a sense of dramatic intensity and urgency.

In *The Life of Julius Caesar* Plutarch provides numerous accounts of the great commander's character and military exploits. In regard to Caesar's treatment of his legions Plutarch writes:

> Now Caesar self did breed this noble courage and life in them. First, for that he gave them bountifully, and did honour them also, showing thereby, that he did not heap up riches in the wars to maintain his life afterwards in wantonness and pleasure, but that he did keep it in store, honourably to reward their valiant service: and that by so much he thought himself rich, by how much he was liberal in rewarding of them that had deserved it. (*Selected Lives from the Lives of the Noble Grecians and Romans*, ed. Paul Turner, 2 vols. [Carbondale: Southern Illinois UP, 1963], 2.11)

Plutarch writes of Caesar's use of military force to achieve his political ambitions:

> Caesar . . . like a wrestler that studieth for tricks to overthrow his adversary . . . went far from Rome, to exercise himself in the wars of Gaul, where he did train his army, and presently by his valiant deeds did increase his fame and honour. By these means became Caesar as famous as Pompey in his doings. (Ibid., 2.19)

The following words of Plutarch attest to Caesar's insurmountable power and energy:

> [Caesar] went forthwith to set upon the camp of Afranius, the which he took at the first onset, and the camp of the Numidians also, King Juba being fled. Thus in a little piece of the day only, he took three camps, and slew fifty thousand of his enemies, and lost but fifty of his soldiers. (Ibid., 2.35)

Another example of Plutarch's portrayal of Caesar is his reaction to the presentation to him of the head of his enemy Pompey the Great: "[H]e came into Alexandria, after Pompey was slain: and detested Theodorus that presented him Pompey's head, and turned his head at toe side because he would not see it. Notwithstanding, he took his seal, and beholding it, wept" (ibid., 2.32).

Not once in this play does Shakespeare refer to Caesar's abilities and character traits that the above citations attest to, except perhaps in the first scene when the tribune Murellus refers derogatorily to Caesar's victory over Pompey's sons: "What conquest brings he home? / What tributaries follow him to Rome, / To grace in captive bonds his chariot-wheels?" (1.1.32–34).

Not only did Shakespeare not use Plutarch's positive passages about Caesar, he took one such passage and altered it in a negative manner to be spoken by Cassius. Here is the passage from Plutarch:

> Concerning the constitution of his body, he was lean, white, and soft skinned, and often subject to headache, and otherwhile to the falling sickness [epilespsy]: (the which took him the first time, as it is reported, in Corduba, a city of Spain) but yet therefore yielded not to the disease of his body, to make it a cloak to cherish him withal, but contrarily, took the pains of war, as a medicine to cure his sick body fighting always with his disease, travelling continually, living soberly, and commonly lying abroad in the field. (Ibid., 2.11–12)

Trying covertly to enlist Brutus in the conspiracy, Cassius says of Caesar in one of the longest speeches in the play:

> He had a fever when he was in Spain,
> And when the fit was on him, I did mark
> How he did shake—'tis true, this god did shake;
> His coward lips did from their color fly,
> And that same eye whose bend doth awe the world
> Did lose his luster; I did hear him groan;
> Ay, and that tongue of his that bade the Romans
> Mark him, and write his speeches in their books,
> Alas, it cried, "Give me some drink, Titinius,"
> As a sick girl. (1.2.119–128)

The point should be clear that Shakespeare's use of Plutarch's full-fleshed portrait of Julius Caesar is reductive and generally unfavorable.

Plutarch's portrayal of Brutus is uniformly favorable. Plutarch shows him to be a merciful, resourceful, and brave warrior who is beloved of his troops. He is portrayed as a great patriot who put the good of Rome before all else, including his wife. Plutarch writes that when he is informed of Portia's sudden illness, "[I]t grieved him, as it is to be presupposed: yet he left not off the case of his country and commonwealth, neither went home to his house for any news he heard." He prides himself on being a direct descendent of Lucius Junius Brutus, the Roman hero who defeated the Tarquins at the end of the sixth century B.C. In contrast to his choleric and malicious ancestor, Marcus Brutus, according to Plutarch, framed his life "by the rules of virtue and study of philosophy." His wit "was gentle and constant, in attending of great things." His very enemies accede that Brutus, alone of the conspirators, acted out of noble motives. Such words as the following from *The Life of Brutus* are characteristic:

> For as Brutus' gravity and constant mind would not grant all men their requests that sued unto him, but being moved with reason and discretion, did always incline to that which was good and honest: even so when it was moved to follow any manner, he used a kind of forcible and vehement persuasion that calmed not, till he had obtained his desire. (Turner, ed., p. 2.165)

Shakespeare complicates Plutarch's account by presenting Brutus as a proud patrician of great persuasive powers but one whose judgment is seriously flawed. He is that destructive type of a well-meaning individual: a misguided idealist who is so sure of his cause that he will entertain no opinions different from his own. It can be argued that Brutus's mistakes, which Shakespeare so clearly demonstrates, lead to the catastrophic consequences of this play. Paradoxically, Shakespeare's Brutus, although greatly altered from Plutarch's highly finished portrait, is altogether more interesting and complex than Plutarch's uniformly virtuous model.

*The Life of Antonius* is the longest of Plutarch's *Lives*, and it gives the most complete sense of the nature of power politics and the ever-shifting allegiances of the political players of ancient Rome. In *Julius Caesar* Shakespeare makes no use of this large body of information. There is no sense in the play of Antony's tumultuous career prior to 44 B.C. nor of his complicated relations with Octavius after Julius Caesar's assassination. In Shakespeare's portrayal of Antony there is lacking that sense of denigration from his sources that is the case with Caesar. Caesar speaks positively of Antony's love of plays as opposed to the ascetic tastes of Cassius. The severe Brutus says that Antony "is given / To sports, to wildness, and much company" (2.1.188–189), therefore posing no danger to the conspirators after the assassination, and Cassius dismisses him before the Battle of Philippi as "a masker and a reveler!" (5.1.62). These few passing remarks trivialize Antony's wanton lifestyle as set forth in Plutarch. His drunkenness and revelry, together with his insolence, made the Roman people hate him. Antony occupied the house of Pompey the Great and, according to Plutarch, "[I]t grieved them [the Roman populace] to see the gates commonly shut against the captains, magistrates of the city, and also ambassadors of strange nations, which were sometimes thrust from the gate with violence: and that the house within was full of tumblers, antic dancers, jugglers, players, jesters, and drunkards, quaffing and guzzling, and that on them he [Antony] spent and bestowed the most part of his money he got by all kind of possible extortions, bribery and policy" (ibid., 2.116–117).

Shakespeare uses Plutarch's description of the cold-blooded purge by the triumvirate, but he stops short at using the following passage from Plutarch depicting Antony's barbarian cruelty:

> Antonius . . . commanded them to whom he had given commission to kill Cicero, that they should strike off his head and right hand, with the which he had written the invective orations (called Philippides) against Antonius. So when the murtherers brought him Cicero's head and hand cut off, he beheld them a long time with great joy, and laughed heartily, and that oftentimes for the great joy he felt. Then when he had taken his pleasure of the sight of them, he caused them to be set up in an open place over the pulpit for orations . . . , as if he had done the dead man hurt, and not blemished his own fortune, showing himself (to his great shame and infamy) a cruel man, and unworthy the office and authority he bare. (Ibid., 2.116)

This is clearly not the Antony of Shakespeare. Shakespeare portrays Antony as a shrewd, even Machiavellian, figure who loved Julius Caesar and loathed his murderers, a man whose major strength may well be his being underestimated by his enemies as a mere hedonist.

Shakespeare's use of his major source raises interesting questions about his intentions. Various theories have been put forward regarding them: that Shakespeare shared the view held by Dante and Chaucer that Brutus and Cassius were traitors deserving the direst of punishments for betraying their established master; or that the play takes the Renaissance view, advocated by Ben Jonson and Sir Phillip Sydney, that Caesar was a tyrant and Brutus and Cassius would-be liberators. A study entitled "Honourable Men: Militancy and Masculinity in Julius Caesar," by Eugene Giddens of Cambridge University (*Renaissance Forum* 5.2 [Winter 2001] www.hull.ac.uk/renforum/v5no2/) argues that the play is a subtle commentary on the factions in Queen Elizabeth's court regarding the necessity of military valor as a means of validating one's masculinity and worth. Giddens argues that the lust for reputation drives the conspirators and that after the assassination Antony devalues military valor in favor of a more sophisticated and strategic policy to achieve victory over one's opponents. Hence, *Julius Caesar* is a defense of Queen Elizabeth's cautious approach in foreign affairs. For various reasons this is an interesting but not entirely compelling addition to criticism of the play: if *Julius Caesar* is indeed a commentary on the political climate surrounding the nature of valor in the late 1590s, the commentary is too adumbrated to be noticed by an Elizabethan audience; moreover, as Harold Bloom points out in his *Shakespeare: The Invention of the Human*, Shakespeare was far too cautious to politicize his plays, having the dire examples of Marlowe (murdered) and Thomas Kyd (imprisoned, tortured) before him. In all likelihood, Bloom is correct when he writes, "Shakespeare's politics, like his religion, forever will be unknown to us" (113).

## STRUCTURE AND PLOTTING

*Julius Caesar* is a beautifully crafted play with character, language, and setting focusing in a kind of classical unity on the overarching question of governance: which is better for Rome, an absolute monarchy or a republic? *Julius Caesar* is unlike any other of Shakespeare's tragedies. After *Macbeth* it is the shortest; the title character is killed off half-way through the play, and he speaks fewer than 150 lines. At first blush, one would wonder how Shakespeare could sustain the audience's interest for two and a half acts after the climax. If one subscribed to a nineteenth-century view that Brutus rather than Caesar is the main character, maintaining interest would be still more difficult if not impossible. It is clear to most scholars today that Caesar is the protagonist. Not only is the play named after him, but his presence looms larger after his death than it did in life. Moreover, the assassination of Caesar was as deeply embedded in the collective consciousness of the Renaissance as the myths that inform the plays of Aeschylus, Sophocles, and Euripides were enmeshed in the minds of the ancient Greeks. Thus, the question of suspense is irrelevant. The audience knew ahead of time what was going to happen.

Shakespeare resorted to irony rather than suspense as a way of focusing the audience's attention. Irony permeates the play from the first scene, when Flavius directs Murellus to remove the trophies from Caesar's statues lest Caesar become too powerful, to the last scene but two when Cassius commits suicide on his birthday because of a fatal misunderstanding. Irony in this play is encapsulated in Antony's line in his funeral oration that "Brutus is an honorable man" (3.2.82ff). Almost everyone in the play except Caesar knows that he will be assassinated on the Ides of March, and to watch him on his way to the Capitol accompanied by the conspirators in haughty disregard of the Soothsayer and Artemidorus must have been riveting for the audience.

Structurally this play is divided into two parts. The first part takes place in Rome, on its streets and in three interiors in daytime and at night. It consists of the formation of the conspiracy accompanied by portents and violent storms, the assassination, and its aftermath. In typical disregard of the neoclassical unity of place, Shakespeare shifts part two to Sardis in Asia Minor and the plains of Philippi. In this latter part Shakespeare shows the near-violent confrontation between the brothers-in-law Brutus and Cassius and their reconciliation, the buildup to the final battle with various bad omens, the verbal exchange between Antony and Octavius on the one hand and Brutus and Cassius on the other, the vicissitudes of the battle itself, and the ultimate victory of Antony and Octavius. Both parts are punctuated by dark atmospheric scenes bound to capture the audience's attention: Brutus in his dark study agonizing over the assassination (2.1.10–34); the visitation of the Ghost of Caesar in Brutus's dark tent before the battle at Philippi (4.3). These scenes, filled with nervous tension and the presence of the supernatural, look forward to similar ones in *Hamlet* and *Macbeth*.

Much has been written about Shakespeare's refusal to use more detail from his sources to deepen a sense of his characters and to provide reasons for certain actions, a practice that Harold Bloom refers to as foregrounding. There may be psychological reasons that Shakespeare failed to pursue the possible father-son relationship between Caesar and Brutus, but the practical reason for the absence of foregrounding is that he simply wanted to write a fast-paced play to entertain his audience. His manipulation of historical time illustrates this point well. Historically, the first scene of Caesar's triumphal entry into Rome after his defeat of Pompey's sons takes place in October 45 B.C. Scene 2 fast-forwards to February 15, 44 B.C., the Feast of Lupercal. Caesar is warned to "Beware the Ides of March" (1.2.18) exactly one month in the future, but the following scenes of act 1 are continuous, moving into the next day, the day of the assassination. The time of the rest of the play is similarly concentrated. For example, the Battle of Philippi actually consisted of two engagements separated by about three weeks. Shakespeare reduces these to a single day's fighting.

Yet another device this play uses to appeal to the audience is anachronism. The first scene resembles in some ways Elizabethan London more than ancient Rome. According to A. L. Rowse (*The Annotated Shakespeare*, 3 vols. [New York: Clarkson N. Potter, 1978], 3.135), Murellus's outburst in the following lines recalls Essex's expedition departing London for Ireland:

> O you hard hearts, you cruel men of Rome,
> Knew you not Pompey? Many a time and oft
> Have you climbed up to walls and battlements,
> To towers and windows, yea, to chimney tops,
> Your infants in your arms, and there have sat
> The livelong day, with patient expectation,
> To see great Pompey pass the streets of Rome. (1.1.36–42)

Regardless of the validity of Rowse's surmise, the lines no doubt allowed the audience to identify with the scene. So, too, Casca's description of the Roman populace when Caesar refused Antony's offer of a crown makes them seem like a London crowd:

[H]e put it the third time by; and still as he refused it, the rabblement howted, and clapped their chopp'd hands, and threw up their sweaty nightcaps, and utter'd such a deal of stinking breath because Caesar refus'd the crown, that it had, almost, chok'd Caesar, for he swounded, and fell down at it. (1.3.243–249)

A final anachronism with which the audience could identify would be the striking of the clock in the first and second scenes of the second act. Mechanical clocks would have been familiar in Elizabethan London, but they were not invented until more than a millennium after Caesar's death.

In sum, in writing *Julius Caesar* Shakespeare was driven by dramatic appeal, which he hoped would translate into commercial success. Various contemporary accounts indicate that he succeeded in this attempt.

## MAIN CHARACTERS

### Julius Caesar

Many modern historians regard Julius Caesar as the greatest general of the ancient world after Alexander the Great. His conquest of Gaul (present-day France and Belgium) changed the course of Western civilization by extending the Roman Empire beyond the Mediterranean into Northern Europe. His lasting imprint is seen in the German "Kaiser," the Russian "Czar," and perhaps the Persian "Shah," all versions of "Caesar." The emperors of the Roman Empire adopted the name of Caesar to share his reflected glory. His military achievements and his *Commentaries*, which are models of military history, were simply means to his end of becoming sole ruler of Rome. Cicero says that Caesar was first of all a realist, not above groveling for momentary advantage. He could be a sophisticated and charming aristocrat and a ruthless politician at the same time. His military victories, his oratorical skills, and his lavish bribes won him election to the Senate; as a consummate politician he allied himself with Crassus, Rome's richest man, and Pompey. When he was only forty-one he became one of the two Consuls, and he so intimidated the other that Bibulus stayed at home, leaving Caesar to rule alone. By the end of this two-year term the Senate, outraged by Caesar's domineering rule, tried to bring him to trial on charges of corruption, but Caesar outmaneuvered the Senate by becoming immune as a provincial governor. Caesar named the month of July after himself, and after defeating his old comrade Pompey in a series of battles, he returned to Rome knowing that he had mortal enemies, but he refused a bodyguard on the ground that it was better to die once than live always in the fear of death.

The preceding is a glimpse of the historical Caesar. How different is the anemic and attenuated Caesar of Shakespeare's play. The differences between the historical Caesar and Shakespeare's figure have often been noted, at least since the writing of William Hazlitt in the nineteenth century. Shakespeare's figure is undoubtedly a man of physical courage but physically infirm, deaf in the left ear, and fatally hubristic. There is no record of Caesar's deafness, and Shakespeare not only ignores his legendary energy but portrays him as essentially quiescent. Characters in drama can be delineated in three ways: by what they say, by what they do, and by what others say about them. By all of these methods Shakespeare portrays Caesar as a figure of exponential egocentricity. Caesar can be extremely perceptive in his observations of others. Shakespeare subtly suggests this point by having Brutus note the "angry spot . . . on Caesar's brow" (1.2.183) as Caesar returns from the games. Caesar had refused Antony's offer of a crown because he inferred that the populace did not want him to accept it. The shouting heard offstage was the approval of Caesar's rejection of the crown. Moreover, in all probability Caesar knew that the Senate was about to make him king. Another example of Caesar's ability to read other people is his remark to Antony concerning Cassius:

> Such men as he be never at heart's ease
> Whiles they behold a greater than themselves,
> And therefore are they very dangerous. (1.2.208–210)

His accurate assessment of other people is ironically counterbalanced by his near total lack of self-understanding. This defect is seen in the words that directly follow the above: "I rather tell thee what is to be fear'd / Than what I fear; for always I am Caesar" (1.2.211–212). He is so caught up in being a public man that he seems incapable of introspection. Calpurnia's incisive warning to him—"Your wisdom is consum'd in confidence" (2.2.49)—goes unheeded. The following excerpts from his dialogue exemplify his fatal hubris:

> Caesar shall forth; the things that threaten'd me
> Ne'er look'd but on my back; when they shall see
> The face of Caesar, they are vanished. (2.2.10–12)

> Caesar should be a beast without a heart
> If he should stay at home to-day for fear.
> No, Caesar shall not; Danger knows full well
> That Caesar is more dangerous than he.
> We are two lions litter'd in one day,
> And I the elder and more terrible. (2.2.42–47)

> I am constant as the northern star,
> Of whose true-fix'd and resting quality
> There is no fellow in the firmament. . . .
> So in the world: 'tis furnish'd well with men,
> And men are flesh and blood, and apprehensive;
> Yet in the number I do know but one
> That unassailable holds on his rank,
> Unshak'd of motion; and that I am he. (3.1.60–70)

A few lines after these remarks Caesar is stabbed to death, his final dying word being his own name. To quote from George Meredith's *Modern Love*, Caesar is "betrayed by what is false within" (*Poems* [New York: Scribner's, 1922], 45).

### Brutus

Brutus is an enigmatic and ironic character. His very ancestry is subject to question. Plutarch reports that he was in all probability a direct descendent of Lucius Junius Brutus, the iconic founder of the Roman Republic. Junius slew his eldest sons for treason but spared his youngest, from whom Marcus was apparently descended. Plutarch, following Suetonius, also suggests that Julius Caesar thought Brutus was his natural son by Servilia and forbade any harm to Brutus after the defeat of Pompey (on whose side Brutus was aligned), but Shakespeare does not directly address this possible relationship. Shakespeare's Brutus is a republican whose mistakes of policy and practice contribute to the long dictatorship of Octavius Caesar. Brutus on stage is a high-minded idealist whose counsels of Machiavellian deception are worthy of Lady Macbeth, a rationalist who resorts to irrational rationalization to justify Caesar's death, a skilled orator whose persuasive rhetoric invariably leads to disaster, an esteemed intellectual who refuses to entertain opinions that differ from his own, and finally a Stoic who takes his own life.

Although the prevailing views of Brutus expressed by both the other characters in the play and by commentators on it are positive, he comes across as a rather cold and distant figure. His warmth for his servant Lucius appears as an aberration. Unlike Caesar, Brutus is introspective. He has been troubled by the prospects of a Roman dictatorship, and Portia and Cassius have noticed his changed demeanor. The inability to hide one's innermost feelings was potentially fatal in the dangerous political environment of Caesarian Rome. David Bevington writes that Brutus "is too high-minded and genteel a man for the troubled times in which he lived" (*The Complete Works of Shakespeare* [New York: HarperCollins, 1992], 1023). The nineteenth-century poet Algernon Charles Swinburne in his *A Study of Shakespeare* (London: Chatto & Windus, 1880), avers that Brutus is the "very noblest figure of a typical and ideal republican in all the literature of the world" (159).

Because of his high reputation for good judgment, even wisdom, Brutus's participation in the conspiracy was required to legitimize it, but that reputation is not supported by his actions as Shakespeare delineates them. He makes a number of errors of judgment, any one of which would have destroyed his vision of a Roman Republic. His most serious is his refusal, in defiance of Cassius's good advice, to allow Antony to be killed along with Caesar. His rejection of an oath of secrecy for the conspiracy allows word of it to get out, as evidenced by Artemidorus's detailed paper and Popilius's comment at 3.1.13. Anyone of normal intelligence would know the advantage of having the last word in public oratory, yet Brutus allows Antony not only to speak at Caesar's funeral but even to do so without supervision, after Brutus has left the scene.

His military misjudgments are equally egregious. Before the final battle at Philippi Cassius counsels Brutus to keep their armies on the high ground. Brutus peremptorily overrules his brother-in-law in often-quoted words of misguided eloquence:

> Our legions are brimful, our cause is ripe:
> The enemy increaseth every day;
> We, at the height, are ready to decline.
> There is a tide in the affairs of men,
> Which taken at the flood, leads on to fortune;
> Omitted, all the voyage of their life
> Is bound in shallows and in miseries. (4.3.215–221)

A final example of Brutus's military ineptitude is when he commands his legions to attack Octavius's forces prematurely, thereby giving Antony a tactical advantage. (According to Plutarch, Brutus had the advantage of Octavius in an engagement.)

There is a noticeable deterioration of Brutus's character in the final movements of the play. His refusal to acknowledge Portia's death to Messala has yet to be convincingly addressed. In the elegiac first scene of the last act his answer to Cassius's question of what he intends to do if they should lose the coming battle is a prevarication:

> Even by the rule of that philosophy
> By which I did blame Cato for the death
> Which he did give himself—I know not how,
> But I do find it cowardly and vile,
> For fear of what might fall, so to prevent
> The time of life—arming myself with patience
> To stay the providence of some high powers
> That govern us below. (5.1.100–107)

Several scenes after he speaks these words, in defiance of his philosophy of Stoicism, Brutus commits suicide—but not before ignominiously asking each of his companions in turn to assist him in doing so and being turned down by everyone except the just-awakened servant, Strato. Mark Antony's eulogistic judgment that Brutus "was the noblest Roman of them all" (5.5.68) is not a misstatement. It simply attests to Shakespeare's unrivaled ability to create characters of opaque complexity.

## Cassius

Although Plutarch does not have a great deal to say about Cassius, Shakespeare makes him one of the key players in *Julius Caesar*. Like Tybalt in *Romeo and Juliet*, Cassius is a catalytic character: that is, a person without whom the action of the play could not proceed. Shakespeare ignores the reasons why Cassius despises Julius Caesar as recorded in Plutarch and presents him as a figure of envy and malicious manipulation. He plays upon Brutus as Rosencrantz and Guildenstern try to play upon Hamlet, but Cassius is far more perceptive and intelligent than they. In fact, Cassius is a master psychologist whose counsels regarding the conspiracy and its aftermath are invariably on the mark, and they are always rejected by Brutus. Cassius's acquiescence to Brutus in every matter of disagreement is inexplicable since Cassius is older and more experienced, especially in military strategy. Cassius is a consummate liar whose false tales of Caesar's cowardice obviously have an influence on Brutus, who says, "Since Cassius first did whet me against Caesar, / I have not slept" (2.1.61–62). Cassius's intelligence is consistent with Shakespeare's practice of creating intellectually superior villains. Next to Mark Antony, Cassius is the closest thing to a Machiavel in the play.

## Mark Antony

Deception is central to all of Shakespeare's plays, and in *Julius Caesar* Mark Antony is an absolute master of it. Beneath Antony's veneer of bluff bonhomie beats the heart of a sociopathic Machiavel. In the final act, when he says to Brutus and Cassius, "You show'd your teeth like apes, and fawn'd like hounds, / And bow'd like bondmen, kissing Caesar's feet; / Whilst damned Casca, like a cur, behind / Strook Caesar on the neck" (5.1.42–45), he gives the conspirators a lesson in deception. In the first half of the play Antony speaks no more than five lines, but after Caesar's assassination he is a dominating figure. His funeral speech is a recognized masterpiece of persuasive and ironic rhetoric, and his soliloquy near the end of act 3 evidences his total hatred of the conspirators in his willingness to cause Rome unimaginable suffering in order to destroy them. His prophecy that "Blood and destruction shall be so in use, / And dreadful objects so familiar, / That mothers shall but smile when they behold / Their infants quartered with the hands of war" (3.1.265–268) eerily evokes photographic images of Nazi-occupied Poland in the early 1940s. In fact, Antony is a kind of prototype of that sort of evil dictator that Brutus describes: "'tis a common proof / That lowliness is young ambition's ladder, / Whereto the climber-upward turns his face; / But when he once attains the upmost round, / He then unto the ladder turns his back, / Looks in the clouds, scorning the base degrees / By which he did ascend" (2.1.21–27). The brutal opening scene of act 4, in which the triumvirate of Antony, Octavius, and Lepidus draw up a list of political enemies to be executed, is strangely prophetic of the summary liquidation of Hitler's enemies after the Night of the Long Knives in June 1934 or Joseph Stalin's purges. In this scene Antony regards Lepidus as merely a thing to be used rather than as a person (committing what the philosopher Martin Buber regards as the greatest of sins) and nonchalantly agrees to the death of his own nephew. In *Antony and Cleopatra*, the great tragedy yet to come, Antony takes on the flesh and blood of an emotional human being, but in this play he is presented mainly as a cunning and ruthless avenger.

## Octavius

Octavius is arguably the most frightening character in *Julius Caesar*. Only eighteen when his great-uncle and adoptive father was assassinated, and although Julius Caesar named him his successor in his will, Octavius had to overcome major obstacles over a protracted period to secure his position as Rome's first emperor under the cognomen of Augustus. Shakespeare passes over the intricate intrigues and shifting alliances after Caesar's death and presents Octavius as a colorless personality who speaks fewer than thirty-five lines in the play. It is just this absence of affect that makes him such a menacing presence. At the Battle of Philippi Octavius takes away from the older and more experienced Antony the prestigious right wing of the assault:

> *Antony*: Octavius, lead your battle softly on,
> Upon the left hand of the even field.
> *Octavius*: Upon the right hand, I. Keep thou the left.
> *Antony*: Why do you cross me in this exigent?
> *Octavius*: I do not cross you, but I will do so. (5.1.16–19)

His bland speech is in striking contrast to Brutus's style, as is his deadly efficiency. Shakespeare gives Octavius the last words of the play in anticipation of his future grandeur.

## Casca

Although Casca is only briefly mentioned by Plutarch, Shakespeare makes him a significant figure. His acerbic personality is immediately established by his account of Caesar's refusal of Antony's offer of a crown. He speaks largely in prose, in keeping with his persona. The bluntness of his character is economically summed up in his reply to Cassius's invitation to dine with him: "Ay, if I be alive, and your mind hold, and your dinner worth the eating" (1.2.291–292). This reply elicits from Brutus some doubt of Casca's intelligence: "What a blunt fellow is this grown to be! / He was quick mettle when he went to school" (1.2.295–296). Cassius, always Brutus's better in his evaluation of others, is quick to reply:

> So is he now in execution
> Of any bold or noble enterprise,
> However he puts on this tardy form.
> This rudeness is a sauce to his good wit,
> Which gives men stomach to digest his words
> With better appetite. (1.2.297–302)

Casca's unrefined exterior belies his political disaffection with Caesar and contributes to the central theme of deception. When Caesar first enters the stage, Casca commands silence of the multitude: "Peace, ho! Caesar speaks" (1.2.1), and shortly afterward he again silences the crowd so that Caesar can hear the Soothsayer's warning. He is the one who escorts Caesar home after the games, but under his unsophisticated demeanor he hides a dangerous sycophancy. He is the first to stab Caesar. Antony mentions Casca twice in the rest of the play: "See what a rent the envious Casca made" (3.2.175) as he displays Caesar's bloody mantle to the Roman plebeians, and in the lines previously cited (5.1.41ff) as he confronts Brutus and Cassius before the final onslaught.

## Portia and Calpurnia

Shakespeare did much to expand and deepen the importance of women in drama. When he came to write *Julius Caesar* in 1599 he had already created some of the most memorable women in all of drama: Juliet, the quintessential romantic heroine; the clever Beatrice of *Much Ado about Nothing*; and Portia, the dominant figure of *The Merchant of Venice*. Although Caesarian Rome was decidedly patriarchal, women of high estate were well regarded and on occasion wielded considerable influence beyond their immediate household. Portia and Calpurnia are at the highest tier of Roman society, articulate and educated, but they are pitifully marginalized by their husbands. In the play neither has real influence on her husband's behavior, although Brutus assures Portia that she is his "true and honorable wife" (2.1.288), and her behavior in 2.4 suggests that Brutus had confided in her about the conspiracy, as he said he would, before he set out for the Senate. Portia's cutting herself in her thigh (a detail from Plutarch) to make "strong proof of [her] constancy" (2.1.299), that is, prove her Stoicism, speaks volumes about her need for Brutus's respect. She so loves her husband that she later takes her life in defiance of her philosophy when she fears for his defeat in battle. His reaction to her death, while exemplifying his Stoic beliefs, reflects little warmth toward her.

Calpurnia speaks fewer than twenty-five lines, but she comes across as just as intelligent and perceptive as Portia. She pleads with her husband, kneeling before him as Portia did before Brutus, and she relies on omens and dreams to dissuade him from going to the Senate. When Caesar discounts the night's portents as pertaining to the world at large as much as to himself, Calpurnia wisely replies: "When beggars die there are no comets seen; / The heavens themselves blaze forth the death of princes" (2.2.30–31). And when Caesar blusters about being more dangerous than danger itself, Calpurnia perceptively says, "Your wisdom is consum'd in confidence" (2.2.49). When she tells Decius Brutus to say to the senators that Caesar is sick and is overruled by her husband, she says nothing else for the duration of the scene or, for that matter, the rest of the play. She simply disappears—a nonentity. It is all too obvious that the only two women in this play, despite their intelligence and even wisdom, are dealing with difficult men at trying moments, and neither is a match for the male ego in this patriarchal age.

## DEVICES AND TECHNIQUES

In his observations on the language of *Julius Caesar*, Samuel Johnson writes the following:

> Of this tragedy many particular passages deserve regard, and the contention and reconcilement of Brutus and Cassius is universally celebrated; but I have never been strongly agitated in perusing it, and think it somewhat cold and unaffecting, compared with some other of Shakespeare's plays; his adherence to the real story, and to Roman manners, seems to have impeded the natural vigour of his genius. (quoted in *Johnson on Shakespeare*, ed. Arthur Sherbo, The Yale Edition of the Works of Samuel Johnson [New Haven: Yale UP, 1968], 8.836)

Rowse remarks that Johnson "preferred Shakespeare's characteristic mixture [of style], the more colored texture, the richer variousness—and perhaps this betrays a latent romanticism in the soul of the great Augustan" (*The Annotated Shakespeare*, 3.134). Bloom agrees that something inhibited Shakespeare's language in this play, whether it was the contemporary tyrannicide controversy or the relationship between Caesar and Brutus. Caroline Spurgeon remarks that *Julius Caesar* is "almost bare in style" (*Shakespeare's Imagery and What It Tells Us* [Boston: Beacon P, 1935], 346), and Frank Kermode speaks of "the deliberately restricted range of the verse" (*The Riverside Shakespeare*, 1150).

As valid as these critical judgments may be, it would be a mistake to conclude that the language of this play is uniformly simple and direct. Some passages require explication, and the critic Arthur Quinn identifies in the play no fewer than ten rhetorical devices. David Bevington believes that *Julius Caesar* "gives us a range of rhetorical styles, from the deliberative (having to do with careful consideration of choices) to the forensic (analogous to pleading at law, maintaining one side or the other of a given question), to the epideictic (or display, as in set orations)" (*The

*Complete Works of Shakespeare*, 1023). Bevington also sees a richer panoply of imagery than Spurgeon.

For a highly charged political drama dealing with such grand public issues as governance, political assassination, freedom and tyranny, war and peace, Shakespeare had to develop a different style of dramatic poetry, one that would be neutral to contemporary political sensibilities. He met this need by developing what may be referred to as a public, rather impersonal style.

Clearly, one purpose of a public style would be to create the illusion of an objective historical document instead of a personally created work of art. The language of *Julius Caesar* has a kind of marmoreal quality that to some degree depersonalizes the characters. Virtually every character in this play speaks ceremoniously, as if by rote. Much of the dialogue, and certainly all of the set speeches, seem self-conscious, even memorized. The language lacks spontaneity. At times it is almost operatic in its effect. In the first scene the minor characters Murellus and Flavius speak as if they are playing a role, as if they have memorized their lines:

> Wherefore rejoice? What conquest brings he home?
> What tributaries follow him [Caesar] to Rome,
> To grace in captive bonds his chariot wheels?
> You blocks, you stones, you worse than senseless things! (1.1.32–35)

The studied parallelism of these lines, a stylistic trait most pronounced in the funeral orations of Brutus and Antony, is evident throughout the play. Consider, for example, the manner of Portia's speech:

> Is Brutus sick? And is it physical
> To walk unbraced and suck up the humors
> Of the dank morning? What, is Brutus sick?
> And will he steal out of his wholesome bed
> To dare the vile contagion of the night? (2.1.261–265)

or, later:

> I grant I am a woman; but withal
> A woman that Lord Brutus took to wife.
> I grant I am a woman; but withal
> A woman well reputed, Cato's daughter. (2.1.292–295)

Two more examples of this way of speaking must suffice. Caesar's language is generally declamatory and filled with parallel constructions, as in his famous observation, "Cowards die many times before their deaths, / The valiant never taste of death but once" (2.2.32–33). A final example of this public, ceremonial style characterized by a pronounced parallelism (among other devices) is the farewell of Brutus and Cassius before the battle at Philippi:

> *Brutus*: For ever, and for ever, farewell, Cassius!
> If we do meet again, why, we shall smile;
> If not, why then this parting was well made.

> *Cassius*: For ever, and for ever, farewell, Brutus!
> If we do meet again, we'll smile indeed;
> If not, 'tis true this parting was well made. (5.1.116–121)

In addition to creating the aura of a historical record this public style is intricately connected to the characters. One would expect the hubristic Caesar to speak as if his words were to be immortalized in marble. Brutus resorts frequently to the use of aphorisms to prevail in argument and to rationalize his role in the conspiracy. "It is the bright day that brings forth the adder, / And that craves wary walking" (2.1.14–15). "Th' abuse of greatness is when it disjoins / Remorse from power" (2.1.18–19). "But 'tis a common proof / That lowliness is young ambition's ladder" (2.1.21–22). These pithy sayings, truisms per se, are taken from Brutus's soliloquy at the beginning of the second act, in which he seeks to justify killing Caesar to prevent his potential abuse of power. Perhaps they provide for Brutus a psychic distance from the actual act of assassination. This is surely the case with Brutus's euphemistic words to his fellow conspirators: "Let's carve him as a dish fit for the gods, / Not hew him as a carcass fit for hounds" (2.1.173–174).

Antony, in contrast, sees the dead Caesar as a "bleeding piece of earth" and the conspirators as "butchers" (3.1.254, 255). Antony appears purposely to focus on the physical horrors of Caesar's wounds to fuel his revenge. Bevington writes that Brutus is "unsuited for the stern exigencies of assassination and civil war" (*The Complete Works of Shakespeare*, 1022). Certainly the same cannot be said of Antony.

Just as the style of *Julius Caesar* must be evaluated differently from the styles of Shakespeare's greatest tragedies, so must the imagery. Spurgeon asserts the lack of a "dominating image" in the play, although she mentions briefly "a certain persistence in the comparison of the characters to animals" and gives several examples. She is correct that the animal imagery in *Julius Caesar* "is not nearly so marked as in either *King Lear* or *Othello*" (*Shakespeare's Imagery and What It Tells Us*, 347), but there are two salient image clusters in the play: one of animals, the other of blood. Antony regards Lepidus as an "ass" or "horse" (4.1.21, 29) fit only to do burdensome work at the bidding of its master, and he refers to the duplicitous conspirators as "apes" and "hounds." Casca is "a cur" (5.1.41, 43). Animals figure prominently in the different omens: for example, the whelping lioness, the lion that glared at Casca, the owl shrieking even "at noonday upon the marketplace" (1.3.27), the beast without a heart, the two eagles that accompanied the lead standard of Cassius's legion to Philippi— where they flew away to be replaced by "ravens, crows, and kites," which in the words of Cassius "downward look on us / As we were sickly prey" (5.2.88–89). Despite the frequent references to animals throughout *Julius Caesar*, they are not conjoined into a motif as in *King Lear*, where they represent the bestial savagery of human experience, or in *Othello*, where they represent gross sexuality.

The image of blood is prominent throughout, from Brutus's first mention of it among the conspirators, to Antony's near obsession with it after the assassination, to the final act when Titinius says of the dead Cassius, "So in his red blood Cassius' day is set!" (5.3.62). Given the numerous references to blood and its variant forms it is remarkable that C. T. Onions in his *A Shakespeare Glossary* (rev. Robert D. Eagleson [Oxford: Clarendon P, 1986]) refers to its use in *Julius Caesar* only once. It may be that the scattered nature of the image in this play makes it less memorable than it is in *Macbeth*, where it is the predominant motif, representing regicide. No reference to blood in this play captures the power of Lady Macbeth's "Yet who would have thought the old man to have had so much blood in him?" (5.1.39–40).

Although the style and imagery of *Julius Caesar* lack the richness and complexity of the language of Shakespeare's greatest plays, they are by no means as straightforward and constricted as some critics have made them out to be. No other playwright of the Elizabethan and Jacobean periods could have written *Julius Caesar*, not even Ben Jonson, Shakespeare's superior in classical learning but whose *Sejanus* and *Catiline* pale in comparison with this play.

## THEMES AND MEANINGS

The major theme of *Julius Caesar* is governance. The historical significance of whether Rome would be better off as a republic or a monarchy cannot be inferred from the play itself because Shakespeare does not—and no doubt could not in the confines of a five-act play—provide enough historical background to enable his audience to draw meaningful conclusions. A playgoer or reader requires some knowledge of Roman history to grasp adequately the motivations of the conspirators to assassinate Julius Caesar. Such knowledge is especially crucial to understanding the motives of Brutus. Brutus no doubt idealized the republic founded by his possible ancestor Lucius Junius Brutus over four centuries in the past, although that republic was in effect a patrician state in which the plebeians led truly miserable lives. For Brutus to have been the true idealist that various critics make him out to be, he would have had to be ignorant of the personal cruelty of his iconic ancestor and the nature of the republic that he established. In fact, the conspirators generally must have had short memories because the Roman republic in the period immediately preceding the time of the play, under the control of Sulla and Pompey, experienced repeated turmoil. Sulla began a reign of terror, putting his enemies to death without a trial; and Pompey's tenure was overtaken by famine and ochlocracy (mob rule).

While the question of governance is the salient theme in this play, there are many other major ideas that also appear in a number of Shakespeare's other plays, such as the unpredictability of history and the vagaries of fortune, the transience of power and the danger of hubris, the irrationality of blind idealism, the omnipotence of change, and the ubiquity of deception. *Julius Caesar* is a tragedy of good intentions in that Brutus wanted to avoid the monarchical rule of Caesar and to establish an ideal republic. Instead, his misguided and shortsighted intentions led to the reign of Caesar Augustus, a long period that proved no more desirable than Caesar's rule would probably have been and perhaps worse.

Brutus, the intellectual, does not understand the nature of history and human inability to control future events. This is a recurrent idea in many of Shakespeare's plays, particularly the histories and tragedies. For example, in *Romeo and Juliet* the well-meaning Friar Lawrence, thinking he can manage human experience as if it were under rigorous laboratory control, unwittingly brings about the deaths of the two young lovers. The villainous Iago in *Othello* makes the same mistake. So do Macbeth and Richard III. This idea that one can manage the future is in itself a form of hubris, and it is obviously not limited to those with bad intentions. Shakespeare might be saying that it is a characteristic of human nature. After all, people like to believe they are always in control. But they are not always in control in real life—or in Shakespeare's plays.

Inasmuch as change is the only known constant, the vagaries of fortune and the transience of power are inevitable conditions of human experience. They lie at the heart of Greek tragedy, and Shakespeare invariably incorporates them in his tragedies and histories. In all but name in 44 B.C. Julius Caesar held absolute power in Rome. Political absolutism was the driving force of his life, and the fact that he is killed on the very day that he would be given the imprimatur of that power by being proclaimed king is the height of irony. The irony is intensified by the knowledge that he had narrowly escaped death on more than one occasion in his numerous military campaigns. Had Caesar not been so self-assured, he might well have escaped assassination. While waiting for Caesar to pass on his way to the Capitol, Artemidorus says of his paper incriminating the conspirators: "If thou read this, O Caesar, thou mayest live; / If not, the Fates with traitors do contrive" (2.3.15–16). Artemidorus does not understand that character determines fate.

The power, even omnipotence, of change can be more explicitly observed in David Bevington's account of the successive rise and fall of the paramount men of Rome, starting with Pompey before the play, proceeding to Caesar at the height of his power "and his imminent decline to death," moving on to the prominence of Brutus and Cassius, who are replaced by Antony and Octavius, and finally to the triumph of Octavius over Antony (*Complete Works of Shakespeare*, 1024). Each of these men (with the exception of Octavius) is brought low by a fatal defect of character, a phenomenon that Shakespeare richly explores in *Antony and Cleopatra*.

Deception, whether it be self-deception or deception by others, is essential to Shakespearean tragedy. Caesar is easily deceived because of his vanity. As Decius Brutus says of Caesar to his fellow conspirators, "when I tell him he hates flatterers / He says he does, being then most flattered" (2.1.207–208). Every character in the play, with the exception of the Soothsayer and Artemidorus, is deceived by the conspirators, even Antony, although Calpurnia instinctively fears a coming danger. Shakespeare does not make it clear how she regards the conspirators when they come to take her husband to the Capitol. Cicero and Popilius might suspect something untoward, but Shakespeare does not pursue their possible suspicions. The scenes in the play that most clearly demonstrate deception are 2.2 (when the conspirators come to Caesar's house to escort him to his death) and 3.1 (when Antony appears before the conspirators in apparent friendship).

The prevailing opinion regarding Brutus is that he is a high-minded idealist. In reality, he is a masterful deceiver. In a short soliloquy before the conspirators enter his house Brutus speaks the following:

> O Conspiracy,
> Sham'st thou to show thy dang'rous brow by night,
> When evils are most free? O then, by day
> Where wilt thou find a cavern dark enough
> To mask thy monstrous visage? Seek none, Conspiracy!
> Hide it in smiles and affability. (2.1.77–82)

As the conspirators leave his house on the night before the assassination, Brutus says to them: "Good gentlemen, look fresh and merrily; / Let not our looks put on our purposes" (2.1.224–225). These lines sound more like Lady Macbeth than a noble idealist. It may be that the commentators who see Brutus in an exclusively favorable light are basing their views on Plutarch instead of Shakespeare. If one takes a medieval view of Brutus, his subsequent deception by Antony is well deserved.

Brutus is also a master of self-deception. He can call the conspirators "sacrificers, but not butchers" (2.1.166). He says that they oppose "the spirit of Caesar, / And in the spirit of men there is no blood" (2.1.167–168). He finds no evidence that Caesar will govern badly, yet he persuades himself that Caesar is like "a serpent's egg" that must be crushed (2.1.32). He is convinced that Antony is harmless. In sum, he never doubts himself, and thus he resembles Shakespeare's other self-assured tragic heroes, such as Othello, Macbeth, and Coriolanus.

This play is rich in ideas; it is, however, open-ended, and the major theme of governance is not clearly resolved. The dispute over the justness of the conspirators' cause continued through the Renaissance, and even today there is no consensus regarding it. The sub-themes are perennial issues of discussion and debate.

## CRITICAL CONTROVERSIES

In the eighteenth century there was more critical carping about *Julius Caesar* than there was critical controversy. Neoclassical critics, with the singular exception of Samuel Johnson, faulted the play for its lack of unity, its "vulgar" use of the mob, and its historical inaccuracy. Romantic critics, such as William Hazlitt and Samuel Taylor Coleridge, were less troubled by the play's supposed lack of dramatic unity but still held that it was a series of great scenes rather than a dramatic whole, and there was some question as to the identity of the protagonist: Caesar or Brutus?

Today *Julius Caesar* does not prompt the same level of critical controversy inspired by some of the great tragedies. There is general consensus that the play is unified and that Caesar is the protagonist. The play does not present the textual problems of *King Lear* and *Macbeth* or the question of character interpretation of *Hamlet*. All of the characters in this play, except Brutus, are relatively easy to understand, and even Brutus is far more accessible than Hamlet as a character. The critical questions that this play raises are essentially unanswerable: Why did Shakespeare not use more foregrounding? Did he have a political motive in writing the play? Problems of creative intent are generally intractable, especially in the impersonal genre of drama. And Shakespeare is the most inscrutable of writers, as Matthew Arnold observes in his sonnet "Shakespeare": "Others abide our question. Thou art free. / We ask and ask—Thou smilest and art still, / Out-topping knowledge."

## PRODUCTION HISTORY

There is scant but reliable evidence that *Julius Caesar* was popular with playgoers from its first performances in 1599 to well into the seventeenth century. A Swiss traveler to London saw one of the first performances at the Globe and in his diary described it as "very well acted." Leonard Digges wrote in his poem for the First Folio that the play had no equal among contemporary dramas. In an amplified version of the poem for the 1640 edition of Shakespeare's poems ("Upon Master

William Shakespeare, the Deceased Author, and his Poems" [London: Tho. Cotes for John Benson]) he wrote:

> So I have seen, when Caesar would appear,
> And on the stage at half-sword parley were
> Brutus and Cassius, oh how the audience
> Were ravished, with what wonder they went thence;
> When some new day they would not brook a line
> Of tedious, though well-laboured, *Catiline*.

Both Digges and Jonson were dead when these lines appeared, but they tell us that Jonson's rival, despite what Jonson called Shakespeare's "small Latin and less Greek," could write a Roman play with more audience appeal than his own and that the play had remained popular through the years. In fact, the play was consistently performed, though until the mid-eighteenth century not in the form that Shakespeare wrote it.

John Ripley acknowledges that the stage history of *Julius Caesar* is one of "unrealized potential" (275). Little is known about the number and quality of performances of this play in the seventeen century other than that the actor Thomas Betterton played the role of Brutus beginning in 1684 and continuing for almost a quarter of a century. His interpretation of Brutus as the hero prevailed through the next two centuries, an interpretation reinforced by the sense of patriotism in England and America at various times during the eighteenth century.

In the early years of the eighteenth century a version allegedly adapted by John Dryden and William Davenant (published in 1719) was mainly used. This version alters Shakespeare's text considerably, cutting lines and characters, eliminating entire scenes to speed up the action, and bowdlerizing the language (for example, Portia cuts herself in the arm instead of the thigh) to conform to the tastes of the age. The reductive alterations of Shakespeare's text were made for several reasons: to save money, to speed and unify the action (though paradoxically the alterations often turned the play into a series of significant scenes instead of an organic whole), to "improve" on the original text, and to highlight the role of Brutus, a role always taken by the dominant actor of the time. Moreover, during the eighteenth and nineteenth centuries there were not enough first-rate actors at any given moment to perform adequately all four of the major male speaking roles.

Twentieth-century stage productions of *Julius Caesar* were frequently characterized by directorial experimentation, which was sometimes so extreme as to render the original text virtually unrecognizable. Two such examples are the productions of Orson Welles (1937) and Jonathan Miller (1972). Orson Welles's *Julius Caesar* was the first production of the recently established Mercury Theatre, created by John Houseman and Welles. Subtitled "Death of a Dictator," the play, in the words of John Houseman, was "a political melodrama with clear contemporary parallels" (quoted in Ripley, p. 222). Welles used Shakespeare's play as a vehicle to dramatize the mindless brutality of fascism, which was rearing its ugly head in Germany and Italy. To accomplish this goal he wrote an abridgement of Shakespeare, reducing the original number of fifty-eight players to eighteen speaking parts, eliminating acts and scenes, virtually excising the last two acts, and reducing the acting time to about an hour and a half. The focus was on Caesar and Brutus; all else was expendable. The actor who played Caesar, Joseph Holland, bore an uncanny resemblance to Mussolini, immediately recognizable to an audience inundated by newsreel footage of Il Duce. "The production begins with Caesar, dressed in a green uniform, scowling behind the masklike face of a modern dictator. His first gesture is a fascist salute that the others returned" (Richard France, *The Theatre of Orson Welles* [Lewisburg: Bucknell UP, 1977], 109). He is at once recognizable as a symbol of an absolute dictator. The petty conspirators "were portrayed as modern day racketeers with turned-up collars, black hats pulled low around their ears, and that gun-in-the-pocket look about them" (France, p. 109). This is the image of Hitler's Gestapo thugs.

The action takes place on a three-tiered bare stage with no curtain, and it is accented by shafts of light from above or below, the latter coming from openings in the stage floor, sometimes creating the effect of a Nazi rally at Nuremburg. The background throughout is a stark red-brick wall. An ominous tension is created by the dramatic use of utter darkness from which come sounds of voices and the stamping of feet. Marc Blitzstein's musical score, identified as "The Fascist March," also adds greatly to the atmosphere. The scene showing the murder of Cinna the Poet (3.3), eliminated in eighteenth- and nineteenth-century productions, is perhaps the most compelling one in the play. In Welles's production the scene is more terrifying than in Shakespeare, as the hapless Cinna is literally surrounded and then engulfed by the mindless mob. His name could be Bernstein in Hitler's Germany. Another highlight of this fast-paced production is Antony's funeral oration, counterpointed by the growing impatience and potential violence of the mob. Brutus is the naive intellectual idealist unfit to combat the brutality of fascism, and the play ends with shafts of light shooting up from the floor to reveal Antony standing over Brutus's dead body.

Although a few critics failed to grasp Welles's allusions to the political turmoil in Europe, all critics apparently failed to understand Jonathan Miller's treatment of Shakespeare's *Julius Caesar*. Miller produced his interpretation for the Oxford and Cambridge Shakespeare Company and in 1972 presented it at various universities. Later, it enjoyed a brief run at London's New Theatre, where it created the same confusion among audiences as it had on the university tour. Miller's *Julius Caesar* was staged "as an expressionistic fantasy with the terrifying illogic and persuasive reality of dreams" (Ripley, p. 268). But who was the dreamer? And what was he dreaming about? The critic Jeremy Kingston hazarded that the play was "a nightmare fantasy on parricide. Brutus and Cassius destroy the tyrant father-figure and then become inhibited with guilt, bickering blunderers who lack the wish to survive. Antony and Octavius identify themselves with the father and go on to triumph" (quoted in Ripley, p. 268). Most other critics simply refused to speculate about the play's "meaning," merely accepting it as Miller's private interpretation.

The backdrop was suggestive of "a blood-red medieval Italian fortress with a soaring panel behind" (Ripley, p. 269). Movement throughout was dreamlike and sometimes frozen. Costuming was bizarre, with Caesar appearing "as a southern gambler, complete with white frock coat and top hat, cigar and cane" (Ripley, p. 269). The assassination of Caesar was accomplished by a karate blow instead of knives, and Antony's funeral speech "was spouted at a masked mob who remained totally silent. The final battles were wrestling-matches in hypnotic slow-motion as

Marlon Brando as Marc Antony in Joseph L. Mankiewicz's 1953 film *Julius Caesar*. Courtesy of Photofest.

if underwater" (Ripley, p. 269). The brilliant John Mortimer could only conclude that this production began "at some distant and private point and coincides only occasionally with the author's intentions" (Ripley, p. 270), which is surely an understatement. While these two productions are examples of extreme directorial interpretation of *Julius Caesar*, they represent the general trend to "reinterpret" the play to conform to a particular vision.

As heretical as it may seem to some, Shakespeare's play may be too grand in this age of visual pyrotechnics for the stage or even for television. Modern audiences, conditioned by visual realism, do not possess the capacity of past generations to suspend their disbelief for the moment, to have what the nineteenth-century critic Samuel Taylor Coleridge defined as "poetic faith." The big screen cinema can capture the battle scenes of *Julius Caesar* in a way that is more satisfying to the contemporary audience than can the stage. Although the cinema clearly lacks the intimacy and excitement of stage performance, modern cinematography can capture close-ups of emotional feelings and other subtle nuances of expression better than the stage. The John Houseman film production of *Julius Caesar*, directed by Joseph Mankiewicz in 1953, used an all-star cast, including Marlon Brando as Marc Antony, to create a powerful reproduction of Shakespeare's text and of ancient Rome. After half a century it remains the finest film treatment of the play. Perhaps the time is ripe for another director to use more recent technologies to produce a new *Julius Caesar*.

## EXPLICATION OF KEY PASSAGES

**2.1.10–34. "It must be by his death; . . . And kill him in the shell."** In *Julius Caesar* the most problematic passage is Brutus's soliloquy at the beginning of the second act in which he seeks to justify Caesar's death. For a good while Brutus has thought of eliminating Caesar as a threat to the Republic, and now, apparently after an inner struggle, he has decided that Caesar must die.

This passage is illogical in the extreme, a gross rationalization that makes no sense on its face. Samuel Taylor Coleridge was troubled by it, as any clear-thinking person with a sense of fairness would be (in Terence Hawkes, *Coleridge's Writings on Shakespeare* [New York: Capricorn Books, 1959], 244–245). In view of the fact that Brutus was the first praetor (chief judge) of Rome and respected for his sagacity, this soliloquy is nothing short of astonishing. Brutus admits that he bears Caesar no personal animus and that he has never known Caesar to allow his passions to overrule his reason. Brutus does not judge Caesar for his past and present actions but rather by what he might do as king. The passage contains one use of the word *might* and three uses of *may*.

Since Brutus must certainly perceive the injustice of putting a person to death on the basis of possible future actions, he resorts to aphorisms and metaphors, comparing Caesar as king to a poisonous snake. Inasmuch as Caesar is already the most powerful person in Rome, not some young upwardly mobile politician, lines twenty-one through twenty-eight are inappropriate and irrelevant. They are all the more so when one recalls that Caesar forgave Brutus for fighting on Pompey's side and eventually made him first praetor, thereby incurring the enmity of the older and more experienced Cassius.

**2.1.61–69. "Since Cassius first did whet me against Caesar, . . . The nature of an insurrection."** Various editors have interpreted these lines in rather different ways. For example, Samuel Johnson writes that "Shakespeare is describing what passes in a single bosom, the 'insurrection' which a conspirator feels agitating the 'little kingdom' of his own mind . . . when the desire of action and the care of safety, keep the mind in continual fluctuation and disturbance" (Sherbo, p. 828). Hardin Craig writes that "The *Genius* is used to signify the soul; the *mortal instruments* are the spirits, which are the agents of reason and the will" (*The Complete Works of Shakespeare* [Glenview, IL: Scott, Foresman, 1961], 778). Bevington is somewhat more specific: "The immortal part of humanity, the rational soul, deliberates or debates violently with the lower or moral faculties, the physical and passionate side" (*The Complete Works of Shakespeare*, 1033). Rowse merely identifies the mortal instruments as "The powers of the body" (*The Annotated Shakespeare*, 3:152), following Kermode's explanation that "the reasonable soul takes counsel with its lower powers (called 'mortal' because they animate the body)" (*The Riverside Shakespeare*, 1158n). Despite the different editorial readings the general meaning is clear: the spirit is in conflict with the emotions or the body itself as it is affected by them. What is more important, however, about these lines is the way Brutus moves from a personal statement of inner conflict in the first line to a generalized comparison of his inner conflict with the civil war of "a little kingdom" (2.1.68). In a moment of apparent personal anguish this immediate resort to such an intellectual concept as the microcosm-macrocosm connection must be his way of objectifying his part in the conspiracy, trying psychically to distance himself from it. Again, one is forced to take note of Shakespeare's depiction of Brutus as a man substantially different from Plutarch's, Antony's, and numerous commentators' images of him.

**3.2.73–252. "Friends, Romans, countrymen, . . . when comes such another?"** Antony's funeral oration takes up approximately 80 percent of scene 2 of act 3, and in this speech Antony proves himself to be a virtuoso orator and actor. Instead of appealing to reasoned argument as Brutus had done in his speech (in prose) to the Roman populace (3.2.13–47), Antony's blank verse resorts to emotion and theatrics to stir the crowd to his side, transforming his listeners into a murderous rabble. His words are heavy with irony, misinformation, and suspense. He is also a master of rhetorical devices. He asks his audience to "lend me your ears" (3.2.73), a classic example of metonymy. He reverses the expected eulogy by saying that he comes "to bury Caesar, not to praise him" (3.2.74), thereby putting the audience that has just supported Brutus somewhat off guard. The first part of his address appears to the uninitiated to support Brutus and his cohorts: "For Brutus is an honorable man, / So are they all, all honorable men" (3.2.82–83). This reference to "honorable men" becomes a powerful ironic refrain.

Antony also appeals to the memory of his listeners. He reminds them that "on the Lupercal / I thrice presented him a kingly crown, / Which he did thrice refuse" (3.2.95–97). Brutus says that Caesar was ambitious, and Brutus "is an honorable man." Yet Antony suggests that "Ambition should be made of sterner stuff" (3.2.92) than Caesar was.

Antony mentions Caesar's will, which he implies bequeaths great gifts to the populace but that he says he will not read. In his treatment of the will, Antony shows himself a master manipulator. He does not divulge its contents until the conclusion of his speech. The mention of the will is the turning point in Antony's control of the crowd. The crowd wants to hear it, but Antony puts them off with the masterstroke of displaying Caesar's bloody mantle, declaring which tear was made by which assassin. "See what a rent the envious Casca made; / Through this the well-beloved Brutus stabb'd" (3.2.175–176). Of course, this is total fabrication, but it is dramatically effective, especially since Caesar's corpse is on display. With the partial reading of the will, Antony stirs the crowd to attack Caesar's murderers.

**4.3.213–224. "Under your pardon . . . Or lose our ventures."** These words clearly illuminate three important facets of Brutus's character: his patrician certainty in the soundness of his views, his persuasive rhetoric, and his naive impracticality. These must be considered in their dramatic context for their full import to be recognized. Brutus and his brother-in-law, Cassius, enjoy a strategically advantageous position in the coming battle with Antony and Octavius. Cassius wants their armies to hold the high ground they occupy and wait for the enemy to attack them. He is arguing his case when Brutus interrupts him. Brutus argues, wrongly, that the enemy is gaining recruits daily, while the conspirators' armies are as large as they will get and "are ready to decline" (4.3.217). But why should the legions of Brutus and Cassius be diminished while waiting for Antony and Octavius to arrive? There is no reason for them to decline.

Brutus's famous remark about the "tide in the affairs of men" (4.3.218) uses a complex nautical metaphor regarding a vessel having to leave the shore at high tide to proceed to the open sea or else remain grounded forever. Again, though, the reasoning is spurious. In fact, the high tide will come back, although Shakespeare's contemporaries might have grown impatient crossing the Thames if they missed the proper tide. In current parlance Brutus's point could be expressed as "opportunity knocks only once. If you do not take advantage of it, it will never come again." Brutus's words are eloquent, but they are shallow and false. Their spurious reasoning is highlighted by Octavius's comment at the beginning of act 5: "Now, Antony, our hopes are answered. / You said the enemy would not come down, / But keep the hills and upper regions" (5.1.1–3).

**5.5.68–75. "This was the noblest . . . 'This was a man!' "** Antony's eulogy of Brutus at the end of the play is well known, but it may not seem connected to the funeral oration for Caesar. Yet in both speeches Antony speaks authoritatively of matters about which he must have incomplete knowledge. In the funeral speech he could not possibly have known which rent was made by which conspirator, and in his eulogy for Brutus he could not know that all the conspirators except Brutus acted out of envy.

Nevertheless, the eulogy for Brutus shows Antony as magnanimous. His mention of Brutus as "gentle" (5.5.73) is historically accurate. His reference to the "elements" (ibid.) that comprised Brutus refers to the idea that the body consists of the four humors of blood, choler or yellow bile, phlegm, and black bile (melancholy) and to the four elements (earth, air, fire, water) that make up everything in nature. Antony is saying that Brutus was an ideal combination of these elements and hence that nature could proclaim him an ideal or perfect man.

## Annotated Bibliography

Bloom, Harold. *Shakespeare: The Invention of the Human*. New York: Riverhead Books, 1998. This study of all of Shakespeare's plays by an illustrious humanist-scholar is clearly and unpretentiously written while showing Bloom's catholic grasp of literature. The chapter on *Julius Caesar* consists of cogent insights into the characters of Caesar and Brutus. If his comment that Caesar's "estimate of Cassius shows him to be the best analyst of another human being in all of Shakespeare" (106) is somewhat excessive, his view that Freud's *Totem and Taboo* could be considered a rewriting of *Julius Caesar* is tantalizing. Bloom sees the play as at least inhibited if not cold because Shakespeare for some unknown reason chose not to explore the tradition that Brutus was Caesar's natural son. This chapter also contains perceptive analyses of two soliloquies by Brutus: "It must be by his death" and "Between the acting of a dreadful thing."

Charney, Maurice. *Shakespeare's Roman Plays: The Function of Imagery in the Drama*. Cambridge, MA: Harvard UP, 1961. In a close examination of the text Charney explores the images of blood, fire, the storm and portents, and dramatic character. His modus operandi is to give a running account of the play in terms of each image under consideration. Each image has a double-edged meaning: for example, fire as inflammatory or purifying, blood as Caesarian tyranny or healthy new life of the body politic. His discussion of the character "Julius Caesar the individual" and "Julius Caesar the public figure" is especially enlightening. The duality of these images is never resolved.

Goddard, Harold C. *The Meaning of Shakespeare*. 2 vols. Chicago: U of Chicago P, 1951. Goddard sees *Julius Caesar* as the tragedy of Brutus, who "undertakes a role for which nature never intended him." He is Everyman "in the sense that every man is Brutus at some hour of his life." He has his good (Lucius and Portia) and his evil (Caesar and Cassius) angels, and the evil ones take possession of his soul. Although Goddard does not mention Edgar Allan Poe on perversity as a wellspring of human action, he well could have because his Brutus is a study in perversity. Cassius is seen as no more than a seducer, albeit a wily one. One of the strengths of this work is Goddard's ability to place *Julius Caesar* in the context of other plays of Shakespeare. He sees the major point of the play as an indictment of violent opposition to imperialism, a refinement of the theme of *Henry V*. "The path of violence and the path of the violent opposition to violence can easily be the same."

Knight, G. Wilson. *The Imperial Theme*. London: Methuen, 1963. Chapter three, "The Eroticism of *Julius Caesar*," is valuable (in spite of its misleading title) for Knight's original insight into the character of Brutus as a dissociative character who sacrifices everything—love, even his life—for honor and ends up wreaking havoc on everyone around him. According to Knight, Brutus "fails in life and dies sadly, pathetically searching at the end for some one 'honourable' enough to slay him." Knight sees Cassius, the "lover of the republican ideal," and Antony, the "lover of Caesar," as "positive forces," while "Brutus is negative, because his fine intellect sees equally with the vision of the other two" (95). A refreshingly different interpretation of Brutus and Cassius suitable for the advanced student.

——. *The Wheel of Fire*. London: Methuen, 1965. Chapter six of this study, "Brutus and Macbeth," is an acute psychological analysis of these two characters and the effects that their actions have on the outer world. Against their better natures both commit murders. Both are characters of disintegration and disorder, self-disgust and perversity. Though Knight focuses on the similarities of Brutus and Macbeth, he distinguishes between the portents in the two plays: "The storm-imagery in *Macbeth* . . . is less fiery and bright and scintillating: more black, smoky, foul" (130). The disturbances in the natural world reflect the inner turmoil and agony of Brutus and Macbeth but have no effect on Cassius or Lady Macbeth, both of whom are being true to their own natures in their descent into evil. One of Knight's most perceptive insights is that Brutus and Macbeth fail in their schemes "not so much because of outward events and forces, but through the working of that part of their natures which originally forbade murder" (128).

Ripley, John. *Julius Caesar on Stage in England and America, 1599–1973*. Cambridge: Cambridge UP, 1980. Essential to all students of Shakespearean production, this book includes a chronological handlist of performances of *Julius Caesar* from 1599 to 1973, documentary notes, bibliography, and index. The text consists of twelve chapters covering every imaginable aspect of performance indicated in the title.

Traversi, Derek A. *An Approach to Shakespeare*. Garden City, NY: Doubleday, 1969. Recommended for the advanced student, Traversi's chapter on *Julius Caesar* takes the reader through the main movements of the play by way of in-depth analyses of Caesar, Brutus, Cassius, Antony, and especially the Quarrel scene of Brutus and Cassius (4.3). Caesar is seen as a dual figure of public image and personal identity; Brutus as one who never truly knows himself and "in seeking the clarification of his own motives, gives the action its dynamic quality" (495). He "is seen as one more example of that typical Shakespearean creation, the man who, willing an end, is ready to deceive himself concerning the means necessary to gain it" (500). Cassius is a shrewd manipulator of Brutus, motivated largely by envy of Caesar; and Antony is a cold power player who is later defeated by an even colder Octavius. The highlight of Traversi's chapter is the subtle analysis of the Quarrel scene (4.2) in which Brutus is seen as something of a sadist. Traversi's characteristic style is always challenging and sometimes almost Jamesian in complexity.

# *Hamlet*

## Jay L. Halio

### PLOT SUMMARY

**1.1.** *Hamlet* opens at night. Francisco, a guard, is on duty on the ramparts of Elsinore Castle. Hamlet's friend, Horatio, and two other guards, Marcellus and Bernardo, approach and relieve Francisco. The guards are worried because they have twice seen a Ghost dressed in armor; they have brought the skeptic Horatio to see whether the Ghost will speak to him. As they are talking, the Ghost of Hamlet's father (Old Hamlet) appears. Horatio is now convinced that, though the Ghost will not answer his challenges, it is real, and he determines to relay the news to young Hamlet. Meanwhile, he and the others discuss the impending trouble of young Fortinbras's threatened invasion from Norway, which has occasioned the round-the-clock armed watch at Elsinore.

**1.2.** The next scene begins as the new King of Denmark, Claudius, Old Hamlet's brother, addresses the court. He explains (more for the benefit of the theater audience than the stage audience) why he has married Gertrude, his "sister" (that is, sister-in-law) and Old Hamlet's widow, so soon after his brother's funeral. He then speaks of Fortinbras's threat and sends Voltimand and Cornelius as ambassadors to Norway to deal with it. He turns next to Laertes, who desires to return to Paris. With the consent of Polonius, Laertes' father, Claudius grants the request. Finally, he turns to Hamlet, dressed all in black, and questions why he is still mourning his father. Gertrude joins in the appeal to her son to discard his "nighted color" (1.2.68) and be friendlier to Claudius.

Hamlet is sullen and rejects their appeals. When Claudius asks him not to return to his studies in Wittenberg, Gertrude seconds the request, and Hamlet agrees to her, not Claudius's, appeal. The court withdraws, and Hamlet is left alone. In a soliloquy, Hamlet explains why he would like to commit suicide: his mother's hasty remarriage troubles him, he despises Claudius, and their marriage is incestuous. (To Shakespeare's audience it would be, for to marry a sister-in-law was tantamount to marrying one's sister, since Elizabethans took the marriage ceremony literally: husband and wife are become one flesh. This is what Hamlet alludes to later on in act 4 when he mocks Claudius, calling him his "mother," 4.3.49.)

Just as Hamlet says he is unable to do anything about the situation, which he feels will come to no good, Horatio and Marcellus enter and tell him about seeing the Ghost. They agree to meet together that night on the ramparts to see whether it will come again. Hamlet ends the scene with another brief soliloquy, in which he says he suspects some "foul play" (1.2.255) is involved in the death of his father, since his Ghost has appeared.

**1.3.** Laertes warns his sister, Ophelia, not to have anything more to do with young Hamlet, who has apparently been wooing her. Polonius enters, bids his son farewell with some sententious remarks, and turns to Ophelia. With an even sterner warning, he forbids her to have anything more to do with Hamlet, as the prince is so above her station that marrying her is out of the question. Hamlet must only be trifling with her, Polonius believes, and Ophelia reluctantly agrees to follow her father's orders.

**1.4–5.** The next two scenes—really linked to each other—take place that night. Hamlet, Horatio, and Marcellus are on the ramparts, while Claudius and the court carouse below them in the castle. As Hamlet delivers a discourse on drinking, the Ghost suddenly appears. Against his friends' entreaties, Hamlet follows the Ghost to another part of the ramparts, where the Ghost speaks to him alone. The Ghost declares that he is the spirit of Hamlet's father, who was murdered by Claudius. He demands revenge, telling Hamlet to break up the royal bed of Denmark but to be careful not to taint his mind or proceed against his mother, who is to be left to heaven and her own guilty conscience (1.5.82–88). The Ghost, however, does not tell Hamlet how to carry out his commands. He departs, leaving Hamlet amazed.

Hamlet does not reveal anything to the others when they find him, except that he believes it is an "honest" Ghost (that is, a real one and not a devil, 1.5.138). He also says that he may put on an "antic disposition" (that is, pretend to be mad, 1.5.172) from time to time and makes them swear that they will not reveal that this is only a ploy. As he gets them to swear to his secrets, the Ghost moves under the stage and repeats, "Swear" (1.5.149, 155, 161).

**2.1.** Polonius sends his servant, Reynaldo, to Paris to check on Laertes. Ophelia enters distressed and tells her father of Hamlet's visitation to her chambers (2.1.74–97). Polonius is convinced that Hamlet, who has been acting strangely, is mad for love of Ophelia, who has rejected him on her father's orders. Polonius determines to go to the King and Queen and tell them his theory.

**2.2.** Before Polonius gets there, Claudius and Gertrude talk with Rosencrantz and Guildenstern, old school friends of Hamlet, whom they have summoned from Wittenberg. The King and Queen want them to help find the cause of Hamlet's melancholic disposition. When Rosencrantz and Guildenstern exit, Polonius enters and says that the ambassadors to Norway have returned with good news and that he has found the cause of Hamlet's indisposition. Before he discusses that matter, he leaves and reenters with the ambassadors, who announce that Fortinbras's uncle, Old Norway, who rules Norway, has prevailed on his nephew not to invade Denmark after all but merely to seek permission to cross Denmark and attack the Poles instead. Voltimand and Cornelius leave, and Polonius in a long-winded speech discloses his theory of the cause of Hamlet's madness.

Although Claudius is skeptical and Gertrude still thinks the cause of Hamlet's melancholy is Old Hamlet's death and her quick marriage, they decide to adopt Polonius's plan to test the theory by using Ophelia as a decoy. Just then Hamlet enters reading, and Polonius asks Claudius and Gertrude to leave while he examines the prince. Hamlet puts on a good act, using his "antic disposition" to befuddle the old man. When Polonius leaves, Rosencrantz and Guildenstern reenter and begin their own testing of Hamlet, repeatedly suggesting that ambition preoccupies him. Hamlet perceives that they have been sent for to learn his thoughts, gets them to confess as much, and no longer trusts his erstwhile friends.

Rosencrantz changes the subject to announce that actors are coming to Elsinore to entertain the court, being driven out of the city by "the late innovation" (2.2.333), an allusion to the competition Shakespeare's troupe was facing from the children's companies. When the actors enter, Hamlet has their leader deliver a speech drawn from book 2 of the *Aeneid*, about how Pyrrhus attacked and killed the Trojan King, old Priam. This image of a bloody avenger reflects what Hamlet may be thinking about regarding himself.

Before the scene ends, Hamlet gets the leader to agree to play "The Murder of Gonzago" the next night before the court with a speech he will add to the script. Hamlet then concludes the scene with a long soliloquy in which he upbraids himself for not acting yet against Claudius. He expresses the hope that the play, which mirrors the murder of his father, will so affect the King that Claudius will confess his crime or at least give evidence to confirm the Ghost's story.

**3.1.** Act 3 begins as Polonius, Claudius, and Gertrude set Ophelia up to test Hamlet to see whether Polonius's theory concerning his madness is correct. Gertrude leaves, and Claudius and Polonius hide behind a curtain or tapestry as Hamlet enters. Failing to see Ophelia kneeling at prayer, he speaks his "To be or not to be" soliloquy (3.1.55–89). He debates which is nobler: to suffer or to act, then contemplates suicide again. He rejects it this time only because one cannot know what comes after death. He then notices Ophelia, and their dialogue begins as she returns some gifts to him, calling him "unkind" (3.1.100). He reacts violently, seems to detect the spies, and orders her to a nunnery. When he leaves, Ophelia laments, "O what a noble mind is here o'erthrown" (3.1.150), in the process anticipating her own later breakdown.

Polonius and Claudius reenter. Claudius believes it is not at all rejected love that affects Hamlet. He therefore determines to send him away to England. Polonius, however, still clings to his theory and suggests that Gertrude test Hamlet further after the play is performed that night while he again hides to overhear their conversation.

**3.2.** Before the play within the play begins, Hamlet gives instructions to the actors on how to perform. The court enters, and after some bawdy byplay with Ophelia, Hamlet sits down beside her to watch first the dumb show, then the action proper. When the Player King lies down to sleep, the murderer Lucianus enters, whom Hamlet identifies as "nephew to the king," not brother (3.2.244). When he pours poison into the sleeping king's ear, Claudius rises, upset, calls for lights, and departs, disrupting the proceedings, which Polonius cancels abruptly.

Left alone with Horatio, whom he has asked to observe Claudius carefully, Hamlet exults in his success in getting the evidence he feels he needs to confirm the Ghost's story. When Rosencrantz and Guildenstern enter with Gertrude's message to come to her chambers, Hamlet mercilessly teases them. Polonius also enters with the summons to the Queen, and Hamlet teases him, too. Alone, Hamlet soliloquizes that though he could now "drink hot blood," he "will speak daggers" to his mother "but use none" when he sees her (3.2.388–399).

**3.3.** Rosencrantz and Guildenstern advise the King to protect himself, for the welfare of the state depends on his safety. They leave, and Claudius kneels in prayer. He recognizes that to repent he must give up "My crown, mine own ambition, and my queen" (3.3.55). As he prays for some angelic help, Hamlet enters. Finding Claudius alone, he raises his sword to kill him but then halts. He feels that killing Claudius at this moment, while he is praying and presumably in a state of grace, is inadequate revenge. Hence, he sheathes his sword and leaves. Claudius rises, ironically confessing that his prayer was insincere.

**3.4.** Polonius instructs Gertrude to speak to Hamlet sternly. He then hides behind a curtain as Hamlet enters and immediately takes the offensive. Frightened, Gertrude cries out. Polonius echoes her cries, whereupon Hamlet stabs through the curtain and kills him. Dismissing Polonius as a "wretched, rash, intruding fool" (3.4.31), Hamlet turns again to Gertrude and begins to upbraid her for marrying Claudius, in the process suggesting that she was an accessory to killing her husband. Gertrude admits she has sinned but is shocked at Hamlet's accusation. As their dialogue continues and grows more heated, the Ghost enters, warning Hamlet not to forget his "almost blunted purpose" (3.4.111) and disappears. Gertrude does not see or hear the Ghost; only Hamlet does. Thus she thinks that Hamlet is hallucinating. The scene ends with Gertrude in remorse, asking her son what to do. Hamlet tells her not to go to Claudius's bed anymore and mentions that he is being sent off to England with Rosencrantz and Guildenstern. He suspects it is a plot against him and suggests he will foil it somehow.

**4.1.** As act 4 opens, Claudius and Gertrude console each other on what has been happening.

**4.2.** Hamlet leads Rosencrantz and Guildenstern a merry chase around the castle when they try to discover where Hamlet has hidden Polonius's body.

**4.3.** After a tendentious talk with Hamlet, Claudius admits in a concluding soliloquy that he is sending Hamlet to England to be killed.

**4.4.** Fortinbras appears for the first time, leading his army across Denmark to attack the Poles. Hamlet sees the young prince and comments in his last soliloquy on "How all occasions do inform against me, / And spur my dull revenge!" (4.4.32–33). He praises Fortinbras's courage and swears that from this time forth his thoughts will be "bloody" (4.4.66) as Rosencrantz and Guildenstern lead him to the ship that will carry them to England.

**4.5.** Ophelia enters, mad, and Laertes returns from Paris bent on revenge for his father's murder. Claudius enlists Laertes to kill Hamlet.

**4.6.** Hamlet has escaped from the ship that was taking him to England, after secretly revising Claudius's diplomatic packet so that Rosencrantz and Guildenstern's names replace his as the persons to be executed. He sends letters home to Claudius and Horatio announcing his return to Denmark.

**4.7.** Claudius and Laertes lay plans for Hamlet's murder by means of a fencing match. Gertrude announces that Ophelia has drowned, possibly a suicide.

**5.1.** Two gravediggers are preparing a grave as Hamlet and Horatio enter. After a punning dialogue with one of the undertakers, Hamlet sees the funeral entourage approaching and discovers that Ophelia is dead. He and Horatio hide. Laertes is upset with the priests because the funeral is abbreviated, and he jumps into the grave to embrace Ophelia's dead body. Hamlet emerges, swears his love for Ophelia, too, and he and Laertes grapple. They are separated, and Gertrude blames Hamlet's madness for his conduct.

**5.2.** Hamlet recounts to Horatio his adventures at sea, including the way he was rescued by pirates, who returned him to Denmark. The courtier Osric approaches them and tells Hamlet of the fencing match Claudius has arranged between the prince and Laertes. Although Hamlet has some presentiments of disaster, he accepts the challenge, thinking it is only to be a friendly bout. He does not know that Claudius and Laertes have together planned to have Laertes' foil poisoned and not blunted ("unbated" 5.2.317). Moreover, Claudius puts a poisoned pearl into a cup of wine that he plans to have Hamlet drink at some point. Before the bout begins, Hamlet apologizes to Laertes for his behavior in the cemetery. Hamlet gets the better of Laertes in the first two passes, angering Laertes so much that between passes he wounds Hamlet with the poisoned rapier. Meanwhile, Gertrude drinks from the poisoned cup. Furious now at Laertes for his cowardly act, Hamlet duels with him, gets control of the unbated rapier, and wounds Laertes. The Queen dies, and in the uproar that follows Laertes confesses his villainy and Claudius's; he then dies. Hamlet, mortally wounded too, has just strength enough left to run Claudius through with the unbated rapier and force him to drink the remaining liquor in the poisoned cup. Claudius dies, and before Hamlet also dies, he asks Horatio to deliver his story to the world instead of joining him in death. At this point Fortinbras enters, sees the results of the melee, and claims his rights to the kingdom, as he orders Hamlet to be taken up and carried like a soldier to the "stage" (5.2.396), that is, a raised platform for exhibiting the body.

## PUBLICATION HISTORY

The date of composition of *Hamlet* is uncertain, but it was probably written between 1600 and 1602, when it was entered in the Stationers' Register (that is, the record of printers and booksellers) on July 16. What its relation is to an older play called *Hamlet*, no longer extant, is still more of a problem. Possible allusions to the older play, referred to by scholars as Ur-*Hamlet*, appear as early as 1589 in Thomas Nashe's preface to Robert Greene's *Menaphon*. The entrepreneur Philip Henslowe records a performance of a play called *Hamlet* on June 9, 1594; and a couple of years later, Thomas Heywood alludes to a ghostly figure calling "*Hamlet, revenge!*" in his *Wit's Miserie* (1596). The author of Ur-*Hamlet* is unknown, although some scholars speculate that it may have been Thomas Kyd, famous for another revenge tragedy, *The Spanish Tragedy*, published in 1592 but written earlier.

Shakespeare's *Hamlet* first appeared in quarto in 1603 (Q1), followed shortly afterward in 1604 by another quarto edition (Q2) that contains a much fuller text. Many years later a still different version appeared in the First Folio (1623)—the first collected edition of Shakespeare's plays compiled by Shakespeare's colleagues John Heminge and Henry Condell. The Folio text is much closer to that of Q2 but cuts a number of lines, most notably Hamlet's last soliloquy (4.4.32–66), and adds some other lines not found in either quarto.

Various theories have been proposed to explain the appearance of the two quartos, which are so different from one another. One theory is that Q1 represents a memorial reconstruction of the play as it was performed in the provinces. An actor who played Marcellus and one or two other small parts is said to have been the one to reconstruct the play from memory, since the scenes in which he appears are the most textually accurate of any. This theory, though widely held, remains unproven, however, as no hard evidence exists to show that any of Shakespeare's plays was ever published from such "stolne and surreptitious" copies as Heminge and Condell maintain in their preface to the First Folio. Certainly, it is a shortened version, presumably an acting script, whereas most scholars believe that Q2 was printed from Shakespeare's own manuscript. Q2, therefore, is considered to be the most authentic version of the play and the one that is the basis for almost all scholarly editions.

Shakespeare's *Hamlet* is a pivotal play in the development of revenge tragedies, which were popular in the 1590s. Capitalizing on that vogue and on the success of Kyd's *The Spanish Tragedy*, Shakespeare wrote his first tragedy, *Titus Andronicus* (ca. 1590; published 1594), as a violent and bloody revenge drama, very much in the current mode. Although revenge is a motif in many of his plays, including such comedies as *The Merchant of Venice*, it appears that Shakespeare had doubts about taking personal vengeance. The secular authorities and the church vehemently attacked personal revenge, which was both unlawful and unsanctified, indeed a sin and a crime. In *As You Like It*, Shakespeare shows his protagonist, Orlando, grappling with the problem of revenge when he sees his wicked older brother lying asleep under a tree about to be attacked by a starving lioness. He starts to abandon his brother, but then realizing that "kindness" is "nobler ever than revenge" (4.3.128) he turns back and saves Oliver from the lioness. Similarly, in *The Tempest*, one of Shakespeare last plays, Prospero also has to struggle with the problem of revenge and, like Orlando, finds that "The rarer action is / In virtue than in vengeance" (5.1.27–28). Penitence on the part of the malefactors is the important thing, not revenge, as both of these plays dramatically represent.

This may be an underlying reason for Hamlet's delay in taking his revenge. Certainly revenge tragedies after *Hamlet*, like Cyril Tourneur's *The Atheist's Tragedy* (1611) and George Chapman's *The Revenge of Bussy D'Ambois* (1613), reflect this attitude toward personal vengeance. In Tourneur's play, a father, murdered by someone who has taken his dukedom, returns as a ghost but specifically orders his son *not* to take action against the criminal duke, who dies at the end ironically by his own hand as he tries to execute the son on a trumped-up charge. The revenge tragedies after *Hamlet* are thus very different from the plays before it that treated the subject of revenge. *Hamlet* also refers to the "War of the Theatres" between adult and children's acting companies from 1600 to 1601 (2.2).

## SOURCES FOR THE PLAY

The story of Hamlet goes back many centuries, at least to Saxo Grammaticus's twelfth-century tale in his *Historicae Danicae*, first published in 1514. It is a very primitive revenge story about a young man, Amleth, whose father has defeated the King of Norway in a duel and is then murdered by Amleth's uncle, Feng, who aspires to his crown and marries Gerutha, the Queen. To protect himself from his murderous uncle, Amleth pretends to be mad (an idiot could not be executed) but speaks in riddles and otherwise suggests that he may not be completely insane. To determine how mad Amleth is, Feng decides to test him by discovering whether he can be seduced by a pretty lady put in his way. He is seduced, but Amleth gets the young woman to swear not to reveal what they have done. A friend of Feng then suggests that he test Amleth further by having his mother question him while the friend hides. Amleth discovers the eavesdropper and kills him, dismembering his body and feeding the parts to the pigs. Returning to his mother, he upbraids her for her actions in forgetting her husband and marrying Feng, and he wins her to repentance.

Feng decides to get rid of Amleth by sending him to England in the company of two retainers, but Amleth discovers the document they are carrying and substitutes their names for his as the ones to be executed. He adds that the English King should give his daughter to Amleth to be married. This happens, and Amleth spends several years in England before returning to Denmark, setting fire to the palace, and finally killing Feng. He then hides, waiting to see how the people will react, and emerges declaring what he has done and why. The people applaud his deeds, and he becomes King, ruling over the country and having other adventures before he himself dies in battle.

Whether Shakespeare read Saxo Grammaticus's tale, we do not know. He could, of course, read Latin, but whether he had access to the *Historicae Danae* is unknown. No English translation was available until 1608, but a French version appeared in 1570. It was included in François de Belleforest's *Histoires Tragiques*, published in later editions as well. It is here that Shakespeare probably first read the story, unless he simply got the essentials from Ur-*Hamlet* and rewrote that play. Belleforest's version of the Hamlet story is interesting partly for his editorializing: he sermonizes against the pagan Danes and comments at the outset that revenge is never to be countenanced. Or if it is, he says, it is understandable only in the situation where a son's father is murdered and justice has not been forthcoming.

Belleforest's version is also interesting for two innovations. First, Fengon (as he is now called) has an adulterous affair with the queen before he kills the king. Second, after Hamlet confronts his mother with her guilt, she admits her wicked ways, agrees to keep his secret, encourages him to take revenge, and hopes to see him as King of Denmark. In neither Saxo's tale nor Belleforest's version does a ghost appear to the dead king's son, and at the end, Hamlet does not die after killing the new king but ascends to the throne. Shakespeare adds Laertes and Fortinbras to his dramatis personae, alters considerably the character of the woman who loves Hamlet, and brings in the players. Most importantly, Shakespeare, possibly taking a hint from Belleforest (unless he was following the Ur-*Hamlet*), places the story in a Christian rather than a pagan context.

## STRUCTURE AND PLOTTING

Analysis of *Hamlet* suggests that the play has three main movements: act 1, acts 2–3, acts 4–5. The movement of act 1 begins with the soldiers on guard and Horatio's confrontation with the Ghost and proceeds in 1.2 to the first of three major court scenes. There, everyone except Hamlet seems pleased with Claudius's ascension to the throne, his marriage to Gertrude, and his ability to handle the Norwegian threat by Fortinbras. Tension mounts as Hamlet, still dressed in mourning for his father, crosses verbal swords with Claudius, whom he hates. In his first of several important soliloquies, Hamlet also expresses the deep pain he feels at his mother's hasty remarriage to Claudius, a marriage he regards as incestuous. He ends by stating how impotent he feels to do anything about a situation that is not good and cannot come to good. This first soliloquy is a pivot to the next part of the scene, when Horatio and Marcellus enter to inform Hamlet about the Ghost they have seen. Tension continues to mount as Hamlet agrees to visit the ramparts with them that very night.

Act 1, scene 3 is an interlude with the family of Polonius, as Laertes takes his leave of Denmark, not returning until act 4 after his father has been killed. Both he and Polonius warn Ophelia about Hamlet, and, albeit reluctantly, she agrees to cut off contact with him. The next two scenes, which form a continuous action, occur that night and reach the play's first momentous climax as Hamlet confronts the Ghost of his father, learns about the murder, and swears to take revenge.

Act 2, which begins the second movement, opens two months later, as we learn from Ophelia's remark later at 3.2.128. (Shakespeare gives specific time signals when tension mounts but is much more vague when he relaxes the dramatic tension, as here.) Hamlet's strange behavior to Ophelia prompts Polonius to go to the King and Queen in the next scene with his theory of the cause of Hamlet's madness, Ophelia's rejection of him as her lover. But Claudius and Gertrude have other ideas and send Rosencrantz and Guildenstern to probe Hamlet. Claudius suspects Hamlet's ambition, that he is upset at not getting the throne after Old Hamlet's death; Gertrude, however, is convinced that her son's melancholy is the result of her hasty remarriage.

Tension builds slowly in the very long 2.2, which has several parts—a portmanteau scene, as it may be called. It reaches its highest point in Hamlet's second long soliloquy (2.2.550–605), which ends with his plan "to catch the conscience of the king" (2.2.605) by putting on a play that mirrors Claudius's murder of Old Hamlet. Tension has also been raised in Hamlet's dialogue with Rosencrantz and Guidenstern, when he detects their real purpose in coming to Elsinore. But the true climax of this second movement of the play does not come until the next act.

Tension in act 3, in fact, peaks several times. The first time is when Hamlet meets with Ophelia. If he seems despondent and unsure of whether to proceed with his revenge in the soliloquy immediately before he sees Ophelia, when he is with her he senses the trap that Polonius and Claudius have laid for him, as they eavesdrop, and makes a thinly veiled threat against the King. At the same time, he orders Ophelia to a nunnery. Her soliloquy expresses the turmoil she—and the audience—feels because of what is happening to Hamlet. Her soliloquy is also a precursor to her own mental breakdown later in act 4.

Tension drops in the next scene, as Hamlet calmly advises the players on how to act and then praises Horatio as a man who "in suff'ring all . . . suffers nothing" (3.2.66). But tension begins to mount again as the King, Queen, and others enter for the second of the three major court scenes. Hamlet adopts his antic disposition once more in speaking with Polonius and is especially bitter in his conversation with Ophelia. The performance of "The Murder of Gonzago" is another high point in the play and represents a pivot of the main action. For it is here, in Claudius's reaction, that Hamlet gets the confirmation of the Ghost's story that he feels he needs. He exults in his success, even though Claudius has not revealed his guilt publicly. Summoned to his mother's closet, Hamlet is ready for what he has to do; as he says in his soliloquy, which ends the scene, "Now could I drink hot blood, / And do such bitter business as the day / Would quake to look on" (3.2.390–392).

Before Hamlet gets to Gertrude's room, he passes Claudius at prayer. This is the one time in the play that they are alone together—a moment of high tension indeed, for Hamlet realizes that right now he could kill Claudius. But he desists, because he believes that sending Claudius to heaven would be "hire and salary, not revenge" (3.3.79). In wishing Claudius damned, Hamlet comes close to damning his own soul; in the next scene he is punished for his thoughts by killing the wrong man.

In 3.4 Hamlet confronts his mother and kills Polonius, thus leading to Ophelia's madness and Laertes' return to Denmark to exact the revenge that will unfold in 5.2.

The action is continuous through the first three scenes of act 4, which begin the third and final movement of the play. (Alternatively, the final movement may be said to begin with 4.5, after Hamlet disappears from the action for several scenes.) Tension continues to drop following the last appearance of the Ghost and the point at which Hamlet is sent to England. Claudius's heart has now hardened after his failure to pray successfully for repentance in 3.3. En route to board the ship, Hamlet passes the army of Fortinbras. He sees in Fortinbras a noble prince who is acting, whereas Hamlet feels that in contrast he himself is too slow to take revenge. Except for his conversations with Horatio in act 5, this is the last time Hamlet speaks his mind confidentially to the audience. Concluding, he promises that from now on his thoughts will be "bloody, or be nothing worth" (4.4.66), but under the circumstances of his being led away from Denmark the promise seems empty.

Tensions mount again later in act 4, first as Ophelia appears thoroughly mad, and still more when Laertes returns from Paris bent on taking revenge against Claudius, who he suspects is responsible for Polonius's death. Claudius manages to calm Laertes, and when news arrives in 4.7 that Hamlet has returned to Denmark, the King and Laertes plot to kill Hamlet in a duel. While Claudius and Laertes are talking, Gertrude enters with a very moving description of how Ophelia drowned in a brook. Tension grows higher as Laertes is even more determined now to take vengeance on Hamlet, whom he blames for all the bad things that have befallen his family.

Act 5 opens in a graveyard. As the two clowns, or gravediggers, engage in what is a comic interlude, the tension generated by the end of act 4 drops considerably, only to build again to the end of 5.1 and once more in 5.2. Hamlet and Horatio enter after one of the gravediggers leaves, and Hamlet engages the other in some witty dialogue. When Ophelia's funeral cortege arrives, Hamlet and Horatio hide to eavesdrop on the proceedings. After Laertes jumps into the grave to embrace Ophelia's body, Hamlet emerges, declaring himself "Hamlet the Dane," that is, the rightful King of Denmark (5.1.258). Laertes attacks him, and they grapple together until separated. In an emotional speech, Hamlet declares that he loved Ophelia far more than any brother could. Claudius and Gertrude try to excuse him as mad, and eventually he leaves in the care of Horatio, as Claudius asks Laertes to be patient until they can carry out their plan.

The last scene of the play (another portmanteau scene) begins as Hamlet tells Horatio what happened while he was at sea and how he foiled Claudius's plot and sent Rosencrantz and Guildenstern to be executed in his place. As they converse,

Osric enters with the proposal from Claudius for the fencing match with Laertes. The dialogue with the affected courtier is another comic interlude before the final climactic action. Despite presentiments of danger and even death, Hamlet agrees to the match, notwithstanding Horatio's pleas for him to refrain. Hamlet here shows a more resolute attitude and an acceptance of the will of Providence—something he seemed to be resisting all through acts 1–3.

The match takes place in the hall where Hamlet and Horatio have been talking. Claudius, Gertrude, and others enter with fanfare for the third and final court scene. With qualification, Laertes accepts Hamlet's proferred apology for his behavior the day before, and the duel begins. Unable to hit Hamlet with the unbated and poisoned rapier while fencing, Laertes stabs him while Hamlet's back is turned. Incensed, Hamlet swiftly retaliates when he gains possession of the fatal rapier. Meanwhile, despite Claudius's warning, Gertrude drinks from the poisoned chalice and a few moments later dies. Feeling guilty for his role in the conspiracy, Laertes confesses everything to Hamlet, who goes after the King, wounds him, and forces him to drink from the chalice, too. Knowing they are going to die, Laertes and Hamlet exchange forgiveness. With his dying breath, Hamlet then prophesies that the new King of Denmark will be Fortinbras, who then enters and takes possession of the crown.

This is the overall dramatic structure of *Hamlet*. Another way of viewing it, however, is to see the central action of the play as a movement of oscillating rhythm, framed by Hamlet's incomplete knowledge for most of act 1 and his considerable change in attitude in act 5, after his return from the sea voyage. For the two months separating acts 1 and 2, Hamlet has done nothing. He seems unsure how to carry out the Ghost's commands and speculates at the end of act 2 that he may have been deceived by the apparition. He wants surer grounds for action than a Ghost's story because the Ghost could be a devil in disguise seeking to mislead Hamlet into damning himself. By putting on "The Murder of Gonzago" he hopes to get the evidence he needs. By now he has whipped himself up to a frenzy similar to what he experienced when he first confronted the Ghost and seemed determined to take action. But in the very next scene (3.1), only a few moments of playing time later, he speaks his famous "To be or not to be" soliloquy, debating with himself "whether 'tis nobler in the mind" to act—revenge, in his case—or "to suffer the slings and arrows of outrageous fortune," that is, to engage in Christian forbearance (3.1.56–57). This up-and-down movement of Hamlet's emotions, or his blowing alternatively hot and cold, characterizes him and the action of the play through the next several scenes. For example, after becoming excited when he speaks to Ophelia after his soliloquy, he is calm again in the following scene, giving instruction to the players and then praising Horatio as one who suffers "Fortune's buffets and rewards . . . with equal thanks" (3.2.67–68). This oscillating movement continues throughout this scene and the ones following, until Hamlet's final soliloquy in 4.4. When Hamlet returns from sea, he briefly reverts to that frenzied state when he and Laertes grapple at Ophelia's grave, but on the whole throughout this act he seems quietly resigned to let Providence control his destiny, until he finally kills Claudius. It is important in this connection to note that when Hamlet comes back to Denmark and lists all of Claudius's villainies up to that point (5.2.64–67), he does not have any plan of action. He is ready at last to "let be" what will be (5.2.224).

## MAIN CHARACTERS

In the prologue to his famous film of the play, Laurence Olivier said the story of *Hamlet* was that of a man "who could not make up his mind." This is a gross oversimplification of Hamlet's character, which is far more complex, as indeed the entire play is.

### Hamlet

To begin with, Hamlet is apparently the only person in Denmark who still mourns his father's sudden death. He reluctantly agrees to stay in Denmark rather than return to Wittenberg, where he has been a student, so that he can remain under the watchful care of his mother, Queen Gertrude, and his stepfather/uncle, King Claudius. Hamlet dislikes Claudius intensely and contrasts him unfavorably with Old Hamlet, who was, compared to Claudius, "Hyperion to a satyr" (1.2.140), he says. He is thus unhappy about his mother's hasty remarriage to Claudius, all the more so because he regards the marriage as incestuous.

When Hamlet first enters in 1.2, he knows nothing about the Ghost of his father, who has appeared on the ramparts, and nothing about his father's murder. Nevertheless, he feels that because of the incestuous union of Gertrude and Claudius, the situation in Denmark is very bad. But since he is isolated—the entire court, according to Claudius, has approved the new King's actions—he feels completely impotent to do anything about it. When Horatio and Marcellus enter and tell him what they witnessed the previous night, Hamlet carefully cross-examines them and then decides to join them on watch that very evening. But before he sees or even hears about the Ghost, he knows that things are bad enough to demand redress. He nevertheless feels compelled to hold his tongue, even though it breaks his heart to do so.

When the Ghost tells Hamlet the story of the murder, Hamlet's first reaction— "O my prophetic soul!" (1.5.40)—shows, like his earlier lines in 1.2, how intensely he dislikes his uncle and that he had intuited Claudius's foul play. He now resolves to take revenge, as the Ghost demands. But under the Ghost's injunctions, which include not tainting his mind or proceeding against his mother, Hamlet has a problem: how to accomplish the goal of breaking up the incestuous union. This may be one reason for his delay in taking any quick action. Another may be his doubts about the validity of the Ghost and his story. Although Hamlet is a person who may act impulsively at times, as when he later kills Polonius or boards the pirate ship while at sea, he is also a contemplative young man. Indeed, his alternation between these two sides of his personality is a large part of his problem. Unlike Horatio, whom he praises in 3.2 just before the play within the play, Hamlet is not one who easily adopts a stoical attitude; he is not one who can take "Fortune's buffets and rewards" with equanimity (3.2.67).

After his first meeting with the Ghost, Hamlet decides to put on an antic disposition (1.5.172), that is, pretend to be mad. Apparently, he adopts this behavior as a kind of shield or protection against Claudius and others who may try to pry out his secret and foil his revenge. In addition, this behavior will give him time to plan his course of action against Claudius. He clearly acts mad when talking with Polonius in 2.2, but at other times his behavior is such that it is difficult to tell whether he is really mad or just pretending to be. One such occasion is in the so-called Nunnery Scene (3.1), when he speaks so furiously against Ophelia that she thinks he has truly lost his mind.

Another reason for Hamlet's delay may be that, isolated as he is, he cannot marshal the resources for action against Claudius. Moreover, killing a king would be a very serious, even a damnable, action, as Shakespeare's audience would recognize. As Laertes says when he returns from Paris intent on exacting revenge for his father's murder, he is willing to dare damnation; for he is willing to kill Claudius, who at that moment he thinks is responsible for Polonius's death. But unlike Polonius's rash son, and in spite of his impulsive actions at times, Hamlet is mostly a man of thought. He recognizes this tendency in himself, however, and at one point he criticizes those who are cowards for "thinking too precisely on th' event," that is, for worrying too much about the consequences of an action (see 4.4.41). In his case, that would mean pondering too carefully on what killing Claudius would entail, should he bring himself to do it. Finally, as if he did not have enough problems, Ophelia, whom he loves, rejects him under her father's orders not to have anything further to do with him.

All of these considerations may account for Hamlet's inaction. From a Freudian point of view, he may also be inhibited by an Oedipus complex. Although not prominent in the play, two clues indicate that this may indeed be a concern. For example, when Hamlet asks the First Player to recite "Aeneas' Tale to Dido" (2.2.446) and begins the speech himself, the figure that Pyrrhus attacks is much more like Old Hamlet than Claudius. Again, in "The Murder of Gonzago" Hamlet identifies the King's murderer not as his brother but as his nephew. These instances suggest that unconsciously Hamlet wishes to kill his father so that he may have access to his mother as her lover, as in the classical case of an Oedipus complex. But that is far less a problem for Hamlet than is his concern over the justice of killing Claudius, which is the only way he can think of to carry out the revenge the Ghost has demanded.

Hamlet's reluctance to take action against Claudius seems to be resolved when the players arrive and he asks them to put on "The Murder of Gonzago," with a speech that he will write and have them insert into the dialogue. He hopes that by seeing a mirror reflection of his murder of Old Hamlet, Claudius will confess his crime. At the very least, Claudius will so give himself away that Hamlet will get all the evidence he needs to confirm the Ghost's story. For by now, two months after seeing the Ghost, Hamlet has some doubts regarding the Ghost's authenticity. Despite his initial intuitive acceptance of the murder story, Hamlet thinks that the Ghost might be a devil in disguise, tempting Hamlet to the damnable deed of killing the king.

After he kills Polonius, thinking it was really Claudius behind the arras in his mother's chamber, Hamlet at first dismisses the old man as a foolish intruder. But he later realizes that his action may be a punishment for some misdeed and that he must be both "scourge and minister" to Denmark (3.4.175). His misdeed, as some critics believe, may have been wishing Claudius damned when he came upon him at prayer in the preceding scene. At any rate, he now seems to accept the role that he evidently had been resisting—a resistance that had hitherto caused him to delay action against Claudius.

Still, he does not devise a plan of action after the play within the play. Instead, accepting heaven's decree as he understands it, he places himself in the hands of providence. Thus, the play strongly suggests Hamlet's changing attitude, as seems clear from his behavior in act 5, where he recounts to Horatio his adventures at sea. He tells how he sensed what Rosencrantz and Guildenstern were about and how he acted swiftly to counteract them. He attributes his intuitive action to the "divinity that shapes our ends" (5.2.10) and later, when he describes how he had his father's signet ring with him to seal the altered commission Rosencrantz and Guildenstern were carrying, he says "even in that was heaven ordinant" (5.2.48). Finally, when Osric delivers the invitation to fight Laertes in a duel, Hamlet has presentiments of danger. But he is unwilling to follow Horatio's entreaty to avoid or postpone the match. Again, he cites the will of providence and is ready to "let be" what will be (5.2.224). He knows now that he does not need a plan against Claudius, that heaven will determine the outcome. "The readiness is all" (5.2.222), he tells Horatio, meaning that when heaven is ready, he will act as required. And he does, even though acting costs him his life.

## Claudius

Although Claudius may appear as a hardened criminal, he is far from that at first. At the outset (1.2) he tries to be conciliatory to Hamlet, despite the prince's obvious dislike of him. He is also a peacemaker and by sending his ambassadors to Norway successfully prevents Fortinbras from going to war with Denmark. He has a conscience, too, as several asides (see, for instance, 3.1.48–53) and his attempt to pray for forgiveness indicate. He is also a very successful politician. How else could he have managed to win the entire court to elect him King and then to raise no objection to his marrying his brother's widow? As he says in his opening speech in 1.2, the court, with whom he has consulted from the first, has granted him everything he has wanted.

Claudius is also very perceptive. Although he is willing to test Polonius's theory of love madness to explain Hamlet's strange behavior, he has his own theory. For this reason he has sent for Rosencrantz and Guildenstern, Hamlet's friends, so that they can probe the prince and try to discover what has upset him so much. Claudius believes it must be because he instead of Hamlet, the dead King's son and presumed heir to the throne, has taken the crown. After Hamlet's behavior in the Nunnery Scene, Claudius is by no means convinced that Hamlet has gone mad because of love for Ophelia. He recognizes then, as he does again later, Hamlet's not so thinly veiled threat against him and resolves to deal with it quickly by sending Hamlet to England. After "The Murder of Gonzago," in which Hamlet identifies Lucianus as "nephew to the king," Claudius knows for certain that Hamlet wants to kill him and decides to have Hamlet killed in England instead.

But before he sends Hamlet away, Claudius tries to repent. In his soliloquy in the Prayer Scene (3.3.36–72), he indicates that he is fully aware of his most heinous sin. He says it has "the primal eldest curse upon't, / A brother's murther" (3.3.37–38). His strong sense of guilt, however, prevents him from praying effectively. Besides, he recognizes that for true repentance he must surrender those things for which he committed his sin: his crown, his ambition, and his queen. He forces himself to kneel and try to pray, appealing to angels for help. For with that help, "All may be well" (3.3.72).

Instead of an angel who might help Claudius, Hamlet enters lusting for revenge. He spares Claudius only because he thinks the King might be in a state of grace, unlike Old Hamlet, who was killed before he could confess to heaven his sins, which therefore must be burned away in purgatory. Hamlet wants to kill Claudius when Claudius is in a sinful situation. Claudius is entirely unaware of Hamlet's presence. The irony is that he has not been able to pray effectively at all, and henceforward he becomes the hardened villain he was not at the outset.

As an example of Claudius's villainy, not only does he send Hamlet to England to be killed, but when he discovers that Hamlet has evaded that trap, he co-opts Laertes into a devilish scheme to murder Hamlet in a duel. To be doubly sure of this plan's success, Claudius has a poisoned cup prepared in addition to the un-bated and poison-tipped rapier Laertes will use. The plan backfires when Gertrude, not Hamlet, drinks the poison and Laertes is unable to win any of the bouts. Guilt-stricken at what he has done when he finally wounds Hamlet and Hamlet wounds him, Laertes exposes the plot. Hamlet at last takes his revenge and kills Claudius, calling him an "incestuous, murd'rous, damned Dane" (5.2.325).

## Gertrude

Like the other major characters, Gertrude is also complex. Hamlet thinks she was an accomplice to her husband's murder, but there is no evidence to show that he is right. On the contrary, when he accuses her in the Closet Scene (3.4) of killing a king and marrying with his brother, she is shocked and does not seem to understand his allusion. She may have had an adulterous affair with Claudius while Old Hamlet was alive, but for that we have only the Ghost's word in 1.5 and the inference we may draw from her hasty remarriage.

That Gertrude cares about her son and worries about him is certain. She attributes his strange melancholy to her hasty remarriage; its effect on him troubles her, as she tells Claudius when they send Rosencrantz and Guildenstern to probe his sickness. It is unclear how effective Hamlet's "shriving" of her is in 3.4. She feels guilty for her sins—probably for her union with Claudius, which both Hamlet and the Ghost call incestuous, as well as for her hasty remarriage—but whether she takes her son's advice to abstain from further intercourse with Claudius is not clear.

Gertrude's most beautiful lines in the play are her eulogy of Ophelia (4.7.166–183). Later, as Gertrude strews flowers over Ophelia's grave, she also mentions that she had hoped that Hamlet and Ophelia would marry, but earlier she does not voice this wish and even goes along with Polonius's plot to use Ophelia as a decoy in 3.1. She is ineffectual, moreover, in chastising her son, as Polonius tells her to do in 3.4.

Overall, Gertrude appears to be a weak but compassionate woman. Claudius is obviously strongly attracted to her, as she is one of the main reasons he has killed her husband. As he tells Laertes, "She is so conjunctive to my life and soul, / That, as the star moves not but in his sphere, / I could not but by her" (4.7.14–16). Freudian critics also see her as sexually attractive to her son, who cannot understand how she could become involved with Claudius. Their dialogue in 3.4 is sometimes presented on the stage or in films as erotically charged, but that interpretation may overdo Shakespeare's intention.

## Polonius

Actors usually have to decide between two basic ways of portraying Polonius, the King's chief adviser and the father of both Laertes and Ophelia. Either he is a doddering old fool who loves to pry into others' affairs, as Hamlet describes him after killing him (3.4.31–33), or he is an elderly and wise councilor who has at least the nominal respect of the King (2.2.129–130). Probably he is a little of both and should be played that way. He is also something of a Machiavellian schemer, as he shows himself when at the beginning of 2.1 he plots with Reynaldo to spy on his son, Laertes, and later when he devises various schemes to discover what ails Hamlet.

A caring father, Polonius displays concern for his children, as when he delivers his precepts to Laertes upon his departure for Paris (1.3.59–81). He justifies forbidding his daughter to have anything to do with Hamlet because he recognizes, as Laertes does, that Hamlet is "a prince out of [her] star" (2.2.141). That is, Hamlet as royalty will have to marry for reasons of state someone of higher rank than hers (compare 1.3.14–28).

After Ophelia reluctantly obeys her father, Hamlet's strange behavior toward her inspires Polonius's theory that the Prince is mad for love; it is the underlying cause of his melancholy. Polonius has no qualms about using Ophelia as a decoy in 3.1 to test his theory. He has no qualms, either, about eavesdropping on Hamlet then and later (3.4) to further test his theory, an action that leads to his death. He is thoroughly given to sententious phrases and to wordplay, as when he tries to explain his theory concerning Hamlet's melancholy to the King and Queen (2.2.86–95). Hamlet enjoys teasing him, putting on his antic disposition, but Polonius is wise enough to see how "pregnant" his replies are, and how, though they seem mad, there is some "method" in them (2.2.209, 206).

In college Polonius was an actor (3.2.99–106), and to some extent he is always acting. He loves staging a scene, like the attempt to trap Hamlet by using Ophelia as a decoy in 3.1 and placing himself behind an arras in Gertrude's closet in an attempt to overhear her conversation with her son.

## Ophelia

Doubtless the most innocent of those who suffer in *Hamlet*, Ophelia is both the lovely young woman who has won Hamlet's heart and the obedient daughter who is compelled to reject him. She is also the beloved sister of Laertes, who worries that Hamlet is only toying with her and advises her to be extremely careful not to let her emotions get the better of her. While she promises to take her brother's words seriously, she warns him to follow his own advice. Apparently, she knows Laertes well. But when her father extracts from her what Laertes was saying and then forbids her to see Hamlet anymore, she feels compelled to yield to his demands, dutiful daughter that she is.

Ophelia becomes upset, therefore, when Hamlet pays her a visit while she is sewing in her closet and acts so strangely. She tells her father about the visit, and this information provides the basis for his theory about Hamlet's melancholy. She accedes to his demand in 3.1 that she test Hamlet by pretending to pray, even though Polonius recognizes how deceitful the action is and says as much to her. When Hamlet sees her, she tries to carry out her part in the charade, but she somehow, unintentionally or not, gives it all away, and Hamlet becomes furious. He verbally attacks her so vehemently that she becomes extremely agitated after he leaves and shows that her own mind is beginning to crack. Still, in the Play Scene (3.2) she is able to respond to Hamlet with some equanimity and even engage in gentle repartee with him; she is not quite a wilting violet, though not quite as strong as Shakespeare's comic heroines or Cordelia in *King Lear*.

After Hamlet kills Polonius and Claudius sends the Prince to England, Ophelia goes mad. Her mad scene in 4.5 is filled with pathos. Her songs reflect the sexuality that she evidently has repressed but that her psychosis has released, especially since her erstwhile lover is guilty of killing her father. When she gives various herbs or flowers to those who behold her, she reveals a method to her own madness, reflecting the "happiness that madness hits on, which reason and sanity could not so prosperously be deliver'd of," as Polonius says of Hamlet in 2.2.209–211. That is especially true when she gives Laertes rosemary for remembrance and pansies for thoughts, and when she gives rue (an emblem of repentance) to Gertrude and a daisy (emblem of dissembling) to Claudius.

Ophelia's death by drowning is ambiguous, as Gertrude describes it at the end of 4.7. Gathering weeds to make a coronet and to hang on the boughs of a willow, Ophelia drops into the adjacent brook. She floats awhile chanting some old hymns, either unaware of her danger or feeling she is—like a mermaid or some other creature—part of the element, until her soaked clothing pulls her down under the water. The ambiguity of her death—accidental drowning or suicide—results in the abbreviated funeral rites that outrage her brother, Laertes. She is buried in hallowed ground only because the King and Queen have interceded. It is at the funeral that Gertrude says she had hoped that Ophelia would have married Hamlet (5.1.244), and it is there that Hamlet emerges and announces that he loved Ophelia more than any brother could.

Ophelia's death recalls Rosencrantz's lines at 3.3.11–23: that the "cess of majesty" is like "a massy wheel" to which "ten thousand lesser things are mortised and adjoined," and when it falls, they fall, too. The death of Old Hamlet, King of Denmark, has begun to take its toll—first, Polonius and his daughter, eventually the rest of his family, and finally the entire Danish royal line.

### Laertes

Laertes, the other member of Polonius's family and among the three young men whom Claudius addresses in his opening speech, has an important if secondary role in *Hamlet*. He appears partly to advance the action but also to contrast with the other two young men. Unlike Hamlet, who interrupts his studies at Wittenberg to attend his father's funeral and his mother's second wedding, Laertes has been away at Paris, to which he wants to return as soon as he can get permission from his father and from Claudius.

In 1.3 Laertes appears as a loving and concerned brother to Ophelia. He is worried about her romance with Hamlet and warns her about it. He specifically warns her that Hamlet may only be trifling with her, but in so doing he paints a portrait not so much of the Prince as perhaps himself. Laertes does not appear again until after Polonius is murdered; then Laertes returns, hellbent on revenge. Here again he contrasts with Hamlet, who has delayed his revenge for his father's murder and seems unable for various reasons to act effectively for two months after hearing about it. Unlike Hamlet, who has just as mighty a cause for revenge but proceeds with cautious deliberation, Laertes acts rashly; he brooks no delay.

He wants to kill Claudius, but Claudius is able to reason with Laertes and deflect his anger and desire for revenge toward Hamlet. Laertes is so incensed that he agrees with Claudius that "revenge should have no bounds" (4.7.128); he says he would cut Hamlet's throat even "i' the church" (4.7.126). In the event, Laertes begins to have some qualms of conscience. He finally does manage to wound Hamlet; but after Gertrude falls and he himself lies wounded by the poisoned rapier, he reveals the plot to Hamlet, who kills Claudius. Laertes then asks him to exchange forgiveness with him, and both die.

## Rosencrantz and Guildenstern

Claudius and Gertrude send for Rosencrantz and Guildenstern to come from Wittenberg, where they have been friends and fellow students with Hamlet, so that they may try to discover what ails the prince. They agree with alacrity, and their language demonstrates how servile to the King and Queen they are and will remain. Callow young men, they crudely try to probe Hamlet's thoughts, but they give themselves away and admit under Hamlet's questioning that they indeed have been sent for (2.2.252–292). After this confession Hamlet no longer trusts them and treats them contemptuously after the play within the play, accusing them of trying to play on him as they would on musical instruments, like the recorders (3.2.350–373).

Hamlet continues to treat them this way when Claudius sends them after him to find out where he has hidden Polonius's body. By this time Hamlet knows that he is being sent to England in their care, and he tells Gertrude that he will trust them as he would "adders fang'd" (3.4.203). He knows that they are a part of Claudius's plot to deal with him and takes some pleasure in contemplating how he will hoist them with their own petard and "blow them at the moon" (3.4.209). During the sea voyage, Hamlet uncovers the details of the plot by stealing the commission they carry while they are asleep. He switches their names with his, thus sending them to their deaths. When he tells Horatio all this in the last scene, he feels no remorse or guilt. As he says, they "did make love" to their employment by Claudius, and so "their defeat / Does by their own insinuation grow" (5.2.57, 58–59).

## Fortinbras

Fortinbras appears only twice in *Hamlet*, and then only briefly, but he is from the first scene onward a presence of some importance. Initially, he seems to be a hot-headed young man and, like Laertes, hellbent on revenge but with not nearly as much justification. According to Horatio (1.1.80–107), Hamlet's father, Old Hamlet, defeated Fortinbras's father, Old Fortinbras, in a duel, and by prior agreement, the loser forfeited with his life all the lands he had conquered. Now young Fortinbras, apparently sensing an opportune moment with the death of the Old King, has enlisted a band of desperadoes to reclaim the lands lost by his father. But before Fortinbras invades Denmark, Claudius sends Cornelius and Voltimand to speak with Fortinbras's uncle, Old Norway, to dissuade him from the invasion.

As a tribute to the young man's ability to listen to reason and obey his uncle, Fortinbras agrees to attack not the Danes but the Poles instead. He requests and receives permission to cross over Denmark peacefully for that purpose. Fortinbras is heard of no more until 4.4, when he appears leading his army across Denmark to fight for a small patch of ground that the Poles refuse to relinquish. When Hamlet learns of this impending exploit, he compares himself unfavorably with Fortinbras, the "delicate and tender prince, / Whose spirit with divine ambition [is] puff'd" (4.4.48–49). By contrast, he feels that he lets all "[e]xcitements" to his reason and passion lie sleeping (4.4.58).

Reasons such as these encourage Hamlet as he lies dying to support the candidacy of Fortinbras in the election of the next King of Denmark. When Fortinbras soon afterward enters, he in fact claims the throne, which lies vacant after the death of Claudius and Hamlet. In a way, he has earned the kingship by the example he has set as a reasonable but nonetheless brave young man. He is also a perceptive man, recognizing in the play's last speech that Hamlet "was likely . . . / To have prov'd most royal"; accordingly, he orders four captains to take Hamlet's body to the platform accompanied by "[t]he soldiers' music and the rite of war" (5.2.395–400).

## The Ghost of Hamlet's Father

The Ghost of Hamlet's father appears in only four scenes, and he speaks in just two. His appearance is so ambiguous that not only Hamlet but also generations of scholars have questioned his authenticity. Although Hamlet at first intuitively accepts the Ghost as "honest" (1.5.138), that is, both real and genuine, not a devil in disguise, after the young Prince has cooled down he has second thoughts. He feels he must have more conclusive evidence to endorse the Ghost's validity and his story of Old Hamlet's murder. Hamlet believes he gets that evidence from Claudius's reaction to "The Murder of Gonzago."

The Ghost is problematic in another way, too. While he commands Hamlet to take revenge, he does not spell out the kind of revenge he means. All he specifies is in the following charge:

> Let not the royal bed of Denmark be
> A couch for luxury and damned incest.
> But howsomever thou pursues this act,
> Taint not thy mind, nor let thy soul contrive
> Against thy mother aught. Leave her to heaven. (1.5.82–86)

He nowhere says "Kill Claudius!" although Hamlet assumes—as would most of a Shakespearean (or modern) audience—that the order to take revenge means just that. Shakespeare, however, was well aware of both state and clerical injunctions against personal vengeance. The Ghost's charge thus implicitly puts Hamlet into a double bind. How can he break up the royal bed of Denmark without morally tainting his mind and without enlisting his mother's aid?

The Ghost appears last in 3.4, the Closet Scene, when Hamlet gets increasingly agitated against his mother. The Ghost says he comes to whet Hamlet's appetite for revenge, even though Hamlet has just killed Polonius, mistaking him for Claudius. The real reason for his appearance in the scene, however, may be to intercede on Gertrude's behalf and to prevent Hamlet from getting further carried away and harming her. He thus appears to be a very considerate Ghost, if also a very puzzling one.

## DEVICES AND TECHNIQUES

*Hamlet* is rich in various kinds of imagery, for Shakespeare obviously thought in images. One of the many patterns of imagery is that relating to gardens, which Hamlet uses in his first soliloquy. Here he speaks of the "unweeded garden / That grows to seed" (1.2.135–136). The Ghost also uses similar imagery when he speaks to Hamlet (1.5.32–34). This imagery suggests that whereas Denmark once seemed Edenic, at least to Hamlet and his father, it is now quite otherwise. The use of garden imagery by both Hamlet and the Ghost further suggests the way they seem to be groping toward each other in act 1, culminating in their dialogue in the last scene of that act.

Another powerful image pattern centers on disease. Hamlet uses it when he addresses his mother in the Closet Scene, saying that her senses must be "apoplexed" to prefer Claudius to her first husband (3.4.73), and again describing Gertrude's rationalization about his madness as opposed to her sin. He tells her not to lay that excuse as a "flattering unction" to her soul since it will only "skin and film the ulcerous place" (3.4.145, 147). Claudius also uses disease imagery when he refers to Hamlet as the "hectic" in his blood (4.3.66), that is, a chronic fever that troubles him. England must cure him of it, he says, by executing the Prince, for "Diseases desperate grown / By desperate appliance are reliev'd, / Or not at all" (4.3.8–10). Earlier, when speaking with Rosencrantz and Guildenstern in 3.2, Hamlet says that Claudius's doctor should purge him of his "choler," not he, since his ministrations might plunge Claudius into far more anger (3.2.304–307).

Closely allied to disease imagery is the imagery of corruption. "Something is rotten in the state of Denmark," Marcellus says (1.4.90) when he sees Hamlet following the Ghost, and indeed it also appears that way to Hamlet. Laertes fears that Hamlet may corrupt his sister: "The canker galls the infants of the spring / Too oft before their buttons be disclos'd," he warns her, "And in the morn and liquid dew of youth / Contagious blastments [blights] are most imminent" (1.3.39–42). As he tries to pray (unsuccessfully), Claudius recognizes that his sin is "rank" and "smells to heaven" (3.3.36).

In some ways *Hamlet* is Shakespeare's most ambiguous play, and its abundance of wordplay is one indication of the prevailing ambiguity. Hamlet's opening lines are loaded with puns. When Claudius addresses him at 1.2.64, "But now, my cousin Hamlet, and my son—", Hamlet comments in an aside: "A little more than kin, and less than kind" (1.2.65), thereby using "kin" (relation, likeness) and "kind" (type, well-disposed) in various senses of the words. Claudius then completes his address, "How is it that the clouds still hang on you?", and Hamlet keeps on punning: "Not so my lord, I am too much in the sun" (1.2.66–67), playing on sun/son but also on the various meanings of the metaphor of being too much in the sun (that is, being in the "sun" of Claudius's good favor, being in the open, too gaudily dressed). Hamlet uses some of the more acceptable senses of the word as a verbal shield behind which he thrusts a more tendentious meaning.

Hamlet is not the only one adept at verbal ambiguity. When Claudius asks Hamlet to remain in Denmark instead of returning to Wittenberg, he says: "we beseech you bend you to remain" (1.2.115), where "bend" may have the sense of "beg" and "compel." Polonius, by contrast, is more obvious in his use of wordplay, and he is quite conscious of it: for example, he tells Gertrude at 2.2.96 that he uses no "art" at all, just after he has played on the word "mad" and otherwise engaged in verbal foolery. He is more sinister when talking with Ophelia in 1.3. When she innocently claims that Hamlet has made her some "tenders / Of his affection" (1.3.99–100), Polonius pounces on the word and warns her against tendering him a fool.

Shakespeare uses a variety of styles in *Hamlet*, in both prose and verse. While his major verse style is iambic pentameter, he also uses a more archaic verse form to set off the play within the play. "The Murder of Gonzago" is in rhymed couplets, a verse form used a generation earlier in plays like *Ralph Roister Doister* and *Gammer Gurton's Needle*. It is sometimes forgotten that Shakespeare was also a master of prose, and some of his best prose appears in the dialogue between Hamlet and the Gravedigger in 5.1. Ophelia uses prose in her mad scenes, but she also sings songs. Shakespeare may have borrowed some of these from old ballads, but he uses them effectively to convey what is in Ophelia's disturbed mind. Hamlet's letters to Horatio and Claudius are in prose, following the conventions that Shakespeare adopted, wherein madness and epistles were invariably in prose.

## THEMES AND MEANINGS

The most obvious theme that Shakespeare develops in *Hamlet* is revenge, which was a popular one during the last decade of the sixteenth century. But by the time Shakespeare wrote *Hamlet* at the end of that decade, he had begun to question revenge. While Hamlet's long delay in carrying out what the Ghost commands him to do follows a tradition of earlier revenge tragedies, Shakespeare treats the delay with a difference. It is occasioned, at least in part, by the curious nature of the Ghost's specific commands (see above). In the event, Hamlet violates both of the Ghost's negative injunctions—not to taint his mind and not to involve his mother—and it is only at the end, when his blood is up and Laertes informs him of Claudius's further villainy, that Hamlet kills Claudius. By that time Hamlet himself is dying, a sacrifice (as some might see it) to the code of revenge that Shakespeare has implicitly questioned in this tragedy.

Both church and state by this time had long opposed any kind of personal blood vengeance. St. Paul in Romans 12.19 wrote, "Dearly beloved, avenge not yourselves, but rather give place unto wrath: for it is written, Vengeance is mine, I will repay, saith the Lord." This is what the Bible taught and church ministers preached. State officials similarly opposed duels and all other forms of vengeful acts because of the civil disorder that inevitably results. Shakespeare had dramatized this problem vividly in the opening scene of *Romeo and Juliet*, written a few years before *Hamlet*, and it remained a serious issue for years afterward.

Not only Hamlet but also other characters raise the question of what is the noblest course of action a person should take, especially someone in the position that

Hamlet finds himself at the beginning of the play as well as later after he hears the Ghost's story. At first Hamlet recognizes that all is not well in Denmark, but he feels impotent to do anything about it (1.2.158–159). When he meets the Ghost, he receives further incitements to act and seems determined to carry out the Ghost's demand for revenge. But the question before Hamlet, as he articulates it in his famous "To be or not to be" soliloquy, is whether it is "nobler in the mind to suffer," that is, to exercise (Christian) forbearance, or "to take arms against a sea of troubles," that is, to act vigorously and oppose those afflictions (3.1.55–59). He does not resolve the dilemma in these terms but drifts off to contemplate suicide, which will end all problems, and then rejects it because of the uncertainty of what follows after death.

The Ghost also invokes nobility of mind when he speaks to Hamlet and refers to him as "thou noble youth" (1.5.38). Ophelia is more specific in her soliloquy after the Nunnery Scene when she begins, "O, what a noble mind is here o'erthrown!" (3.1.150). She recognizes in Hamlet "The courtier's, soldier's, scholar's, eye, tongue, sword, / The expectation and rose of the fair state" (3.1.151–152) and deplores his present condition. She empathizes with him completely: "I of ladies most deject and wretched, / . . . Now see that noble and most sovereign reason / Like sweet bells jangled out of tune and harsh" (3.1.155–158). Earlier, she refers to her own nobility of mind when returning Hamlet's gifts: "for to the noble mind," she says, "Rich gifts wax poor when givers prove unkind" (3.1.99–100).

In Hamlet's last soliloquy (4.4.32–66) his dilemma is just as acute as it was in his "To be or not to be" speech. Seeing Fortinbras lead his army over Denmark, he wonders (wrongly, since he has just killed Polonius, mistaking him for Claudius) whether it is "Bestial oblivion" or cowardice ("some craven scruple") that has occasioned his delay in executing his revenge against Claudius (4.4.40). He admires Fortinbras and his army for being willing to risk death by fighting over a worthless piece of land and concludes: "Rightly to be great / Is not to stir without great argument, / But greatly to find quarrel in a straw / When honor's at the stake" (4.4.53–56). He then compares himself—someone who has "a father killed, a mother stained, / . . . And let all sleep" (4.4.57–59)—with Fortinbras and his men. Implicit in his meditation is the question of his nobility of mind, his "godlike reason" (4.4.38) that he seems not to be using effectively to help him carry out his appointed task. In his great speech generalizing on "What a piece of work is a man," the first attribute that Hamlet cites is "how noble in reason" (2.2.303–304). At the end, as Hamlet dies, Horatio comments, "Now cracks a noble heart" (5.2.359); and Fortinbras, ordering his body taken to the stage, says that had he lived, Hamlet would have proved "most royal" (5.2.398).

Hamlet at the outset is convinced that his mother and Claudius have sinned deeply by getting married in what he regards as an incestuous union. This is precisely what the Ghost in 1.5 tells Hamlet to break up. Since the whole court appears to go along with Claudius's marriage as well as his claim to the throne (see below), the whole court is implicated in this sin. This may explain the dire consequences that Denmark suffers by the end of the play.

Claudius in the Prayer Scene realizes the nature of his sin. Referring to the murder of his brother, Old Hamlet, he says: "It hath the primal eldest curse upon't" (3.3.37), that is, the sin of Cain's murder of Abel in Genesis. Although he does not speak of his marriage as incestuous, he recognizes that a major motive in his crime is his desire to marry Gertrude. He also recognizes that to repent truly and sincerely, he must give up his crown, his ambition, and his queen. But he finds this impossible to do, so his attempt to pray, to repent, fails.

Under Hamlet's vigorous shriving in 3.4, Gertrude confesses that she has very black sins indeed. She is aghast when Hamlet indicates that he believes that she has been involved in the murder of Old Hamlet, and she is probably innocent of that crime. She may, however, be guilty of adultery, as both Hamlet and the Ghost believe, though she does not confess to it. After the Ghost appears to Hamlet and then disappears, she asks Hamlet what she should do, and he tells her not to consort with Claudius any more (3.4.181–196). Whether she does or not is not clear, but in the rest of the play an apparent coolness on her part toward her husband may be evident. How aware she is that the chalice is poisoned when she drinks from it in 5.2 is also unclear, but despite Claudius's warning not to drink, she goes ahead; as a result, she dies. Does she deliberately defy Claudius and take the poison to end her life, or is her death accidental?

After killing Polonius in 3.4, Hamlet at first dismisses the old man as a mere busybody, but later he reconsiders his action. He says, "For this same lord, / I do repent; but heaven hath pleased it so / To punish me with this, and this with me, / That I must be their scourge and minister" (3.4.172–175). Polonius is punished for his interference and eavesdropping, though death seems a disproportionate punishment for that sin. More significant is Hamlet's recognition that he is being punished by killing Polonius. But for what? For delaying in carrying out the Ghost's commands? For not killing Claudius when, a few moments earlier, he had the one chance so far to do so? Or for his wish to damn Claudius, as no true Christian should desire?

Laertes is punished for his nefarious scheme with Claudius to kill Hamlet in the duel in 5.2 by getting killed himself. After he confesses his sin to Hamlet, he asks him to exchange forgiveness with him, and Hamlet agrees (5.2.329–332). His sister Ophelia's death is more problematic. Does she commit suicide by drowning? Her death is sufficiently ambiguous as to make the priests question whether she should be buried in consecrated ground and to abbreviate the funeral rites, much to Laertes' outrage. Looked at from another standpoint, her death is one of those that occur to innocent victims caught in the kind of struggle in which Hamlet and Claudius are engaged. Similarly, Rosencrantz and Guildenstern are sent to their deaths by Hamlet, who feels no remorse, let alone repentance, for the deed. They have come "Between the pass and fell incensed points / Of mighty opposites" (5.2.61–62), as Hamlet says, and suffer accordingly. The reason that Hamlet feels neither remorse nor repentance is that they delighted in their employment by Claudius (5.2.57). But that he sends them to their deaths "Not shriving time allow'd" (5.2.47) suggests that Hamlet once again is acting in an un-Christian manner.

Christianity is very much an issue in this play. Hamlet invokes the "canon 'gainst self-slaughter" (1.2.132) in his very first soliloquy—the Christian injunction, that is, against suicide. Ophelia's burial is also presented in a Christian framework. When confronting his mother, Hamlet urges Gertrude to confess herself to heaven. Claudius himself recognizes the need for a proper repentance, which requires not only remorse but also surrender of the gains gotten from sin as well as the leading of a purer life henceforth. These are all references to Christian doctrine, as is Hamlet's own need to repent for the death of Polonius.

While politics is not a primary theme in *Hamlet*, it is definitely part of the complex fabric of this play. From the very beginning, politics enters when Horatio describes young Fortinbras's reasons for wanting to invade Denmark (1.1.80–107). Claudius deals with this problem, which turns out to be a kind of red herring in the drama, when he sends Voltimand and Cornelius to Norway. They are successful in their negotiations, as they report in 2.2; but by then problems of another kind, more internal to Denmark, have become Claudius's paramount concerns.

Shakespeare's audience might well wonder why Hamlet, the King's son, is not on the throne of Denmark instead of Claudius in 1.2. They would be thinking of the rule of primogeniture, which determined the line of succession and which Shakespeare had dramatized in previous plays, for example, *King Richard II* and *1 Henry IV*. Claudius wants to keep Hamlet in Elsinore so that he can keep an eye on him, probably suspecting that Hamlet has ambitions to seize the throne. From all of his soliloquies it appears that Hamlet has no such desire, though Rosencrantz and Guildenstern, directed by Claudius, try to find out otherwise. It is only later, when Hamlet taunts them in 3.2, that he says he lacks "advancement" (3.2.340) though how serious he is remains doubtful. In contrast, when in 5.2 he speaks with Horatio and lists all the injustices of which Claudius is guilty, he mentions that Claudius "Popp'd in between th' election and my hopes" (5.2.65). Hamlet refers to the Danish method of choosing their king and apparently regrets that he was not selected. But this admission comes very late in the play and is far less significant than the crimes Hamlet mentions first: Claudius's murder of his father and seduction of his mother.

Polonius also figures as a political animal in *Hamlet*, determined as he is to curry favor with the King and Queen by revealing the basis for Hamlet's melancholy in act 2. He sets the stage for the Nunnery Scene and later eavesdrops in the Closet Scene, determined to prove to the King and Queen that his theory of Hamlet's love madness is correct. For this act he pays with his life. Similarly, Rosencrantz and Guildenstern are only too eager to please Claudius, betraying their friendship with the Prince in the process. England figures in as a tribute-paying country that Claudius can command to act as he wishes and execute Hamlet, but Hamlet foils that attempt.

One aspect of politics in the play opposes Machiavellian politics (Claudius and Polonius) to anti-Machiavellian approaches to statecraft. Hamlet is far from the Machiavel that the King and his councilor appear to be. As Ophelia describes him in her monologue (3.1.150–161), he is the epitome of a Renaissance prince. As such, his character and actions derive from Castiglione's *The Courtier* rather than Machiavelli's *The Prince*. For example, Hamlet rejects "seeming" (1.2.76–78); he is much more a man of integrity. By contrast, Claudius seems to be the considerate stepfather as well as the efficient ruler of the kingdom, aided and abetted by similarly minded courtiers, Polonius in particular. He wants Hamlet to stop mourning for Old Hamlet and to think of him instead as his father; moreover, as part of his attempt to deflect Hamlet's hostility, Claudius proclaims him the immediate heir to the throne (1.2.106–112). Laertes, who might otherwise appear more like Hamlet, falls under Claudius's influence into Machiavellian scheming, as they plan the deceitful duel to dispose of Hamlet.

Shakespeare presents various kinds of love in *Hamlet*. Among them are a son's love for his mother and father, a parent's love for his or her child, a man's love for his wife, a young person's love for his or her sweetheart, and a man's love for his sister. The last named concerns Laertes' love for his sister, Ophelia. Laertes and Polonius warn her about Hamlet, and Polonius forbids her to have anything more to do with the Prince. Reluctantly, though she loves Hamlet deeply, Ophelia obeys. Her apparent rejection of Hamlet becomes one of the contributing causes of his melancholy, already afflicting him because of his beloved father's death and his mother's overhasty remarriage. Her actions reinforce his belief that "Frailty, thy name is woman!" (1.2.146).

Claudius sees Hamlet's love for his father, his prolonged and deep mourning after his death, as at once sick and unmanly (1.2.87–108). Claudius even goes so far as to maintain that Hamlet's mourning for his father "shows a will most incorrect to heaven," that is, a willingness not to accept heaven's decree (1.2.95). Hamlet rejects both Claudius's criticisms and his mother's, when she argues that "all that lives must die" and questions why it seems so "particular" with him (1.2.72, 75). In his rejoinder, he satirizes her use of the term "seems" and argues that his grief is far deeper than any apparent shows of mourning can suggest. In his first soliloquy after this dialogue and later in the Closet Scene, he compares his father with Claudius— "Hyperion to a satyr" (1.2.140, 3.4.53–65)—and criticizes his mother's failure to mourn her husband's death longer.

Hamlet loves his mother as well as his father; therefore, her quick remarriage to Claudius disturbs him deeply. That she loves her son is clear from the beginning when, worried over his state of mind, she begs him not to return to Wittenberg but to remain in Elsinore. She also shows her concern for him when she agrees to let Rosencrantz and Guildenstern, and then Polonius, try to find out what is so deeply troubling Hamlet that he acts as strangely as he does for two months following the events of act 1.

Apart from his desire for the crown, Claudius's love for Gertrude certainly is a main motive for his murder of Old Hamlet. Whether or not he engaged with her in an adulterous affair before the murder is, like so many things in *Hamlet*, ambiguous. Nevertheless, he shows how deeply he feels for her when he finds it impossible to repent in the Prayer Scene (3.3). He also reveals the depth of his passion for her in his dialogue with Laertes in 4.7. Laertes questions why he did not take swifter action against Hamlet, who he saw was dangerous, and Claudius replies that he was afraid of hurting Gertrude, who is deeply attached to her son; moreover, he maintains that "She is so conjunctive to my life and soul, / That, as the star moves not but in his sphere, / I could not but by her" (4.7.14–16).

The love Hamlet bears for Ophelia and she for him also forms part of this thematic development. That Ophelia loves Hamlet deeply is clear from her reluctance to give him up under her father's orders and later in her monologue as the Nunnery Scene ends. That Hamlet loves Ophelia is not as clear at first. His strange behavior in her chamber, which she reports to her father in 2.1, suggests that he is taking her rejection badly; and again in the Nunnery Scene, when she returns his gifts to her, he reacts violently against her. But at her funeral he declares he loved her more than forty thousand brothers and would undertake the outlandish deeds he mentions to prove that claim (5.1.269–284). Before his outburst, Gertrude confides that she had hoped Ophelia would have been Hamlet's wife. But whether Ophelia and Hamlet had an affair or engaged in sexual intercourse, as Kenneth

Branagh's 1996 film indicates, is by no means explicit anywhere in Shakespeare's text. (The Branagh production is available through Columbia Tri-Star Video.)

## CRITICAL CONTROVERSIES

Among the longstanding controversies concerning *Hamlet* is the nature of the Ghost. Is he a devil assuming the shape of Hamlet's dead father, or is he a valid spirit from the dead? The Ghost calls for revenge, and therefore he may be tempting Hamlet to commit a damnable crime in killing Claudius. Or if he is a devil, he may be tempting Hamlet to commit suicide, which is what Horatio fears at 1.4.69–78 when Hamlet first confronts the spirit. Although Hamlet's first reaction on hearing the Ghost's story is to believe he is "an honest ghost" (1.5.138), he later begins to have some doubts, notwithstanding the fact that the Ghost has not really commanded him to do anything damnable. On the contrary, the Ghost has only asked him to break up the King and Queen's incestuous union and in the process to be careful not to taint his mind or to proceed against his mother. Nowhere does he demand that Hamlet kill Claudius.

The Ghost is nevertheless ambiguous. He claims to come from where he must wait till his sins are all "burnt and purg'd away," obviously a reference to Purgatory (1.5.13). But Protestant Christianity, the official religion of Shakespeare's audience, rejects Purgatory as a Catholic notion. Moreover, Hamlet is from Wittenberg, Martin Luther's university, and hence linked to Protestantism. Finally, in his last appearance the Ghost says that he has come to "whet thy almost blunted purpose" (3.4.111), even though it is only moments since Hamlet has killed Polonius. Like much else in this play, the evidence regarding the nature of the Ghost is inconclusive. Hence, at least one critic (J. A. Bryant) has argued persuasively that this Ghost is neither good nor bad but ambiguous.

Another controversy focuses on Hamlet's duty to revenge. Some critics have maintained that Hamlet should confront Claudius publicly and denounce him for the criminal that he is. The problem is, of course, that Hamlet is thoroughly isolated—he lacks political support. It is clear from the beginning (1.2) that Claudius has cleverly manipulated the court to accept not only his ascent to the throne, but even his incestuous union with Gertrude. Hamlet hopes that he will not have to denounce Claudius or do anything at all; as he says in his soliloquy at the end of act 2, he hopes that "The Murder of Gonzago" will so stir Claudius's conscience that the King will be moved to confess his crime (2.2.588–594). Justice would then take its course naturally. But while Claudius is moved, even to the point of trying to pray for forgiveness in 3.3, he does not give himself away publicly.

More acutely, controversy centers over Hamlet's behavior in the Prayer Scene. Should not Hamlet have killed Claudius then and there? This is the only time in the play when they are alone together, and Hamlet gained enough evidence from Claudius's reaction a few moments earlier during "The Murder of Gonzago" to convince him that the Ghost was telling the truth. In killing Claudius, the regicide, fratricide, and incestuous husband, would he not be acting as heaven's avenger? He later recognizes, after killing Polonius, that he must be Denmark's "scourge and minister" (3.4.175). The Prayer Scene would have been the best chance for him to assume the role assigned to him by heaven and to execute revenge.

But, as other critics have noted, in 3.3 Hamlet does not see himself as heaven's scourge at all. Instead, he wants to kill Claudius not while he is at prayer and presumably in a state of grace; he wants to kill him when he can be sure the man will go straight to hell. Hamlet thus acts not as a true Christian, but as a killer lusting after revenge. In so doing, he may come close to damning himself, and his murder of Polonius in the following scene may be the punishment he accordingly receives.

Finally, perhaps Hamlet should do nothing at all. He himself contemplates this alternative at 3.1.55–57 and later more indirectly in his praise of Horatio (3.2.65–74). But Hamlet is an impulsive individual, unable like Horatio to balance "Fortune's buffets and rewards" with equanimity (3.2.67). Or what if, when he saw Claudius praying in 3.3—the same Claudius who pleads for some angel to "make assay" (3.3.69) and help him to repent (though Hamlet does not hear this plea)—Hamlet fell to his knees and prayed with him? This would seem to be what a truly pious Christian should do. But though he is mindful of the canons of Christian theology, Hamlet is also a man of passion. The action of a pious Christian requires the virtue of a saint, and Hamlet is not quite a saint. Therein lies his tragedy.

In his "dram of ev'l" speech (1.4.13–38), Hamlet discusses the nature of a tragic flaw without specifically naming it as such. He notes how "the stamp of one defect" (1.4.31) can bring down someone whose virtues otherwise may be "as pure as grace, / As infinite as man may undergo" (1.4.33–34). Critics have long argued over the nature of Hamlet's "one defect."

One way of regarding Hamlet's hamartia, or tragic flaw, is to see him as too determined to avenge his father's death. Another is to see Hamlet as he sees himself, as someone unlike Horatio, one who cannot properly balance passion and reason in himself. As the play repeatedly demonstrates, he oscillates from one extreme to the other, from impulsive action to hesitation and contemplation, and then back again. He finally is able to kill Claudius only when he is enraged and not he but Claudius has prepared the conditions for the end.

Yet another way of looking at Hamlet is to see him not as a man who could not make up his mind, but as a man so burdened with problems that he becomes paralyzed and cannot act to carry out the Ghost's problematic demands. His father has been murdered; his mother has remarried the murderer and may have been—or so Hamlet believes—an accomplice; all the nobility of Denmark have gone along with Claudius, making him King and accepting his incestuous union with Gertrude; and his sweetheart has refused to see him anymore. On top of all this, Hamlet is entirely alone, except for his confidant, the stoical Horatio. Even his former friends Rosencrantz and Guildenstern have betrayed him. Furthermore, he has only a Ghost's word for the story of his father's murder. No wonder Hamlet does not act, and when he does, he acts disastrously, initially killing the wrong man—his sweetheart's father.

## PRODUCTION HISTORY

*Hamlet* was doubtless a popular play from the very beginning. The title page of the first quarto comments on the play's success not only in London but even in the university towns of Cambridge and Oxford. The publication of Q2 the very next year further attests to the play's popularity. A German version of the play, *Der bestrafte Brudermord*, dating from the early eighteenth century, is probably based on the play that English actors touring the continent performed as early as 1603–1604. Many allusions to *Hamlet* occur in the dramatic and other literature of the time. The play was performed by an English crew off the coast of Sierra Leone in 1608, and the Pilgrim leader William Bradford quotes from it in his *Of Plymouth Plantation* (written 1630–1650).

While we do not know for certain who played all the parts in the first performances of *Hamlet* in London, Richard Burbage, as the company's leading actor, doubtless undertook the role of the Prince. Tradition holds that Shakespeare, still acting in the company at this time, played the Ghost. Many of the parts had to be doubled, of course, since the King's Men comprised only about a dozen shareholders and several boys. (Hired men played walk-ons or minor roles.) The actor who played Marcellus, for example, may also have played Voltimand in act 2 and Lucianus in act 3. Costumes were contemporary, and at the Globe few props were required and little scenery. The actors relied on natural light in the outdoor Globe Theatre. Characters entered and exited by one or the other of the stage doors, and the Ghost descended in 1.5 via a trapdoor and subsequently moved about under the stage. Action was swift, and no intervals separated the acts.

Much changed in the late seventeenth century after the Restoration of the monarchy in 1660. Charles returned from France, bringing with him French styles in acting as in much else. Women now performed women's roles, and indoor theaters were used, since all of the old structures, including the Globe, had been torn down after the closing of the theaters in 1642. Thomas Betterton assayed the role of Hamlet, and women played Gertrude and Ophelia. Candlelight illuminated the stage, which had begun to use some painted stage sets on movable panels. Scripts, based on the Folio text, were severely cut. The Players' Quarto of 1676 reveals the following omissions, among others: the roles of Voltimand and Cornelius in their entirety; the dialogue between Polonius and Reynaldo at the beginning of 2.1; Hamlet's advice to the players in 3.2; and all of the Fortinbras scene in 4.4. Laertes' advice to Ophelia was heavily curtailed along with Polonius's advice to his son in 1.3. Even Hamlet's soliloquy at the end of 2.2 was shortened and his last one, in 4.4, omitted; but the gravediggers were retained, possibly because their low comedy had become familiar and popular among audiences.

The eighteenth century was a period of great editorial activity, beginning with Nicholas Rowe's edition of 1709, based on the Fourth Folio. Lewis Theobald was the first to conflate the quarto version (Q2) with the Folio, giving a much longer play than was ever yet seen on the boards. It was not until 1899, in fact, that Sir Frank Benson produced this "unabridged" *Hamlet* at the Shakespeare Memorial Theatre in Stratford-upon-Avon. In the meantime, actor-managers did what they have always done: they adapted the play to suit their interpretation and/or the taste (as they perceived it) of their audience. In our time, only Kenneth Branagh has attempted to produce an unabridged *Hamlet* in his otherwise somewhat updated and refashioned film of the play.

In the eighteenth century David Garrick was the greatest Shakespearean actor of his time, and his Hamlet was the most notable. Aggressive action and passion characterized his representation of the role. By contrast, John Philip Kemble, who succeeded Garrick at the end of the century, was austere and grave. He dressed elegantly and performed accordingly. His was a "sweet" Hamlet as opposed to Garrick's "strong" one, to use Marvin Rosenberg's terms (95–96).

The nineteenth century sought historical accuracy, and with the improvement of technology, stage sets were far more elaborate than ever before. Scripts were cut to allow for the time needed to change sets. Among the great Hamlets of the period were Edmund Kean, Charles Macready, and Henry Irving, while in America Edwin Booth was the most famous Hamlet on record. Kean's Hamlet "exploded" on the stage in 1814 in his new interpretation of a grieved, wronged Prince, which not all critics approved. Macready was also passionate and used Hamlet's antic disposition to an extreme, but he lacked the inwardness we associate with the character. In America Edwin Forrest was famous in the role as a strong Hamlet; even though he recognized the "sweet and noble elements of the courtier," he could not subdue his natural disposition so as to reveal those aspects. Booth, in contrast, was "the slender, romantic, and nervous figure" that the great Italian actor, Salvini, admired and did his best to portray despite his huge size. (Quoted phrases are from Marvin Rosenberg, 97, 108.)

The greatest Hamlet of the nineteenth century was Henry Irving, who probed Hamlet's depth magnificently and easily captured the sympathy of the audience. Following Irving, Herbert Beerbohm Tree beautified the role, stressing what was soft and loving in Hamlet, whom he saw afflicted with an overactive intelligence. Johnston Forbes-Robertson was another "sweet" Hamlet, or, in his own words, "a philosopher with a great sense of humour, a poet, a dreamer, a lover, an affectionate friend, a gracious gentleman, but vague, weak, uncertain, vacillating, *impish* . . . but not mad." He could be, and was, at appropriate moments, however, filled with passion and energy.

The twentieth century saw many outstanding Hamlets, both on the stage and in films. Among them were John Gielgud, John Barrymore, Laurence Olivier, Michael Pennington, Derek Jacobi, David Warner, Mark Rylance, Kevin Kline, Mel Gibson, and Kenneth Branagh. Gielgud first played Hamlet in 1930, when he was twenty-five years old but looked like a teenager; hence, the Gravedigger's lines (5.1.143–148), which indicate that Hamlet is thirty years old, were altered to reflect his youthfulness. He played Hamlet several more times over the next fifteen years, with increasing maturity if less fire and freshness, as one reviewer commented and he himself admitted.

John Barrymore intellectualized Hamlet to some extent but with no loss of power and passion. His cry, "O vengeance!" bordered on the hysterical, as some thought, but his style was generally natural and effective. He tended to simplify the role rather than add to its complexity, and to this end he cut the text severely. He was one of the first actors, however, to suggest Hamlet's oedipal problem. At thirty, he was an attractive young man, well suited for the part, though except for playing Mercutio once and despite his success as Hamlet, he never attempted Shakespeare again.

Although he had played Hamlet on the stage, Laurence Olivier is best remembered for his 1948 film of the play. He rearranged the text, transposing many scenes, and eliminated minor roles, such as Voltimand and Cornelius, Fortinbras, and the First Gravedigger. Under the influence of Ernest Jones's *Hamlet and Oedipus* (1947), he emphasized Hamlet's oedipal problem, so that the Closet Scene (3.4) was played mainly on a bed in Gertrude's chamber. He used deep-focus black-and-white photography rather than technicolor, and the sets reflected the deep melancholy and moodiness of the prince. Olivier bleached his hair blonde, wore the customary black

Laurence Olivier as Hamlet in Olivier's 1948 film *Hamlet*. Courtesy of Photofest.

tights—costumes were Renaissance style—and acted with all the fire and passion of the thoroughly neurotic young man he portrayed. He had an experienced supporting cast, except for Jean Simmons; Ophelia was the first Shakespearean role she had ever attempted. Nevertheless, she captured the pathos of the character well enough. One interesting feature of the film was Olivier's use of insets to picture Hamlet's visit as Ophelia describes it in 2.1 and Hamlet's boarding of the pirate ship.

Many actors, young and not so young, followed after World War II in England, America, and throughout the world, as Shakespeare's plays became part of the world's dramatic literature. Gielgud directed Richard Burton in *Hamlet* in the centennial year 1964 in New York. The stage production was filmed and showed throughout the country on one day only and was not made available again. Hume Cronin played Polonius, and he, like the rest of the cast, appeared in rehearsal clothes. Burton kept the cast on their toes by refusing to reveal beforehand any of the several possible ways he would interpret a particular scene.

At Stratford-upon-Avon, Peter Hall directed twenty-four year-old David Warner in the Royal Shakespeare Company's production of *Hamlet* in 1965. Warner played Hamlet as a young college dropout, or hippie: this was, after all, the sixties, and the production attracted a good many young people who sympathized with the apathy and alienation Warner's Hamlet represented. Derek Jacobi's Hamlet for the British Broadcasting Company television series, by contrast, was again the Renaissance Prince. Michael Pennington in John Barton's Royal Shakespeare Company production in 1981 was a sweet but tortured soul. The staging was innovative, emphasizing the "actions that a man might play" (1.2.84); within the stage proper was a slightly raised platform on which the action took place, and alongside were suits of armor and other stage props emphasizing Barton's "production concept" for the play, or its self-reflexive aspects.

In America, the best Hamlet since Barrymore's was unquestionably Kevin Kline's, who performed in two different productions for the New York Shakespeare Festival. The second one he himself directed. The setting was very sparse and claustrophobic, which is how Hamlet seemed to feel in Kline's interpretation. Lines were very well spoken in American, not British accents. The production was filmed for television and is available on videotape. Zeffirelli's film, starring Mel Gibson, is also available on video. Gibson surprised many by his excellent portrayal of Hamlet as a deeply disturbed, angry young man. Glenn Close as Gertrude and Alan Bates as Claudius were well cast, but Zeffirelli so heavily cut the text that Bates had very few lines and appeared little more than a cardboard figure. Indeed, Zeffirelli's treatment of the text was the most problematic aspect of an otherwise fine film.

Kenneth Branagh's film, the uncut version, lasts a full four hours. It is set in the nineteenth century in a very palatial Elsinore (Blenheim Palace was used)—by no means the gloomy castle that Olivier's black-and-white film displayed. Branagh's set was in full color. But though Branagh retained a conflated text, he was not averse to tampering with it in other ways. For example, at the very end, instead of a peaceful Fortinbras entering to claim his right to the now empty Danish throne, Branagh staged a wholesale attack on the palace by the Norwegian army.

This brief and highly selective survey of productions shows something of the great variety of interpretations and representations that Shakespeare's great revenge tragedy can inspire. The text is so rich that it continues to reveal depths to actors and directors, as well as critics and scholars. The play fascinates audiences and readers alike, who continue to come to the theater and to the print editions to plumb those depths for the countless riches they may reveal.

## EXPLICATION OF KEY PASSAGES

**1.4.23–38. "So, oft it chances . . . his own scandal."** These lines (Q2 only, not in the First Folio) follow immediately after Hamlet lectures Horatio and Marcellus on the "heavy-headed revel" in which Claudius and the court are engaged (1.4.17). Excessive drinking is a vice that Hamlet deplores, because it detracts from all the virtues for which the Danish people are otherwise famous. From this macrocosm, he theorizes on the individual person who may also be blamed for a single fault, or shortcoming, no matter how fine he or she may be otherwise. The fault may be inherent ("some vicious mole of nature in them," 1.4.24) and grow to excess beyond reason's control; or it may be the result of a bad habit that likewise becomes excessive and permeates an otherwise pleasing personality. Whatever the case, the defect is what people notice and emphasize—regardless of the person's virtues, no matter how great he or she is—and criticize accordingly. This is Shakespeare's version of Aristotle's hamartia, or tragic flaw, which brings down the noble hero.

**1.5.82–88. "Let not . . . sting her."** These lines are the Ghost's specific commands to Hamlet after the general command to avenge his death. Note that the Ghost nowhere says, "Kill Claudius!" He wants the incestuous lovemaking between Claudius and Gertrude to stop, but he does not tell Hamlet how to accomplish this goal. He then gives Hamlet two negative injunctions: not to morally contaminate his mind and not to involve his mother. She is to be left to her own conscience, her sense of sin ("those thorns that in her bosom lodge" 1.5.87) and to heaven's justice. Hamlet will violate both of these injunctions in 3.3–4. Whether he succeeds in breaking up the incestuous union between Claudius and Gertrude is unclear. It depends in part on how Gertrude reacts to Hamlet's lines at 3.4.181–196, but the action of the play gives little indication of how successful Hamlet is.

**2.2.292–310. "My lord, . . . to say so."** This prose speech—and we need to remember that Shakespeare was one of the greatest prose writers as well as poets—comes at the end of Hamlet's first dialogue with Rosencrantz and Guildenstern. He recognizes why they were sent for, and by anticipating their explanation (that they are to probe the causes of Hamlet's melancholy) he gets them off the hook where Claudius is concerned. He admits his despondency but cannot explain its cause. In describing his symptoms, he pays tribute to the glory of creation and to human supremacy among all creatures. This is one of the finest encomiums ever penned and typical of Renaissance attitudes toward the nobility of human beings. The lines are also self-reflexive insofar as they may allude to the Globe Theatre, the underside of whose canopy, which overhung the thrust stage, was made to look like the heavens, painted blue and "fretted" with stars ("golden fire" 2.2.301).

The smiles that Hamlet sees crossing the faces of Rosencrantz and Guildenstern at the end of his speech, when he says, "Man delights not me" (2.2.309), lead directly into their announcement of the players' arrival in Elsinore and the next part of this portmanteau scene.

**2.2.452–497. " 'The rugged Pyrrhus . . . as to the fiends!' "** Hamlet begins these lines, quoting them from memory, which the First Player continues. They are significant insofar as they may indicate what Hamlet has been thinking about since he first heard the Ghost command him to take revenge. Pyrrhus, who was Achilles' son in the Greek story of the Trojan War, was also out to avenge his father's death. Hamlet may therefore be imagining himself as Pyrrhus, a part of him wishing he could be as ruthless as the Greek appears in this speech, covered with the "blood of fathers, mothers, daughters, sons" (2.2.458). The imagined parallel, and an anticipation of the action of 3.3, continues as Pyrrhus finds Priam, the Trojan King, but is unable at once to kill him with his sword. But the parallel breaks down insofar as the image of Priam resembles Old Hamlet more than it does Claudius. It thus gives some credence to critics who see an oedipal complex operating in Hamlet's inability to take immediate action against Claudius.

**3.1.55–87. "To be, or not to be, . . . name of action."** The first ten lines of Hamlet's most famous soliloquy have sometimes been misunderstood as a meditation on suicide. Hamlet begins, rather, contemplating the alternatives of action or forbearance. Only later does he think about the consequences of either alternative that might result in his death, and the thought of death leads him to contemplate suicide. From a Christian standpoint, death is not something "Devoutly to be wish'd" (3.1.63), far less is suicide. But the "canon 'gainst self-slaughter" (1.2.132) is not here (unlike his contemplation of suicide in his first soliloquy, 1.2.129–160) what prevents him from taking his own life; rather, it is "the dread of something after death" (3.1.77) that makes him hesitate. Hence, even though he recognizes the many evils that attend life, that fear of what will happen after death "Must give us pause" (3.1.67). When Hamlet says that "conscience does make cowards of us all" (3.1.82), he seems to sum up his own situation. By "conscience" he means both the modern definition and reflection. Either or both of these meanings indicate what keeps him from fulfilling his promise to the Ghost to "sweep to my revenge" (1.5.31).

**3.3.36–72. "O, my offense is rank, . . . All may be well."** Claudius's prayer, or his attempt to pray, for forgiveness is an excellent and unsentimental statement of his present condition. He knows very well what he has done: committed a murder equal to Cain's ("It hath the primal eldest curse upon't," 3.3.37). He would like to repent of his sin, but what holds him back is the knowledge that true repentance requires him to give up the effects he gained by that act. In Claudius's case, that means giving up the crown, his ambition, and his queen (3.3.55). Interestingly, "queen" comes at the end of the line and thereby gets the greatest emphasis, and we learn later on (4.7.11–16) how dear Gertrude is to Claudius. He therefore stands "like a man in double business bound" (3.3.41), unable to move in either direction. He knows very well that however it is on earth, where gold sometimes corrupts justice, it is not so in heaven. There the truth is absolutely clear, and sinners must give evidence regardless of their wish to hide their faults.

Nevertheless, Claudius decides to pray for pardon. He forces himself to kneel, to adopt the attitude of prayer, hoping some angel will come and help him to break free of the chains of guilt that have so far prevented him from sincere repentance. But no angel appears to assist him. Instead Hamlet enters, lusting after his uncle's damnation and sparing his life only out of fear that Claudius is in a state of grace. The irony of the situation, of course, as we learn at the end of the scene, is that Claudius has in fact been unsuccessful in his attempt to repent. As he says, "My words fly up, my thoughts remain below: / Words without thoughts never to heaven go" (3.3.97–98).

**3.4.140–52. "My pulse as yours . . . To make them ranker."** Hamlet speaks these lines to his mother after the Ghost has interceded to remind him of his "almost blunted purpose" (3.4.111) and to urge him to comfort Gertrude, who is confused by what is happening. Gertrude does not see the Ghost; therefore, she thinks her son is imagining things and is probably mad. Hamlet pleads with her to believe him and to attend carefully to what he says, for he is by no means mad and is willing to let her test him to prove his sanity. He asks her to follow a regimen of repentance: she should first confess her sins, sincerely repent them, and avoid sinning in the future. Using a garden metaphor, he begs her not to "spread the compost on the weeds" (3.4.151), that is, she should not continue to sin and thereby aggravate her fault.

Hamlet also uses a medical metaphor. He asks his mother not to let the assumption that he is mad serve as a kind of salve ("flattering unction," 3.4.145) to cover over her guilt, while her sinfulness continues to undermine her virtue like a disease and spreads the infection invisibly throughout her soul. The play does not make clear whether Gertrude follows Hamlet's advice.

**4.4.31–66. "How all occasions . . . be nothing worth!"** Hamlet speaks his last soliloquy just after he sees Fortinbras leading Norwegian troops across Denmark to attack Poland. He contemplates the nature of man and especially the function of reason, which he realizes must be used. But in using it to visualize the possible effects of an action, a person must be careful not to let "some craven scruple / Of thinking too precisely on th' event" (4.4.40–41) inhibit action. In other words, one must take chances and not be overly careful. Implicitly, that "conscience" (3.1.82) may be what Hamlet thinks has prevented him so far from taking effective action against Claudius. But he deceives himself in this, as he does later, when he says he has "will, and strength, and means / To" act (4.4.45–46). He certainly does not have either the strength or the means to do anything against Claudius in the present circumstances, as he is being led away by Rosencrantz and Guildenstern to a ship that is to carry him to England. And we might question his will as well.

Hamlet believes it is important to find "quarrel in a straw / When honor's at the stake" (4.4.55–56). He feels that he has "let all sleep" (4.4.59), but he has certainly not done so recently. He has put on a play designed to trap Claudius (which gave Agatha Christie the title for her long-running hit "The Mousetrap") and has killed Polonius, thinking him the King. He compares himself unfavorably, however, with the Norwegians who will fight for a small piece of land that is not very valuable, in fact too small to bury all those who will die in the encounter. He ends by promising himself that from now on his thoughts will be bloody, but that may be precisely his problem: his thoughts, like his image of Pyrrhus in 2.2, may be bloody enough, but his actions—except for killing Polonius—do not reflect his thoughts.

**5.2.209–224. "You will lose, . . . let be."** Hamlet has accepted the invitation to fence with Laertes and believes he will win "at the odds" (5.2.211–212), though Horatio is doubtful. (Exactly what these odds are [5.2.166–167] is unclear, though in the end they do not matter.) Hamlet has a presentiment, or foreboding, about the fencing match, but he tries to dismiss his fears. Horatio, however, takes them seriously and urges Hamlet not to go through with the match. But Hamlet is determined to "defy augury" (5.2.219). His justification is that he, like everyone else, is in the hand of providence. Alluding to scripture (Matthew 10:29), he argues that providence guides every living being, so why not him? Besides, what will happen, will happen. No one knows when his time has come; it will come when it will come. The important thing is to be ready.

What Hamlet means by "the readiness is all" (5.2.222) may be understood by Edgar's similar pronouncement in *King Lear*, when he counsels his despairing father, Gloucester: "Men must endure / Their going hence even as their coming hither, / Ripeness is all" (5.2.9–11). The important thing is "readiness" or "ripeness." If providence controls our destinies, then we must endure the time of our death even as we abide our being born. Providence, not man, determines the right time for our deaths. Hamlet has come to accept whatever providence has ordained and so has reached the enlightenment one expects of the tragic hero.

**Annotated Bibliography**

Bloom, Harold. *"Hamlet": Unlimited Poem*. New York: Riverside/Penguin, 2003. This small book is a supplement to what Bloom wrote in *Shakespeare: The Invention of the Human* (New York: Riverside Books, 1998). There the author spent too much time, he says, on the origins of the text and not its themes. About half of this little book is on the last act and its implications.

Fergusson, Francis. *The Idea of a Theater*. Princeton: Princeton UP, 1949. 98–142. The essay on *Hamlet* is one of the best ever written about the play. Among other subjects, it examines the structure of the tragedy and the evidence for Hamlet's oedipal conflict.

Frye, Roland Mushat. *The Renaissance "Hamlet": Issues and Responses in 1600*. Princeton: Princeton UP, 1984. Takes a historical approach to the play, trying to see *Hamlet* in the context of the audience for which it was first written. Discusses Elizabethan attitudes toward rebellion, revenge, the nature of ghosts, and so forth. Abundantly illustrated.

Greenblatt, Stephen. *"Hamlet" in Purgatory*. Princeton: Princeton UP, 2001. Explores the medieval origins of the concept of Purgatory and the Protestant rejection of it, with specific applications to our understanding of *Hamlet*.

Kastan, David Scott, ed. *Critical Essays on Shakespeare's "Hamlet."* New York: G. K. Hall, 1995. Contains many stimulating essays, including Stephen Booth's "On the Value of *Hamlet*" and Michael Goldman's "*Hamlet* and Our Problems."

King, Walter. *Hamlet's Search for Meaning*. Athens: U of Georgia P, 1982. As the title suggests, King discusses in great detail the philosophical aspects of the play in the light of Renaissance and modern philosophy.

Kitto, H.D.F. *Form and Meaning in Drama*. London: Methuen, 1956. 246–337. While a good part of the book is on Greek drama, Kitto spends a long chapter on *Hamlet* and its archetypal patterns.

Levin, Harry. *The Question of "Hamlet."* New York: Oxford UP, 1949. Examines the interrogatory nature of Shakespeare's play, which is filled with questions from its opening line.

Price, Joseph G., ed. *"Hamlet": Critical Essays*. New York: Garland, 1986. Contains many useful essays, including Fergusson's, parts of Kitto's and Levin's (see above), and a large number of historical accounts. Maynard Mack's "The World of *Hamlet*" is perhaps the best short discussion of the play.

Rosenberg, Marvin. *The Masks of "Hamlet."* Newark: U of Delaware P, 1992. This is the most extensive and detailed study of the play's stage history, with many insights into and interpretations of characters, scenes, and dramatic structure. Rosenberg displays an encyclopedic knowledge of productions of *Hamlet* all over the world and is especially good on the nineteenth and twentieth centuries.

# *Othello*

### Robert F. Willson Jr.

## PLOT SUMMARY

**1.1.** The tragedy of *Othello* begins in the middle of the night on a dark Venetian street in the midst of a conversation between Othello's ensign, Iago, and Iago's supposed friend Roderigo, a foolish, lustful fellow who desires to marry, or at least sleep with, the beautiful Desdemona, daughter to the respected senator Brabantio. Roderigo is angry with Iago, who has kept an important secret from him concerning the marriage of Desdemona and Othello, a Moor in service to Venice as a captain (or, in modern parlance, general) in the army. Iago explains to Roderigo that he is angry with Othello, who, despite Iago's long and loyal service to the Moor, has chosen as his lieutenant an inexperienced Florentine named Michael Cassio. When Roderigo commiserates with his friend, Iago declares that the decision only reflects the way of the world, according to which advancement depends more on influence than on loyalty. He will take his cue from such signs and in the future be true only to himself.

The two men decide to wake the sleeping Brabantio to warn him that Othello has stolen away his daughter and plans to marry her. The senator is at first angry about the disturbance, recognizing Roderigo as a suitor whom he and his daughter have rejected. When he discovers that Desdemona is not in her bed, however, his suspicions begin to increase, and he gradually loses control of his emotions, even theorizing that the Moor has used witchcraft to seduce his daughter. Iago proves effective in provoking Brabantio's fears by painting the verbal picture of his daughter in "the gross clasps of a lascivious Moor" (1.1.126). Now embracing Roderigo as his future son-in-law, the angry and frightened father heads into the night to apprehend his wayward daughter and her lover.

**1.2.** At the same time, the two-faced Iago rushes to Othello's side to warn him of Brabantio's intention to effect a divorce. Othello coolly dismisses the warning and proudly announces that his love for Desdemona is both just and unbending. Cassio and other officers arrive to announce that the Duke of Venice has sent for Othello on a matter of great urgency; they are followed by Brabantio, Roderigo, and others with their swords drawn. Othello tells his accusers to put up their swords, after which he calmly exits with them to attend the Duke and his council.

**1.3.** Before Othello and his party arrive at the council chamber, the Duke and his advisers are pondering a serious threat that the Islamic Turks pose to Christian Cyprus. The Duke plans to send troops there to defend the garrison and its citizens. When the angry Brabantio arrives to spit out his complaint against Othello, the Duke calls upon his captain to make his case. In an eloquent speech, Othello declares that his only offense is the marriage, which followed from a normal courtship conducted under Brabantio's own roof; he won the senator's daughter by telling her of his military exploits in plain, unadorned language. When Desdemona arrives to confirm her husband's story, arguing that she must naturally show the same love to Othello that Brabantio's wife showed him, her father relents, encouraged by the Duke to forgive and forget. Brabantio proves unable to overlook his hurt, however, and as the newlyweds leave for Cyprus (Othello will command the garrison), he warns Othello: "Look to her, Moor, if thou hast eyes to see. / She has deceiv'd her father, and may thee" (1.3.292–293). Othello's reply ominously foreshadows the play's subsequent events: "My life upon her faith!" (1.3.294).

Devastated by the marriage and his beloved's departure for Cyprus, Roderigo declares to Iago his intention to drown himself. In a mocking tone, Iago brushes away such suicidal notions and tells his friend that Desdemona will soon tire of her husband, giving them an opportunity to cuckold the Moor. Relying on Roderigo's funds, Iago promises he will work tirelessly to bring Desdemona and her suitor together. When a reinvigorated Roderigo leaves, Iago outlines for the audience his nascent plan, motivated by his hatred for Othello and a rumor that the Moor has slept with Iago's wife. He will begin by crafting rumors that Cassio is having an affair with Desdemona, thereby destroying all his victims in one ingenious scheme.

**2.1.** The scene shifts to Cyprus as certain gentlemen discuss the destructive force of a storm that has miraculously wrecked the Turkish fleet. Montano, who has been governing the island, greets Cassio, the first of the officers to arrive. As Cassio expresses concern for his captain's fate, a sail is spotted. Aboard this vessel are Desdemona, Iago, and Emilia (Iago's wife and attendant to Desdemona). While the party waits for Othello's arrival, they engage in humorous banter about how to go about praising a fair woman. Iago's bawdy joking and playful philosophizing reveal his sometimes too frank views on such topics; his intention seems to be to reinforce his reputation for being honest to a fault. In an aside, he also takes note of the affectionate way in which Cassio holds Desdemona's hand and how devotedly his kisses her fingers. These innocent gestures will later serve as "evidence" of intimacy when Iago begins to arouse suspicions in Othello.

Othello finally disembarks to the delight of the townspeople, and he embraces Desdemona with the passion of one who is both relieved and invigorated. As they head off to their quarters, Iago engages Roderigo in a scheme to damage Cassio's reputation by provoking a fight while the lieutenant mounts guard that night. He also asserts that Cassio and Desdemona are deeply involved in an affair, and that Desdemona will switch her affections to Roderigo when Cassio is out of the picture. When Roderigo leaves, Iago, alone on the stage, declares that he has a kind of love for Desdemona and repeats his suspicion that Othello has had sex with Emilia; in his warped mind, his vengeful act against Othello and Desdemona is justified as "wife for wife" (2.1.299).

**2.2.** A herald proclaims a celebration for the defeat of the Turks and Othello's marriage.

**2.3.** Entrusted with the duty of standing watch, Cassio at first refuses Iago's offer of drink at the festivities. But he finally gives in and soon is carousing with Iago and other officers. At Iago's direction, Roderigo picks a quarrel with Cassio, and the two begin a duel, which Montano tries to stop; enraged, Cassio not only beats Roderigo but wounds Montano. Suddenly an alarum bell is ringing, prompting Othello to rise from his bed to investigate the riot. After Iago is urged by Othello to give an honest account of what happened, the Moor decides to punish Cassio by removing him from the lieutenancy. In a state of utter despair Cassio turns to Iago to bemoan his demotion and the damage to his reputation. Feigning friendship, Iago urges him not to worry about his reputation, which he characterizes as "oft got without merit, and lost without deserving" (2.3.269–270) and to approach Desdemona with a request to help him regain Othello's trust. "Our general's wife is now the general" (2.3.314–315) is Iago's reassuring observation.

**3.1–3.** Emilia is enlisted by her husband to entreat Desdemona to meet with Cassio and pursue his case for reinstatement. Desdemona agrees and promises to press his suit every waking hour. Just as Cassio is leaving Desdemona, Iago and Othello enter. Iago hints that Cassio may be sneaking away to avoid being seen. When Desdemona begins vigorously defending Cassio and urging her husband to take him back, her honest but forceful entreaties are regarded suspiciously by Othello. Dropping hints that Cassio may have been wooing for himself when he brought messages to Desdemona from Othello, Iago begins to arouse the "green-ey'd monster" jealousy in his master's imagination (3.3.166). He repeats false beliefs about women's natures being changeable, reminds Othello that Desdemona deceived her father, and hints that Desdemona's only concern is keeping her deceit hidden. Believing blindly in Iago's honesty, Othello slowly begins to suspect his wife and urges his ensign to observe her closely for any signs of infidelity.

When Desdemona enters to call her husband to supper, he informs her he has a headache. She offers him a handkerchief embroidered with strawberries to bind his brows, but it is too small and Othello lets it drop to the floor as he leaves. Emilia takes up the handkerchief, the first gift that Othello gave Desdemona, because she recalls her husband's frequently asking her to steal it; she reluctantly gives it to him, after which he decides to place it in Cassio's lodging.

Angry and frustrated by his ensign's insinuations, Othello confronts him, demanding "ocular proof" that Desdemona is unfaithful (3.3.360). He threatens to kill Iago if the latter cannot prove his insinuations. Iago assumes the role of wounded innocence cursed by his innate habit of speaking only the truth. What evidence short of discovering Desdemona and Cassio in bed can he possibly deliver? But Iago reluctantly tells Othello that he overheard Cassio speaking these words in his sleep: "Sweet Desdemona, / Let us be wary, let us hide our loves" (3.3.419–420). The ensign elaborates by claiming that Cassio, believing in his dream that Iago was Desdemona, kissed him and laid his leg over his thigh. His final blow is to inform Othello that he saw Cassio with the handkerchief Othello had given to Desdemona.

Declaring that he is a man of resolve, never doubting himself once he has made a decision, Othello promises vengeance on both Cassio and his "strumpet" wife (4.2.81). He kneels to confirm this vow, and Iago kneels with him; as they rise, Iago promises to kill his "friend" Cassio (3.3.474) within three days as he receives from

Othello his new office of lieutenant. The Moor will find "some swift means of death / For the fair devil" (3.3.477–478).

**3.4.** When Othello encounters Desdemona, she vigorously implores her lord to reinstate Cassio. He demands instead that she produce the handkerchief; when she ignores his request, he stalks away. Emilia observes Othello's jealousy but does not mention her part in taking the handkerchief. When Cassio, at Iago's urging, again approaches Desdemona to seek her help, she tells him now is not the time to confront her angry lord. Nonetheless, she agrees to try one more time and departs with Emilia. Alone, Cassio encounters his mistress, Bianca, to whom he gives the handkerchief he has found in his rooms (where Iago planted it) so that she can embroider a copy before the owner advertises for it. Though suspicious, Bianca agrees to do so.

**4.1.** Iago has continued working on Othello's psyche to increase his jealous feelings. When he claims that he has heard Cassio boast about sleeping with Desdemona, the overwrought Othello falls into a kind of fit or trance, which Cassio observes when he enters. Iago makes Cassio temporarily withdraw. When Othello revives, he assures Iago he will watch the parties carefully and be sure of his wife's infidelity before acting.

Iago then arranges for Othello to spy on a conversation he has with Cassio. Iago tells Othello that they will talk of Cassio's affair with Desdemona, though in fact the subject of the discussion is Bianca. Othello naturally misconstrues Cassio's gestures and laughter.

Bianca appears, jealous because she is certain that the handkerchief Cassio gave her comes from another woman. She then exits angrily. Iago urges Cassio to go after her and calm her. After Cassio and Bianca leave, Othello steps out of hiding and restates his intention to "chop her [Desdemona] into messes" (4.1.200). Iago instead convinces him to strangle her in bed, the very bed she has "contaminated" (4.1.208).

As Iago and Othello are talking, Lodovico arrives from Venice with a letter from the Duke informing Othello that Cassio will replace him as governor. Now, in Othello's mind, Cassio has stolen his place in bed and in office. Desdemona, glad to be returning to Venice, expresses her happiness. But Othello believes that she is rejoicing over her lover Cassio's promotion. Losing control, Othello turns suddenly on Desdemona and strikes her, an act that so surprises Lodovico he declares it would not be believed in Venice.

**4.2.** As night approaches, Othello meets Emilia in one of the castle's rooms and demands that she tell him of any secret meetings between his wife and Cassio. Emilia protests that her mistress is utterly loyal to him; as she exits she declares that anyone who has called Desdemona unfaithful should be cursed. When Desdemona enters, her lord angrily challenges her to swear to her honesty. Bewildered by this assault, she denies his accusations, further enraging him. It is clear that Othello has already convicted her in his own mind and that he believes everyone is mocking him as a cuckold.

Near distraction herself, Desdemona turns to Iago for help in understanding her husband's threatening conduct and in winning his love again. Iago assures her that Othello is only distracted by affairs of state, but Emilia has no doubt he has been provoked to jealousy by some "eternal villain, / Some busy and insinuating rogue, / Some cogging, cozening slave, to get some office" (4.2.130–132). When the women leave, Roderigo confronts Iago, claiming he is fed up with being deceived and mis-led; now he plans to approach Desdemona himself to press his case. A desperate Iago informs Roderigo of the imminent departure of the Moor and his wife, who will only stay behind if some "accident" occurs to Cassio (4.2.226). To that end, he enlists his friend's help in hatching a plot to surprise and kill Cassio that very evening. Roderigo agrees.

**4.3.** That night after dinner, as Othello prepares to escort Lodovico to the Venetian's lodging, he instructs Desdemona to retire to their bedroom and dismiss her attendants. As Desdemona prepares for bed, she and Emilia talk. Desdemona sings a poignant song she learned from her maid named Barbary, who was forsaken by the man she loved; in the song the woman sheds tears and dies as she sits near a green willow, the symbol of unrequited love.

Desdemona and Emilia then speculate about what kind of woman would cheat on her husband. Emilia asserts that if the deed would advance her husband's fortunes she would not hesitate to sleep with another man. Besides, she observes, men feel free to engage in such illicit behavior without guilt; why should women not do so as well? By contrast, Desdemona states her unwillingness to do the deed for the whole world. As Desdemona retires, she expresses her fond hope that all will be well between her and Othello.

**5.1.** On a dark Cyprus street, Iago and Roderigo lie in wait for Cassio. When he arrives, Roderigo sets upon him but is instead wounded by Cassio's sword. Iago rushes forward, stabs Cassio in the leg, and quickly exits. Othello enters to observe the villains' handiwork. Mistakenly assuming that Cassio is dead, Othello then exits. Help arrives in the form of Lodovico and Gratiano. Seeing that Roderigo is still alive, Iago rushes to kill him before Roderigo can reveal the plot or demand restitution of all the money he has given Iago to give Desdemona. Cassio asks for Iago's help just as Bianca comes in to aid her lover; Iago immediately casts suspicion on her as someone involved in the attack on Cassio. Emilia then enters to be told what has happened and is urged by Iago to go inform Othello and Desdemona. The wounded Cassio is carried off in a chair.

**5.2.** Othello enters Desdemona's bedchamber with a candle and delivers a soliloquy in which he rationalizes the killing of his wife by claiming to be an impartial servant of Justice. Seeing her asleep, he yields to the impulse to give her one last kiss. When she wakes and sees Othello standing over her, she feebly attempts to defend herself as he accuses her of giving her body and the handkerchief to Cassio. She refuses to confess a sin she has not committed, urging him to ask Cassio if she gave him the token. He informs her that Iago has killed him. Desdemona begins to weep for him, thus further enraging Othello, who smothers her with a pillow.

Emilia now calls to Othello and pleads to speak with him. When she enters, she tells him that Roderigo is dead but that Cassio lives, news that prompts Othello to observe that "sweet revenge grows harsh" (5.2.116). Hearing Desdemona's last-breath claim that she has been falsely murdered, Emilia rushes to her lady's side in time to hear her accuse herself of her own murder. When Othello says that he killed her, defending his act by charging that "Cassio did top her" (5.2.136) and stating that Emilia's own husband told him, Emilia launches into a verbal attack on her master and her husband, showing no concern for her own safety.

When Iago and the others arrive to discover the body, Emilia confronts her lying husband and even in the face of his threats tells Othello that she stole the handkerchief and gave it not to Cassio but to her husband. Iago stabs Emilia and flees, but he is soon captured. As Othello seeks the motive for his ensign's designs against his life, Othello wounds Iago, who steadfastly refuses to explain his actions. So distraught is Othello that he characterizes Iago as the devil himself. Lodovico then orders Othello disarmed.

In response to Cassio's claim that he never gave Othello reason to suspect him, Othello asks his pardon but also questions how he got hold of the handkerchief. When Cassio tells him he found it in his room, Othello fully realizes how honest Emilia and Desdemona were and also what a fool he has been. The full extent of Iago's treachery is discovered by letters found by Lodivico in Roderigo's pocket. Turning to Othello, Lodovico informs him of the necessity of returning to Venice, but Othello asks for a moment to plead the case for his service to the state. He likens his distrust of Desdemona to the blindness of the "base Indian [who] threw a pearl away / Richer than all his tribe" (5.2.347–348). Then, surprising everyone, he produces yet another weapon, which he uses to stab himself. He dies kissing Desdemona. Lodovico speaks the final lines of the play, urging Cassio to punish Iago. Lodovico himself will return to Venice "and to the state / This heavy act with heavy heart relate" (5.2.370–371).

## PUBLICATION HISTORY

*Othello* was first performed at King James I's court on November 1, 1604, under the title "The Moor of Venis," according to the "Revels Accounts." Although we have no positive proof of its date of composition, most scholars concur that 1603 seems most likely. This places it after *Hamlet* and before *King Lear*; these plays and *Macbeth* comprise Shakespeare's brilliantly successful experiment with tragedies of evil. *Othello* was not published until six years after the playwright's death, but this circumstance was not unusual because a total of eighteen plays (about half) now assigned to him appeared in print only after his demise. The tragedy was entered in the Stationers' Register (which lists pending publications) on October 21, 1621, for Thomas Walkley and was published by Nicholas Okes the next year in quarto form. Quarto sheets were folded twice to make eight pages of about six-by-four inches on which to print. It was the typical size for publications of this type; all of Shakespeare's plays published in his lifetime appeared as quartos. It seems that Walkley owned the manuscript of the play and then paid Okes to publish numerous copies of it for sale in bookstalls located near St. Paul's Cathedral. One year later, *Othello* was included in the First Folio (printed on pages that were 13½ by 8¼ inches; folio sheets were folded once to create four printed pages). This was the earliest collection of Shakespeare's plays and was edited by two of his actor friends, John Heminge and Henry Condell.

The folio version of Othello has 160 more lines than appear in the quarto text. Many textual scholars believe that the quarto was set up from a transcription of a performance in provincial England, and that the folio is based on a copy of the first quarto with additional material taken from either Shakespeare's original manuscript (called foul papers) or the theater's promptbook. Promptbooks were complete copies of the plays used to help forgetful actors, who were given hand-written copies containing only their individual lines and cues. No contemporary promptbooks for Shakespeare's plays have survived.

Modern editors rely heavily on the First Folio version as their copy text, but there are some problems with that version. For example, some attempt has been made—perhaps by Shakespeare's colleagues?—to remove profanity from the play, and the compositor (typesetter) has committed several errors. The first quarto's readings are therefore preferable in some cases. Two later quartos (published in 1630 and 1655) and subsequent folios have no authority because they were printed from the earlier editions.

Still, there are relatively few textual problems. As already stated, the Folio editors sought to remove profanity. "God" is regularly replaced with "Heaven," and such oaths as "Zounds" ("God's wounds") and "'Sblood" ("God's blood") are simply deleted. Stage directions are entered at different points in some cases, a problem easily solved by following the dialogue clues. The most controversial reading occurs near the end of the tragedy when Othello is about to stab himself. Speaking to Lodovico and Gratiano, he asks them to report his career fairly to the Duke and Senate (5.2.348–366); if they do so, they must describe him as "one that loved not wisely but too well," who, "Like the base Indian, threw a pearl away / Richer than all his tribe." "Indian" is the reading from the quarto; the Folio version has "Judean." Many editors have struggled with the exact meaning of the hero's remark: Does he see himself as a savage unable to appreciate the value of a precious jewel? Or is he a pagan who, like Judas or Herod, destroyed an innocent person seeking to effect his salvation? Most modern editors opt for "Indian," following the lead of earlier textual scholars, such as George Lyman Kittredge, who argued that the reference to savages ignorant of the value of gems had become proverbial by 1603. If one reads the play as relying heavily on Christian imagery, however, Iago's betrayal of his master leads to the Christ-like sacrifice of Desdemona. Responsible editors will outline the controversy in considerable detail, leaving the matter up to the reader to decide.

## SOURCES FOR THE PLAY

Although Shakespeare had written a tragedy in which a Moor played an important villain's role (Aaron in *Titus Andronicus* [1594]), *Othello* was the first tragedy on the Elizabethan-Jacobean stage featuring a Moor as a tragic hero. For his source he turned to a collection of short stories, or novellas, by an Italian writer named C. B. Giraldi Cinthio; titled the *Hecatommithi* (one hundred stories) and published in 1565, the collection consists of tales teaching moral truths about domestic relationships. Many of these tales were based on true stories about the lives of prominent Italians. The seventh tale concerns a Moorish captain (he isn't named) who falls in love with a beautiful Venetian woman named Disdemona. She is attracted to him because of his *virtu*, an Italian term meaning strength of will, although her relatives had hoped she would marry someone else.

All is well until the Moor is ordered to Cyprus to defend the island against an expected attack by the Turks. While quartered there, the Moor's ensign becomes sexually fixated on Disdemona, who does not respond to his advances, a rejection that the ensign blames on her supposed affection for the squadron leader. Using innuendo and lies, the ensign suggests to the Moor that his wife is cuckolding him and that she is driven by weariness with their marriage. When the squadron leader is punished and demoted for fighting while on duty, Disdemona pleads with the

Moor to reinstate him. Her determined arguments make the Moor suspicious, and the ensign confirms these suspicions by claiming that the squadron leader has proudly told him of his "success" with Disdemona.

The ensign steals from Disdemona a keepsake handkerchief that the Moor has given her and leaves it in the squadron leader's rooms, later pointing out to the Moor the handkerchief in the squadron leader's possession to advance his plot with apparently irrefutable circumstantial evidence of the wife's infidelity. The Moor asks the ensign's help in killing both Disdemona and the squadron leader; they will surprise the latter on the street at night and stab him, then beat the former to death in her bed with a sock stuffed with sand, making her death look like an accident by pulling down the bedroom's ceiling on her body. After the murders, the Moor becomes grief-stricken at his loss while the ensign accuses him of killing both victims; although he refuses to confess, even after being tortured by his Venetian masters, the Moor is exiled and eventually murdered by members of Disdemona's family. The ensign escapes unscathed, but he is eventually tortured to death for his involvement in another, unrelated scheme. Following his death, his wife, who had been fearful about speaking out while her husband was alive (who can blame her!), relates the truth about the affair to all who will listen.

Shakespeare modifies this fascinating source story in several interesting ways, adapting a prose tale to the conventions of stage performance. He gives all of his characters names—Othello, Iago, Cassio—some of which have special significance: Iago is at one point compared to a dog by his accusers, a label that echoes the sound of his name; the two "o's" at the beginning and end of the hero's name seem to repeat the mournful sound associated with his fate. Shakespeare also invents characters not mentioned in Cinthio's tale: Brabantio, Desdemona's father; Roderigo, Iago's supposed friend and dupe; Bianca, the prostitute to whom Cassio gives the handkerchief to copy; and the minor but important nobles Gratiano and Lodovico, relatives to Brabantio, who come to Cyprus near the play's end and are shocked witnesses of the mayhem. He changes Iago's motive from revenge for rejection of his lust to revenge for being passed over for promotion, although it soon becomes clear that he hates Othello for no particular reason and is determined to destroy his and Desdemona's happiness. In Cinthio, the Iago character steals the handkerchief from Disdemona when she is playing distractedly with an infant; in Shakespeare, Emilia, Iago's wife and servant to Desdemona, picks it up when her mistress drops it and later gives it to Iago, who will turn it into so-called incriminating evidence. Emilia also plays a key role in the tragedy's ending when she accuses Iago of plotting the murderous plan and is stabbed by him for speaking out.

As for the deaths of Othello and Desdemona, Shakespeare creates more powerfully dramatic scenes than are found in his source. Instead of being bludgeoned to death with a sand-filled sock, Desdemona is suffocated in her bed by her blindly jealous husband, even after she denies vigorously any suggestion that she would ever deceive him. Making the scene more poignant is the playwright's decision to have the tragic heroine dressed in her wedding-night gown in order to win back the affection of her suspicious mate. By having Othello stab himself after discovering the truth, Shakespeare allows him a final moment of tragic power that gives the highly emotional drama a fitting ending. The diabolical Iago is arrested for his treachery but refuses to explain his motives or express remorse; he remains defiant to the end. Whereas in Cinthio's tale the fates of his characters exhibit God's rightful punishment for ambition and jealousy, Shakespeare avoids moralizing and instead focuses on the pathos that attends those who "lov'd not wisely but too well" (5.2.344).

## STRUCTURE AND PLOTTING

*Othello* is structured in five acts, following the model provided to Elizabethan-Jacobean dramatists by the Roman dramatist Seneca. The number of scenes in each act varies, depending on the entrances and exits of the characters or changes of location.

When the play begins, we are reminded early on that Venice is a highly civilized and cultured city whose government is run by wise, civic-minded men. As Brabantio puts it in 1.1.105–106, "This is Venice; / My house is not a grange" (isolated farmhouse). When news of the Turks' movements reach the Duke, who must decide whether to defend Cyprus or Rhodes, he sifts the messages carefully and rightly concludes that Cyprus is the more likely target. And when an emotional, distraught Brabantio tries to use his status as a senator to force the Duke to annul the marriage of Desdemona, the wise leader overrules him, observing after hearing everyone speak: "If virtue no delighted beauty lack, / Your son-in-law is far more fair than black" (1.3.289–290). There is no doubt as well that the Othello we are introduced to in Venice is a cool, calm, experienced leader; he would never indulge in the kind of witchcraft Brabantio accuses him of using on his daughter.

Even though Othello describes himself as rough of speech, his address to the Duke and senate exhibits the balanced elegance of a gifted public speaker. In every respect, then, Venice and Othello represent powerful reason in control of potentially destructive passion.

The voyage to Cyprus marks a significant change in locale and in the hero's behavior. Cyprus is an island, far away from the mainland; it is threatened not only by the elements but also by the forces of barbarism. It is an outpost ruled not by a duke and senators but by a single governor. Almost from the moment he arrives, Othello begins to lose control of his emotions, a change that later erodes law and order on the island. Cassio's drunken brawl is the first sign that soldierly discipline can no longer be maintained among Othello's troops. The ringing bell that wakes up the general seems to announce the widespread chaos and riot that undermine authority. Iago is, of course, the chief cause of this unruliness because Cyprus offers an environment in which his form of mischief making can flourish. Some critics have convincingly argued that he is, in fact, the Turk who has burrowed under the castle walls to practice his kind of paganism from within rather than without. It is ironic indeed that the visible pagan threat has been thwarted, but the invisible one has survived and is slowly but surely undermining Christian society. Passion, not reason, rules Cyprus, as can be seen not only in Othello's epileptic-like seizure but also in his blind acceptance of Iago's outrageous claims about Desdemona's honesty. The tragedy's plot can thus be described as a rapid movement from civilization to barbarism, Christianity to paganism, and reason to passion with the consequences represented in the hero's decline and fall. The terrible storm signals not only the revolt of nature but also a revolt of the passions; it foreshadows the fate of Othello and Desdemona by suggesting that though they have survived nature's tempest, they will soon enough "drown" in their own tempest-tossed "seas."

Accordingly, the unfolding tragedy achieves a level of tension that ascends until it reaches a climax late in the third act of the play. Here is the play's turning point, where the action changes direction in such a way that the hero's fate becomes inexorably determined. Othello's suspicions about Desdemona's loyalty are practically nonexistent as the action begins, but Iago manages to eat away at his confidence until by the end of act 3 he not only seeks the death of Cassio and Desdemona but the assistance of Iago. There is a moment of relief following this act, but the intensity reaches another high point when Othello strikes Desdemona in act 4. The final upswing in emotion and tension comes with his murder of Desdemona and his suicide.

Unlike *Hamlet* and *King Lear*, *Othello* features only one main plot: the love tragedy of Othello and Desdemona. There is no secondary or comic plot to relieve the pathos of the central story. As has also been noted, the location of the action moves from Venice to Cyprus, and these locations are bridged by the storm that separates Othello's fleet and destroys the Turkish armada. It is probable that Shakespeare intended to attach some symbolic significance to each place in *Othello*, especially considering the emotional shift in the hero's psyche.

Iago's role in the "plotting" of *Othello* cannot be overstated. From the beginning, he is in control of the audience, seeking its complicity in the schemes he will craft. His ingenuity and spontaneity keep our attention; he fascinates us because he seems to be making up the plot as he goes along. It is important to notice in this connection that every concerned character at some point comes to Iago for advice and counsel. Because this is so, he has access to intimate details about their lives that they would not divulge to anyone else. He uses this information not to aid but to destroy them, relying heavily on his reputation for honesty to gain their confidence. He could be described as the stage manager or prompter of the play, the only one with the full text in his possession. His creative, deviant mind can use even the smallest detail—a handkerchief, for instance—to achieve success. The rapid pace of the plot also guarantees that audiences will not have time to ponder its inconsistencies and improbabilities.

## MAIN CHARACTERS

The major characters of *Othello* are, of course, the title character, Iago, Desdemona, and Cassio. Brabantio and Roderigo play important but secondary roles. In creating Othello, Shakespeare had Cinthio's tale to work with, but he fashions a much more complex figure than the Moor in the Italian novella. As is true of other Shakespearean tragic heroes, Othello is an essentially good man in a position of authority (though not a prince or king, he is the commander of an army) whose character is marked or marred by a blind spot or moral flaw. His jealous rage destroys himself and his wife, but he seems predisposed to such feelings because of his career, personality, and social standing.

### Othello

Othello is a proven leader of men in the field, but early on in the play he admits to a lack of social graces and an inability to speak in the language of lovers or politicians (1.3.76–94). As a military man, moreover, he is accustomed to trusting implicitly those who serve him. Such loyalty unfortunately inclines him to believe anything that "honest Iago," as he is repeatedly called, might say. While this is an admirable trait in a general, such blind faith does not serve him well in domestic matters, where rumors and innuendoes must be carefully scrutinized. In addition, Othello's career has led him to believe in the vital importance of sound decision making; once an order has been given or infidelity has been discovered, he rejects any tendency to second-guess that order or discovery (3.3.176–192).

Shakespeare concentrates heavily on representing Othello as a man of great nobility who finds himself out of his element. Historically, Moors made their home in Spain and northern Africa during the Middle Ages, where they developed an advanced culture based on their religion and military prowess. In 1492, King Ferdinand and Queen Isabella undertook a project to Christianize Spain and ordered that Moors, Jews, and other minorities must convert or leave the country. Many Moors who decided to leave settled in Italy, where their military expertise was welcomed by city-states like Florence, Milan, and Venice. They soon found themselves in charge of mercenary armies that were hired to advance the interests of these city-states. Yet while the Moorish captains and generals occupied an important place in these city-states, they were still considered outsiders by the native population. When Othello receives word in act 5 that he is being replaced by Cassio as governor of Cyprus, the news only seems to exacerbate his feeling of alienation from his European "masters."

Even though Shakespeare makes the daring decision to feature Othello as a tragic hero—Moors, such as his Aaron from *Titus Andronicus*, were usually depicted as caricatures or villains—he nonetheless sensationalizes his fall by relying on the stereotyped belief that Moors were unable to control their passions. Othello's blind rage precipitates his trance in 4.1, a state that seems to demonstrate a kind of destructive barbarism barely kept in check by the restraints of civilization. When he confronts Desdemona in her bedchamber, his fearful determination and his unwillingness to consider her denials act as further proofs of his decline into a beast-like avenger. This condition qualifies his status as tragic hero, as does his readiness to believe anything Iago tells him; given that Iago tries to shape our opinion of the hero as an easily duped fool, the audience must struggle to sympathize with his suffering.

Yet Shakespeare strives to depict Othello as one whose character changes radically over the course of the play. His self-control and temperate behavior when confronted by Brabantio underscore the qualities we associate with someone who must lead. The respect shown him by the Duke and the devotion demonstrated by Cassio point to a man whose reputation is firmly established. Shakespeare likens his state of mind to a calm sea not easily disturbed by storms or tempests. On Cyprus, however, he becomes an endangered island in the midst of a violent storm of passion; unable to hold back the waves of jealousy, he is inundated by those passions and eventually drowns. As he tells Iago in 3.3.453–460, his bloody thoughts are like the unstoppable current of the Pontic Sea that shall "nev'r ebb to humble love, / Till that a capable and wide revenge / Swallow them up."

As these lines show, despite his claim that he is "rude of speech," he regularly expresses his feelings in powerful poetic form. He obviously displayed that ability during his wooing of Desdemona, who admits to falling in love with him because of the vivid and moving way he described his adventures as a warrior. His lyrical, even hyperbolic greeting of Desdemona when he arrives on Cyprus also reveals a poetic soul (2.1.183–193). His deeply felt joy is richly conveyed here, again through sea imagery, but the speech is also pivotal because of its unintended note of prophecy: "My soul hath her content so absolute / That not another comfort like to this / Succeeds in unknown fate" (2.1.191–193). Othello's corrosive jealousy will soon make this the last moment of unadulterated love between them.

### Iago

Iago is without doubt one of Shakespeare's most fascinating villains. The playwright took Cinthio's ensign as his model, but as was the case with Othello, Shakespeare filled out the character with compelling and complex details. Iago relies heavily on what today might be called psychological disguise to achieve his ends; so successful is he in his disguise that everyone in the play—including his wife—regards him as "honest Iago." In the play's first scene, however, he confesses to the audience: "I am not what I am" (1.1.65). This statement inverts the definition of God in Exodus, that is, "I am what I am." Iago may thus be understood as God's antithesis, the devil (or the principle of evil). His deception recalls that of earlier villains, such as Aaron in *Titus Andronicus* and Richard Gloucester in *Richard III*. By sharing his thoughts and schemes with the audience, he involves us in his plotting and encourages us to view Othello and the others as he does: as fools. His wit and ingenuity make him irresistible, thus posing a critical problem for audiences aware at the same time of his murderous intentions.

His ostensible reason for disguising his intentions is to gain revenge against Othello for being passed over for promotion to lieutenant. He complains to Roderigo in the opening scene that Cassio, a bookish Florentine, got the position because he had well-placed friends who unduly influenced Othello's decision. At the outset, then, Iago tries to represent himself as the underdog whose faithful service and experience have been devalued. While he later offers other reasons for revenge—Othello has supposedly slept with Iago's wife; Iago lusts after Desdemona; and so forth—Iago emerges as one who hates the fact that Othello and Desdemona are happy and enjoys doing evil for its own sake. Given this characteristic along with his comic wit and his skill as a deceiver, many critics have argued that he is based on the Vice of medieval morality plays. It was Vice's job to tempt characters like Mankind to forgo virtuous deeds and to embrace worldly delights; his relationship with Roderigo, from whom he takes money and valuables supposedly to win Roderigo's favor with Desdemona, resembles that between Vice and the heroes in morality plays.

He is also like Vice in his utter contempt for the values that hold civilization together. Even though he plays the role of friend with Roderigo, Cassio, Othello, and even Desdemona, he clearly has contempt for anyone who does not place selfish personal desires first. Thus, he is constitutionally unable to be anyone's friend, even though he plays the part with ease. He also holds love to be nothing more than "a lust of the blood and a permission of the will" (1.3.334–335). He cannot understand the great love that Othello and Desdemona share, nor can he imagine that anyone would sacrifice himself for love. As for reputation, he makes his views clear to Cassio when the former lieutenant comes to him to bemoan the loss of that virtue: "Reputation is an idle and most false imposition; oft got without merit, and lost without deserving. You have lost no reputation at all, unless you repute yourself such a loser" (2.3.268–271).

The irony in this claim is that Iago relies heavily on his own reputation for honesty to bring about the tragedy. This paradox is regularly reinforced in his seeming friendships with others. He has promised the rich Roderigo, who is blinded by desire for Desdemona, to work tirelessly to bring the two together. Even though this scheme does not seem to be succeeding, Roderigo continues to believe in Iago's abilities and continues to fill his purse. Only near the play's end, when Roderigo receives the final wound from Iago's sword, does he fully realize he has been duped. Iago has kept him around just to use him at the right moment in his plot against Cassio, and he apparently enjoys keeping Roderigo from killing himself and helping him sail from Venice to Cyprus in pursuit of his beloved. One might say that Iago rehearses his techniques of deception on Roderigo, the least intelligent of his victims; he is a diversion for the villain, who needs to be amused while hatching larger schemes.

Cassio proves an easy target because of his naive personality makeup and his good looks. Iago seems jealous of Cassio's attractiveness, which he sees as another reason he was chosen for the lieutenancy. Part of Iago's profile as a plain-spoken, truth-telling fellow is based on his cool understanding of the way of the world, something the outsider Othello believes he himself lacks. When a devastated Cassio comes to Iago to complain of his loss of position and reputation, Iago not only consoles him but even urges him to regain his place by working through Desdemona. He takes advantage of his friend's trust to further trap him in the web of his plot; here Iago is the spider and Cassio is the fly.

Iago's relationships with Emilia and Desdemona likewise depend on his reputation for honesty. He sees Emilia as his servant, a good wife who will do his bidding without question or argument. She steals the handkerchief for him and remains silent when Othello rages about its loss. It seems amazing and improbable that she could live with Iago for years and never glimpse the diabolical figure he is. When Iago stabs her in the back at play's end, he demonstrates contempt for yet another custom—marriage—held dear by society. It is ironic, however, that the woman from whom he expected total obedience was in the end the one who violated his trust and accused him of treachery.

Given his inclination toward jealousy, it is surprising that Othello never seems to have noticed that Iago and Desdemona sailed to Cyprus on the same ship. If anyone had the opportunity to cuckold the Moor during the voyage, it was his ensign. Desdemona likewise never seems to question Iago's honesty; she even turns to him after Othello strikes her to seek his aid in winning back her lord. He consoles her and dismisses Othello's behavior as resulting from the "business of the state" (4.2.166) with which he must concern himself.

Iago's relationship with Othello is the central one in the tragedy. The Moor relies on him as both friend and soldier, and it is clear that Iago has worked tirelessly to build his reputation for honesty with his general. Even though Iago uses Roderigo to provoke the quarrel that gets Cassio dismissed, Iago is, ironically, the one that Othello calls on to give an honest account of the fight. In 3.3, the play's turning point, Iago uses Cassio's sudden departure from Desdemona to suggest that the two had been meeting as lovers. Once the seed is planted, Iago works like a careful gardener watering and feeding Othello's jealousy with the story about Cassio's kissing him in his sleep and wiping his beard with the fateful handkerchief. All the time, Iago behaves as the reluctant witness, cursing his honesty, wishing he could lie to protect his "friend" Cassio and the beautiful Desdemona. This performance makes him even more convincing to Othello, who believes he must threaten Iago with bodily harm to hear what prove to be nothing more than bold-faced lies. At the close of 3.3, Iago not only has persuaded Othello of the necessity of murdering the "lovers" but also has attained the lieutenancy he complained about losing at the play's opening. However, it is clear at this point that the appointment was never his main goal. Now he has become his captain's captain as he directs the final movement of the tragedy.

When Othello finally acknowledges Iago's guilt, Othello attempts to kill him. Before striking him, Othello declares, "I look down towards his feet; but that's a fable. / If that thou be'st a devil, I cannot kill thee" (5.2.286–287). Satan's feet were thought to be cloven, a belief that Othello alludes to in his remark, and this reference reinforces the impression that Iago, like Satan, commits evil acts solely for the sake of evil. That he escapes death in the finale has concerned many critics who feel the play lacks a moral message because the villain goes unpunished. Others have argued that Iago's plot is so diabolic that he could not explain or justify it in any believable way; a confession would therefore be improbable. Though he is called a "Spartan dog" by Lodovico (5.2.361), an epithet suggesting both ferocity and inhuman coldness, to modern audiences Iago's personality more closely resembles that of the sociopath. His final, defiant words could have been spoken by John F. Kennedy's assasin, Lee Harvey Oswald, or James Earl Ray, the killer of Martin Luther King Jr.: "Demand me nothing; what you know, you know: / From this time forth I never will speak word" (5.2.303–304). Like the devil or the principle of evil, he can be wounded "but not kill'd" (5.2.288).

## Desdemona

The only character in Cinthio's tale to be given a proper name (spelled "Disdemona" in Cinthio), the play's tragic heroine is something of a puzzle. Her behavior throughout exhibits many admirable traits: loyalty, trust, friendship, honesty, even wisdom. At the same time, her naïveté about the way of the world and her blind faith in others suggest an immaturity that is not commensurate with her bold decision to marry a Moor. She appears to be the model of a hopeless romantic when Othello describes her reaction to his accounts of his adventures:

> My story being done,
> She gave me for my pains a world of sighs;
> She swore, in faith 'twas strange, 'twas passing strange;
> 'Twas pitiful, 'twas wondrous pitiful. . . .
>     She thank'd me,
> And bade me, if I had a friend that lov'd her,
> I should but teach him how to tell my story,
> And that would woo her. (1.3.158–161; 163–166)

This schoolgirl-like behavior does not square, however, with the confident, wise argument she offers to her father later in the scene, when he asks her to choose between him and Othello (1.3.181–188). Shakespeare seems to be saying here that hero and heroine, at least in the play's opening, display similar insight into their feelings for one another. Despite their differences in age, social standing, and color, they are a noble match indeed, something the Duke clearly sees and embraces. It requires Iago's diabolical scheming to destroy that love, which otherwise, Shakespeare implies, would have grown and prospered.

Indeed, many critics who identify the Iago-Satan connection suggest that *Othello* is a heavily allegorical play, with Othello and Desdemona representing Adam and Eve. The suggestion that their story is a version of the fall from Paradise is a tempting one, but it clearly oversimplifies this richly psychological tragedy. For example, Desdemona remains innocent of any deception throughout; any idea of deceiving her lord would never enter her head. This fact becomes clear in her conversation with Emilia shortly before her death. She tells Emilia that she would not betray her husband even to gain the whole world, clearly echoing the biblical passage about gaining the world but losing one's soul.

The key to understanding Desdemona's character hinges on Shakespeare's use of the word "honest." To his audience, the word meant truth-telling, but it also referred to a wife's "honesty" or loyalty to her husband; a "dishonest" wife was one who had an affair, thereby cuckolding her husband. Cuckolds were depicted in drawings and paintings throughout Renaissance Europe, and they were typically pictured wearing elk horns and being pointed at behind their backs by chuckling citizens. The point of the joke was that others can see the horns but the cuckold cannot, just as he cannot see—but everyone else can—his wife's cheating on him. Once Othello believes his wife has been "dishonest" with Cassio, he almost immediately believes that he is a cuckold. This point is confirmed in 3.3 when Othello, troubled by Iago's insinuations, tells Desdemona he has a "pain upon [his] forehead" (3.3.284), and she offers her handkerchief to bind it as a cure. The audience would know immediately that Othello's pain was caused by the growing horns of the cuckold.

Much of Desdemona's character and dilemma are revealed as she tries to help her husband—a gesture of love and selflessness that causes her to drop the very handkerchief that will convict her. Once Othello believes she is disloyal, her beauty and selflessness immediately become in his mind a disguise intended to keep him from suspecting her dishonesty. Indeed, all of her virtues are suddenly transformed into vices in his eyes. Her unflinching effort to have Cassio reappointed, for instance, only proves to Othello that she is trying to help her lover. By reminding her husband that it was his friend Cassio who came to woo her for him, she only persuades Othello that Cassio was in fact wooing her for himself on those occasions. Her utter shock and disbelief at his behavior over the lost handkerchief and his striking her in public are signs to Othello that she is simply covering up her sins. The central irony of the tragedy is that "honest Iago" works assiduously to hide the truth yet is consistently believed, while Desdemona's inability to lie and her loyalty to her friends and her lord are seen by Othello as lies for which he punishes her by death.

In Desdemona's relationship with Emilia, Shakespeare creates a parallel to and contrast with that between Othello and Iago. Both Iago and Emila are trusted confidants, a condition that allows Othello and Desdemona to unburden their hearts to them. But while Emilia keeps her mistress's trust, Iago uses anything his lord tells him to weave his web of deceit. Even though Emilia does not tell Othello about the handkerchief until it is too late—perhaps because her husband has threatened her—she remains loyal to the end; by contrast, Iago is disloyal from the beginning. In an act of heroic loyalty and selflessness, Emilia accuses her husband in the final scene and is rewarded with death; both wives are murdered for their honesty. That Desdemona inspires such loyalty in her attendant is further evidence of the essential goodness of her character.

Desdemona's unwillingness to accuse her husband on her deathbed has disturbed many feminist critics. She remains loyal to him even after she has no reason to love or respect him. When asked by Emilia who has smothered her, Desdemona declares: "Nobody; I myself. Farewell! / Commend me to my kind lord. O, farewell!" (5.2.124–125). Such a statement sounds to many modern ears as if it is yet another example of the woman-victim blaming herself for her husband's cruelty. If this is an attempt by Shakespeare to idealize his heroine by making her an icon of constancy, it also denies her any opportunity to acknowledge and exhibit her individual suffering and outrage. Like so much else about Desdemona, her final words offer a puzzle that both perplexes and fascinates.

### Brabantio

The roles of lesser characters like Brabantio, Roderigo, and Cassio seem intended, like the role of Emilia, as mirrors for the main characters. Brabantio, like Othello, is duped into believing that Desdemona is deceitful; like Othello, his pride leads him to disown her. Both men allow passion to blind their reason. When Brabantio warns Othello about Desdemona before they leave for Cyprus, he plants the seed of doubt in the Moor's mind just as a father might pass on a piece of wisdom to his son: "Look to her, Moor, if thou hast eyes to see; / She has deceiv'd her father, and may thee" (1.3.292–293).

### Roderigo

Roderigo, too, mirrors elements of Othello's character, especially in his gullibility and unquestioning faith in Iago. Both men are in love with Desdemona, but Roderigo's passion is more lustful and mundane than Othello's. Like the puppeteer, Iago holds the strings to both of these "puppets," making them do his bidding throughout and finally bringing about their deaths.

### Cassio

Like Desdemona, Cassio proves loyal to Othello throughout; his concern for his loss of reputation is as acute as Desdemona's concern over the loss of her lord's affection. Both are objects of Iago's treachery because they possess a kind of innocence and beauty that he lacks. Cassio's survival and appointment to the governorship of Cyprus signal the triumph of virtue over vice and the return to honest, principled leadership.

## DEVICES AND TECHNIQUES

To reinforce Iago's vision of men as beasts, Shakespeare uses animal imagery throughout the play. In the opening scene, the ensign shouts up to Brabantio that "an old black ram / Is tupping your white ewe" (1.1.88–89), a particularly disgusting vision of Othello and Desdemona's having sex. The citizens Iago tells the senator to wake up are described as "snorting" in their sleep (1.1.90). In response to Roderigo's claim that he intends to drown himself for love of Desdemona, Iago declares: "Ere I would say I would drown myself for the love of a guinea hen, I would change my humanity with a baboon" (1.3.314–316). Showing contempt for Othello's trustfulness, he observes:

> The Moor is of a free and open nature,
> That thinks men honest that but seem to be so,
> And will as tenderly be led by th' nose
> As asses are. (1.3.399–402)

Othello's transformation under Iago's spell is evident in 3.3. As soon as Iago departs, Othello remarks, "If I do prove her haggard, / Though her jesses were my dear heart-strings, / I'ld whistle her off" (3.3.260–262). His imagery here is drawn from falconry, indicating that he already sees Desdemona as something less than human. It is also a sign that Othello himself has fallen into the realm of the beasts where the monster jealousy rules.

In the following act Othello again sounds much like Iago when he speaks of Desdemona as "a cistern for foul toads / To knot and gender in!" (4.2.61–62) and likens her to "summer flies . . . in the shambles, / That quicken even with blowing" (4.2.66–67). Othello's use of animal imagery shows that he has come to accept Iago's dim view of humanity and his belief that people are driven solely by their sensual desires, just as animals are. Hence he can readily believe that Desdemona has cuckolded him to satisfy the lust he now thinks governs everyone.

In the opening of the play Iago tells Roderigo that Othello is lodging at an inn called the Sagittary (1.1.158). No inn of that name existed in Shakespeare's London or in Venice: it is Shakespeare's invention. Sagittarius is, of course, a centaur: half man, half horse. This is a fitting image of people, who combine the spiritual and the earthly. This view goes back at least to Plato, who imagines the soul as a charioteer trying to govern two horses (that is, desires): one pulling upward, the other downward. Othello must decide which he thinks prevails, and to do so he must choose between the earthly, animalistic Iago and the divine Desdemona.

The difficulty of deciding is accented by the prevalence of darkness in the play, much of which takes place at night. The clarity of daylight is largely absent, and this ambiguity is repeatedly reinforced. Do the Turks intend to attack Rhodes or Cyprus? When Brabantio is awakened and comes to his window he asks Roderigo, "[W]hat are you?" (1.1.94). Roderigo disguises himself on Cyprus; Iago disguises himself everywhere. After Roderigo attacks Cassio in the dark, Iago calls out, "Who's there? Whose noise is this that cries on murther?" To which Lodovico replies, "We do not know" (5.1.48–49). Othello thinks that Cassio has been slain when in fact it is Roderigo. Shortly afterward Othello himself responds to Emilia's knocking on his door, "Who's there?" (5.2.89).

That is the key question. Othello agrees that "men should be what they seem" (3.3.128). Indeed, his problem may be that he cannot tolerate ambiguity: "to be once in doubt / Is once to be resolved" (3.3.179–180). He lacks faith, that evidence of things unseen. At the end of 3.3 he rejects heaven for hell, love for hate, Desdemona for Iago. At the end of the play he kills himself exactly as he says he once killed "a malignant and a turban'd Turk" (5.2.353), that is, an infidel. He thus finally recognizes that he has abandoned the teaching of Christianity and in lacking faith has also lost hope and love.

In addition to jealousy, *Othello* presents the theme of civilization versus barbarism. This theme is dramatized by the opposition of Venice and Cyprus, Christians and Turks, reason and passion. The movement of the action from Venice, home of civil society and deliberative government, to Cyprus—an island in the sea subject to invasion from without and disorder from within—mirrors the decline and fall of Othello. While in Venice Othello exhibits the calm self-control and authority that are likewise found in the Duke and senators. Through reason the senators and Duke can see through the Turkish feints and rightly determine that the goal of the Turkish fleet is Cyprus rather than Rhodes. Brabantio's passion is blunted by those wiser councilors, who notably approve of the union between Othello and Desdemona. Iago's ability to disrupt has only limited effect in Venice, whose leaders are adept at piercing appearance to discover the truth beneath.

By contrast, Cyprus emerges as a place of chaos, where Othello's inability to rule his passions seriously hampers his ability to rule the citizens. It lies between rational, Christian Venice and the wild and heathen Turks. It is an island fortress surrounded by treacherous seas. It is, in short, a middle ground, an ambiguous place.

Because of his proximity to the Moor, a condition brought about by the demotion of Cassio, Iago can more effectively weave his web without interruption. He is aided, moreover, by the sudden destruction of the Turks, which means his general has time on his hands to fret about his wife's behavior. Ironically, the barbaric army has been defeated but the barbaric character of Iago, who opposes civilized, Christian values, has infiltrated the highest levels of rule on Cyprus.

The transition between these two "worlds" requires a sea voyage. The Venetian ships encounter the same tempest that sank the Turkish fleet, but they suffer only separation and manage to survive. No such storm is described in the Cinthio tale, suggesting that Shakespeare had a specific thematic purpose for creating it. This purpose may have been to warn the characters that they are sailing into uncertain, troubling waters. Given that Shakespeare associates the sea with Othello's emotional state, the storm could also function as a specific foreshadowing of his tidal-wave-like jealousy. The separation of the ships might also signal the coming separation between friends (Cassio and Othello) and spouses (Othello and Desdemona). When in his final speech Othello refers to himself as both a "base Indian" and "turban'd Turk," we sense that the transformation from civilization to barbarism is complete.

## THEMES AND MEANINGS

Because it is a tragedy, *Othello* depicts the main theme of the hero's fall from a successful military leader and loving husband to a jealous, murdering monster. This theme can be traced back through the medieval Fall of Princes genre to classical Greek and Roman tragedy, in which the heroes exhibit tragic flaws that lead to their downfalls. In Othello's case, his flaw is his great passion; paradoxically, it is also his great strength. No one else in the play speaks as powerfully or poetically about love, but, once doubt and suspicion set in, no one else speaks as compellingly and frighteningly about being "deceived."

Linked to the theme of love, of course, is the theme of jealousy. This tragedy offers a careful examination of the destructive emotion of jealousy—its origins and consequences. In the play's beginning, we overhear Iago's jealous remarks about Cassio's promotion and the supposedly unfair way he got it; we also witness Roderigo's jealous attitude toward Othello, who has married Roderigo's imagined beloved. As the action develops, we soon discover that Iago is, in fact, jealous of Othello and Desdemona's capacity to love and their love for each other, and intends to destroy this love at all costs.

Because Iago's character is linked to Satan's, Shakespeare gives Iago the ability to transform appearance into reality; he can make the Moor believe he sees infidelity when it does not exist. He first convinces Othello that Desdemona's desire for him is unnatural because he is old and black, the total opposite of the young Italians to whom she should be attracted. Her choice of Othello shows, in Iago's words, "a will most rank, / Foul disproportions, thoughts unnatural" (3.233–234). Once that seed is planted, Iago goes on to talk freely about how the wives of Venice regularly deceive their husbands and work carefully to keep their affairs secret. Othello is particularly vulnerable to Iago's insinuations about Venetian life because he is an outsider who relies on his ensign's experience and honesty.

Iago is successful as well because of his special gift of imagination, the art of painting a picture of what in fact does not exist. He gives that imagination free reign when he recounts the story of Cassio's talking in his sleep and embracing Iago while supposedly thinking Iago is Desdemona (3.3.413–426). The sheer audacity of this account proves that Iago's imagination and cruel will know no bounds. Using the lost handkerchief to focus his victim's attention, he concludes this sequence of deception by informing Othello that he saw Cassio wipe his beard with it that very day! What makes him even more believable to Othello is that Iago throughout has resisted speaking out because he does not wish to hurt his friend Cassio. Once Othello becomes the victim of the "green-ey'd monster," he proves blind to any evidence of his wife's faithfulness; indeed, he takes on Iago's vision of a world where all people are either liars or fools. For him, appearance functions as disguise to cover up human beings' bestial nature, and the world becomes a place where only the fittest survive. Like other Shakespearean tragic heroes, Othello needs to see better.

One of Shakespeare's favorite themes throughout his plays involves the definition of loyal service. Iago immediately declares himself opposed to such a principle in the following speech to Roderigo:

> I follow him [Othello] to serve my turn upon him.
> We cannot all be masters, nor all masters
> Cannot be truly follow'd. You shall mark
> Many a duteous and knee-crooking knave
> That (doting on his own obsequious bondage)
> Wears out his time, much like his master's ass,
> For nought but provender; and when he's old, cashier'd.
> Whip me such honest knaves. Others there are
> Who, trimm'd in forms and visages of duty,
> Keep yet their hearts attending on themselves,
> And, throwing but shows of service on their lords,
> Do well thrive by them; and when they have lin'd their coats,

Do themselves homage. These fellows have some soul,
And such a one do I profess myself. (1.1.42–55)

The master-servant relationship was the bedrock of Elizabethan-Jacobean society because each party was expected to perform his role in harmony with nature's rule of order and degree. Satan's revolt in heaven was caused by the servant's impulse to unseat his master on the grounds that he was his master's equal. The result was Satan's expulsion from heaven, along with other rebellious angels, and the creation of hell as a new home for the rebels. Adam and Eve's fall from Paradise followed from Satan's revolt as he attempted to gain revenge by tempting God's creatures with the promise of godlike intelligence. Such rebelliousness could not be tolerated in heaven or on earth if society was going to function according to hierarchical principles; this meant that each link in the chain of being had to accept its proper place. The heresy that Iago speaks here exhibits his Satan-like contempt for loyal service—a contempt that is based on the idea that anyone who serves someone else without attending to his own desires is a fool.

Just as Iago corrupts the principle of loyal service, Othello corrupts the rule of law in his decision to kill Desdemona. In order to dramatize this theme, Shakespeare relies heavily on imagery related to sight and seeing. Early on Brabantio warned Othello to follow closely the actions of his daughter "if you [Othello] have eyes to see" (1.3.292). This prompts the Moor, with Iago's aid, to become a spy; when he sees Cassio steal away from Desdemona's side in 3.3, Iago suggests that what he has witnessed is the hurried end of an illicit meeting. As the play progresses, Iago directs Othello's sight, making him see what is not there. Driven to distraction, Othello demands "ocular proof" of Desdemona's infidelity (3.3.360), and his ensign promptly produces not the handkerchief itself but a story in which Desdemona has given the handkerchief to Cassio. Jealousy, when it preys on Othello, is a "green-ey'd monster" (3.3.166), suggesting that the jealous man sees with distorted vision. And when Othello enters Desdemona's bedchamber in 5.2, he comes with a candle that symbolizes the dim vision or understanding he has of her true character. He refuses to accept what his eyes tell him; her beauty and innocence argue not for corruption but for chastity. Othello, however, has rationalized his role here as that of Justice, the figure that is supposed to represent impartiality by covering her eyes. What he really seeks, however, is to punish her for making him a cuckold, and he is blind not because of impartiality but because of anger. Only after Desdemona's death and Emilia's accusation does Othello begin to gain the insight necessary to understand the horrible consequences of his deed, to begin once again to see clearly and judge fairly.

Perhaps most obviously, *Othello* is a play about love. Just before Iago begins to corrupt Othello, the latter says of Desdemona, "Perdition catch my soul / But I do love thee! And when I love thee not, / Chaos is come again" (3.3.90–92). Here is dramatic irony at its greatest. Othello rightly says that if he fails to love Desdemona he is damned, and chaos will ensue.

Throughout the Shakespeare canon damnation and chaos are the consequences of a failure to love. In *Romeo and Juliet* old hate breeds civil unrest and destroys young love. In *King Lear* Goneril and Regan breed civil war and effect their own deaths. In the comedies the triumph of love restores order and happiness. Here, Othello is "ensnar'd . . . soul and body" (5.2.302), Cyprus is at least temporarily thrown into turmoil, and by the end of the play Roderigo, Emilia, Desdemona, and Othello have perished. Shakespeare would agree with W. H. Auden's statement, "We must love one another, or die."

## CRITICAL CONTROVERSIES

Three major critical controversies have been cited in analyses of *Othello*: its status as a domestic tragedy; Iago's "motiveless malignity"; and the time problem. Other questions related to race and Desdemona's character have preoccupied more recent cultural critics of the play.

Thomas Rymer, a seventeenth-century critic of *Othello*, offered the following review of the play in his *Short View of Tragedy* (1692): "plainly none other, than a Bloody Farce, without salt or savour." He concluded that the moral of the play was directed at "all good Wives, that they look well to their Linen." Rymer was a classicist who believed in strict rules of tragic construction, following the practice of Greek and Roman playwrights. These required that the hero be a man of "high degree," preferably a king, whose individual fate has a destructive effect on the state. Because Othello is both a Moor and a military officer, he does not qualify for hero status in Rymer's eyes. His tragedy, moreover, affects primarily his marriage, or "domestic affairs," and has no impact on the state or its citizens. Rymer also believed that the action of tragedies should take place in one locale during the period of no more than one day because audiences should not be asked to imagine a shift from Venice to Cyprus. Such a shift was thought to be unrealistic and would lead viewers to suspect that what they were watching was not in fact action with a moral purpose. That action should be serious, formal, and tragic throughout; there should be no comic episodes to distract from the play's serious message. Rymer maintained that Shakespeare probably was only dimly aware of these rules, which in any case he violated throughout the play, because he lacked a university education and wrote for a popular audience that simply wished to be entertained.

Perhaps the most persistent critical question posed over the play's lifetime concerns Iago's motivation. Samuel Taylor Coleridge, the English Romantic poet and critic, described Iago's soliloquies as "the motive-hunting of motiveless malignity." What Coleridge means is that the ensign seems to be trying out several reasons to justify his hatred of Othello as he goes along; yet no one of those motives is itself sufficient justification. Is being passed over for promotion an adequate motive? Does Iago's hatred of Moors drive him to act? Is he the avenging husband out to kill the man he thinks slept with his wife? The implication of these questions is that the play is weakened if the villain must search for reasons to engage in such heinous deeds; while Iago certainly seems ambitious and vengeful, his primary motivation appears to be to engage in evil for evil's sake. This squares with Shakespeare's apparent aim of linking the ensign with Satan: the Devil has the specific goal of destroying God's creatures. Yet the Satan designation also oversimplifies a character who so clearly reveals a psyche that can only be called complex. Perhaps in this day of serial murderers and workers "going postal" we can better understand why sociopaths like Iago are never likely to produce a rational motive or explanation for their actions.

The problem of time in *Othello* has also been a long-standing concern of critics. It appears from the text that Othello and Desdemona use their first night on Cyprus to consummate their marriage. (In Cinthio, the couple live happily in Venice for several weeks before leaving for Cyprus.) Given that the parties were separated on the voyage to Cyprus and that they spend only a short time on the island before Iago hatches his plot, it appears that Desdemona has had little time to engage in an affair with Cassio or anyone else. Shakespeare certainly intended for the plot to move rapidly and for Othello to have little time to consult anyone other than Iago. Yet he seems to be aware that an audience might have doubts about probability, so he creates what critics have called "double time." This means that the action progresses on two time lines at once. Through references to Othello's dining with his officers and the arrival in act 4 of the representatives from Venice, Shakespeare implies that time is passing at a slower pace than it appears to be in the main action. Several scenes begin with characters entering already engaged in full conversation about events that have taken place "offstage." The double-time scheme creates a somewhat more realistic mood in the play, but it is not entirely believable for readers, as opposed to viewers, of the tragedy. As Harley Granville-Barker observed, however, "Shakespeare . . . is not essentially concerned with time or the calendar at all. . . . [T]he play's essential action lies in the process of thought and feeling by which the characters are moved and the story is forwarded" (*Prefaces to Shakespeare* [Princeton: Princeton UP, 1963], 147).

The tragedy's improbable plot has also earned it considerable criticism from those concerned with formal excellence in literature. Shakespeare uses the handkerchief as a key prop by arranging for Desdemona to lose it, then having Emilia find it and give it to her husband (who, she claims, has asked her to steal it "a hundred times," 3.3.292) so he can plant it in Cassio's lodging. He also has Othello describe to Desdemona how an Egyptian charmer who gave it to his mother told her that as long as she possessed it she would have the power to keep her husband's love. But if she lost it or gave it away, her husband would reject her and "hunt / After new fancies" (3.4.62–63). This account comes only after Iago has told him that he saw Cassio wipe his beard with the napkin. Why did Othello not tell Desdemona about the handkerchief's history when he gave it to her? By placing the story at this point in the plot, it appears to be an afterthought intended to justify Othello's anger at its loss. Such a trick of plotting has seemed to formalist critics an instance of "bad art," a major flaw in an otherwise compelling and aesthetically pleasing story.

The suddenness of Othello's change from a rational, controlled hero to a raging figure of revenge has also concerned formalist critics. In a tragedy like *King Lear*, for instance, the hero's decline and fall are more gradual and can be traced in stages as his daughters implement the strategy to strip him of his kingship. Othello's transformation, by contrast, happens with lightning speed as he believes unquestioningly the lies of his ensign; indeed, the loss of his faith in Desdemona's honesty seems to occur before our disbelieving eyes in 3.3. The rapid pace of the action does mean that an audience has little time to think about the plot's improbabilities, but upon reflection viewers must certainly question Othello's gullibility and his failure to doubt any piece in Iago's elaborate puzzle.

## PRODUCTION HISTORY

Little is known about the 1604 production at court, but the play was performed later at Oxford (1610), possibly with Richard Burbage as Othello, and the apprentice boy playing Desdemona was able to provoke tears from the audience during her death scene. The diarist Samuel Pepys reports on performances at the Cockpit in 1660 and the Theatre Royal in 1669 in which women played the parts of Emilia and Desdemona. These productions were very popular even though critics like Rymer were concerned with the tragedy's plot and apparent lack of a moral message.

During the eighteenth century, Shakespeare's texts were refined and regularized, especially to give Othello lines that emphasized his nobility and heroic status. Oath swearing and epithets were often cut. Records of productions of *Othello* can be found for all but seven years of the century. Among the actors who played the lead role were Thomas Betterton, who emphasized the agony of the hero's loss, and Barton Booth, who attempted to project an Othello working hard to keep his emotions in check. Colley Cibber frequently played the role of Iago in productions from the middle 1700s, and his interpretation heavily stressed the Machiavellian aspects of the villain's character. The famous actor David Garrick, who created a more natural style and restored many of the scenes cut by other editors, was a failure in the part; he was short and physically unimposing, and his conception of a violent Moor did not fit the taste of the age.

John Philip Kemble played Othello in a production at the Drury Lane Theatre in March of 1785. His sister Mrs. Siddons played Desdemona and received high praise from critics. The acting team was legendary for its interpretations of Shakespearean characters, but in this play Kemble's treatment was too stately and solemn, failing to catch the rage of Othello in key scenes (Rosenberg, pp. 43–44).

The nineteenth century saw extensive editing of the Shakespearean text; the focus of that editing was the elimination of swearing and of bawdy, sexually suggestive language. The bowdlerization process seriously affected Iago's character because so much of his language is marked by bawdiness and sexual innuendo. Two kinds of Othello dominated the stage during this period: the restrained and dignified intellectual and the passionate, wildly jealous Moor. The former type was embraced by the famous actors Charles Macready and Henry Irving, although Macready, influenced by the natural style, sometimes played the part in a more expressive way. Irving teamed with Ellen Terry (Desdemona) and Edwin Booth (Iago) in an 1881 production that was a great commercial success. Booth was likewise successful in the title role, playing the Moor as a kind of black nobleman who never seems to lose control.

Edmund Kean's performances in 1814 and 1832–1833 were praised as admirable representations of the passionate Othello. Unlike previous actors of the part, Kean used tawny rather than black makeup, and he produced a jealous state that approached insanity. The critic William Hazlitt called his interpretation "the finest piece of acting in the world." During his last performance in 1833, he became mortally ill and was carried off the stage just after completing Othello's "Farewell the tranquil mind" speech at 3.3.345–357.

Iago's role was of great interest to the actors of the Victorian age because they were challenged to create a plausible motive and to represent his disguise of honesty in a believable way. Macready and Irving played Iago with some success, but Booth was generally recognized as the best Iago of the age; he managed to enthrall audiences with his magnetic personality and to take them along with him as he hatched his plot.

At the beginning of the twentieth century, Johnston Forbes-Robertson and Oscar Asche mounted productions that enjoyed some commercial success. Though widely

Laurence Fishburne as Othello and Kenneth Branagh as Iago in Oliver Parker's 1995 film *Othello*. © Corbis Sygma.

admired, Forbes-Robertson lacked the intensity that Kean had brought to the role, and Asche was not successful in interpreting Othello's poetry. Godfrey Tearle managed to attract appreciative audiences to his performances of Othello between 1921 and 1950. He had a classical style of delivery but was also able to communicate the character's fierce passion. Orson Welles received critical acclaim for his Othello in the 1930s; his was a larger-than-life Moor who used exaggerated gestures and a melodramatic style of speaking to impress critics and audiences alike. He made a film of the play in 1952 (it is available from Academy Entertainment).

All of these actors of course wore makeup to approximate Othello's blackness. Ira Aldridge was the first black actor to play the role on the stage, although the performance by an African American that prompted the highest critical praise was by Paul Robeson in the 1930s. Robeson's powerful voice and physical presence created an Othello of both great strength and gentleness. Robeson also injected the element of race into the play, which opened it up for other black actors, such as James Earl Jones. Jose Ferrer played Iago in the Robeson production, and he was widely praised for his technical excellence. Laurence Olivier's Othello of the early 1960s had a West Indian accent and somewhat wild expressions, emphasizing his alienation from Venetian society; when he lapses into his fit, he attains a kind of voodoo-inspired state that is fascinating to watch. His performance is recorded in a 1965 film directed by Stuart Burge. Frank Finlay delivers a memorable performance as Iago.

More recent performances by James Earle Jones at the New York Shakespeare in the Park festival and by Laurence Fishburne in the 1995 film directed by Oliver Parker (Kenneth Branagh plays Iago) demonstrate how the play continues to speak to racial and cultural issues today. A more recent film, *O* (2001), directed by Tim Blake Nelson, with Mekhi Phifer as the Othello character, Julia Stiles in the Desdemona role, and Josh Hartnett playing the Iago persona, set the play in a private high school in the United States and dealt to a certain extent with racism. No doubt *Othello* will continue to appeal to repertory companies and filmmakers of the future, since its themes and characters, like those in so many other Shakespearean plays, are universal and timeless.

## EXPLICATION OF KEY PASSAGES

**2.3.336–362. "And what's he then . . . enmesh them all."** Early in the play Iago reveals his "occupation" to the audiences in a soliloquy that proves he would never give up his profession of ensnaring victims for anything. He has just told Cassio that the way to be reinstated in Othello's good graces is to employ Desdemona as his champion. After Cassio leaves, the villain reflects cynically on his disguise. Iago's opening pronouncement points directly at his technique for turning Othello's world upside down. His disguise of honesty, a divine virtue, is intended soley to cover up his hellish plot. By calling Cassio "honest fool" (2.3.353) he reveals just how much contempt he has for people who genuinely believe in telling the truth. Though he does not mean that he will actually pour poison in Othello's ear, his figure of speech aptly describes the corrosive language he will use to dupe his captain. This skill with rhetoric and storytelling is meant to recall the seductive speech of Satan, who won over Eve by painting an irresistible picture of the godlike powers she would have after eating the apple. The disturbing description of the effect of Desdemona's pleading for Cassio, the turning of her virtue into "pitch," suggests blackening her reputation but also the trapping of birds in nets or flies in spider webs. Pitch was often put on birds' tails to make escape from the snare more difficult. Indeed, the vision of Iago's victims becoming more fully ensnared as they struggle mightily to get free is a powerful one. Moreover, his improvisational talent, his ability to lead the audience along as he decides on his next move, keeps our attention riveted on him even as we realize that we too are his victims.

**3.3.345–357. "I had been happy . . . Othello's occupation's gone."** Once Othello becomes convinced of Desdemona's disloyalty, he speaks movingly of how that deceit has also destroyed his career. This linking of his cuckolding with his professional status initiates Othello's decline and fall, which is inevitable once we realize how closely he identifies with the military role that has given his life meaning. The repetition of "farewell" gives the speech a sense of finality even though we are only in the middle of the play. Othello's catalogue of all that has been lost along with his honor—the sights and sounds of war—proves particularly moving because it indicates how dearly he has relished these things. As a Moor and an outsider, moreover, his military ability is in effect the only quality that gives him status in European society; once it is gone, he no longer has a "place" or purpose that he values. Shakespeare's use of the word "occupation" is particularly significant because the root "occupy" points directly at the concept of holding a valued place in society. Finally, the numerous exclamation points underscore the height of emotion attached to his words of farewell; he seems to be speaking not only to himself but also to the troops he can no longer lead.

**5.2.1–22. "It is the cause . . . where it doth love."** Othello's soliloquy, delivered just before he smothers Desdemona in her bed, exhibits his self-deception about his role as avenger. He tries to persuade himself that he is acting as an instrument of Justice here, not a bloody murderer. In order to steel his will, he must also characterize his victim's beauty and innocence as a disguise designed to deter him from his mission. By repeating the word "cause," Othello reveals that he has made his personal jealousy into a legal cause in which he has become the judge, jury, and executioner. The candle he carries becomes a focal point as it symbolizes the light of Desdemona's spotless life that he is about to extinguish. What is perhaps most frightening about this speech is that Othello can see so clearly the consequences of his deed but still persuades himself of the righteousness of it.

He does not name the cause perhaps because he cannot, since in reality he has no justification for murdering his wife. How much he has become like Iago is evident in his false logic in claiming that his "sorrow's heavenly, / It strikes where it doth love" (5.2.21–22). Here is Iago's "divinity of hell" (2.3.350) and yet another proof of how self-deluded Othello has become.

**5.2.338–356. "Soft you . . . smote him—thus."** Othello's final lines act as a kind of summary of his life; they are marked by the calm, reasoning tone of his earliest speeches. The tempest is over. He asks Lodovico and Gratiano to remind the state of his good service to it, but he also urges them to "Speak of me as I am" (5.2.342). Just as his first speech in this act shows his kinship with Iago, so this speech demonstrates his distancing himself from his betrayer. For here Othello inverts Iago's line, "I am not what I am" (1.1.65). He admits to his destructive jealousy, which has overpowered "one that lov'd not wisely, but too well" (5.2.344). Such insight is typical of Shakespeare's tragic heroes before their deaths, an illumination that comes too late and only after terrible suffering and loss. In this play, however, a tinge of irony accompanies Othello's claim of loving too well and not wisely because although the observation is intended to describe his relationship with Desdemona, it can apply as well to his love for Iago. Had he but sought proof from anyone other than his ensign, Shakespeare implies, he might have avoided the "green-ey'd monster" jealousy and its consequences.

### Annotated Bibliography

Adamson, Jane. *"Othello" as Tragedy: Some Problems of Judgment and Feeling*. Cambridge: Cambridge UP, 1980. A close study of Othello's complex character that pays attention to his changes of mood and his contradictory states of mind. Adamson relies heavily on selected principles of psychological analysis to demonstrate why Othello is so vulnerable to Iago's lies and insinuations. She also explores Desdemona's character to determine her ability to judge and to feel.

Boose, Lynda E. "Othello's Handkerchief: 'The Recognizance and Pledge of Love.'" *English Literary Renaissance* 5 (1975): 360–374. Boose examines the keepsake handkerchief as a plot device, prop, symbol of Desdemona's honor, and so forth. She argues that its link to Othello's love for Desdemona cannot be denied even though his account of its history comes long after he has given it to her. The discussion of the pattern of strawberries and its significance is particularly interesting.

Heilman, Robert B. *Magic in the Web: Action and Language in "Othello."* Lexington: U of Kentucky P, 1956. A standard formalist discussion of the tragedy that focuses on the handkerchief as a symbol of the web that ensnares Othello and Desdemona. Heilman examines the rich imagery of the play to demonstrate that the tragedy forms an artistic whole that is both complex and aesthetically satisfying. He offers an especially pointed analysis of Iago's evil.

Hyman, Stanley Edgar. *Iago: Some Approaches to the Illusion of His Motivation*. New York: Macmillan, 1970. A thorough review of the debate about Iago's motivation starting with Coleridge's comment about his "motiveless malignity." Hyman argues that attempts to pin down one motive for his actions are fruitless, that the fascinating talent of the character lies in his ability to create motives that sound plausible but have no basis in fact.

Kirsch, Arthur. *The Passions of Shakespeare's Tragic Heroes*. Charlottesville: U of Virginia P, 1990. Kirsch uses medieval and Renaissance religious ideas to study the emotional and spiritual suffering of Shakespeare's major tragic heroes. He challenges the findings of cultural critics who claim that the idea of the individual is a modern one that did not exist in the Renaissance. He uses both St. Paul and Freud to analyze the contrary states in Othello's mind as they relate to his intense preoccupation with his sexual relationship with Desdemona. In the end, he seems to confirm the traditional claim that Othello, like other Shakespearean heroes, is a "slave of passion."

Orkin, Martin. "Othello and the 'plain face' of Racism." *Shakespeare Quarterly* 38 (1987): 166–188. An important study of how racism in Shakespeare's time is similar to and differs from modern attitudes. Orkin carefully explores the standing of Moors in European society, especially as it relates to their cultural development in Spain and Africa. He takes a close look at terms like "thick-lips" (1.1.65) and "sooty bosom" (1.2.70) to determine their significance to a Jacobean audience.

Rosenberg, Marvin. *The Masks of "Othello."* Berkeley: U of California P, 1961. The study combines an account of the tragedy's performance history and a close reading of the text to suggest various "masks" or ways of playing Othello. Rosenberg finds several variations on two basic models: the restrained, somewhat aloof intellectual not easily moved to anger and the passionate, explosive victim of jealousy who reverts to the "beast." His analysis is consistently perceptive and suggestive.

# King Lear

Jay L. Halio

## PLOT SUMMARY

**1.1.** *King Lear* opens with a short dialogue between the earls of Gloucester and Kent concerning which of Lear's two sons-in-law, the Duke of Albany, married to Goneril, or the Duke of Cornwall, married to Regan, the King favors in the division of his kingdom. Apparently, Lear prefers neither one over the other. Standing nearby is Gloucester's illegitimate son, Edmund, whom his father introduces to Kent with some locker-room humor regarding the youth's genesis. King Lear and his train then enter.

Lear sends Gloucester to fetch the King of France and the Duke of Burgundy, who are suitors for the hand of his youngest daughter, Cordelia. Meanwhile, he declares the reasons why he has decided to abdicate and divide up his kingdom among his heirs. Although the division has already been determined, he asks each of his daughters in turn to declare how much she loves him so that he can decide who gets the best portion. First, Goneril, the eldest, professes in extravagant terms her love for Lear. Regan follows and tries to outdo her sister. In a couple of asides, Cordelia expresses her dilemma. She cannot express her love in words, she feels, and when Lear asks her, she repeatedly answers that she can say nothing: she loves her father according to her "bond, no more, nor less" (1.1.93). This response infuriates Lear, who promptly disowns her. Kent tries to intercede, but is banished for his pains.

When France and Burgundy enter, Lear offers Cordelia first to Burgundy, then to France, with no dowry whatsoever. Burgundy balks, but France sees that Cordelia is "herself a dowry" (1.1.241), and he claims her as his bride. Lear and the rest of the court exit. Then Cordelia parts from her sisters in a short leave-taking, recognizing the danger for her father while in their care, since he, together with a hundred knights of his own choosing, is now to spend one month alternatively with each daughter. This, and retaining the title though not the powers or responsibilities of kingship, is the condition of his gifts of the kingdom to them.

**1.2.** The next scene begins the parallel plot of Gloucester and his two sons, Edgar and Edmund. Edmund devises a scheme by which Gloucester will disinherit Edgar and proclaim Edmund as his heir instead. The device works, and Edmund gloats, easily getting Edgar to fall into his plot.

**1.3–4.** These scenes are set in Goneril's palace. Displeased with her father and his hundred knights, she plots to get rid of him and at least half his train. Kent returns in disguise to continue to serve his old master. Lear becomes outraged at Goneril's treatment and her insistence that he cut his train in half; cursing her, he leaves for Regan's palace. The Fool, who has been missing since the start of the play, enters during 1.4 and tries to awaken in Lear a sense of his foolish behavior, but Lear seems unable to comprehend what the Fool is saying. Lear sends Kent ahead to notify Regan and her husband, the Duke of Cornwall, of his impending arrival. Goneril has already sent her steward, Oswald, to Regan with a similar purpose.

**1.5.** Lear and the Fool have a short dialogue in which Lear expresses his fear of going mad as a result of his daughter's harsh treatment. The Fool offers insight though small comfort, suggesting in his riddling idiom that Regan will be much like Goneril.

**2.1.** Curan, a courier, informs Edmund of trouble brewing between the dukes of Albany and Cornwall, each of whom apparently wants to take over the entire kingdom of Britain—precisely what Lear had hoped to avoid in dividing up his kingdom. Curan also informs Edmund, who is delighted to hear the news, that Regan and Cornwall are coming to Gloucester's castle. This short interlude gives way to Edmund's plot to get rid of his brother and to further antagonize their father against Edgar. When Regan and Cornwall arrive, they endorse Gloucester's efforts to apprehend Edgar, who they believe was "companion with the riotous knights" that attended Lear (2.1.94). When Gloucester informs them how Edmund has helped him uncover Edgar's "plot," they immediately begin to favor the younger son.

**2.2.** Outside the castle, Kent in disguise confronts Oswald, whom he has earlier tripped up in Goneril's palace (1.4.86) and thereby gained Lear's favor. He picks a fight with the cowardly steward, who cries out and awakens the household. Plain-spoken Kent affronts Cornwall and is placed in the stocks despite Kent's status as the King's messenger. Gloucester is upset at this treatment of Kent, but is powerless to alter the situation. Left alone in the stocks, Kent reads a letter from Cordelia suggesting that help may be forthcoming.

**2.3.** Recognizing his danger, Edgar decides to adopt the disguise of a madman and beggar, Tom o' Bedlam. He tears off his clothes and covers his features with filth, tying his hair in knots to make himself look utterly repugnant, and declares, "Edgar I nothing am" (2.3.21).

**2.4.** Act 2, scene 4 is really a continuation of 2.2 (as some editions indicate by not assigning 2.3 a separate scene designation). Lear, the Fool, and a Gentleman (or one of his knights) arrive at Gloucester's castle. The first thing they see is Kent in the stocks. Lear can hardly believe that his daughter and son-in-law would treat his emissary in such a way. Lear enters the castle to find Gloucester, and when they emerge, Lear demands to speak with Regan and Cornwall. Gloucester extemporizes, but Lear insists. When he returns with the Duke and Duchess, Lear greets them as cordially as he can, but before long Regan begins treating him in much the same way Goneril did, if somewhat more suavely. She tells him to return to her sister's palace, as she herself is in no position now in Gloucester's castle to do anything for him; but Lear refuses. A trumpet soon announces Goneril's arrival, and a three-way confrontation among Lear and his two daughters begins, during which Kent is silently released from the stocks. Between them, the daughters decide that Lear needs no knights at all, let alone the fifty that Goneril agreed to permit or the twenty-five Regan at first said she could accommodate. Furious at his daughters' ingratitude, Lear rushes out into the gathering storm, followed by the Fool. Gloucester again tries to mediate, but unsuccessfully, as the doors of his castle are shut against the storm and the old King.

**3.1.** The storm rages throughout most of act 3. Kent apparently has lost Lear in all the confusion and sets out with a gentleman to find him. He also asks the man to go on to Dover, where he says a power from France has landed. There he can find Cordelia and inform her of what has been happening. They part, going separate ways to search for Lear.

**3.2.** Lear shouts his defiance at the storm, while the poor Fool, drenched, tries to get him to return to the castle for shelter. Lear refuses; he has truly begun to go mad by now, when Kent appears and leads him and the Fool to a hovel nearby.

**3.3.** Events of this night—not only the way Regan and Goneril have treated their father but also the way his castle has been commandeered by his guests—determine Gloucester to take action on behalf of King Lear. Still trusting Edmund, he confides in him a letter he has received, apparently from Cordelia, and says that they must support the King. In a brief soliloquy, Edmund decides to inform on his father to Cornwall, thus hoping to gain further favor.

**3.4.** Kent gets Lear and the Fool to a small hovel, which turns out to be where Edgar, as Tom o' Bedlam, has found shelter. Lear tells the Fool to enter in first while he utters a prayer on behalf of the "[p]oor naked wretches" whom he has failed to care for sufficiently while in power (3.4.28). Frightened, the Fool runs out of the hovel, followed by Edgar as Tom, uttering his wild, mad talk of demons and devils. Struck by this image of "unaccommodated man" (3.4.106–107), Lear begins to tear off his own clothes, when Gloucester arrives on the scene to lead them to a more comfortable shelter. He does not, of course, recognize the disguised Edgar, who Lear insists should come along with them, too.

**3.5.** Having informed against his father, Edmund becomes the new Earl of Gloucester, proclaimed as such by Cornwall, who regards Edmund's father as a traitor.

**3.6.** Lear, Kent, the Fool, and Edgar are in the shelter that Gloucester has provided. Now quite mad, Lear insists on trying his daughters, Goneril and Regan, for their ingratitude, setting Kent, Edgar, and the Fool as justices to hear the case. Gloucester returns with orders for the others to take Lear, who has fallen asleep exhausted, to Dover, while he returns to his castle.

**3.7.** In Gloucester's castle Cornwall, Regan, and Goneril apprehend Gloucester as a traitor. Cornwall sends Goneril and Edmund back to Albany to prepare for war against the threatened invasion from France, while he and Regan deal with Gloucester. They have the old man bound to a chair, and Cornwall proceeds to take out Gloucester's eyes. One of Cornwall's servants tries to prevent him and wounds him fatally, as Regan, taking a sword from another servant, kills the first one. Gloucester calls on Edmund for help, only to learn then that it was he who had informed against him. In that way, Gloucester learns who his loyal son really is.

**4.1.** Edgar sees his father, his eyes bandaged, led by an Old Man. Gloucester gets Edgar, still in disguise as mad Tom, to lead him to Dover, where he plans to kill himself by leaping from a cliff.

**4.2.** Goneril and Edmund arrive at Goneril's castle. They have obviously formed an amorous relationship, and when Goneril learns how passively Albany has taken the news of the French invasion, she sends Edmund back to Cornwall and Regan; he is to "Hasten his [that is, Cornwall's] musters and conduct his pow'rs" (4.2.16), while she deals with her husband. Albany by now is thoroughly disgusted with Goneril and accuses her of inhuman behavior, but Goneril treats him with disdain. A messenger arrives with the news of Gloucester's blinding and Cornwall's death, which horrify Albany. Goneril takes the news as both good and bad, as far as she is concerned—good insofar as a serious threat to her supremacy in the land has been eliminated, bad insofar as Regan is now free again to marry.

**4.3–4.** Kent and a Gentleman discuss the current situation and particularly Cordelia's return to Britain with a French army in Dover. Lear, ashamed, has refused to see her, although she still loves him and has returned only to aid him in his distress.

**4.5.** Oswald has come to Regan to find Edmund and deliver a letter from Goneril. Regan tries to get the steward to let her see the letter; but out of loyalty to his mistress, Oswald refuses. Edmund is away, already leading Cornwall's army to Dover. Regan tells Oswald to find Gloucester and kill him, as his sorry state is moving people against her and Goneril. He agrees.

**4.6.** Edgar, who has changed his disguise, leads Gloucester to what the old man believes is a tall cliff overlooking the sea, though actually the ground is flat. He knows Gloucester wants to commit suicide. He deceives his father deliberately in order to cure his despair, though still not revealing his identity. The deception works, and Gloucester thinks his life has been saved by a miracle, as Edgar, again changing his voice, makes him believe. Suddenly, Lear appears, quite mad, and engages Gloucester in dialogue. Though blind, Gloucester recognizes Lear and grieves for him. Some of Cordelia's people appear to carry Lear to his daughter, but he runs off, with them in pursuit. Oswald next comes on the scene and prepares to kill Gloucester. Assuming now the voice as well as the garb of a peasant, Edgar fights and kills Oswald, who asks him to deliver Goneril's letter to Edmund. Edgar opens the packet and sees that Goneril is plotting with Edmund to get rid of Albany. The sounds of drums and impending battle are heard, as Edgar leads Gloucester to shelter.

**4.7.** Cordelia has found her father and put him in the care of a doctor. She talks with Kent, who tells her who he really is but says he is not ready to reveal himself to Lear. Lear is brought in still asleep; as he awakens, he and Cordelia begin a beautiful reconciliation, which includes Lear's recognition of his foolish behavior. He has begun to regain his sanity.

**5.1.** The rivalry between Goneril and Regan, especially as it concerns Edmund's favor, grows, even as they prepare for war. Privately, Edgar gives Albany Goneril's letter to Edmund and says that if the British triumph, he will appear to prove what the letter says. He leaves, and Albany exits to get ready for battle. The scene ends with Edmund's soliloquy expressing his dilemma insofar as both Goneril and Regan want him for their husband. He also says that if they defeat Cordelia's army, he will see to it that she and Lear never receive Albany's intended pardon.

**5.2.** The battle occurs offstage. Edgar has hidden his father and returns to take him elsewhere for shelter after Goneril and Regan's forces triumph.

**5.3.** Lear and Cordelia are led away by a captain, commissioned by Edmund to execute them. Albany enters with Goneril and Regan, and the confrontations among the victorious British begin. Albany demands the captives from Edmund, who demurs. Regan intercedes, and she and Goneril begin quarreling. Albany produces the letter from Goneril that Edgar had given him and arrests Edmund and

Goneril for capital treason. He then orders the trumpet to sound for his champion, as both he and Edmund throw down their gloves in defiance of one another.

Edgar appears in yet another disguise as the challenger, and in the ensuing duel he fatally wounds Edmund. Revealing himself, he and Edmund exchange forgiveness. Edgar then relates how he cared for Gloucester, who died after Edgar revealed himself just before the duel. As Edgar continues to say how he encountered Kent, a man with a bloody knife enters to announce the deaths of both Regan and Goneril. Kent enters to inquire after Lear, reminding the others of the King's capture. Experiencing a change of heart, Edmund tells them to send for Lear and Cordelia before it is too late. But it is too late. Lear enters moments later with Cordelia in his arms. She has been hanged. Lear tries to revive her, all in vain. He then dies, too, as Albany cedes the kingdom to Edgar.

## PUBLICATION HISTORY

Shakespeare probably began composition of *King Lear* sometime in 1605—just when, we cannot be sure. The reference to "These late eclipses in the sun and moon" (1.2.103) may allude to actual eclipses in September and October of 1605. King James I (James VI of Scotland) had recently ascended the English throne after the death of Elizabeth I (1603), and one of his main concerns was unification of Scotland and England. This issue might have given Shakespeare the idea for a play about King Lear, to show what happens when a kingdom is divided. An old play, *The moste famous Chronicle historye of Leire kinge of England and His Three Daughters* (ca. 1590), published around May 1605, may also have prompted Shakespeare to think about writing his own version. The only definite piece of evidence we have, however, is that Shakespeare's *King Lear* was performed at King James's court on St. Stephen's Day (December 26) during the Christmas holidays in 1606. It was an appropriate choice for performance, since the readings from scripture on that day urged patience in adversity. The festivities, moreover, emphasized hospitality, especially to the poor, themes developed in Shakespeare's play.

The first publication of *King Lear* was the quarto of 1608. Its title page reads as follows:

> M. William Shak-speare: / *HIS* / True Chronicle Historie of the life and / death of King LEAR and his three / Daughters. / *With the vnfortunate life of* Edgar, *sonne* / and heire to the Earle of Gloster, and his / sullen and assumed humor of / TOM of Bedlam: / *As it was played before the Kings Maiestie at Whitehall vpon* / S. Stephans *night in Christmas Hollidayes.* / By his Maiesties seruants playing vsually at the Gloabe / on the Bancke-side. / [Printer's device] / *LONDON,* / Printed for *Nathaniel Butter,* and are to be sold at his shop in *Pauls* / Church-yard at the signe of the Pide Bull neere / St. *Austins* Gate. 1 6 0 8.

This quarto, also known as the "Pied Bull" quarto, was printed in the shop of Nicholas Okes for the publisher Nathaniel Butter. How Butter or Okes got the manuscript, we do not know.

Okes had never before printed a play, and his two compositors, who set the type, obviously had trouble with the handwriting; hence, some verse is printed as prose, some prose as verse, and other errors, mainly misreadings, abound. Scholars rightly assume that the copy from which Okes's compositors set the type was Shakespeare's own manuscript, written over in places and revised, sometimes in the margins, making the manuscript difficult to read and thus occasioning the many errors. Some of the errors were corrected—or attempts were made to correct them—by proofreading during the printing process, with the result that some extant copies have corrected pages and some do not.

A second quarto (Q2) was printed in Isaac Jaggard's printing shop in 1619 as part of the abortive attempt by Thomas Pavier to publish a collected edition of Shakespeare's plays. The project was halted, probably because of copyright problems. Not to lose his entire investment, Pavier assigned false dates to the plays already printed, trying to pass them off as the original editions. Hence, Q2 bears the date 1608. It is simply a reprint of Q1, making some corrections while introducing other errors. It has no authority whatsoever, except for part of a line consisting of a speech ascription and two words, which appear at 4.6.197. This brief bit may have appeared in a copy of Q1 no longer extant from which Q2 was printed.

The other authoritative text of *King Lear* appears in the great First Folio (1623). It is significantly different from Q1 in many respects, omitting some lines and a whole scene (4.3), while adding other lines not found in Q1. Many alternative readings, or variants, also appear throughout the First Folio. For a long time, scholars believed that Q1 was based on a memorial reconstruction of Shakespeare's play, but most now accept the two-text theory: that is, that Shakespeare (or someone else, but probably Shakespeare for the most part) revised the play, possibly more than once, in the period between its first performances in 1605 and publication in 1623. Whereas many modern editions conflate, or splice together, Q1 and the First Folio so that none of Shakespeare's lines are lost, more recent editions prefer to base their texts on one or the other authoritative text, correcting as necessary from the other, but maintaining the integrity of the control text—either Q1 or the First Folio—as far as possible.

Differences between the two texts include the following examples and may be attributed to a variety of causes, about which textual scholars can only speculate:

- Many of the omissions in the First Folio of passages found only in the quartos (Q) are from act 4 and may be explained as attempts to shorten an already long play. Not only is all of 4.3 omitted, but much of Albany's dialogue in 4.2 is also cut.

- In the First Folio the Fool's curious prophecy is added at the end of 3.2, and his final words are added in 3.6, suggesting that Shakespeare knew when revising that the Fool would never appear again and therefore gave him a good closing line.

- The ending of *King Lear* is also significantly different. In Q, Albany has the last lines of the play; in the Folio, the last lines are given to Edgar, whose character, after various alterations have been made in the Folio, appears to be stronger than Albany's.

- Lear's final lines are also changed, with lines 5.3.311–312 added in the Folio.

Students should be aware of the many alterations that distinguish the two texts and that have led some editors (see, for example, Oxford's *Complete Works* and *The Norton Shakespeare*) to print both texts. Norton even includes a third version: a conflated *King Lear*. The two texts are distinguished by their titles as well: Q has *The History of King Lear*, whereas the Folio has *The Tragedy of King Lear*.

In 1681 Nahum Tate rewrote Shakespeare's *King Lear*, restoring the happy ending from the earlier renditions of the story. In addition, he added a love interest between Edgar and Cordelia, eliminated the Fool, and introduced a new character: Arante, Cordelia's confidante. Much of the language as well as the structure and plot of Shakespeare's play is different in Tate's version, designed more closely to suit the taste of the age. The changed ending in particular held the stage for the next 150 years; not until 1838 did the Fool appear again as part of the dramatis personae, when William Charles Macready cast a woman in the role.

## SOURCES FOR THE PLAY

Shakespeare borrowed from a variety of sources for *King Lear*. The Lear plot comes from an old legend, whose earliest written form is found in Geoffrey of Monmouth's *Historia Regum Brittaniae* (ca. 1135). Shakespeare may have read the original Latin version or its derivatives in many later accounts, such as Raphael Holinshed's *Chronicles of England, Scotland, and Ireland* (1577, 2nd ed. 1587) although most likely the old play *King Leir* was his most immediate source. Other works that contain the Lear story include John Higgins's *A Mirror for Magistrates* (1574 edition) and Edmund Spenser's *The Faerie Queene*, book II (1590). The Lear story itself owes much to still older sources, folk tales like the Cinderella story, and to legends such as "Love like Salt" (in which a daughter tells her father that she loves him like salt and then explains that he, like salt, is essential to her) that scholars have found and named. In addition, a contemporary scandal involving an old knight, Sir Brian Annesley, and his three daughters, one of whom was named Cordell, may also have influenced Shakespeare.

Shakespeare's play differs in many important respects from its major source in the anonymous play *King Leir*. Whereas the older play is full of pieties and is in fact set in a Christian context, Shakespeare's play is an interesting mixture of pagan and Christian allusions and ideas. Some of most important differences between Shakespeare's play and his source include his introduction of the Gloucester plot, which not only universalizes his themes, as some critics have argued, but also contrasts the ways in which Lear and Gloucester confront their fate at the hands of their children. Shakespeare also introduced new characters into the Lear plot, such as Oswald the steward and the Fool. Lear's madness and the storm are other innovations. The role of the Gallian king in the old play is far more substantial than that of the King of France in *King Lear*, possibly because Shakespeare wished to downplay (for political reasons) the conflict between England and France, especially in the Folio version of his play, and to enhance the role of Cordelia. For other reasons, Shakespeare omitted the low comedy in *King Leir* as well as some melodramatic incidents, though the main outlines of the story, with one notable exception—the ending—remain the same.

All the preceding accounts of King Lear and his daughters have a happy ending: the forces of Cordelia are victorious over those of her sisters, and Lear is restored to his throne. Shakespeare was the first and only writer to make the story end tragically. Why he did so is hard to explain. Perhaps his reading in Sidney's *Arcadia*, which provided the source for the Gloucester plot (see below), suggested the tragic implications of the Lear story. Undoubtedly, Shakespeare chose to deepen the tragedy almost beyond human endurance. Despite the promises of a happier outcome, as when Lear and Cordelia are reconciled at the end of act 4, Edgar's victory over Edmund, and other indications that all may yet be well, Shakespeare brings his play to a devastating conclusion. Refusing to sentimentalize, he forces us to confront the starkest version of potential outcomes.

The Gloucester plot derives directly from Sir Philip Sidney's *The Countess of Pembroke's Arcadia* (1590) and the story of the Paphlagonian King and his two sons, Leonatus and Plexirtus. The latter is an illegitimate son who deposes his father and blinds him. The good son comes to the King's aid and saves him from suicide. For Edgar's language as mad Tom o' Bedlam, however, Shakespeare had recourse to Samuel Harsnett's *Declaration of Egregious Popish Impostures* (1603). Many of the devils Edgar mentions while impersonating mad Tom are those Harsnett describes in his tractate against exorcism.

## STRUCTURE AND PLOTTING

Basically, *King Lear* presents two parallel plots that serve to contrast with and comment upon each other. They do not simply echo one another, despite certain obvious similarities. Although the Lear plot is primary, the Gloucester plot is also fully developed. In both plots a father is deceived by his children: Lear by his older daughters, Goneril and Regan, into believing they love him extremely well; Gloucester by his younger son, Edmund, into believing that his older son Edgar wants to murder him. Lear's youngest daughter speaks truthfully and is banished for her pains; Gloucester's older son does not even have the opportunity to speak to his father and refute the charges against him. Cordelia knows her sisters well and as she leaves for exile in France predicts in general terms that things will not go well for Lear. Edgar, as the *vir bonus*—the good man who is so innocent and naive that he suspects no evil—accepts his brother's urging in 2.1 to flee from their father's wrath. He then assumes a disguise that permits him to remain on the scene, where he comes directly into contact with evil and learns, as Cordelia already understands, the wicked ways of the world. Lear meets his fate with fierce defiance; Gloucester meets his with despair so deep that he wishes to commit suicide.

Shakespeare alternates scenes to move both plots forward, as it were, almost simultaneously. The first scene of the play at once disposes of the love contest and Cordelia's consequent banishment. In the following scene, Edmund quickly initiates his plot to get rid of Edgar. Indeed, the action of *King Lear* is so swift that things begin to happen before anyone quite realizes it. Gloucester wonders in amazement at what Lear has done in banishing both Cordelia and Kent (1.2.104–117), while he himself falls victim to Edmund's strategy. By the end of act 1, Goneril has successfully put her own plan into action to humiliate and ultimately destroy Lear. In the very next scene, Edmund completes his plan to have Edgar run for his life. Learning of the impending visit of the Duke of Cornwall and his wife, Edmund begins to think of further ways to aggrandize himself.

Thus the rising action of the play moves forward at nearly breakneck speed and reaches a climax by the end of act 2. Incidents such as Kent's being put in the stocks, Regan's initial refusal to greet her father, and Goneril's arrival at Gloucester's castle build to the point where Lear, who has increasingly feared incipient madness, abandons all attempts to reason with his daughters to gain their respect and gratitude. He rushes out into a raging storm with only the Fool accompanying him. Gloucester tries to ameliorate the situation, but in vain. Nevertheless, the incidents in act 2 coupled with those in act 1 have helped to make him realize that he must soon take a stand in support of the old King, his master.

Act 3 is mostly concerned with Lear's accelerating madness as he confronts the storm with titanic defiance. Kent's efforts (he finally has caught up with him) and those of the Fool to calm Lear down and get him to seek shelter at first meet with sturdy resistance. But in 3.4 Lear begins to realize what is happening to others besides himself. Just after he puts concern for the Fool's pitiful condition before his own (3.4.26), he begins to pray for the unfortunates for whom he failed to provide while in power (3.4.28–36). This marks a major turning point in Lear's development, which paradoxically coincides with his descent into madness. When Edgar emerges from his hovel as mad Tom o' Bedlam, frightening the Fool nearly to death, Lear sees a reflection of what he himself will soon become. He cannot conceive of anything other than Edgar's daughters' ingratitude that would result in Edgar's condition as the Bedlam beggar.

Meanwhile, Gloucester has confided in Edmund that he has decided to side with King Lear. This marks a turning point in Gloucester's development: from a temporizing, weak individual in 2.2 and 2.4 to someone prepared to act on the side of compassion and justice. He finds Lear outside Edgar's hovel and leads him and the others to a better shelter. He does not recognize his son in disguise, who he still believes intended to murder him (3.4.165–170).

After Edmund informs Cornwall of his father's intentions (3.3.21–25), thus gaining for himself Gloucester's title, two scenes follow that comment upon each other significantly. Within the shelter Gloucester has provided, Lear conducts a mock trial of his daughters. He is by now thoroughly out of his mind, as he sets about indicting a couple of join-stools as his ungrateful daughters, Goneril and Regan (3.6.46–54), and appoints Tom o' Bedlam, the Fool, and Kent as the justices to hear his prosecution. In the Folio version, most of this part of the scene is cut for reasons difficult to ascertain. In the scene immediately following, Gloucester is arraigned as a traitor by Cornwall and Regan. Their trial of the poor old earl stands in direct contrast to Lear's trial of his daughters and implicitly raises the question: Which trial is crazier? Cornwall himself admits that he is exceeding even the form of justice in what he is about to do (3.7.24–27), but he willfully goes ahead anyway. Regan torments Gloucester, but the worst torture occurs when Cornwall takes out first one, then the other of Gloucester's eyes. At this moment, Gloucester calls on his son Edmund for help, only to learn that it was Edmund who informed against him. He realizes at last that Edgar was innocent (3.7.91). The horror of these proceedings is so great that one of Cornwall's servants tries to intervene and stop the Duke before he takes out Gloucester's second eye. He wounds the Duke fatally, and in the process is himself killed by Regan. The scene ends as the remaining servants take pity on Gloucester and condemn those who acted against him; these lines are found only in the quarto version.

At the end of 3.6, Lear, exhausted and asleep, is carried off in a litter to Dover, not to be seen again until well into act 4. This sleep and his change of garments symbolize a change in character; similarly, another sleep and change of clothes at the end of act 4 also symbolize an important transformation. Most of act 4 is devoted to the aftermath of the climactic scenes in act 3 and preparations for the culminating events of act 5. Edgar begins the act in soliloquy, commenting on his situation vis-à-vis what he has recently witnessed, when he sees his father, his eyes bandaged, led by the Old Man. The sight prompts him to recognize that no matter how bad things appear, they can still get worse. When he agrees as mad Tom to lead Gloucester to Dover, hope is engendered that things now really cannot get any worse: Gloucester's good son has him in hand, and Lear is en route to safety, too. But Shakespeare's tragic strategy in this play is to raise such hopes repeatedly, only to dash them later on; or, in other words, to promise happy endings that then turn out to be anything but.

The hope for a good outcome, already aroused by news in a letter Kent has received from Cordelia (2.2.165–173) and again in Gloucester's letter (3.3), is reinforced by several other events in act 4. Albany upbraids Goneril severely for her behavior toward her father in 4.2 and is shocked to learn about what has happened to Gloucester. Kent and the Gentleman in the next scene (4.3, omitted from the First Folio) comment on Cordelia's return to England with a French army to rescue Lear, and in 4.4 Cordelia herself appears. She has changed a great deal from in 1.1; she is much more conciliatory toward her father, whom she sends some of her people to find and bring to her. Added to these positive elements are indications that the solidarity between Goneril and Regan has begun to split badly because of their jealousy over Edmund. By the end of act 4, when Lear recovers from madness and Cordelia and he are finally reconciled, hope for a happy outcome is at its highest. But the battle between Cordelia's forces and the British, led by Edmund and Albany, has yet to take place.

Other hopeful signs occur in act 4. For example, Edgar saves Gloucester from despair by tricking the old man into believing that the gods have saved his life. He also saves Gloucester from Oswald's attempt to kill him, and in so doing he uncovers Goneril's plan to get her husband, Albany, killed so that she can wed Edmund. When Edgar delivers Goneril's letter to Albany instead of Edmund in act 5, the hope that the evildoers will fall and the virtuous will be saved peaks again—only to be almost completely dashed by the outcome of the battle.

Tracing Lear's madness reveals other aspects of the play's dramatic structure. In the first two acts, Lear experiences various rebuffs from his daughters and fears he will go mad. During the storm in act 3, which echoes his mental turmoil, he rapidly breaks down; and when he meets Edgar as Tom o' Bedlam, he is propelled into nearly complete madness, as he appears in the mock trial of his daughters. At the end of 3.6 he falls asleep—a transitional state, as often in Shakespeare. When Lear reappears in act 4, meeting Gloucester at Dover Beach, he is utterly mad and runs away from those who try to aid him. In the last scene of act 4, he is asleep again, but this time when he awakens he has begun to recover his sense. He has also changed into a more perceptive person, a process that began as early as 3.4 (see above) and culminates with the self-knowledge that he is "a very foolish fond old man" (4.7.59).

Gloucester's development parallels and contrasts with Lear's. At first he temporizes and goes along with events that he recognizes are terrible. Like Lear, he falls into his wicked child's trap. But in act 3 he knows that he must take sides against the malefactors. His shift costs him his eyes and brings him knowledge of the error of his ways. Where Lear's perception and growing self-knowledge lead him at first to mad defiance and only later to reconciliation and acceptance, Gloucester's lead him to profound despair. In act 4, just as Cordelia helps her father to recover from his illness, Edgar helps his father, using quite different tactics, those more appropriate to Gloucester's condition.

In act 5, the various strands of the dramatic structure come together with tragic results. Cordelia's army loses the battle; she and her father are taken prisoner and condemned to death by Edmund. Edgar in a new disguise appears, challenges his brother in a duel, and kills him. Their rivalry grown to fever pitch, Goneril meanwhile poisons her sister, but when she sees Edmund dying, she takes her own life. Gloucester also dies, his "flaw'd heart / . . . / 'Twixt two extremes of passion, joy and grief," having "[b]urst smilingly" (5.3.197–200). The last hope for a happier ending is dashed when Lear enters with Cordelia in his arms. Though he has gained much self-knowledge and repented his sins, he too dies soon afterward, much like Gloucester, joy and grief warring in his anguished soul.

It is left now for the survivors to rebuild the kingdom. Albany proposes to turn over rule to Edgar and Kent. But Kent is already dying and declines. It is left to Edgar—who by now has learned so much about the ways of the world—to take over, and he does.

## MAIN CHARACTERS

### King Lear

King Lear dominates the action of most of the play, except for the first four or five scenes of act 4. His development from an egocentric, imperceptive, arrogant old tyrant to someone with greater understanding not only of himself but also of others is the most important aspect of his character. The changes, however, do not come easily to Lear, who undergoes the fires of an earthly purgatory before he realizes fully what he has done and who he is.

Lear's initial actions are highly irrational. As those in Shakespeare's audience would immediately grasp, his decision to divide up his kingdom is deeply wrong; it can and does lead to disaster. His motives seem reasonable enough: he is old and wants to give up the responsibilities of ruling his kingdom to "younger strengths" (1.1.40). By dividing his kingdom now among his daughters, furthermore, he hopes to prevent future strife (1.1.44–45). In this expectation he is badly mistaken, for division of the kingdom almost immediately leads to strife, as Curan informs Edmund (2.1.6–13). Finally, he foolishly thinks he can keep the title and honors of a king even as he gives away all of his royal powers and prerogatives.

Lear's decision to hold a contest among his three daughters to determine who loves him most, and thus to award the appropriate portions of his kingdom, is also absurd. In the first place, it is absurd to try to measure love quantitatively. Then, as Gloucester and Kent discuss the situation at the very start of the play, Lear has already decided who will get what lands. When Goneril and Regan profess their love for Lear, he awards them two-thirds of the kingdom, hardly distinguishing between them, and leaves only a third. When it comes time for Cordelia to speak to get "a third more opulent than [her] sisters" (1.1.86), all she can say is "Nothing" (1.1.87, 89). Lear's surprise, embarrassment, and increasing anger (for all of this action takes place in open court) show that he does not know what he is doing any more than he understands why Cordelia is acting as she is. Although she tries to explain her behavior in reasonable and honest terms, Lear will have none of it. He summarily disowns her and banishes her from his sight without any dowry whatsoever. Although he had "thought to set [his] rest / On [Cordelia's] kind nursery" (1.1.123–124), Lear informs his other two daughters that he will henceforward reside with each of them a month at a time, along with a hundred knights that he has reserved as his retinue.

That Lear expects his daughters to put up with him in his old age accompanied by a hundred knights shows further how irrational and imperceptive the old man is. He knows his children no better than he knows himself, as his elder daughters recognize and plan to act accordingly (1.1.293–308). Things quickly come to a head in Goneril's palace when she decides to precipitate a crisis by showing disrespect for her father. But before those events occur, which propel Lear to search for better comfort with Regan, Kent returns in disguise and seeks service with his old master. When Lear asks why he wants to serve him, Kent answers in words that speak directly to an essential element of Lear's character (1.4.24–30). Despite his erratic behavior in 1.1, Lear still maintains what Kent sees in him as "[a]uthority" (1.4.30).

Lear becomes angry when Goneril criticizes his knights' comportment and becomes further outraged when she demands that he reduce his train by half. Taking her demand—as it was probably intended—as an insult of the vilest kind, Lear leaves precipitously, sending Kent ahead to inform Regan of his imminent arrival. During 1.4–5, the Fool tries to show Lear how foolish he has been and is, but Lear seems to take little notice of the attempts to bring him to greater awareness and insight. He must undergo a good deal of suffering before he gets to that stage.

Lear and his entourage, or what is left of it (we never see more than one or two knights at any time), ride off to find Regan and her husband, Cornwall, who, forewarned by Goneril's letter (1.4.334), have departed at once for Gloucester's castle. When Lear finally arrives there at night, he is shocked to find his servant Kent in the stocks, taking this act as another insult to him and a reflection of the growing disrespect he is experiencing. Though he demands an explanation, he is more concerned with gaining Regan's sympathy, despite the Fool's earlier warning that she is much the same as Goneril. Indeed, she is, and has no sympathy at all for her father, whom she tells to return to Goneril. Lear rejects the suggestion and begins cursing his eldest daughter anew when she also arrives at the castle.

Dismayed at first at the way Goneril and Regan greet each other in so friendly a manner, Lear again tries to make his case and again is rebuffed. He is thoroughly bewildered, it seems, at his daughters' attitude toward him, especially when they begin to question whether he needs any knights at all in his entourage. Although their argument seems rational enough—they have plenty of servants to care for him, so why does he need to have any others?—Lear tries to explain how they miss the point. Overcome with emotion, he breaks down into incoherence and utters loud but empty threats against them (2.4.264–286). He has feared losing his mind before; he realizes now that he is already on the way to madness (2.4.286).

Lear's titanism—for that seems the best way to describe his actions here and at the beginning of act 3—shows itself fully in his defiance of the elements. A terrible storm has broken out, reflecting the turbulence in his mind. But he refuses to take shelter, rejecting the Fool's entreaties to return to the castle and ask his daughters' blessing (3.2.11–12). In his ravings against the elements, his egocentrism is still mingled with self-pity, as he cries, "I am a man / More sinn'd against than sinning" (3.2.59–60). At the same time, he seems to have a greater awareness of others, mainly criminals who he believes are being punished by the storm (3.2.49–59), but also of himself and the Fool, whom he has begun to pity as well (3.2.67–73).

The storm and the events that occur in act 3 bring Lear to the edge and over into the abyss of madness, but it is a madness that paradoxically allows him to see better and understand more than he had done earlier. In his prayer for the "poor naked wretches" in his kingdom, who "bide the pelting of this pitiless storm" (3.4.28, 29) he acknowledges that he has taken too little care of them. These lines reveal his growing sympathy for others, signaled earlier by his concern for the shivering Fool in 3.2. The confrontation with Tom o' Bedlam soon pushes him into insanity; but at the same time it enables him to recognize and articulate better than he could when speaking to his daughters in 2.4 what basic humanity is really about. Tearing off his clothes to becomes less "sophisticated" and more like "the thing itself: unaccommodated man" (3.4.106–107), Lear tries to get on the same level as his "philosopher" (3.4.154), mad Tom, who is himself nearly naked to the elements. However disoriented Lear may seem—as when he conducts his mock trial of his elder daughters in 3.6—his madness, like Hamlet's, has some method in it. He knows, for example, how to ask pointedly, "Is there any cause in nature that make these hard hearts?" (3.6.77–78), as he asks to "anatomize" Regan to help find the answer (3.6.76).

Thanks to Gloucester, Lear, falling asleep at last after his terrible ordeal, is carried off to Dover, where Cordelia has landed with her army from France. We do not see him again until well into act 4, when he appears utterly mad on Dover Beach, dressed differently and crowned with wild flowers and weeds (4.4.1–5). Out of deep shame, he has refused to see Cordelia and runs along the sands until he meets and preaches to Gloucester. Again, although his words lack form a little, they are filled with newfound wisdom, as when he says, "Through tatter'd clothes small vices do appear; / Robes and furr'd gowns hide all" (4.6.165–166). His self-knowledge is also acute. Speaking of his daughters and others, he says: "[T]hey told me I was every thing. 'Tis a lie, I am not ague-proof" (4.6.104–105).

Lear's sex revulsion in this scene is understandable. Although his daughters were all of legitimate birth, Goneril and Regan's behavior fills him with loathing, not only toward them, but toward all of their gender. "Down from the waist they are Centaurs, / Though women all above," he cries; "But to the girdle do the gods inherit, / Beneath is all the fiends'" (4.6.124–127). His irregular verse patterns reflect to some extent his disordered mind, but his comments are nonetheless cogent. When Gloucester claims he cannot read the "challenge" Lear gives him (4.6.138), Lear comments, "Your eyes are in a heavy case, your purse in a light, yet you see how this world goes"; for indeed, "A man may see how this world goes with no eyes" (4.6.146–151).

Still burdened by shame, Lear runs away when Cordelia's Gentleman and attendants find him and try to bring him to her. In the following scene, they have apparently caught him and he has fallen into another deep sleep. His clothes are also changed, signaling once more a shift in character. Awakening before Cordelia, Kent, and a doctor, Lear at first thinks he must be dead, "bound / Upon a wheel of fire," and Cordelia "a soul in bliss" (4.7.45–46). Their reconciliation follows in one of the most poignant scenes ever written. Lear at last knows himself as "a very foolish fond old man" (4.7.59), fully aware of his injustice to his daughter and needing her forgiveness. This is the culmination of his journey to self-knowledge.

In the last act, when Cordelia loses the battle against her sisters' forces, and Edmund captures her and her father, Lear seems to care only that the two of them are together. "Come let's away to prison," he says; "[w]e two alone will sing like birds i' th' cage" (5.3.8–9). Lear is unconcerned with anything else as long as he can be with Cordelia. She is his entire world, and world enough for him. He scoffs at courtiers and their pretensions—"Who loses and who wins; who's in, who's out" (5.3.15)—and tells Cordelia that the two of them will "take upon 's the mystery of things / As if we were God's spies" (5.3.16–17). If Lear here shows himself to be once again overly possessive, entirely unmindful of Cordelia's husband as well as her other commitments and concerns, it is no wonder. Perhaps, under the circumstances he has lived through, it is even excusable. Certainly he recognizes his need for Cordelia's forgiveness, here as earlier (4.7.83, 5.3.10–11). He recognizes, too, the sacrifices that she has made for him and is thus determined never to part from her again (5.3.20–25). His grief is therefore as profound as it is boundless when at the end of the act he enters with her in his arms after she has been hanged.

Whether Cordelia is already dead or nearly so is not clear from the text, for Lear tries desperately to revive her. He is struck to the depths of his heart by the realization that she will "Never, never, never, never, never" (5.3.309) wake again. As he himself dies, his only thoughts are for her; now he directs others to regard not himself, as in 1.1, but to "Look on her! Look her lips, / Look there, look there!" (5.3.311–312). Does he believe she has revived and is still alive, as some interpret the moment; or does he point upward to her soul flying heavenward, as it is sometimes enacted on stage? Does Lear die in joy, or return to madness? Is he redeemed through Cordelia's ministry and his own self-knowledge, or does he die unregenerate after all? These are questions that Shakespeare leaves us to ponder.

## Gloucester

Paralleling Lear's development but also contrasting with him in several important ways is the Earl of Gloucester. One of his children, his bastard son Edmund, deceives him; but unlike Lear, he has no one to advise him against precipitous action. If Lear is willfully blind, Gloucester is foolishly gullible; hence, he too easily falls into Edmund's trap. When he discovers how wrong he has been, Gloucester suffers a profound despair and wishes to kill himself, again unlike Lear, who is powerfully defiant, raging against his fate.

Gloucester is an ordinary old man in many ways. In the dialogue with Kent that opens the play, he speaks of Edmund's birth in jocular terms, or what we would associate today with "locker-room talk." He makes jokes, even as Edmund stands within earshot, suggesting that Gloucester lacks sensitivity as well as morality. While he accepts his responsibility for Edmund and his upbringing, he does not appear keen to keep him at home—not because Edmund disgraces his father but rather because Gloucester feels it may be prudent to educate him elsewhere than in his own house. "He hath been out nine years, and away he shall again" (1.1.32–33).

Like many men of his age and station, Gloucester is protective of his fortune and place in society; any threat to these fills him with anxiety. He is accordingly vulnerable to Edmund's plot to rob his brother Edgar of his birthright. The scheme arouses

Gloucester's anxiety. Quickly duped, Gloucester takes immediate steps to condemn Edgar without so much as a hearing.

Edmund's charges against Edgar are the more disturbing to Gloucester because of recent events involving Lear and the King's family and retainers. Gloucester is superstitious, attributing to the "late eclipses in the sun and moon" the ill effects that have been occurring, such as "Love cools, friendship falls off, brothers divide" (1.2.103, 106–107). He seems especially troubled by "the noble and true-hearted Kent banish'd! his offense, honesty!" (1.2.116–117). Gloucester is thus not without all moral feelings, as subsequent events reveal.

When in act 2 Regan and Cornwall arrive unexpectedly at his castle, Gloucester is glad to see them. He expects them to assist him in apprehending Edgar, who under Edmund's prompting has fled. By now Gloucester is firmly convinced of Edgar's alleged treachery and villainy. When the Duke takes Edmund under his protection (2.1.112–116), Gloucester expresses his gratitude on his son's behalf. Regan explains why they have come suddenly and at night, saying they want the old earl's counsel—Gloucester, utterly imperceptive here as elsewhere, replies, simply, "I serve you, madam. / Your Graces are right welcome" (2.1.128–129). Not until later, and at terrible personal expense, does he learn how ill-advised his welcome is.

In the next scene, when Cornwall places Kent in the stocks, Gloucester regards the act as an affront to the King and tries weakly to intervene, but to no avail (2.2.140–147). It is the beginning of his growing awareness of how evil his guests are, but much worse follows. When in 2.4 Lear arrives with his Fool and one of his gentlemen, or knights, Gloucester is outraged that Regan and Cornwall at first refuse to see the King and tries to temporize (2.4.91–100), citing extenuating circumstances. Regan and Cornwall finally appear, and during the ensuing dialogue— while Goneril arrives and Kent is freed—Gloucester is mainly an onlooker. What he observes, especially after Lear in a fury runs out into the storm, apparently convinces him, as he tells Edmund later, that they must help the King (3.3.13–14). He further confides to his son that he has received a letter about the impending invasion from France and says, "If I die for 't (as no less is threat'ned me), the King my old master must be reliev'd" (3.3.17–19). This misplaced confidence in Edmund spells disaster for the old man.

Meanwhile, Gloucester attempts to succor the King and send him on to Dover, where Cordelia's army is landing. Searching for Lear in the storm, he finds the King outside Poor Tom's hovel and leads him and his motley entourage to a better shelter. Gloucester does not recognize Edgar disguised as Tom o' Bedlam, although something about Tom reminds him of his son (see 4.1.32–35). He says to Kent, who is like Edgar still in disguise, "I'll tell thee, friend, / I am almost mad myself. I had a son, / Now outlaw'd from my blood; he sought my life, / But lately, very late. I lov'd him, friend, / No father his son dearer; true to tell thee, / The grief hath craz'd my wits" (3.4.165–170). Gloucester is still under the delusion that Edgar is his enemy and Edmund his true and loyal son, but very shortly he will become radically undeceived.

For Edmund informs against his father to Cornwall, who then orders him to seek out his father (3.5.17–19). Edmund complies, and Gloucester is brought before Cornwall, Regan, and Goneril as a traitor. Gloucester's "trial" takes place before Cornwall and Regan, who treat him with utter disdain. Gloucester tries to defend himself and pleads with them to remember that they are his guests. When he finally sees that they intend no mercy, he recognizes that he is "tied to th' stake" and "must stand the course" (3.7.54). He tells Regan that he sent Lear to Dover "Because I would not see thy cruel nails / Pluck out his poor old eyes, nor thy fierce sister / In his anointed flesh rash boarish fangs" (3.7.56–58). Cornwall takes his cue and begins plucking Gloucester's eyes out, rejecting (to his cost) his servant's plea to desist after the first eye is gone. As soon as his other eye is out, Gloucester calls for Edmund to requite this terrible act, and it is at this point that he learns the truth about his son from Regan: "Thou call'st on him that hates thee" (3.7.88). Gloucester at last recognizes how badly he has misjudged his sons: "O my follies! then Edgar was abus'd" (3.7.91).

Gloucester's deep despair begins here. Throwing him out of his own house, Regan says he may "smell / His way to Dover" (3.793–794). His self-knowledge also begins here, as he tells the Old Man who leads him outside the castle walls, "I stumbled when I saw" (4.1.19). Fortunately for him, Edgar as mad Tom is nearby. Although Gloucester is deeply depressed and longs to touch his son once more, Edgar does not yet reveal who he really is. Later, we learn his reason is to help his father recover from despair, which Gloucester expresses bitterly: "As flies to wanton boys are we to th' gods, / They kill us for their sport" (4.1.36–37). Like Lear in the storm, he has some feeling for the poor and asks the Old Man to bring the mad beggar some clothing. Gloucester asks Tom to lead him to a high cliff at Dover, from which he plans to commit suicide. Edgar agrees, but has another purpose in mind.

Gloucester and Edgar do not appear again until the beginning of 4.6, where Edgar pretends to help his father climb the high cliff. Once again, Gloucester is deceived, but this time it is for his own benefit. Edgar's vivid description of the heights they supposedly are on convince the blind old man that he is really at a cliff's edge. Giving him another purse with a rich jewel in it, Gloucester prepares to jump. Before doing so, he prays for Edgar.

Gloucester believes he has fallen, thanks to Edgar's clever deception (4.6.45–54, 57–59, 69–72). Edgar proclaims, "Thy life's a miracle" (4.6.55), as all life is, and proceeds to convince his father that "the clearest gods, who make them honors / Of men's impossibilities, have preserved thee" (4.6.73–74). The deception works. Gloucester says, "Henceforth I'll bear / Affliction till it do cry out itself / 'Enough, enough,' and die" (4.6.75–77).

Relieved for the moment of his despair, Gloucester nonetheless is subject to backsliding. Perhaps for this reason Edgar, although he changes disguise several more times, still does not reveal himself to his father. He needs to be sure that Gloucester is fully cured. For example, when later in the scene Oswald comes upon them and wants to kill the old man, Gloucester is altogether willing that he should do so. Again, when Cordelia's army loses the battle, Gloucester is unwilling to let Edgar lead him to safety, saying "a man may rot even here" (5.2.8). Edgar reminds Gloucester of what he should have learned earlier: "What, in ill thoughts again? Men must endure / Their going hence even as their coming hither, / Ripeness is all." To which Gloucester replies, "And that's true too" (5.2.9–11).

This is the last we see of Gloucester. Near the end of the play, after he has defeated Edmund in combat, Edgar recounts Gloucester's death: "Not sure, though hoping of this good success [in the duel], / I ask'd his blessing, and from first to last / Told him our pilgrimage. But his flaw'd heart / (Alack, too weak the conflict to support!) / 'Twixt two extremes of passion, joy and grief, / Burst smilingly"

(5.3.195–199). Gloucester's death, like much else about the end of his life, resembles Lear's, whose emotions and attitude at the end are similarly ambiguous.

### Goneril

Lear's eldest daughter is usually portrayed on the stage as the more vicious of the two wicked sisters, although in the First Folio version Shakespeare adds enough lines to give her behavior some rationale. But in both quarto and Folio she is a domineering, self-confident, and masterful villain. From the first she sizes up the situation accurately and determines to take fullest advantage of it. Concerning her father at the end of 1.1, she says to Regan: "You see how full of changes his age is. . . . He always lov'd our sister most, and with what poor judgment he hath now cast her off appears too grossly" (1.1.288–292). Anticipating difficulties with him, she continues: "The best and soundest of his time hath been but rash; then we must look from his age to receive not alone the imperfections of long-engraff'd condition, but therewithal the unruly waywardness that infirm and choleric years bring with them" (1.1.295–299). She conspires with Regan to deal with Lear accordingly, and in 1.3 and 1.4, we see how she goes about doing this, provoking a confrontation with Lear that leads directly to his cursing her and abandoning her palace to seek out Regan.

To her husband, Albany, Goneril justifies her behavior with some sarcasm, in lines found only in the Folio (1.4.322–327), pointing out the folly and danger of letting Lear keep a private army of a hundred knights. Albany demurs softly, saying that Goneril may "fear too far." But she replies, "Safer than trust too far" (1.4.328).

The situation becomes acute and reaches a climax in 2.4, when Goneril joins Regan at Gloucester's castle. The two daughters unite against Lear and his stipulation, made at the time he divided his realm between them, that he will keep a hundred knights when he spends a month at a time with each of them. Here they query how many knights he really needs, arriving swiftly at the question of whether he needs even one. She is indifferent, as Regan is, when Lear appeals to a deeper rationality, or reasonableness—one that goes beyond mere "need" (2.4.264). When Lear breaks down into incoherence and empty threats, she remains unmoved and lets him run out, bare-headed, into the storm that has been brewing all the while, commenting heartlessly: " 'Tis his own blame hath put himself from rest, / And must needs taste his folly" (2.4.290–291).

Goneril's behavior elicits significant comment later not only from Cordelia (4.3.27–29, 4.7.25–41) and others, such as Gloucester (3.7.57–58), but also from her own husband. Having patiently awaited the outcome of her actions, Albany turns on her fiercely in 4.2. Softening her character here, too, the Folio curtails a good part of Albany's severe criticism of his wife, but enough is retained to make the point. He calls her "Most barbarous, most degenerate" (4.2.42). Far from being chastened, she retorts with equal vehemence, calling Albany a "Milk-liver'd man" and a "vain fool!" (4.2.50, 61). Earlier in this scene Goneril kisses Edmund and puts a chain or some other favor around his neck, indicating that she is ready to betray her husband, as she has her father.

When Goneril's letter to Edmund miscarries after Edgar kills her messenger, Oswald, and delivers the incriminating missive to Albany instead, Goneril at first adopts an arrogant stance before her husband. She claims that the laws are hers, not his, and he cannot arraign her (5.3.159). Meanwhile, she has taken steps to rid herself of her rival for Edmund's affections by poisoning her sister, Regan. But when Edmund loses the duel to Edgar, Goneril is overcome with despair and commits suicide.

## Regan

Like her sister Goneril, Regan plays along with Lear's love contest and proclaims her affection for her father in even more sweeping abstractions. But after he divides his kingdom in half, she is willing to plot against Lear with Goneril. Usually portrayed as the sexier of the two sisters, she is somewhat more subtle but just as bad. Her husband, the Duke of Cornwall, is as different from Albany as she is from Cordelia, as his actions in act 2 show. Prompted by Goneril's message as delivered by Oswald, Regan and Cornwall leave their own home for Gloucester's, where they proceed not only to make themselves at home but to take over completely. When Kent picks a fight with Oswald and Cornwall orders the stocks for him, Regan not only seconds her husband's command to make him sit in them till noon but even goes him one further and orders Kent to sit in the stocks "Till night, . . . and all night too" (2.2.135). She is not at all concerned that Lear will take this action amiss; she is much more concerned that Goneril will be upset at Kent's treatment of her servant.

Regan's behavior toward Lear when he arrives at Gloucester's castle initially arouses the King's ire, since she and Cornwall at first refuse to come down to greet him. When they finally do appear, she says she is glad to see him, but soon afterward she begins to take her sister's part against Lear and defends her actions. Referring to her father's advanced years, she says: "You should be rul'd and led / By some discretion that discerns your state / Better than you yourself" (2.4.148–150); therefore, she urges him to return to Goneril. Of course Lear refuses, but when he resumes cursing Goneril, Regan fears he will start cursing her, too. Lear responds by reassuring Regan that she is much nicer than her sister: "Thy tender-hefted nature shall not give / Thee o'er to harshness" (2.4.171–172). He could not be more wrong, as her subsequent behavior quickly shows.

Goneril appears, and the two sisters join forces in belittling and humiliating Lear, stripping him systematically not merely of half his train but all of it, so that Lear runs from them out into the gathering storm. Neither sister cares. Assuming a semblance of rationality, Regan says: "This house is little, the old man and 's people / Cannot be well bestow'd" (2.4.288–289). Then with a false show of compassion, she adds: "For his particular, I'll receive him gladly, / But not one follower" (2.4.292–293). Finally, she blames her father's own willfulness for what has happened and orders the doors to be shut up against him and his knights. Like Goneril earlier, she again sounds perfectly rational as she warns: "He is attended with a desperate train, / And what they may incense him to, being apt / To have his ear abus'd, wisdom bids fear" (2.4.305–307).

Worse follows in act 3, when Edmund informs against his father and Gloucester is apprehended as a traitor. With Goneril and Edmund sent away by Cornwall, Regan joins with her husband in brutally interrogating and abusing the old earl, plucking him by the beard (3.7.34–36) and demanding his confession. After Cornwall plucks out one of Gloucester's eyes, Regan urges him to pluck out the other, too (l.71). Astonished by the servant's resistance to Cornwall's actions, she grabs a sword and kills him, though not before her husband receives a mortal wound. At Gloucester's cry for Edmund's help, it is she who tells him the truth about his son and then orders him to be thrust out of the gates. When Cornwall, bleeding from his wound, asks her for her arm, some modern editions supplement Shakespeare's simple stage direction, "Exit," with "led by Regan." But it is arguable whether she in fact gives him her arm or stands back, either aghast at the sight or already looking forward to claiming Edmund for her own. On the stage, she has assumed various attitudes.

In act 4 Regan appears only briefly, quizzing Oswald and trying to seduce him into letting her see Goneril's letter to Edmund (4.5). She recognizes now that it was an error to let the blinded Gloucester roam freely instead of executing him, since the pitiful sight turns hearts against her and Goneril; she therefore promises Oswald a reward if he finds and kills him. She also says that she knows Goneril is interested in Edmund, but she tells Oswald that she and Edmund have talked; moreover, now that her husband is dead, Edmund is more "convenient" for her hand than for her sister's (4.5.31). Thus the rivalry between the sisters grows, showing cracks in their erstwhile united front.

The rivalry comes to a head and breaks out into the open in act 5, which begins with a dialogue between Regan and Edmund. Regan tries to learn from Edmund how far he has gone with Goneril, but he fends off her queries. When Goneril and Albany appear with their troops, the cordiality between the sisters disappears. In 5.3, after they have won the battle, and Edgar has delivered Goneril's letter to Albany, the Duke tries to take control of affairs by ordering Edmund to deliver up his prisoners. When Edmund demurs, Regan takes his side and insists he should be regarded as Albany's equal, since he has led her troops as Cornwall would have done, had he lived. She goes further and proclaims him her "lord and master" (5.3.78), which is Goneril's cue to challenge her. But Albany intervenes, produces the letter Edgar has given him, and arrests both his wife and Edmund for capital treason. Goneril refuses to take him seriously, calling his action "An enterlude" (5.3.89), but by this time Regan has begun to feel the effects of Goneril's poison. Crying out that she is sick, she is conveyed to her tent and never seen again until her corpse is brought out near the end of the play.

## Cordelia

In striking contrast to Lear's elder daughters, Cordelia is as honest and straightforward as she is good and compassionate. In 1.1, unlike her sisters, who flatter Lear with empty claims of extreme devotion, she refuses to play their game and speaks straight from her heart. Even her language contrasts with that of her sisters. Whereas they speak hyperbolically and in generalities and abstractions, Cordelia speaks directly, using concrete terms. Cordelia, moreover, is perfectly logical, as she points out her sisters' hypocrisy: "Why have my sisters husbands, if they say / They love you all?" (1.1.98–99). When Lear breaks out into a rage against her, Cordelia stands her ground, despite his determination to banish her forever from his sight. She can be as tough as her father, as this scene shows, though she will be much more compassionate later, after he suffers at the hands of Goneril and Regan.

Cordelia is also perceptive; she rejects Burgundy, who seems more interested in her dowry than in her (1.1.247–249). When it comes time for her to leave with the King of France, she bids her sisters farewell, knowing full well, it seems, what they are like (1.1.269–271). She knows, too, that in time they will reveal themselves for what they truly are, though for the present she is evidently powerless to do anything to prevent what their "plighted cunning" will reveal (1.1.280).

That is the last we see of Cordelia until the middle of act 4. Why she is kept offstage for so long while her counterpart, Edgar, is not may be explained in various ways. Logistically, the boy actor who played Cordelia may also have played the Fool, who is not present in 1.1 and disappears after 3.6, allowing for the same actor to play both roles. Thematically, whereas Edgar is a naive young man who does not suspect any ill-doing from his brother, Cordelia is well acquainted with evil and so does not have to experience it firsthand to recognize it.

When Cordelia discovers what is happening to her father, she resolves to come to his aid despite the way he has treated her. Shakespeare makes clear that the only purpose of her military invasion is to aid her father. As she says, paraphrasing the gospel of Luke, "O dear father, / It is thy business that I go about; / . . . No blown ambition doth our arms incite, / But love, dear love, and our ag'd father's right" (4.4.23–28). Before she even reappears, a Gentleman describes her to Kent in the most poignant and moving terms, likening her tears to "pearls from diamonds dropp'd" (4.3.22), thus characterizing not only her beauty but the high value of her being. The allusion to a pearl without price (an image used earlier in *Othello*, 5.2.347–348) puts Cordelia in a religious context.

The allusions to scripture as well as her death have suggested to some critics that Cordelia is a Christ figure in the play. Whether or not one accepts a Christian interpretation, she is a sacrificial figure who helps Lear find redemption. Their reconciliation scene at the end of act 4 shows how selfless and understanding she is. Upon first awakening, Lear thinks she is "a soul in bliss," a "spirit" or an angel, whereas he is in hell, chained to "a wheel of fire" for his sins (4.7.45–48). Cordelia reassures him, and when she asks for his blessing, he kneels instead, wanting hers. She begs him not to kneel (4.7.58), and when he offers to take poison from her as his punishment, knowing she has some cause, she replies, simply, "No cause, no cause" (4.7.74). They leave together, presumably arm in arm, or Cordelia gently leading him out, now that they are fully reconciled.

After the battle, when Cordelia's forces have lost and she and her father are captured, she is full of regret—but mostly for Lear (5.3.5–6). When she suggests seeing Goneril and Regan, Lear has not the slightest desire to do so. Being with her is all he wants. She has become everything that matters for him:

> We two alone will sing like birds i' th' cage;
> When thou dost ask me blessing, I'll kneel down
> And ask of thee forgiveness. So we'll live,
> And pray, and sing, and tell old tales, and laugh
> At gilded butterflies. (5.3.9–13)

When Cordelia dies, his world dies with her. She has helped bring Lear to the full recognition of himself, or as much self-knowledge as he can bear. At the end, she is his only concern, and her death deeply moves everyone else standing by as well.

For Kent, Edgar, and Albany, the sight is tantamount to a vision of Judgment Day (5.3.264–265).

## Edgar

"He childed as I fathered!" (3.6.110), Edgar says of Lear, when he sees the poor condition to which his daughters have driven the King. It is an apt comment, for as Lear's daughters have treated him, Gloucester has treated Edgar, driving him out of his castle in fear of his life. How did his brother Edmund's clever manipulation bring Edgar to this pass? Because Edgar is naive, an innocent where evil is concerned, he is easily manipulated. As Edmund comments at the end of 1.2: "A credulous father and a brother noble, / Whose nature is so far from doing harms / That he suspects none" (1.2.179–181). Edgar is the *vir bonus* of Roman story, the good man who suspects no evil because he has no experience of evil. The events in the play thus become a powerful learning experience for Edgar, through which he grows to full manhood and knowledge.

Driven from his father's castle by Edmund's scheming, Edgar seeks shelter as a poor beggar, Tom o' Bedlam. His disguise as a naked, mad beggar is the best he can devise, for who would suspect the son of a nobleman in the form of a Bedlam beggar? The irony is that whereas disguise usually involves putting something different on, Edgar discards all of his clothes except for a loincloth. He grimes his face with filth and puts "[p]ins, wooden pricks, nails, sprigs of rosemary" in his arms to add to his disguise (2.3.16), but it is his nakedness to the elements that is most important, as Lear recognizes soon after confronting him in the storm. He thus becomes "unaccommodated man," the "poor, bare, fork'd animal" (3.4.106–108) that Lear admires and wishes to emulate, tearing off his own clothes to become more like him.

Edgar's disguise works, though the scenes he witnesses are such that they almost ruin his "counterfeiting" (3.6.61). As poor Tom he provides good insight into the condition of the realm, where creatures such as he roam about begging help from others in their deep distress. Although an innocent in many ways, he must have seen the poor wretches whom he imitates roaming the countryside.

Edgar acts also as a chorus: for example, at the end of 3.6, when he comments on the sorry spectacle of Lear's going mad (at least in the quarto version of the play; lines 3.6.102–115 are omitted in the First Folio). He recognizes that one's own pain diminishes upon seeing how terribly off others, especially one's "betters," can be (3.6.102). Similarly, at the beginning of 4.1, he comforts himself that he cannot be any worse off than he is—until he sees his father, blinded, led by an old man. Chorus-like again, he comments, "To be worst, / The lowest and most dejected thing of fortune, / Stands still in esperance, lives not in fear" (4.1.2–4). He thinks, that is, that there is nowhere to go but up. Then he sees his father and knows "the worst is not / So long as we can say, 'This is the worst'" (4.1.27–28). Edgar's education continues, as he experiences more and more of the world's wicked ways. But instead of making him cynical, his experience makes him more compassionate as well as more perceptive and knowledgeable.

Edgar does not reveal himself to his father until much later in the play. The reason for his silence is difficult to understand. It may be that he is unsure as yet how his father will receive him, although Gloucester says, perhaps not in his hearing, that he longs to see his "abused" son again in his "touch" (4.1.22–23). Or Edgar may just be biding his time until he feels the moment is right. Later, after he agrees— still in disguise as mad Tom—to lead Gloucester to Dover, where his father wishes to commit suicide, Edgar says he "trifle[s]" with him to cure him of his despair (4.6.33–34). In this he succeeds, although he confesses afterward that he probably waited too long to reveal himself (5.3.193–194).

Edgar assumes yet another mask in revealing to Albany the villainy of Goneril and Edmund. Edgar's versatility in shifting disguises is extraordinary, but it shows how well he is learning to adapt to various situations and deal with them effectively. He defeats his brother in a duel and only then reveals who he is, generously exchanging forgiveness with Edmund.

Edgar's growth in stature as much as his heroism fits him at the end to take over the kingdom, which Albany relinquishes and which Kent, his heart breaking and near death, declines. His growth is more clearly apparent in the Folio version than in the quarto; therefore, the last lines of the play, which the quarto assigns to Albany, are Edgar's in the Folio.

## Edmund

Although Edmund has a few lines at the beginning of 1.1, his real entrance is at the start of 1.2 with his soliloquy, "Thou, Nature, art my goddess" (1.2.1). Nature is an important concept in *King Lear* with a wide range of meanings, used differently by different characters at different times. Here, Edmund alludes to nature raw in tooth and claw, as the poet Tennyson much later described the Darwinian notion of survival of the fittest. It is to the law, or rather the lawlessness, of this nature that Edmund commits himself, as his actions throughout the play clearly demonstrate.

As both a younger and an illegitimate son, Edmund can make no legal claim to inherit his father's title or his land, but he is nevertheless determined to undo his brother Edgar's rightful legacy. His immediate plan is to deceive his father, Gloucester, into believing that Edgar wants to kill him to take over the earldom sooner rather than later. This deception works, largely owing to Gloucester's gullibility and Edgar's naïveté. But Edmund's success in this initial effort leads to other attempts to aggrandize himself, until the edifice of deception and ambition he has built comes crashing down at the end.

It is important to recognize from the outset that Edmund is not an obvious villain. In keeping with the Elizabethan notion of evil seeming fair, Shakespeare makes him very attractive in many ways, both physically and intellectually. That is the source of his success. As the opening lines of 1.1 indicate, his father thinks highly of him. At their first meeting, both Goneril and Regan are drawn to him, and that attraction quickly turns into something much deeper and more dangerous. Edmund is willing to play along with both women, recognizing the advantages they represent for his billowing ambition, until in act 5 he realizes that he has a problem:

> To both of these sisters have I sworn my love;
> Each jealous of the other, as the stung
> Are of the adder. Which of them shall I take?
> Both? one? or neither? (5.1.55–58)

Edmund recognizes that "Neither can be enjoy'd / If both remain alive" (5.1.58–59) but decides to let Goneril work things out, once the battle is over and the British forces have won.

Some critics like to see Edmund as evolving from the medieval morality play figure of the Vice, and he has sometimes been played that way in a very stylized manner. Certainly, he has the wit and cleverness of the Vice, but his intentions are far more wicked than mischievous. Informing against his trusting father in act 3, he allows Gloucester to be apprehended by Cornwall and Regan in his own castle, though he is spared the horror of seeing Cornwall pluck out his father's eyes. His most diabolical action, however, comes when he has captured Cordelia and Lear and arranges for them to be executed. His commission to the captain who is to carry out his orders conveys his attitude and convictions:

> Know thou this, that men
> Are as the time is: to be tender-minded
> Does not become a sword. (5.3.30–32)

In corrupting his subordinate to commit a crime against his prisoners, Edmund here again reveals his contempt for humane attributes and shows himself for what he is: a devil in human form.

Or almost one. After he is fatally wounded by his brother in the duel, Edmund at last sees the folly of his ways and recognizes how the wheel of his machinations has come full circle (5.3.175). Listening to Edgar's account of how he nursed his father (5.3.182–200), Edmund is moved to remorse, though unfortunately not all at once, to do some good. Only after Kent enters and inquires after the King and Cordelia does Albany remember that Edmund has them in his power. After the bodies of Goneril and Regan are brought out, Edmund, knowing that he is dying, says in a kind of deathbed conversion from wickedness, "Some good I mean to do, / Despite of mine own nature" (5.3.244–245). He tells Albany to send to the castle to stop the executions he has ordered. But it is too late.

## The Fool

Shakespeare's audience was familiar with two kinds of fools, as opposed to clowns, such as Peter in *Romeo and Juliet* or Dogberry in *Much Ado about Nothing*. The two kinds were the professional fool, dressed in his motley coat, and the natural fool, or a person whom we would regard today as mentally handicapped. Royal and noble households used both kinds to provide amusement and entertainment. Professional fools, like Touchstone in *As You Like It* or Feste in *Twelfth Night*, could charm their masters or mistresses with their wit, jokes, and songs. They enjoyed privileges in speech that others did not, so long as what they spoke could be construed as funny in some way. Although the Fool (he has no other name) in *King Lear* partakes of many of these attributes, he more closely resembles the natural fool and thus gets away with many utterances that another might not. Lear thinks of himself later in similar terms when in his madness he calls himself "[t]he natural fool of fortune" (4.6.191).

Possibly because the same boy actor played both Cordelia and the Fool, the Fool does not make his appearance until 1.4, after Cordelia has disappeared from the action, not to return again until after the Fool vanishes altogether. The doubling of roles may have some special significance, signaled by something one of Lear's knights says: "Since my young lady's going into France, sir, the Fool hath much pin'd away" (1.4.73–74). Both Cordelia and the Fool serve essentially the same function, though in different ways. They are truth tellers, for one thing, but the Fool, however "all-licens'd," as Goneril notes (1.4.201), has to be careful to clothe his truth telling in riddles, jokes, and snatches of songs. For another thing, both Cordelia and the Fool try to minister to King Lear: the Fool, in the first part of the play right through the storm scenes; Cordelia, after her return from France in act 4 to try to rescue her father from the depredations of her sisters and from madness. The Fool is unsuccessful in his ministry, that is, in staving off Lear's madness; indeed, by constantly reminding Lear of his folly, he may be a contributor to it. Cordelia does better. Her ministry in act 4 is entirely different, and in any case, Lear by then has gone through the purgatory of his insanity.

The Fool also acts as a choral commentator in the scenes in which he appears. For example, when he sees Kent in the stocks in 2.4, he counsels him—and by extension, everyone else: "Let go thy hold when a great wheel runs down a hill, lest it break thy neck with following; but the great one that goes upward, let him draw thee after" (2.4.71–74). This is sound, rational advice. But the Fool immediately afterward contradicts it with his rhyme:

> That sir which serves and seeks for gain,
>     And follows but for form,
> Will pack when it begins to rain,
>     And leave thee in the storm.
> But I will tarry, the Fool will stay,
>     And let the wise man fly.
> The knave turns fool that runs away,
>     The Fool no knave, perdie. (2.4.78–85)

The Fool does stick with Lear and does not abandon him in the storm. But everything that Lear endures throughout acts 2 and 3 apparently wears the Fool out. In addition, he finds a mightier fool in Edgar disguised as Tom o' Bedlam in act 3 and competing with him for Lear's attention largely fails. Whatever the case, by the end of 3.6, the Fool disappears after speaking his last line, "And I'll go to bed at noon," in response to Lear's nonsensical, "We'll go to supper i' th' morning" (3.6.84–85). We do not know what happens to the Fool thereafter. Lear's comment near the end, "And my poor fool is hang'd!" (5.3.306), may refer to him, although it more likely refers to Cordelia, since "fool" was a term of endearment, as Shakespeare's audience knew. But again it suggests another connection between Cordelia and the Fool that, if both roles were played by the same actor, the audience would not miss.

## Kent

The Earl of Kent is Lear's faithful servant and counselor. He knows his master well, but he takes a big chance in speaking up against the King when he intervenes as Lear banishes Cordelia. Lear has invited Kent to speak plainly, but the King hates what he hears; though Kent speaks truly, he too is banished.

What brings Kent back, in disguise, to continue serving Lear? His love for the King, certainly (1.4.6), but something else as well. That becomes clear in his dialogue upon returning. Lear questions him carefully:

*Lear*: Who wouldst thou serve?

*Kent*: You.

*Lear*: Dost thou know me, fellow?

*Kent*: No, sir, but you have that in your countenance which I would fain call master.

*Lear*: What's that?

*Kent*: Authority. (1.4.24–30)

This is an important key to Lear's character; moreover, it is an attribute and a perception that might otherwise be missed from the way Lear's daughters and others treat him, once he surrenders his crown.

Kent's fidelity to Lear is absolute. From the first, he demonstrates his loyalty when he trips up the insolent Oswald a few lines later in 1.4, and again when he picks a fight with him at the beginning of 2.2. He is the very antithesis of Goneril's steward, and that may be one reason for his inclusion in the action. As things continue to disintegrate, Kent helps to carry Lear to Dover, out of the reach of Goneril and Regan and presumably into Cordelia's camp. There, Cordelia asks Kent to drop his disguise, but he declines. Why? He wants Lear to acknowledge him, to make the connection between his servant "Caius," that is, Kent in disguise, and the man he banished. That is the only reward he seeks for his long and difficult service. But he does not get even that. At the end of the play, when Albany wants to turn the kingdom over to him and Edgar, now that Lear and his daughters are all dead, Kent declines. "I have a journey, sir, shortly to go: / My master calls me, I must not say no" (5.3.322–323). Kent will follow his master Lear even into death.

## DEVICES AND TECHNIQUES

Sight imagery pervades almost every aspect of *King Lear* and directly helps to develop one of the play's major themes (see "Themes and Meanings," below). In 1.1, when Lear commands Kent to get out of his sight, Kent replies, "See better, Lear, and let me still remain / The true blank of thine eye" (1.1.158–159). "Blank" refers to a bulls-eye, or target, and the line is usually glossed to mean that Kent asks Lear to direct his sight toward him. But another interpretation is possible: taking "blank" to refer to the pupil of the eye, Kent asks Lear to see with his (Kent's) eyes. Lear is willfully blind and pays the price for his blindness soon enough.

The literal and figurative use of sight imagery dominates the Gloucester plot. When Edmund conspicuously tries to put away the letter he has forged as Edgar's in 1.2, telling his father it is "Nothing," Gloucester says, "Let's see. Come, if it be nothing, I shall not need spectacles" (1.2.31, 34–35). But of course Gloucester does need spectacles, figuratively speaking, to see into the plot that Edmund is weaving. When Edmund pretends to demur, Gloucester insists, "Let's see, let's see" (1.2.43). His curiosity gets the better of him, and then he too easily accepts Edmund's affirmation that the handwriting is Edgar's.

The eyesight/blindness imagery becomes literal at the end of act 3, when Cornwall plucks out Gloucester's eyes. The Duke is led to this action partly by Goneril's cruel sadism (3.7.5) and partly by Gloucester's reply to Regan's asking why he has sent Lear to Dover: "Because I would not see thy cruel nails / Pluck out his poor old eyes" (3.7.56–57). A few lines later he adds: "but I shall see / The winged vengeance overtake such children" (3.7.65–66). This is all Cornwall needs to prompt him to say, "See't shalt thou never" (3.7.67), and to act accordingly.

Once blinded, Gloucester learns the truth about Edmund. In the following scene, when the Old Man tries to take him to some comfort, remarking that he cannot see his way, Gloucester says, "I have no way, and therefore want no eyes; / I stumbled when I saw" (4.1.18–19). Later, when Edgar as mad Tom o' Bedlam agrees to take his father to Dover, Gloucester remarks: "'Tis the time's plague, when madmen lead the blind" (4.1.46). This might well be an epigraph for much of the play.

When the mad King Lear comes upon them on Dover Beach, at one point he asks Gloucester to read a challenge he says he has written and to "mark but the penning of it" (4.6.138–139). Gloucester replies that he cannot, and when Lear insists, he says, "What, with the case of eyes?" (4.6.144). The following dialogue develops the image pattern significantly:

> *Lear*: O ho, are you there with me? No eyes in your head, nor no money in your purse? Your eyes are in a heavy case, your purse in a light, yet you see how this world goes.
>
> *Gloucester*: I see it feelingly. (4.6.145–149)

Both Gloucester and Lear have learned by now through their sufferings, the result of their follies, how to "see," that is, understand, "feelingly."

Other image patterns abound in *King Lear*. Animal imagery, for example, is prevalent. Although Lear refers to himself as a "dragon" (1.1.122) when furious with Cordelia, he never refers to her in animal terms. In contrast, when he falls out with Goneril and Regan, he frequently uses animal imagery. At 1.4.262, for example, he addresses Goneril as "Detested kite" and later refers to her "wolvish visage" (1.4.308). Others also use animal imagery to refer to Lear's two elder daughters. Gloucester refers to Goneril's "boarish fangs" that would gore Lear's "anointed flesh" (3.7.58), and Albany calls them "Tigers, not daughters" (4.2.40). Edgar as mad Tom sings a song about vicious dogs, as Lear's mock trial of his daughters ends (3.6.66–73), and Kent refers to them as Lear's "dog-hearted daughters" (4.3.45). In a play that shows Nature in all its ramifications but especially in its most elemental form, wild animal imagery appears highly appropriate (see "Themes and Meanings," below).

Clothing along with its divestiture is also an important image in *King Lear*, and it relates to another device Shakespeare uses: disguise. Elizabethans recognized the theatrical convention of impenetrable disguise. Thus, when Kent borrows other accents and changes his appearance (1.4.1–4) to assume the role of Caius, a serving man, neither Lear nor anyone else recognizes him for who he really is. Hence, he is able to continue serving his master, Lear, throughout the play despite the decree of banishment (1.1.173–178). Similarly, at 2.3, Edgar assumes a disguise that shields him from discovery when his father, Gloucester, threatens his life (2.1.56–58).

When Lear sees Edgar, he recognizes in him "the thing itself: unaccommodated man" (3.4.106–107). He discards his own clothes to resemble him, to get down to essential humanity and no longer be among the "sophisticated" (3.4.106), that is, artificially altered or adulterated. Later, when he falls asleep, he is dressed in still other clothes and taken to Dover. But there he appears as a madman, bedecked with flowers, "Crown'd with rank femiter [the herb fumitory] and furrow-weeds" (4.4.3) and other base plants, as Cordelia informs us. Finally, when he is found and brought to Cordelia's camp, his clothes are changed again, once more signaling a change in his disposition, as he recovers from madness and begins his reconciliation with his beloved youngest daughter.

Edgar's use of disguise does not end with Tom o' Bedlam. He assumes a series of different personae later in the play. In act 4, dressed in clothes the Old Man has given him, he no longer speaks or acts like mad Tom, and he appears to Gloucester after his false leap from the cliff at Dover as "A most poor man, made tame to fortune's blows" (4.6.221). But when Oswald appears and tries to kill Gloucester, Edgar assumes still another disguise, a peasant or countryman, adopting an appropriate accent to conceal himself further. Finally, when the trumpet summons a champion to meet Albany's challenge to Edmund, Edgar appears in another guise, a more obvious one. He is masked and armed for the duel. Only after he inflicts the mortal wound on his brother does he reveal himself for who he truly is, as they exchange forgiveness (5.3.167–170).

In her book, *Shakespeare's Imagery and What It Tells Us*, Caroline Spurgeon notes the preponderance of images and verbs that convey the atmosphere of buffeting, strain and strife, and bodily tensions to the point of agony, which flow naturally from Lear's sufferings and Gloucester's. She cites, for example, Lear's words and actions at 1.4.270–272:

> O Lear, Lear, Lear!
> Beat at this gate, that let thy folly in
>   [*Striking his head*]
> And thy dear judgment out!

Lear is ashamed that his daughter has the power "to shake [his] manhood thus" (1.4.297), and later during the storm scenes in act 3 he stands defiantly, allowing the tempest to torment him. In act 4, as he awakens in Cordelia's camp, he feels he is "bound / Upon a wheel of fire," his tears scalding him "like molten lead" (4.7.45–47). Gloucester says that his "old heart is crack'd, it's crack'd," when Regan and Cornwall arrive at his castle (2.1.89–90). In the end, "'Twixt two extremes of passion, joy and grief," his heart "burst smilingly" (5.3.199–200), Edgar reports.

Shakespeare uses many biblical allusions, or echoes, in *King Lear*, despite the fact that the play is set in pre-Christian times. For example, as noted above, Cordelia echoes Christ in the temple, as recorded by St. Luke (Luke 2:49), when she says, "O dear father, / It is thy business I go about" (4.4.23–24). Earlier, when she says, "Unhappy that I am, I cannot heave / My heart into my mouth" (1.1.91–92), she is apparently echoing Ecclesiasticus 21:26: "The heart of fools is in the mouth; but the mouth of the wise men is in their heart." Some critics see in the character of Cordelia an emblem of Jesus, even though she is a woman. At the end of the play, when Lear enters with her in his arms, they believe the figure represents an inverted pieta—the image of Mary carrying the body of her son after he has been lowered from the cross.

The love contest at the beginning of *King Lear* and much of what follows brings to mind the exhortation in 1 John 3:18: "My little children, let us not love in word, neither in tongue only; but in deed and in truth." When Gloucester says, referring to Edgar as Tom o' Bedlam, "I' th' last night's storm I such a fellow saw, / Which made me think a man a worm" (4.1.32–33), he echoes Job 25:6, where Bildad the Shuhite says, "How much less man, that is a worm? And the son of man, which is a worm?" Similarly, when Lear asks, "Is man no more than this? Consider him well" (3.4.102–103), he echoes Hebrews 2:6: "What is man, that thou art mindful of him? Or the son of man, that thou visitest him?" The topsy-turveyness that characterizes so much of the world of *King Lear*, as in the sight-blindness motif, or Lear's last exchange with the Fool (3.6.84–85), has its counterpart in Job 5:14: "They meet with darkness in the daytime, and grope in the noonday as in the night."

These and many other allusions and echoes, which Rosalie Colie has noted ("The Energies of Endurance: Biblical Echoes in *King Lear*," in *Some Facets of "King Lear"*: *Essays in Prismatic Criticism*, ed. Rosalie L. Colie and F. T. Flahiff [Toronto: U of Toronto P, 1974], 117–144), suggest that Shakespeare was well aware that although his play was set in pagan times, he was writing for a Christian audience—one that, moreover, was far better versed in scripture than many are today. He could count on, and probably did count on, his audience's ability to pick up many of these biblical allusions and echoes, which provide a larger dimension for the action of his play and its moral content.

## THEMES AND MEANINGS

In a play as intricate and complex as *King Lear*, many of the themes are closely related and intertwined. While some themes may loom larger than others, no single one dominates the whole. The analysis that follows treats the themes discretely, but the reader should be aware of how often and significantly they overlap and interrelate.

The opening dialogue of *King Lear* between Gloucester and Kent about the King's impending division of Britain introduces a theme that would immediately strike Shakespeare's audience with concern, if not horror, especially when the play was performed at King James's court. James was king of both Scotland and England, and one of his first goals when assuming the English throne was to unite the two kingdoms, which had a long history of strife along their common border. The idea of dividing an already united kingdom therefore would be anathema to him and others in the audience who knew that division bred weakness and, worse, conflict.

What prompts Lear, then, to decide to divide up his kingdom? He gives his reasons, such as they are, in his opening speeches. He wants to "shake all cares and business from [his] age," letting "younger strengths" take over (1.1.39–40). In other words, he wants to retire. He has another motive: by dividing up the kingdom now, he believes he will avoid "future strife" between his daughters, or rather their husbands (1.1.44). In this, of course, he is radically deceived; we learn very early on that the two dukes, Albany and Cornwall, have begun planning to fight for control of the entire kingdom (2.1.6–13). Lear is also deceived to think that in giving up his royal powers he may still retain "the name, and all th' addition [honors and pre-rogatives] to a king" (1.1.136). Although Kent tries to stop Lear, the King is adamant. Later, the Fool tries to show Lear the folly of his actions: for example, he cracks an egg and reveals two empty crowns (1.4.155–163). The advice, however, comes too late. The damage has been done.

The disastrous results of Lear's decision to divide up his kingdom are abundantly clear at the end of the play. The country is in shambles. The entire royal family has been wiped out, and the survivors—Albany, Kent, Edgar—are utterly dejected. Albany no longer has the heart to rule in the kingdom. Edgar ends up as the sole ruler, but how capable he will be to repair and restore the state remains unclear.

When Lear determines to test his daughters' love for him and to allocate a portion of his kingdom to them accordingly, he is obviously just playing games. He has already divided up the kingdom, as Gloucester and Kent note in their opening dialogue. Nevertheless, Goneril and Regan decide to go along with the game and to speak in hyperbolic terms of how much they love their father. But Cordelia refuses to play; instead, she speaks honestly and forthrightly. In the context of Goneril and Regan's exaggerated professions of love, her statement strikes Lear as an insult, and he becomes outraged.

For speaking truthfully, Cordelia is banished from the kingdom with nothing for her dowry; the bond between Cordelia and her father, however, is not completely broken. When she learns of the terrible treatment Lear has received at the hands of her sisters, Cordelia comes to her father's aid. In this effort she is unsuccessful—at least in Shakespeare's treatment of the story—but her failure in battle seems less important to Lear than her loyalty and devotion to him, which at last he recognizes for the great gift it is. Their bond reaffirmed, he is willing to go to prison along with her. Their reunion does not last long, though; Cordelia's death finally separates Lear from his beloved youngest daughter.

The parallel plot similarly develops the theme of bonds between parent and child, child and parent. Edmund hardly feels any bond of loyalty to either his father or his brother, as he plans to alienate Edgar from Gloucester and succeeds very quickly in doing so. Credulous Gloucester erroneously believes Edmund's forged letter stating that Edgar wants to get rid of their father so that they can together take over his earldom. In this way, Edmund severs the bond between Gloucester and Edgar, parent and child, although not permanently. When Edgar in disguise as Tom o' Bedlam sees his blinded father led by the Old Man, he willingly agrees to lead Gloucester to Dover. Edgar's love and devotion, like Cordelia's, to the father who wronged him is stronger than any feelings of vindictiveness or resentment. Instead of letting Gloucester carry out his wish to die, Edgar determines to help cure him of despair, and he succeeds despite Gloucester's occasional backsliding. At the end, when Edgar finally reveals himself, Gloucester's flawed heart breaks, battered between the extremes of joy and grief (5.3.193–200).

Other bonds besides those between parent and child, child and parent are also important in *King Lear*. Chief among them is the loyalty that brings the Earl of Kent to serve Lear even after he has been banished from the kingdom for speaking out against Lear's foolish actions in dividing up the realm and banishing Cordelia. His loyalty to Lear is absolute; hence, despite Lear's threat of capital punishment, Kent returns to serve his master, adopting a disguise as a common serving man named Caius.

Kent as Caius first proves himself worthy of service when he trips up Goneril's steward, Oswald, who is impertinent to Lear. Later, he again confronts Oswald at Gloucester's castle and picks a fight with him, which lands Kent in the stocks. The contrast between the two men, both acting as servants to royalty, could not be more striking. Whereas Kent is plainspoken and forthright, Oswald is fawning and obsequious, willing to carry out any of his mistress's orders, no matter how devious or despicable. He is entirely willing, for example, to act as Goneril's go-between in her affair with Edmund (see 4.2.18–19). He will even attempt to kill blind Gloucester and is only prevented from doing so by Edgar.

Another servant who shares Kent's sense of loyalty and devotion is the Fool. Although sad about Cordelia's banishment, he accompanies Lear everywhere, even into the raging storm in act 3; he tries to help the old King see the error of his ways. That Lear seems to pay little heed to his advice does not deter the Fool, although by the end of act 3 he is so worn out with following his master that he disappears from the play. His rhyme about the servant who only seeks for gain and follows "but for form" compared with one who stands by his master regardless of adversity (2.4.78–85) aptly describes both himself and Kent, the true servants in this play.

Issues of loyalty relate to social responsibility, particularly the responsibility of those in power to those they govern. Lear, irresponsible in dividing up his kingdom, soon learns not only how wrong he was but also how badly he had neglected his obligations as King. Stripped of his power, exposed to the raging storm with only the Fool and Kent at his side, he begins to recognize his fault in failing to care for others. When Kent entreats him to enter the poor hovel they have found, Lear uncharacteristically says, "Prithee go in thyself, seek thine own ease" (3.4.23). A moment later he turns to the Fool and urges him to go in first. He then addresses the "houseless poverty" in his kingdom (3.4.26) that he has up to now terribly overlooked and prays:

> Poor naked wretches, wheresoe'er you are,
> That bide the pelting of this pitiless storm,
> How shall your houseless heads and unfed sides,
> Your loop'd and window'd [full of holes] raggedness defend you
> From seasons such as thse? O, I have ta'en
> Too little care of this! Take physic, pomp,
> Expose thyself to feel what wretches feel,
> That thou mayst shake the superflux to them,
> And show the heavens more just. (3.4.28–36)

This speech marks a major turning point in Lear's journey to self-awareness and compassion for others. Recognizing his failure to care sufficiently for the poor in his realm, he urges the wealthy to expose themselves to what the poor experience. In this way they may be moved to divest themselves of excess possessions, which they hardly require, and distribute them to the poor.

Gloucester's experience relates closely to Lear's, as he, too, suffers extreme deprivation and torment. After being blinded, he begins to see things "feelingly" (4.6.149), having "stumbled" when he saw (4.1.19). When the Old Man turns him over to Edgar (in disguise as Tom o' Bedlam), Gloucester asks the beggar to guide him to Dover, where he has sent the King. He gives Edgar money, echoing Lear's sentiments when he says:

> Let the superfluous and lust-dieted man,
> That slaves your ordinance [controls the laws], that will not see
> Because he does not feel, feel your pow'r quickly;
> So distribution should undo excess,
> And each man have enough. (4.1.67–71)

In giving his purse to a man he thinks is a beggar, Gloucester has begun to practice what he preaches; moreover, by his action he fulfills Lear's exhortation in act 3. Shaking his "superflux" to Tom, he takes the "physic," or medicine, that the King prescribes. In the redistribution of wealth, both Lear and Gloucester enact a form of social justice that heretofore they failed to practice.

As John F. Danby has written in *Shakespeare and the Doctrine of Nature* (London: Faber and Faber, 1948), *King Lear* dramatizes a wide range of meanings in the single word "nature." For Elizabethans, nature did not refer to the Wordsworthian concept of a healing or beneficial aspect of creation, to which one might flee for recreation and restoration, for peace and tranquility. For Shakespeare and his contemporaries, nature meant "the visible creation regarded as an orderly arrangement" (Danby, p. 15). "Nature" referred to something normative, a pattern of creation, reason displayed in nature and law as its innermost expression. Self-restraint was important as the basis for the proper observance of custom, upon which law was largely founded in human society.

From the very outset, *King Lear* explores many of these ideas, especially the ways in which nature, once violated, may become a terrible scourge. When Lear enters at the beginning of 1.1, he asks:

> Which of you shall we say doth love us most,
> That we our largest bounty may extend
> Where nature doth with merit challenge? (1.1.51–53)

In these words, Lear sets up a competition not only among his three daughters but also between "nature," or natural affection, and "merit," or deserving. Before the scene is over, we become aware of what a disastrous competition that is. Careful analysis shows how unnatural, because hyperbolical and hypocritical, the protestations of Goneril and Regan are. Although Cordelia and Kent see them for what they are, Lear does not. Instead, he believes Cordelia behaves unnaturally in refusing to say anything at first, and then in responding quite properly how precisely she loves and honors her father (1.1.95–104). For her honesty, Lear denounces and disowns her—a signal act against natural affection and family unity.

In the soliloquy that opens 1.2, Edmund calls upon nature as his goddess and proclaims that he is bound only to her law. His definition of "nature" is what in the nineteenth century would be recognized as a Darwinian concept—the survival of the fittest. Edmund, an illegitimate second son, here determines to prove himself more fit, and thus more innately deserving, than his older, legitimately born brother, Edgar. He thoroughly discounts society's denigration of bastards and claims that he is as well composed as any man conceived in the "dull, stale, tired bed" (1.2.13) of legal matrimony. He dismisses as merely the "curiosity of nations" (1.2.4) the basis of primogeniture and determines to challenge what he calls "the plague of custom" (1.2.3). For a while he succeeds, until more inherently natural and reasonable forces prevail against him.

As Edmund's plot unfolds, Gloucester comments on the way nature finds itself "scourg'd": "Love cools, friendship falls off, brothers divide: in cities, mutinies; in countries, discord; in palaces, treason; and the bond crack'd 'twixt son and father" (1.2.106–109). He attributes these disorders in nature to "the late eclipses in the sun and moon" (1.2.103), disorder, that is, in the natural universe, which Elizabethans believed was organically unified, so that a disturbance in one of its dimensions affected every other. To Edmund, this reasoning is pure nonsense, "the excellent foppery of the world" (1.2.118), mere superstition. Of course, to a modern sensibility it certainly seems so, and Edmund is one of Shakespeare's moderns.

Edmund then proceeds to work his baleful influence on Edgar, "Whose nature is so far from doing harms / That he suspects none" (1.2.180–181). Edmund refers to Edgar's human nature, which is indeed far purer than Edmund's insofar as he neither practices evil himself nor suspects it in others. For all his clever manipulations, however, it is not Edmund's nature but Edgar's, educated by the buffets and abuse he soon experiences, that triumphs in the end.

Meanwhile, the effects of Lear's violations of nature begin to mount. Oswald's insulting behavior to the king early in 1.4, acting under Goneril's commands, is the first sign of disruption. When Goneril confronts her father regarding the behavior of his knights, Lear is astonished and asks, "Are you our daughter?" (1.4.218). He cannot believe she speaks to him as she does. The Fool astutely comments on this perversion of nature, of natural filial respect, when he says, "May not an ass know when the cart draws the horse?" (1.4.223–224). Outraged at her language and haughty attitude, Lear calls Goneril "Degenerate bastard" (1.4.254). He invokes Nature—not Edmund's goddess of unbridled competition but that of procreation and reproduction—to punish Goneril with sterility, or at least with a "child of spleen" (spiteful child) that it may be "a thwart disnatur'd [perverse, unnatural] torment" to her (1.4.282–283). Lear no longer recognizes Goneril as a fully human being so much as a "Detested kite" (1.4.262) and refers to her "wolvish visage" (1.4.308).

Lear flees from Goneril's palace to find Regan, but she offers him no better treatment. Amazed at their disregard for him, he tries vainly to appeal to their better natures. He argues that

> our basest beggars
> Are in the poorest thing superfluous.
> Allow not nature more than nature needs,
> Man's life is cheap as beast's. (2.4.264–267)

In other words, by reducing a person's needs to the lowest possible common denominator, one can no longer distinguish a human being from a beast. Calling his daughters "unnatural hags" (2.4.278), Lear breaks down almost completely and runs out into the storm.

The storm itself reflects the perversions in human nature that have occurred throughout the first two acts of *King Lear*: the unnatural behavior of father to daughter, daughters to father (and their king), brother to brother, father to son, and so forth. In Ulysses' speech on "degree" in *Troilus and Cressida*, Shakespeare gives an excellent account of the theory of an organically unified universe and what happens when it is disturbed:

> Take but degree away, untune that string,
> And hark what discord follows. Each thing meets
> In mere oppugnancy. (1.3.109–111)

*King Lear* dramatizes many of these effects, or versions of them, and in fact uses similar imagery when Albany accuses his wife, Goneril, of unnatural acts against her father, concluding:

> If that the heavens do not their visible spirits
> Send quickly down to tame these vild offenses,
> It will come,
> Humanity must perforce prey upon itself,
> Like monsters of the deep. (4.2.46–50)

During the storm Gloucester, too, recognizes the perversions of nature that are occurring. No longer willing to stand idly by and see what Goneril, Regan, and Cornwall are doing, he resolves to help the King. Mistakenly, he confides in his son, "Alack, alack, Edmund, I like not this unnatural dealing." Edmund hypocritically replies, "Most savage and unnatural!" as indeed it is (3.3.1, 7). But worse follows when Gloucester tells his son that he has received a letter concerning the forces that are assembling to aid Lear and advises that they, too, must support the King. Edmund immediately informs against his father, who is then suddenly apprehended and given cruel and inhuman punishment at the hands of Regan and Cornwall. Edmund does nothing to intervene; his devotion is not to normal human nature but to the goddess he proclaimed at the beginning of 1.2. Instead, one of Cornwall's own servants tries to intercede on Gloucester's behalf but is killed for his attempt after he has fatally wounded Cornwall—another instance of unnatural actions, when a servant crosses swords with his master.

Despite all these perversions of basic human nature, decency prevails at the end, if just barely. Edgar's natural affection for his father motivates him to minister to Gloucester in his adversity, just as Cordelia's devotion to her father prompts her to return from France to aid him. Indeed, it is Cordelia's ministry to Lear that helps restore his sanity in one of the most poignant scenes in Shakespeare (4.7). Though their reunion is cut short by Edmund's vicious plot to have them executed, they share at least a few moments of filial love and devotion. Nor does Gloucester die before recognizing all that Edgar has done to aid him. Opposed to these events of natural human devotion, however, are the rivalry between Goneril and Regan and the duel between Edmund and Edgar, which result in the deaths of three of them. Edmund's change of heart to reprieve Cordelia and Lear from the death sentences he has imposed comes too late to save Cordelia. Nature—the normative aspects of nature as Elizabethans regarded it—has been violated too often and too vehemently by this time for the good that Edmund or anyone else means to do. It remains for the next generation, under Edgar's presumed leadership, to recover and restore nature from the awful depredations depicted in the play.

Closely related to the theme of nature is that of reason and madness. If normative nature reflects the operation of reason, with law as its innermost expression, then madness reflects nature disrupted, or reason perverted. In *King Lear*, even more than in *Hamlet*, Shakespeare explores the relationship between these two mental states—reason and madness, sense and nonsense—in depth. Various kinds of madness are contrasted with each other, and all of them with commonly accepted modes of sanity. Edgar's assumed madness in act 3 as he impersonates Tom o' Bedlam compares or contrasts with the genuine and extreme madness of King Lear in act 4. The rationalist discourses of Goneril, Regan, and Edmund compare with the greater reasonableness of Cordelia and Kent. The Fool's utterances are a special case altogether. Speaking in apparent nonsense, he often makes the greatest sense of all. A good example is his dialogue with Lear in 1.5; another is his speech at the end of 3.2, "Merlin's Prophecy," which is unique to the First Folio but serves as a penetrating comment on the topsy-turvyness of Lear's world.

Is Lear mad at the very beginning of the play, or merely foolish, when he plans to divide up his kingdom among his daughters? Kent gets nowhere when he tries to reason with the King and blurts out in exasperation, "Be Kent unmannerly / When Lear is mad" (1.1.145–146). Kent means that Lear is acting unwisely, not that he has really gone out of his mind. Lear eventually does go mad, driven there not only by the treatment of his daughters, but as much or more by his growing recognition that he has indeed acted foolishly and unjustly, and by his passionate reaction to that perception.

What finally tips Lear over the edge into insanity, ironically, is his confrontation with Edgar in his assumed madness as Tom o' Bedlam. Lear cannot believe that anything less than Tom's gift of everything to his daughters could bring him to his present condition. Lear is still sane enough, however, to realize in Tom's desperate state the basic nature of humanity. "Is man no more than this?" he asks rhetorically, looking at Edgar's near naked body (3.4.102–103). In sympathy, Lear begins to tear off his own clothes, and in 3.6 he plunges headlong into lunacy, desperately trying to convene a trial of Goneril and Regan. In this scene, as later in 4.6, his mad ravings, like the Fool's nonsense, convey an element of sense or wisdom that in his saner moments he lacked. He speaks sense in nonsense, for example, when he preaches to Gloucester at Dover Beach: "A man may see how this world goes with no eyes. Look with thine ears; see how yond justice rails upon yond simple thief. Hark in thine ear: change places, and handy-dandy, which is the justice, which is the thief?" (4.6.150–154).

The difference between Edgar's discourse as mad Tom and Lear's is not merely that one is an assumed madness and the other is real. Edgar's is that of someone hounded by his brother's wickedness and his father's paranoia; Lear's is that of someone driven mad by his own shame and profound humiliation. Both appear afflicted, however, with a strong sense of sex revulsion (compare, for example, Edgar at 3.4.86–92 and Lear at 4.6.109–129). Unlike either Tom or Lear in their mad talk, though related to both, are the Fool's utterances. His rhymes and songs are full of mother wit and wisdom that no one sufficiently heeds, except perhaps Kent, who recognizes that "This is not altogether fool" (1.4.151). Like Edgar as Poor Tom and

Lear in his madness, the Fool also shows an acute sexual awareness, as in his verses on marriage:

> The codpiece that will house
>> Before the head has any,
> The head and he shall louse:
>> So beggars marry many. (3.2.27–30)

In striking contrast to these madmen and fools are the apparently rational characters, Edmund, Goneril, and Regan. But as Shakespeare presents them, he shows that their rationalism is superficial; it is fed, or rather led, by lusts that are deeply irrational—the lust for power and the lust for sex. As a result, these characters overreach themselves and are ultimately defeated. Not satisfied with gaining superiority over his brother, Edmund goes further, betrays his father, and then becomes amorously involved with both Goneril and Regan. His cool-sounding rhetoric is full of hypocrisy when he informs against his father to Cornwall: "How malicious is my fortune, that I must repent to be just! . . . O heavens! that this treason were not; or not I the detector!" (3.5.9–13). After Edgar mortally wounds him, Edmund seems to become more reasonable, when he confesses his ill deeds, exchanges forgiveness with his brother, and then tries to rescind his decree against the lives of Lear and Cordelia.

Goneril's case against Lear in 1.4 is at best plausible, but only that. She may be right that Lear does not need a hundred knights of his own, and that they can threaten the order and security of her castle. However, the text affords little evidence to support her charges against Lear's knights. It soon becomes clear what Goneril and Regan are really up to. In their lust for power, they defy all reasonable limits. Their hubris, like Edmund's, leads them to act irrationally, as in the trial and blinding of Gloucester. Goneril reveals her sadism when she cries out against Gloucester, "Pluck out his eyes" (3.7.5)—a most cruel and unusual punishment for any suspected treason. For all their apparent rationality, the malefactors misstep badly. Finally, as one sister first murders the other and then kills herself, she fulfills Albany's prophecy: that humanity such as theirs will eventually "prey on itself, / Like monsters of the deep" (4.2.49–50).

For the true voice of reason, we have to turn to others: Cordelia, Kent, Albany, and Edgar as himself. Cordelia's behavior in the first scene has already been noted; so has Kent's. They both try to speak reasonably to Lear, but he refuses to listen. These two later go beyond reason in their loyalty and service to the King, risking their lives in the process and illustrating what the Fool has spoken at 2.4.78–85 about the wise man who runs away and the fool who does not. Likewise, Edgar ministers to his father. In a worldly sense they are fools, but they are God's fools; their wisdom and reason transcend those of nature's worshippers, who, in turn, prove most unnatural.

Albany's speeches are perhaps the most dispassionate and reasonable of all, for in a sense the actions of Cordelia, Kent, and the Fool transcend reason. At first, when Albany tries to restrain Goneril from acting as she does against Lear and she demurs, he comments: "How far your eyes may pierce I cannot tell: / Striving to better, oft we mar what's well" (1.4.345–346). But he reserves judgment. He does not appear again until 4.2, and by then much has happened to compel him to turn against Goneril and Regan. A reasonable man, he has seen and heard enough. Under the threat of invasion from France, however, he must defer any action against his wife to deal with matters more pressing. Those settled—and Albany comports himself in 5.1 and 5.3 very reasonably, too—he acts decisively. He accuses both Goneril and Edmund of treason, using the letter Edgar has given him as his evidence. At the end, after Cordelia and Lear have died, he relinquishes the realm to those he feels are more capable of ruling it. Reason mingled with compassion—the best kind of mixture, as events have shown—speaks through him to those who survive and to the audience.

## CRITICAL CONTROVERSIES

Critical controversy regarding *King Lear* may be said to begin with the text of the play. For a discussion of this controversy, see "Publication History," above.

Critics also debate the extent to which *King Lear* has a religious component. Although everyone recognizes the pre-Christian setting of *King Lear*, the numerous biblical and other Christian allusions in the play have led some critics to emphasize a Christian interpretation. Some see the play in terms of a morality structure resembling older forms of drama still popular in Shakespeare's day. Others have gone further and allegorized the structure of *King Lear*, seeing in Cordelia a Christ figure redeeming humanity, represented in the figure of King Lear. To them, *King Lear* is a Christian tragedy, pointing toward the final salvation of Lear along with the punishment of the evildoers: Edmund, Goneril, and Regan.

Although he does not allegorize the play, Roy Battenhouse analyzes *King Lear* from a Christian perspective in *Shakespearean Tragedy: Its Art and Christian Premises* (Bloomington: Indiana UP, 1969). He not only points out many biblical allusions and analogies, he also shows how the play, in his view, offers a Christian interpretation of events in a non-Christian setting. He says, for example, that Edmund's deathbed confession of his guilt and his impulse to do some good despite his own nature are prompted by Edgar's willingness to exchange charity with the brother he has just defeated in a duel. Similarly, Gloucester comes to recognize "[t]he bounty and benison of heaven" (4.6.225) in his unknown guide, the disguised Edgar. Divine providence is further operative in Albany's recognition of Goneril's fate as "This judgment of the heavens" (5.3.232). Her downfall, according to Battenhouse, is related to earlier strokes of justice, such as Edgar's interception of her letter and his victory over Edmund.

Other critics firmly reject such interpretations. It is one thing to notice biblical allusions and echoes; it is quite another to make a biblical narrative out of them. William Elton (1988), for example, sees Cordelia as anything but an emblem or image of Christ. In his view, she represents the pagan *prisca theologica*, or virtuous heathen, of pre-Christian thought, which in some ways prefigured Christian concepts of virtue. Such figures may be seen, Elton argues, in Sir Philip Sidney's *Arcadia* and Sir Thomas More's *Utopia*. It is not necessary to adduce Christian formulations or theories to interpret the play.

Thomas P. Roche initially espoused the view that *King Lear* ends with a kind of transcendence, owing in part to the double plot. Just as Edgar guides Gloucester from despair to acceptance, so Lear is led beyond misery to some transcendent knowledge and redemption. But Roche says that he no longer believes in the "saving grace of double plots" (" 'Nothing Almost Sees Miracles': Tragic Knowledge in *King Lear,*" in *On "King Lear,"* ed. Lawrence Danson [Princeton: Princeton UP, 1981], 136–162). For him, as for others, the ending of the play is bleak and unrewarding; transcendence, rather, is something that we impose on the play. Every gesture of Lear's love is countered by its opposite, a gesture of hatred. Much depends, finally, on the weight given to various aspects of the action, especially in the final moments of *King Lear.*

Another controversy centers on the emphasis the play seems to give to patriarchal structures. Some feminist critics, like Kathleen McLuskie ("The Patriarchal Bard," in *Political Shakespeare,* ed. J. Dollimore [Manchester, Eng.: Manchester UP, 1985], 98–108), analyze the play as a defense of patriarchy, which tends to the political as well as domestic subjugation of women. Women are seen as destroyers in *King Lear,* and patriarchy as the only form of social organization that is capable of forestalling chaos. Cordelia's role is not restoring a redeemed womankind but attempting to restore the very form of masculine control that feminine control almost destroyed. Other critics, like Linda Woodbridge (in *Women and the English Renaissance* [Urbana: U of Illinois P, 1984]), provide historical analyses that offer valuable perspectives. A balanced gender criticism takes into account not only Lear as father but also Lear as King; his rejection of Cordelia affects not only female but also male sensibilities, as does the banishment of Kent. Moreover, this approach includes the parallel plot of Gloucester and his two sons, which some feminist critics tend to overlook.

## PRODUCTION HISTORY

Scarcely any records exist of the earliest performances of *King Lear.* We know from the title page of Q1 that Shakespeare's company, the King's Men, performed the play on St. Stephen's night (December 26), 1606, at court before King James. Doubtless it was performed at the Globe before and after that event, and perhaps at the indoor Blackfriars Theatre after the King's Men started acting there in 1609. We may be sure that Richard Burbage, the company's leading actor, played Lear. Many scholars believe that Robert Armin, who had replaced William Kempe and who had probably assumed the fool's role in *As You Like It* and *Twelfth Night,* acted the Fool in *King Lear.* But a good case can be made that he was Edgar instead, since he was adept at changing roles within a single play, and since a boy could have doubled the roles of Cordelia and the Fool. Given the relatively small number of professionals in the acting company (about fifteen), such doubling was far from unusual, indeed often necessary. The doubling of these roles, morever, from a thematic point of view makes good sense (see The Fool in "Main Characters," above).

No other record of performance in the Stuart period is extant, except for a production by a touring company in 1610 in Yorkshire. Records of professional stagings of *King Lear* in London begin to appear only after the restoration of the monarchy in 1660. Puritans had closed the theaters in 1642, and public acting was not permitted. When Charles II came to the throne from France, where he had sought refuge during the Commonwealth period, he brought with him an abundance of French influences. Actresses now performed women's roles. Movable scenery was introduced, along with the proscenium stage instead of the thrust stages of the Elizabethan playhouses. Indoor theaters replaced the large amphitheaters of the earlier period, which had been torn down; thus artificial lighting was used.

Licensing of plays continued during the Restoration period (and, indeed, well into the twentieth century). Two acting companies were authorized: the King's Company under Thomas Killigrew and the Duke's Company under Sir William Davenant. Davenant's company was given the right to perform *King Lear* along with several other Shakespeare plays, and we know of a performance of Shakespeare's tragedy in January 1664 at Lincoln's Inn Fields and again on June 25, 1675, at the Dorset Garden, a new theater built by Christopher Wren. Although the cast is unknown, probably Thomas Betterton, the leading actor of the Duke's Company, played Lear. The text for these performances must have been based on one of the later Folios, suitably adapted for the new stage and the new era.

*King Lear* as Shakespeare wrote it and as it was revised for performance did not please the taste of the later age; hence, in 1681 Nahum Tate rewrote the play, restoring the happier ending of Shakespeare's sources and making a number of other significant changes. For example, Tate's version opens with Edmund's soliloquy from 1.2, and much of the language was altered for the more "refined" sensibilities of the times. Decorum also dictated elimination of the Fool's role, and a confidante for Cordelia was introduced. The King of France was also dropped; in his stead Edgar became Cordelia's suitor, although in Shakespeare's original they never exchange a word. Tate's redaction of *King Lear* held the stage for 150 years, both in Britain and later in America, although further changes were also introduced by others and several attempts were made to restore at least some of Shakespeare's text. But not until 1838 did the Fool reappear (in William Charles Macready's production); and Shakespeare's ending was restored, though not in every nineteenth-century production.

David Garrick was the most celebrated Lear of the eighteenth century. Small of stature, he played Lear as a feeble old man who moved the audience to tears of pity for his distress. James Boswell records in his *London Journal* (New York: McGraw-Hill, 1950) for May 12, 1763, "I went to Drury Lane [Theatre] and saw Mr. Garrick play *King Lear*. So very high is his reputation, even after playing so long, that the pit was full in ten minutes after four, although the play did not begin until half an hour after six. . . . Mr. Garrick gave me the most perfect satisfaction. I was duly moved, and I shed abundance of tears" (256–257). By contrast, Tommaso Salvini in the next century played Lear as the archetypal titan. A giant of a man, Salvini looked every inch a king. Garrick and Salvini represent two major ways of approaching the role of King Lear, with many subtle variations possible in between those extremes. Laurence Olivier, for example, in the Granada television version (1983), and Yuri Yarvet in Grigori Kozinstev's 1970 film presented a more human rather than titanic or senile interpretation. Ian Holm in the Royal National Theatre production, later adapted for television (British Broadcasting Company, 1998), is perhaps the best recent example of a Lear moving between the very human qualities of a father betrayed by ungrateful daughters and the outraged king cursing those daughters and promising them dire punishments.

Other roles also offer interesting variations in performance. While Goneril is usually portrayed as a cold, heartless woman who knows very well what she is up to—as Irene Worth presented her in Peter Brook's Royal Shakespeare Company (RSC) production (1962)—Regan contrasts with her in a variety of ways. In the

(Left to right) John Laurie as Gloucester and Paul Scofield as King Lear in *King Lear*, 1964.
Courtesy of Photofest.

RSC's 1993 production, for instance, Sally Dexter played Regan as a very sexy, rather
dependent personality, weaker than her older sister but nonetheless vicious, de-
lighting in a sadistic way at Gloucester's blinding. The most difficult woman's role,
however, is doubtless Cordelia's. The actor must resist the temptation to play her
simply as an entirely self-righteous woman who, recognizing her error in responding to Lear in 1.1, becomes the excessively devoted child in acts 4 and 5. Cordelia is
all that and more. Her anxiety as her sisters insincerely protest their love for Lear
must seem very real, as must her bitterness in defeat in act 5. Monique Holt, a deaf-
mute Korean actress, gave an extraordinary performance as Cordelia at the Shakespeare Theatre in Washington, D.C., in 1999. Using sign language to convey her
words, as the Fool spoke her lines, she conveyed both the vulnerability as well as
the indomitability that is at the heart of Cordelia's character. Her small stature and
close-cropped blonde hair coupled with an animated style of acting that stressed
her difficulty in making herself understood made this Cordelia all the more appealing and convincing.

The Fool's role also presents opportunities for diverse interpretations. Although
Lear calls him "Boy," for instance at 3.2.78 and again at 3.4.26, he may be played as
an older man, closer to Lear's own age. He has even been played by a woman, as
Emma Thompson did in the Renaissance Theatre production of 1990 and as Linda
Kerr Scott did in the RSC production the same year, though their interpretations
varied quite a good deal from each other. Thompson's Fool was a mysterious fig-

ure, whereas Scott's poignant portrayal emphasized everything that is close and vulnerable in the Fool's relationship to King Lear, with her wide eyes, knock-kneed walk, windmilling arms, and desperately comic attempts to bring Lear to his senses. Earlier, Antony Sher surprised audiences in the 1982 RSC production by playing the Fool as an outlandish vaudevillian clown, complete with Grock violin, baggy trousers, and red nose, all of which underscored the influence of Samuel Beckett in Adrian Noble's direction of the play.

Set design, including costumes, has sometimes been a problem for modern productions of *King Lear*, though it would not have been at Shakespeare's Globe. There, few props were required and no movable scenery: the trap in the stage would have been sufficient for Edgar's emergence as Poor Tom in 3.4, and metal sheets shaken more or less vigorously backstage provided the sound effects for the storm scenes. Costumes were in Elizabethan dress; indeed, contemporary dress was customary through the eighteenth century. In the nineteenth century, however, actor-managers like Charles Kean became enamored of historical authenticity in mounting Shakespeare's plays. But Kean's set designers could hardly be expected to find detailed descriptions of prehistoric Britain; hence, they settled on an Anglo-Saxon period of about A.D. 800. More recent productions have preferred an indeterminate period—"timeless Jacobean," as it has sometimes been called—although in his 1971 film version Peter Brook attempted a primitive landscape and setting, going to Denmark's Jutland to film in order to convey his intentions. At the other extreme, modern-dress productions have sometimes been mounted, such as Trevor Nunn's RSC production in 1976, which set the play in the period of World War I. Two other film versions that warrant mention are those directed by Peter Brook (1971) and Jonathan Miller (1982). In the former Paul Scofield played Lear. The text is severely cut, and the world of the play is bleakly existential. The latter, for the British Broadcasting Company's Shakespeare series, stars Michael Hordern as Lear. This production closely follows the text but breaks no new ground. It has a claustrophobic feel that mars some of these BBC videos.

As *King Lear* has replaced *Hamlet* in contemporary criticism as Shakespeare's greatest tragedy, more and more stage and film productions have become available for audiences. The trend will almost certainly continue, as directors and actors find additional ways of interpreting the text (whichever text is used, quarto, Folio, or some combination). This is altogether to be desired; the play has infinite depths, worthy of being plumbed by the most talented and capable artists, as they have done most impressively over the centuries. Modern technology, moreover, has contributed a great deal to stage and film representation in ways that Shakespeare could hardly have foreseen, but productions must be careful not to let technology, such as may be used for the storm scenes, overwhelm the actors. As Aristotle long ago maintained, spectacle is the least significant aspect of tragedy.

## EXPLICATION OF KEY PASSAGES

**1.2.1–22. "Thou, Nature, art my goddess, . . . stand up for bastards!"** Edmund's soliloquy is in the manner of the old Vice of the morality plays, or like Richard III's opening soliloquy in which he proclaims his evil intentions. As a soliloquy, it is directed to the audience, revealing to them the speaker's own thoughts. Here, Edmund proclaims no known pagan deity, let alone the Judeo-Christian God, but Nature as his goddess, or ruling power. As Gloucester's "natural" son, this is ironically appropriate. Furthermore, he disclaims the conventional observance of the elder son's right to inherit and blames the "curiosity of nations" (1.2.4), that is, official but capricious legal meddling for putting him down. By repeatedly using the word "base" and its derivatives (1.2.6, 10, 20), he tends to empty the term of meaning. Moreover, he sees himself as in every way physically and mentally equal to any legitimately born son. He therefore encourages the audience to question with him the "plague of custom" (1.2.3) that maintains the privileges of legitimacy and primogeniture.

Edmund's purpose becomes clear at the end of this speech, when he declares that he will get Edgar's legacy through the plan he has contrived (his "invention," 1.2.20), the forged letter he will let Gloucester find on him. If his scheme succeeds, he says, then he, a bastard, will "top" (overcome) Edgar, "th' legitimate" (1.2.21). Edmund ends by foreseeing his success and invokes the pagan gods to applaud him.

**1.4.148–165. "Dost thou call me fool, boy? . . . finds it so."** In this passage the Fool toys with language. He begins by examining the word "fool." He is, of course, given that title, but he suggests that it might better be given to Lear, who, having stripped himself of every other has only that one left. Then the Fool plays upon the various senses of "crown": the crowns of the broken eggshell, Lear's bald head, and the golden crown Lear wore as King. The Fool alludes not to Lear's parting of the coronet but to his division of the kingdom. The reference to bearing an ass on his back is to the fable of the old man who foolishly, out of a mistaken sense of kindness, carried his ass instead of letting the ass carry him, as it properly should. The Fool's comment here, as elsewhere, points up the inversions or perversions of the natural order. The emptiness of the eggs after they have been opened and the meat consumed also alludes to the "nothing" that reverberates throughout the play from Cordelia's first reply to Lear in 1.1. At the conclusion of his speech, the Fool says that whoever calls him foolish for speaking thus should be punished for it, not him for speaking this way. The punning in this episode has its humorous side, but it also highlights the way that language has begun to lose its meaning in this play. What does it mean to be a father? A son? A fool? This loss of linguistic meaning in turn is a sign of the chaos that unfolds in this play.

**2.3.1–21. "I heard myself proclaim'd, . . . Edgar I nothing am."** In this soliloquy Edgar explains how he has escaped the vigorous hunt after him that Gloucester has ordered and Cornwall has reinforced. Determined to save himself, he decides to take the least likely form, that of a poor Bedlam beggar, the lowest form of human appearance next to a beast's, as his best disguise. Accordingly, he discards his nobleman's clothes, dirties his face, knots his hair into elf-locks (tangles), and uses only a cloth to cover his loins. He indicates that there is plenty of precedent for his disguise insofar as many such beggars, hideously decorating themselves with pins and so forth populate the countryside. Hence, in this disguise he will beg his way along paltry villages, lowly farms, mills, and sheep enclosures. Sometimes he will enact the cries of a lunatic, sometimes he will use prayers to beg for charity. He thus descends to the lowest form of human beings, but that is still something, he says; he is no longer Edgar.

How is human identity constructed? Shakespeare had explored this question beginning with his first play, *The Comedy of Errors*, where twins become interchangeable. Is Edagr in some way still himself if he has no rank, no trappings of his former existence? Later in the play Lear says that if the judge and thief trade places, they are indistinguishable (4.6.151–155). What, indeed, is humanity? At the end of this soliloquy Edgar echoes the opening exchange between Lear and Cordelia (1.1.87–90) with his "nothing." In 1.4 Shakespeare shows how words lose their meaning. With Edgar's speech he shows how human identity is following the same course in this play.

**2.4.264–286. "O, reason not the need! . . . I shall go mad!"** Lear replies to his daughters, Goneril and Regan, who have been arguing with him about retaining his hundred knights. They systematically reduce the number he requires until Regan concludes, "What need one?" (2.4.263). To their apparently rational argument, Lear tries to counter with a very different one, going beyond mere reason to more important considerations, such as dignity and stature. The poorest beggar, he says, still has more than he requires, if you are going to argue from the basis of simple need. But human beings require more than basic necessities to distinguish themselves from animals. He points to one of his daughters and notes ironically that the gown she wears, with its deep décolletage, hardly keeps her warm, which is the basic function of clothing; it is worn for other reasons. Similarly, true need must be based on something other than utility. In this part of his speech Lear is once more raising the question of what it takes to be fully oneself, about the construction of identity.

Having lost that identity by being stripped of his retinue and his respect, Lear then breaks off into incoherence, as he is overcome with emotion and cannot go on rationally addressing his daughters. He says that he will be revenged but does yet know how, and he says he will not weep. As his speech suggests, and as his last words confirm, his reason is giving way, and the storm that rages outside provides a macrocosmic analogy to the tempest within. Like Edgar, Lear is losing his identity, and the orderly world of nature is disintegrating as well into nothingness.

**3.4.6–36. "Thou think'st 'tis much . . . heavens more just."** Out in the storm, Kent pleads with Lear to enter the hovel before them, but Lear declines, putting others—Kent and the Fool—before himself. This is the first time that Lear seems to be more concerned for others than for himself. He notes how the storm does not let him dwell on things that would hurt him more (for example, his daughters' ingratitude and his own foolishness). After urging the Fool to precede him into the shelter, Lear begins to pray for the poor in his realm for whom he has hitherto insufficiently cared. He wonders how the homeless, dressed in rags, can withstand the onslaught of the elements and blames his negligence. He then addresses those much better off—the wealthy and mighty—to medicate, or purge, themselves emotionally and spiritually by exposing themselves to what the poor experience. They will thus be encouraged to donate the excess, which they hardly need, to the poor and so demonstrate how the heavens can be more just than we realize.

Lear's speech suggests a growing self-awareness as well as a developing sense of the world around him. But the process will continue. He must lose all, even his reason, and become nothing before he can recover himself and Cordelia.

**3.4.101–109. "Thou wert better . . . Come, unbotton here."** Disguised as the poor naked beggar Tom o' Bedlam, Edgar prompts Lear to this discourse on the nature of basic humanity. In a sense, it is a continuation of his speech at the end of act 2, "O, reason not the need!" (2.4.264ff; see above). He notes that Edgar is bare to the skin, owing nothing to animals for his covering or for perfume. By contrast, he says he and the others (Kent and the Fool), who wear clothing, are "sophisticated," that is, adulterated or artificially altered. "Unaccommodated man" (3.4.106–107), a human being stripped to the barest necessities, is nothing more than the beggar before him. He then begins stripping off his own clothes to be more like poor Tom, "the thing itself" (3.4.106).

Here again Shakespeare explores the question of identity and what makes us human. Lear's journey has been a stripping off of trappings, whether through his own renunciation or through the actions of others. He removes the last of those things given to him, his clothes ("lendings," 3.4.108), stripping himself to his essential being to learn the nature of humanity.

**4.1.64–71. "Here, take this purse, . . . each man have enough."** Gloucester's speech parallels Lear's at 3.4.28 (see above). Giving his purse to Edgar disguised as Poor Tom, blinded Gloucester says that his misfortune is Tom's advantage and prays that the heavens will continue to force others like him to distribute their wealth to those in greater need of it. His prayer focuses on those who wallow in excess, who overindulge their lusts, and who subvert heaven's command to care for the poor. They do not recognize what they do because they do not feel the sufferings of the poor; therefore, Gloucester hopes that they, like him, may be brought to feel what the wretches feel. In this way, a more equitable distribution of wealth would follow, and everyone would have sufficient means to live decently, instead of the rich with far more than they need, and the poor with much less. Like Lear, Gloucester is learning about the world through bitter experience.

**4.6.150–173. "What, art mad? . . . harder, harder—so."** Totally mad here, Lear meets the blinded Gloucester on Dover Beach and preaches to him, as Edgar stands aside. The passage dwells mainly on the theme of perverse human behavior, the topsy-turvy world of the times, where justice and crime are interchangeable, and where anyone in authority, no matter how lowly or unqualified, can rule with impunity. Lear also cites the hypocrisies prevalent in this topsy-turvy world, where the beadle, or parish officer, whips an offending prostitute while simultaneously lusting after her. In lines unique to the First Folio (4.6.165–170), Lear notes how gold can corrupt justice: the poor are sentenced for the slightest offenses while the rich get away with anything. He pretends to engage in just such bribery, offering an imaginary "friend" (4.6.169) money to stop the accusation from going forward against an offender. He ends this part of his speech by citing politicians, who also engage in false behavior.

The speech questions identity and justice. Who is the thief, who the judge? What is justice? Is everything in the world socially constructed? Does universal truth exist?

**5.3.8–19. "No, no, no, no! . . . by th' moon."** The battle has been lost; Lear and Cordelia, taken prisoner. Cordelia asks her father about seeing Goneril and Regan. Lear vehemently rejects the idea, for he is content now just to be alone with his beloved daughter: he uses the touching image of two birds singing in a cage together. As a continuation of their reconciliation in 4.7, he speaks of their kneeling to each other for blessing and forgiveness. His idyllic vision contrasts with and mocks court intrigues, which they will find laughable, as they take upon themselves "the mystery of things" (5.3.16): that is, understanding the hidden workings of the world. As such, they will be like "God's spies" (5.3.17) commissioned and enabled by God, and so outlive the fleeting successes of "great ones" (5.3.18), who rise and fall like tides controlled by the moon.

Lear has lost all only to regain something of his true self. His reason has been restored, and he is at last reunited with the daughter who truly loves him. At the start of the play he had hoped "to set [his] rest / On [Cordelia's] kind nursery" (1.1.123–124), and now he looks forward to doing so.

**5.3.306–312. "And my poor fool . . . [*He dies*]."** Lear's joy at the opening of the scene is short-lived. These are Lear's last words in the play, and the lines contain several important ambiguities. The reference to his fool may be to Cordelia, since "fool" was a term of endearment in Shakespeare's time, or to the actual Fool, who has not been seen since 3.6. (An actor I know believes that Goneril must have finally got to the Fool.) Lear cannot comprehend—nor can many of Shakespeare's readers—why Cordelia must die, and it strikes him at last that her death is final, when he repeats "never." As it has sometimes been enacted, it is after the third "never" that the significance of what he is saying really strikes Lear.

Whose button does Lear want undone—his own, since he is evidently beginning to struggle for breath, or Cordelia's, and who does his bidding? And what does Lear see when he asks the bystanders to look at Cordelia's lips? Does he see them moving, or delude himself into thinking so? Or does he point upward, to where he believes he sees her soul mounting toward the heavens? It has been played both ways. The important thing is that he, unlike Lear in 1.1, now directs others' gaze not to himself, but elsewhere. Lear's transformation, such as it is, is thus complete, as he dies.

**Annotated Bibliography**

Bloom, Harold. *Shakespeare: The Invention of the Human*. New York: Riverhead Books, 1998. 476–515. The chapter on *King Lear* is one of the best things in this book and one of the best ever written on the play. For Bloom, "*King Lear* is arguably the most powerful and inescapable of literary works" (496–497).

Elton, William R. *"King Lear" and the Gods*. 2nd ed. Lexington: UP of Kentucky, 1988. This very learned book, fully documented, makes the strongest case for a non-Christian interpretation of *King Lear*.

Foakes, R. A. *Hamlet versus Lear: Cultural Politics and Shakespeare's Art*. Cambridge: Cambridge UP, 1993. This excellent study includes a survey of much of the important criticism of both plays and shows how *King Lear* has gained ascendancy over *Hamlet* as Shakespeare's greatest tragedy.

Halio, Jay L., ed. *Critical Essays on Shakespeare's "King Lear."* New York: G. K. Hall, 1996. Contains major essays on various aspects of scholarship and criticism, including the essays by Thomas Roche and Kathleen McLuskie cited in this chapter.

———. *The Tragedy of "King Lear."* Cambridge: Cambridge UP, 1992. This edition of the play is based on the Folio text, with Quarto-only passages included in an appendix, fully annotated like the rest of the text. Includes a lengthy analysis of the two-text theory, with many passages reproduced in facsimile and explained.

Leggatt, Alexander. *Shakespeare in Performance: "King Lear."* Manchester, Eng.: Manchester UP, 1991. Contains excellent analyses of several modern productions, both on the stage and in film.

Mack, Maynard. *"King Lear" in Our Time*. Berkeley: U of California P, 1965. Three fine essays included here cover the sources of the play, criticism, and performance.

Rosenberg, Marvin. *The Masks of "King Lear."* Berkeley: U of California P, 1972. Doubtless the best and most thorough study of *King Lear*, combining literary criticism and stage history, up to the date of publication. Using firsthand experience but mainly documented historical sources, Rosenberg shows the various ways the play and its characters have been interpreted, with some suggestions of his own included.

Soellner, Rolf. *Shakespeare's Pattern of Self-Knowledge.* Columbus: Ohio State UP, 1972. 281–326. The chapters on *King Lear* are subtitled "Valuing the Self" and "Stripping the Self." The overall approach develops Lear's and Gloucester's journeys to self-knowledge, beginning with their almost total lack of self-knowledge.

Taylor, Gary, and Michael Warren, eds. *The Division of the Kingdoms: Shakespeare's Two Versions of "King Lear."* Oxford: Clarendon P, 1983. The volume contains a dozen essays that describe and analyze the differences between the quarto and Folio editions of *King Lear* along with detailed explanations that help to account for those changes.

# Macbeth

## Matthew Woodcock

### PLOT SUMMARY

**1.1.** The play begins with a brief meeting between three witches during a thunderstorm. They agree to convene again upon the heath following a battle that will be fought that day and to meet with Macbeth. They depart after calling upon their familiars or attendant spirits, Grimalkin (a cat) and Paddock (a toad).

**1.2.** At a camp near a battlefield, King Duncan of Scotland, his sons Malcolm and Donalbain, and one of his nobles (or "thanes"), Lennox, speak with a bleeding Sergeant returned from fighting. The Sergeant tells how Macbeth valiantly defeated the rebel Macdonwald and, together with fellow noble Banquo, went on to fight the Norwegian lord Sweno. The thanes of Rosse and Angus enter to report that the Norwegian forces, though aided by the treasonous Thane of Cawdor, have been defeated by Macbeth and that Sweno himself now desires to surrender. Impressed at Macbeth's conduct, Duncan awards him the Thane of Cawdor's forfeited title.

**1.3.** The witches meet again on the heath. When asked where she has been, the First Witch replies that, having been insulted by a sailor's wife, she will sail in a sieve to the sailor's ship, named the *Tiger*, and torment him. The First Witch then produces the thumb of a pilot whose ship was wrecked.

Macbeth and Banquo enter, the latter immediately puzzled by the presence of the "wither'd" old women (1.3.40). Macbeth bids them speak. The First Witch greets him, "All hail, Macbeth, hail to thee, Thane of Glamis!"; the Second Witch greets him, "All hail, Macbeth, hail to thee, Thane of Cawdor!"; the Third Witch says, "All hail, Macbeth, that shalt be King hereafter!" (1.3.48–50). Banquo observes that the witches' words have unsettled Macbeth, but he asks whether they have any predictions for him. The witches reply, "Thou shalt get kings, though thou be none" (1.3.67). Macbeth is puzzled as to why he should have been addressed as Thane of Cawdor, since "The Thane of Cawdor lives / A prosperous gentleman" (1.3.72–73) and dismisses the possibility of ever being king.

After the witches' sudden disappearance Macbeth and Banquo begin to doubt their own sanity, until Rosse and Angus enter to tell of Duncan's favor toward Macbeth following the rebels' defeat and of the King's granting the title of Thane of Cawdor to Macbeth. Upon learning that he is the new Thane of Cawdor, Macbeth begins to entertain the idea that the witches' words may prove true and tells Banquo as much. Banquo is more skeptical and advises that the prophecies may be a form of diabolical deception. Macbeth (in his first soliloquy) briefly contemplates the potentially horrific implications of the trajectory plotted by the witches' prophecy. Banquo notes that Macbeth is clearly absorbed with the possibilities raised by the prophecy.

**1.4.** The scene opens with Malcolm's informing King Duncan of the traitor Cawdor's execution. Macbeth and Banquo enter with Rosse and Angus and are greeted as loyal and dutiful kinsmen. Swelled by the loyalty and strength of his retainers Duncan then declares that his eldest son, Malcolm, will inherit the King's title and estate. Malcolm is made Prince of Cumberland. Duncan resolves to ride to Inverness to stay with Macbeth, who deferentially promises to ride ahead and inform his household of the King's approach. As he leaves, Macbeth says in an aside that Malcolm now stands as an added obstacle between him and the prophecy's realization.

**1.5.** At Inverness Lady Macbeth reads a letter from her husband in which he informs her of his encounter with the witches. Macbeth tells her that events have clearly proven that the witches "have more in them than mortal knowledge" (1.5.3), since, just as they declared, he was duly named Thane of Cawdor. He informs her also of the promised greatness suggested in the witches' reference to his being "king hereafter." Lady Macbeth is confident that the prophecy will come to fruition but is also fearful that Macbeth himself is "too full o' th' milk of human kindness" (1.5.17) to take matters into his hands directly and achieve the crown by "the nearest way" (1.5.18), that is, by killing for it. She fears that although he desires the ultimate goal, he is afraid of the means of obtaining that end. She therefore wants Macbeth to hurry back to her so she can persuade him to overcome the obstacles that keep him from what she believes rightfully ordained to be his, the "golden round" of the crown (1.5.28).

**1.6.** The King and his retinue approach Macbeth's castle. Both Duncan and Banquo comment upon the overall "pleasant" and "delicate" nature of the place (1.6.1, 10). Lady Macbeth welcomes Duncan to the castle and speaks of the great honor of lodging the King.

**1.7.** Alone, Macbeth contemplates the implications of assassinating Duncan. Lady Macbeth enters and enjoins her husband to return to the chamber where the King is being entertained. Macbeth tells his wife that they should proceed no further with their deadly plans. She retorts by calling him a coward. She praises the resolve he showed when first he told her of his royal ambitions but criticizes him viciously for failing to capitalize upon the opportunity with which they are now presented, urging him to "screw [his] courage to the sticking-place" (1.7.60). She tells Macbeth of her plan to drug the King's attendants, kill Duncan in his sleep, and then implicate the unconscious servants. Impressed (though shocked) by his wife's courage, Macbeth is once more resolved to kill the King.

**2.1.** It is now late at night and Banquo greets his son Fleance. Banquo is still troubled with "cursed thoughts" concerning the implications of the witches' prophecy (2.1.8). When Macbeth enters, Banquo presents him with a diamond as a token of the King's gratitude for Macbeth's hospitality. Banquo tells Macbeth that he has dreamt about the witches and how—thus far—they appear to have told the truth.

Macbeth dismisses the witches' words but sounds out Banquo's potential loyalty. Banquo and the others leave Macbeth alone. Macbeth sees an imaginary dagger and interprets it as a sign of the "bloody business" (2.1.48) that now must be done.

**2.2.** Elsewhere in the castle Lady Macbeth has drugged the King's grooms. Macbeth enters with two bloody daggers. Lady Macbeth confesses that she was unable to kill the King, but Macbeth bluntly informs her that he has done the deed. Macbeth then notes that he was troubled by the voices of Malcolm and Donalbain as they cried out in their sleep in the room next to the murdered Duncan. Macbeth becomes increasingly troubled by the voices he believes he heard following the murder, though his wife urges him not to think about that. She bids him wash his hands and then go smear the sleeping grooms with the bloody daggers, as she had earlier instructed him. Afraid to return to the scene of the crime, Macbeth refuses. As Lady Macbeth leaves to go and implicate the grooms, a loud knock at the gate is heard. Macbeth is startled by the noise and appalled at the guilt betrayed by his blood-stained hands. Lady Macbeth re-enters to instruct Macbeth to wash his hands and pretend to be asleep. "A little water," she says, "clears us of this deed" (2.2.64).

**2.3.** The Porter at the castle gate responds to each knock with a cry of "Who's there?" and in a series of comic exclamations drunkenly complains about the noise. He eventually admits Lennox and Macduff, Thane of Fife. There is a mocking exchange concerning the Porter's drunken, sluggard nature before Macduff asks after Macbeth. Macbeth enters to report that Duncan is not yet awake. Macduff calls upon the King's chamber while Lennox tells of the unnatural storm of the night before, in which "strange screams of death" (2.3.56) were said to prophesy some terrible event. Macduff enters in a shocked state and, unable to tell of the horrific scene he has just encountered, bids Macbeth and Lennox look into the King's chamber. He calls upon Duncan's sons and Banquo, and a general alarm is raised at the castle. Lady Macbeth enters to inquire innocently about the commotion; she feigns shock when Macduff tells Banquo of Duncan's murder. Duncan's sons enter and are told of their father's murder, and Lennox reports that the King's grooms appear to be to blame. Driven by grief and "violent love" for the slain Duncan (2.3.110), Macbeth, as he reports, has already killed the implicated grooms. When Macduff suspiciously asks why Macbeth did so, Lady Macbeth appears to faint. Everyone else goes off to discuss what should happen now, but Malcolm and Donalbain resolve to flee for safety: the former to England, the latter to Ireland.

**2.4.** An Old Man discourses with Rosse concerning the strange and unnatural things witnessed on the night of Duncan's murder. Rosse says that the King's horses broke from their stalls; the Old Man adds that the horses were seen to eat each other. Macduff enters to tell of Malcolm and Donalbain's flight, and of how this act suggests they were guilty of instigating the murder. In the absence of Duncan's sons Macbeth has been named successor and has gone to Scone (the ancient site of Scottish coronations) to be invested as King. In the meantime Duncan's body has been interred at Colmkill (Iona, the traditional burial site of Scottish kings).

**3.1.** Banquo, alone, meditates upon how all of the witches' prophecies have come true and fears Macbeth has played "most foully for" the crown (3.1.3). Banquo remembers, however, that the witches said that Macbeth would have no heir, but that he (Banquo) would be ancestor of many. Macbeth enters as King, and his wife as Queen; together they invite Banquo to dine with them that evening. An arrangement is also made for Macbeth and Banquo to meet the following day to discuss

affairs of state, including the flight of Duncan's (apparently guilty) sons. Lady Macbeth and the court retinue exit, leaving Macbeth to muse on the danger of leaving
Banquo and his issue alive. A Servant enters, leading in two Murderers. Macbeth
has worked to turn the Murderers against Banquo and now asks them if they are
willing to act upon their nurtured hatred to kill Banquo and Fleance. The Murderers agree to enact what they perceive as their vengeance upon Banquo and his
family. Macbeth promises to advise them where to commit the murders, ensuring
it is done at a sufficient distance from the palace so as not to implicate the new
King. The Murderers leave; Banquo and Fleance are to be murdered that night.

**3.2.** Lady Macbeth, alone, expresses her concern that, despite the murder of Duncan, the Macbeths' situation is not without continuing hazards. Macbeth enters and
voices similar thoughts. The offspring of Duncan and Banquo still present a threat
to their sovereignty and state, and it would be better to be dead like Duncan (and
thus now safe) than remain wracked by doubts. Lady Macbeth tells her husband
that he must disguise any such fears at that evening's feast. Macbeth agrees and is
comforted by considering Banquo and Fleance's mortality.

**3.3.** At a remote location some distance from Macbeth's castle the two Murderers, now aided at Macbeth's behest by a mysterious third, await their intended targets. Horses are heard, and then Banquo and Fleance enter. The Murderers kill
Banquo, whose final words urge his son to flee so "Thou mayst revenge" (3.3.18).
Fleance escapes, and the Murderers exit with Banquo's body.

**3.4.** In the banqueting hall in the palace at Forres, the King and Queen are attended by Rosse, Lennox, and several other Lords. While Lady Macbeth acts as host-
ess, Macbeth surreptitiously meets with the bloodied First Murderer. Macbeth is
pleased at hearing of Banquo's murder but remains troubled by news that Fleance
has escaped. As the Murderer leaves, Lady Macbeth encourages her husband to look
cheerful with his guests and to be a good host. The Ghost of Banquo then enters
and sits in Macbeth's place at the table. Macbeth is shocked at the appearance of
this reminder of the heinous act he ordered. The other nobles, who cannot see Banquo's Ghost, encourage Macbeth to sit down; but the King perceives the table to be
full (as his own place is occupied by the Ghost) and refuses to be seated. Instead
he taunts the Ghost, claiming that it cannot accuse him of the murder. Lady Macbeth attempts to dismiss the incident by saying that Macbeth is simply ill, struck
with a fit that he often manifests. She tries to convince him that this Ghost is just
an illusion or a projection of his fears. As the Ghost exits, Macbeth interprets its
appearance as a sign of the strange, uncanny nature of the recent murders. Lady
Macbeth draws her husband from his startled reverie. He apologizes and bids his
guests drink good health to all. But the Ghost re-enters, Macbeth continues to rant
about the spirit, and consequently Lady Macbeth bids the other guests leave. Macbeth now muses as to why Macduff did not attend the feast. He also plans to return to the witches to discover what further bloody events the future holds for him.
Macbeth blames his over-active conscience on the fact that he is still new to the
business of evil: "We are yet but young in deed" (3.4.143).

**3.5.** At a nondescript location, the three witches meet with Hecate, goddess of
witchcraft. Hecate demands to know why the witches never called upon her in their
previous dealings with Macbeth. To make amends she ordains that the three meet
with her the next day when Macbeth comes to seek knowledge of his destiny. There
Hecate will create such "artificial sprites / As by the strength of their illusion"

(3.5.27–28) Macbeth will continue upon his bloody trajectory, confident that he is safe from future harm. Confidence in his own safety will lead to Macbeth's downfall.

**3.6.** Lennox discourses with another (unnamed) Lord concerning recent events. He begins to reassess the murders of Duncan and Banquo, and the accusations made regarding the perpetrators. He recalls Macbeth's deadly grief at Duncan's grooms' supposed actions. Moving on from voicing such thoughts Lennox reports that Macduff still lives in disgrace for failing to attend Macbeth's feast. The Lord tells Lennox that Duncan's son and heir Malcolm has fled to England to the court of King Edward the Confessor. Macduff has also gone there to attempt to raise the people of Northumberland and the "warlike" noble Siward against Macbeth in order to restore order and security to Scotland.

**4.1.** The witches meet once more. They proceed to cast a long incantation citing all of the noxious, bestial, and monstrous ingredients that must go into their cauldron. Their spell is punctuated by the refrain, "Double, double, toil and trouble; / Fire burn, and cauldron bubble" (4.1.10–11, 20–21, 35–36). Hecate appears, praises the witches, and bids them all dance about the cauldron "Like elves and fairies in a ring" (4.1.42). Macbeth enters and demands that, despite the witches' great powers, they do his bidding and answer his questions. The witches agree to show Macbeth further prophecies, this time in the form of three apparitions. The first is of an armed head who simply warns Macbeth to be beware of Macduff. The second apparition is of a bloody child who encourages Macbeth to be "bloody, bold, and resolute" for he shall be harmed by "none of woman born" (4.1.79–80). Macbeth is emboldened by this news but still is resolved to kill Macduff to ensure his own safety. The third apparition is of a child wearing a crown and bearing a tree in his hand. Macbeth is urged to care not for "conspirers" (4.1.91), for he will not be vanquished until such time as Birnam Wood comes to Dunsinane hill. Macbeth is again heartened by the apparition's words since the forest cannot uproot itself. He believes that he will live out his life's natural course but asks to know of Banquo's issue. The witches' cauldron disappears, and Macbeth is presented with a "show of eight kings" followed by Banquo's Ghost (stage direction after 4.1.111). A spectral pageant of kings passes before Macbeth, who is horrified to see an ever-improving, ever-strengthening line of descendants from Banquo. To improve his spirits the witches dance before suddenly vanishing.

Macbeth encounters Lennox, who reports of Macduff's flight to England. Macbeth is dismayed that Macduff has escaped and resolves henceforth to be more decisive and quick to act. In the first instance he resolves to attack Macduff's castle and slay the Thane of Fife's wife and children.

**4.2.** Lady Macduff, at her castle in Fife, asks Rosse why her husband was forced to flee from Scotland. It was not only unwise of him to leave his family, castle, and title, but was also unnatural, for even the smallest of creatures will fight to protect its young. Rosse ascribes Macduff's actions to the general fearful nature of the times, "when we hold rumor / From what we fear, yet know not what we fear" (4.2.19–20). As Rosse leaves, Lady Macduff resignedly tells her son that she believes her husband is dead. In the exchange that follows, Lady Macduff and her son discuss whether Macduff was indeed a traitor and what that should mean. A messenger enters to urge Lady Macduff and her son to flee. Lady Macduff asks why she should have to flee since she has done no harm. Murderers then enter and call her son a traitor before they strike him down. The scene closes with Lady Macduff pursued by the Murderers.

**4.3.** Malcolm and Macduff are at King Edward's palace in England. Both lament the pitiful state of their country. Macduff vows to act in his country's defense, but Malcolm begins to express certain doubts concerning Macduff's loyalty: Macbeth, who was once thought noble and trustworthy, may have corrupted those around him, and thus far Macduff has not suffered at the hands of the tyrant king. Macduff is also told that he would have much to gain from Macbeth if he were to betray Malcolm. Macduff protests that he is not the villain that Malcolm thinks he might be. Malcolm says that should he himself finally rise to power once Macbeth is defeated Scotland will see an even greater display of vice than any witnessed under the present tyrant. He declares that there would be no end to his depravity, and that he would cut off the Scots nobility from their land, such is his great desire to appropriate all of the country's resources. Macduff is shocked by such claims and protests that the Scottish royalty alone has enough riches to satisfy any such desires. But Malcolm says that he has none of the "king-becoming graces" of virtue and temperance; if he had power he would "Uproar the universal peace, confound / All unity on earth" (4.3.91, 99–100). Macduff laments that it was this kind of evil in Macbeth that forced him to flee Scotland in the first place. Malcolm then reveals that he has been testing Macduff all along and is now convinced of the Thane of Fife's love and loyalty. He says that he is Macduff's and his country's to command. A Doctor enters and reports that King Edward is at hand and engaged in curing a group of his subjects of "The King's Evil" (the skin disease scrofula). Rosse enters with ill tidings from Scotland; Macduff is told about his wife and son's murder. Macduff refuses to accept the fateful news and requires reaffirmation from Rosse. Malcolm urges Macduff to harness his grief and turn it to revenge. Together they vow to gather their forces and return to Scotland to enact retribution upon Macbeth.

**5.1.** At Macbeth's castle at Dunsinane, Lady Macbeth's Waiting-Gentlewoman tells a Doctor how, since Macbeth has been involved with preparing his troops for battle, her mistress has been sleepwalking. Lady Macbeth enters with a candle and is seen to rub her hands constantly, calling out "Out, damned spot! out, I say!" (5.1.35) and talking to herself of Duncan's murder. As she continues to wash the imagined blood from her hands, she speaks of the murder of Macduff's family and Banquo. The Doctor recognizes that these strange actions are the sign of a troubled mind and the result of more dreadful, unnatural deeds that are better cured by divine means than by a physician.

**5.2.** The Scottish nobles opposed to Macbeth meet near Dunsinane and await the English forces led by Malcolm, Siward, and Macduff. The Thanes of Caithness and Angus report that the King is strongly fortified in his castle, though he is troubled by his treasonous actions and served only by those who fear him, rather than by those who love and support him. They all march on toward Birnam Wood.

**5.3.** Macbeth dismisses reports of enemy advances by recalling the words of the prophecies uttered by the conjured apparitions. He is confident of victory in battle, though he realizes that his life is changed forever and will consist of continual struggles to maintain what he believes is rightfully his. Macbeth calls for his armor and hears from the Doctor about his wife's diseased mind. He tells the Doctor to "[c]ure her of that" (5.3.39) and then expresses the wish that the physician knew of some medicine that would "scour these English hence" (5.3.56). In an aside, the Doctor says he wishes he knew how to get away himself. Macbeth still trusts the third apparition's prophecy that he will not die until Birnam Wood comes to Dunsinane.

**5.4.** The English and Scottish forces meet at Birnam Wood. Malcolm instructs the soldier to cut down boughs and carry them as camouflage. There is further report that the Scottish people are revolting against Macbeth and that he is served only by those who feel constrained to give him support.

**5.5.** Macbeth stands defiantly upon the castle walls at Dunsinane, confident that he will be victorious. A cry of women is heard from within. The King's loyal attendant Seyton reports that the sound betokened Lady Macbeth's death. Macbeth responds simply that she would have died at some other time if she had not died then and speaks of the dismal transience of life: "Life's but a walking shadow, a poor player, / That struts and frets his hour upon the stage, / And then is heard no more" (5.5.24–26). A messenger reluctantly reports seeing Birnam Wood begin to move. Macbeth, enraged, threatens the messenger but concedes that if the report is true then the apparition who gave the prophecy must have spoken falsely. Yet Macbeth resolves to fight, come what may.

**5.6.** Malcolm, Siward, Macduff and their forces are gathered before Dunsinane. Malcolm commands them to drop their boughs and commence the assault.

**5.7.** Macbeth appears on the battlefield. Though he feels almost resigned to die, like a bear chained to a stake to be baited, he is emboldened by recalling the second apparition's prophecy that he should fear only one who "was not born of woman" (5.7.3). Young Siward challenges Macbeth but is easily slain by the King.

Macduff hears the noise of that fight and rushes to find Macbeth, swearing that he will continue to be haunted by his wife and son's ghosts if anyone but he strikes down the King. Siward tells Malcolm that the castle has surrendered and that some of Macbeth's forces now fight on their side.

**5.8.** Still, Macbeth fights on, eschewing the "Roman" alternative of honorable suicide. Macduff appears behind Macbeth and demands that the "hell-hound" turn to confront him (5.8.3). As they fight, Macbeth taunts Macduff, declaring that he (Macbeth) lives a "charmed life" (5.8.12) and cannot be killed by anyone born of woman. Macduff replies that he was "Untimely ripped" from his mother's womb (5.8.16), that is to say, delivered by Caesarean section and so not actually "born of woman." Macbeth curses Macduff for telling him this and now dismisses the apparitions' ambiguous prophecies. Macduff bids Macbeth surrender, but the tyrant King refuses to submit to the rule of Malcolm and resolves to "try the last" (5.8.32) despite all of the prophecies' equivocation. Both warriors exit engaged in combat. They re-enter fighting and Macbeth is ultimately slain.

**5.9.** The battle is over. Malcolm, Siward, and Rosse enter with their warriors and nobles. Macduff enters bearing Macbeth's severed head and addresses Malcolm as King; Malcolm is hailed as "King of Scotland" (5.9.25). In the play's final speech Malcolm honors his thanes by making them earls and promises to welcome back all those who fled the tyranny of the "dead butcher and his fiend-like queen" (5.9.35). Malcolm invites all to attend his coronation at Scone.

## PUBLICATION HISTORY

The earliest published version of the play is in the 1623 First Folio. However, the play was composed and first performed during the years immediately following James VI of Scotland's accession to the English throne in 1603, when he became

James I of England and so king of both Scotland and England. *Macbeth* contains allusions to a wide range of ideas, themes, and events of particular pertinence to the new king. Consequently, discussion of the play's date relates closely to examination of the historical background of its production and immediate reception. The earliest reference to a performance of *Macbeth* in Shakespeare's lifetime is in the diary of astrologer and playgoer Simon Forman, who describes a performance acted at the Globe Theatre in 1611. There are several apparent allusions to *Macbeth* in a number of earlier Jacobean plays, including Jasper's evident impersonation of Banquo's ghostly visitation in John Fletcher and Francis Beaumont's 1607 *The Knight of the Burning Pestle* (5.1.6–28).

Topical allusions in *Macbeth* itself link the play to events surrounding the Gunpowder Plot of 1605. Guy Fawkes and a number of other discontented Catholics attempted to blow up the Houses of Parliament as the king opened the parliamentary session on November 5, 1605. Before the plot was carried out they were apprehended and subsequently executed. *Macbeth* can be linked to the attempted regicide by picking up on points of contextual terminology. During his trial, one of the plot's conspirators, Father Henry Garnet, strenuously defended the practice known as equivocation. This term was used in Jesuit doctrine to describe the employment of deliberately ambiguous words in order to promote falsehood—but in such a way that the speaker might salve his conscience with the thought that he was not overtly lying. Garnet argued that equivocation was a means to pay lip-service to a perceived unjust or illegitimate authority; for James, however, this was simply a way of defending deceit. In *Macbeth*, the witches' apparitions are deemed guilty of "equivocation," as Macbeth observes in 5.5.42; their ambiguous prophecies deliberately lead him toward a misinterpretation of the truth. The Porter's claim that "here's an equivocator, that could swear in both the scales against either scale, who committed treason enough for God's sake, yet could not equivocate to heaven" (2.3.8–11), together with the play's subsequent references to equivocation, has long been seen as a mocking allusion to the practices of the would-be regicides. Garnet, who also used the pseudonym "Farmer," was hanged in May 1606, and this event appears to inform the Porter's response to the knocking: "Here's a farmer, that hanged himself on th' expectation of plenty" (2.3.4–5).

Steven Mullaney has explored wider associations between linguistic equivocation and treason within *Macbeth* as a whole (*The Place of the Stage: License, Play, and Power in Renaissance England* [Chicago: U of Chicago P, 1988], 116–134). The Porter's diabolic references are compounded by a topical allusion to a contemporary attempt at the infernal act of regicide. Gunpowder itself was often represented as a devilish invention in early modern texts (see Edmund Spenser, *The Faerie Queene*, ed. A. C. Hamilton [London: Longman, 2001], book 1, canto 7, stanza 13), and Lennox's reference to the "dire combustion" (2.3.58) witnessed on the night of Duncan's murder would have had added resonance after November 1605. Gary Wills even identifies a sub-genre of so-called "Gunpowder plays" on the Jacobean stage post-1605 (*Witches and Jesuits: Shakespeare's "Macbeth"* [New York: Oxford UP, 1995]). *Macbeth* is not the first drama to treat plots to kill James: a now-lost play called *The Tragedy of Gowrie* appears to have dealt with the Earl of Gowrie's attempt to assassinate James in 1600. The play was suppressed for representing the existing king's intended death upon the common stage.

Even without such specific linguistic echoes, *Macbeth* can, of course, also be located within a general climate of widespread public horror at the possibility of regicide. Shakespeare may well have already been working on a play that drew upon Scottish history and represented the new king's lineage as a form of compliment to James. In 1603 James became patron of Shakespeare's theatrical company, the Lord Chamberlain's Men, which was renamed the King's Men. But events surrounding the Gunpowder Plot provide a datable historical context for Shakespeare's play about the political and metaphysical aspects of what it means to kill a king. Given this context, the approximate composition date can be established as being between late 1605 and mid-1606. Specific allusions to equivocation date composition to after the first half of 1606, when the trials and executions took place. This working date for composition is tentatively supported by the suggestion that Shakespeare may have intended *Macbeth* for a royal entertainment performed for James and his brother-in-law, King Christian IV of Denmark, at Hampton Court in August 1606. Following this view, David Farley-Hills argues that the entrances and exits in the Folio text imply a version suited more to the indoor private theaters than to the public stage ("The Entrances and Exits of *Macbeth*," *Notes and Queries* 50 [2003]: 50–55). *Macbeth* is thus one of Shakespeare's last major tragedies, written after *Hamlet*, *Othello*, and *King Lear* and shortly before *Antony and Cleopatra*.

Several particular features of *Macbeth* had a special relevance for James I and form an important part of the thematic and contextual background for the play's audiences, both in royal performance and on the popular stage. The first is James's deep-seated personal interest in witchcraft and its powers; the second is his claim to be descended from Banquo, the Thane of Lochaber. The witches of *Macbeth* are certainly not as fantastic or incongruous within a play about Jacobean kingship as a modern audience may assume. Belief in the power and efficacy of witchcraft was a social and political reality at every level of society, including the ruling and intellectual elites. Individuals accused of witchcraft had been persecuted in England and continental Europe throughout the sixteenth century. During the 1590s James had been personally involved in the prosecution of a group of alleged witches from North Berwick who, he believed, were responsible for bewitching him and attempting to wreck the ship upon which he and his queen were returning from Denmark. The king himself wrote on the reality of powers ascribed to witches in his treatise *Daemonologie* (1597). James attacked contemporary writers who proposed physiological or skeptical accounts of witchcraft, and his theories were heavily influenced by continental demonologists' discussions of demonic pacts between witches and Satan. James argues that witches were the means through which Satan did battle with God's anointed representative on earth—the king—and located his own constitutional role in a vast, cosmic struggle against evil. By the time he came to the English throne James's views on witches were rather more skeptical, but witchcraft was still politically expedient for Stuart conceptions of monarchical authority and an occasion for the king to display his sovereign powers of judgment and punishment. As Peter Stallybrass concludes, "[W]itchcraft beliefs are less a reflection of a real 'evil' than a social construction from which we learn more about the accuser than the accused" ("*Macbeth* and Witchcraft," in *Focus on "Macbeth*," ed. John Russell Brown [London: Routledge, 1982], 190). There was something of a vogue for representing the spectacle of witchcraft on both the private and public stage during the first decade of James's reign. In February 1609 Queen Anne was entertained at court by Ben Jonson's *Masque of Queens*, which featured an anti-masque of witch figures being overcome by exemplars of female rule. Some time after, Thomas Middleton sought to capitalize upon the fashion for witchcraft entertainments in *The Witch* (ca. 1615), a play that included many of the costumes, properties, and dances used in Jonson's masque.

James's interest in the Macbeth story was also founded on his apparent belief that he was descended from Banquo. It was a common practice during the medieval and early modern periods for royalty and the nobility to embellish their lineage by claiming descent from a historical or mythical ancestor. A succession of Tudor monarchs employed mythography, professing their descent from King Arthur. With similar intent, the "purely imaginary" character Banquo was introduced into Hector Boece's *Scotorum historiae* (1527 and 1575) to provide a legitimate ancestry for the Stuarts (M. C. Bradbrook, "The Sources of *Macbeth*," in *Aspects of "Macbeth*," ed. Kenneth Muir and Philip Edwards [Cambridge: Cambridge UP, 1977], 16). A woodcut in John Leslie's *De Origine, Moribus, et Rebus Gestis Scotorum* (1578) depicted a family tree of James's descent from Banquo, and this lineage was also represented in a pageant by Matthew Gwynne, *Tres Sibyllae*, performed for the king in Oxford on August 27, 1605 (see Geoffrey Bullough, *Narrative and Dramatic Sources of Shakespeare*, 8 vols. [New York: Columbia UP, 1957–1975], 7: 516, 470–472). The pageant showed Macbeth and Banquo encountering three witches and may have inspired Shakespeare's choice of material for a play to compliment James. The king's professed ancestry certainly affects the presentation of Banquo in *Macbeth*. Banquo's descendants are mentioned from early on in the play; and, after hearing of Macbeth's prophesied royal trajectory, Banquo learns from the witches that "Thou shalt get kings, though thou be none" (1.3.67). The witches present a "show of eight kings" to Macbeth—effectively an embedded masque for James—that alludes to the eight Stuart kings who had ruled Scotland by the time *Macbeth* was performed. Banquo's ghost follows the eight carrying a "glass" or mirror signifying the means through which the future might be viewed. As part of his potential panegyric strategy Shakespeare ameliorates the character of Banquo (see "Main Characters," below) found in his principal source, Raphael Holinshed's *Chronicles* (1587).

The composition of *Macbeth*, whether or not the play was intended for a specific royal performance, demonstrates a continuation of Shakespeare's wide-ranging fascination with the nature and limitations of different forms of political leadership, particularly kingship. Shakespeare had already produced an extensive anatomization of monarchical power in the nine English history plays of the 1590s (ten if including *Edward III*), and the dramatic exploration continues into the Jacobean period in the major tragedies and Roman plays. E.M.W. Tillyard is one of several critics who found it useful to examine *Macbeth* in relation to the English histories, not least due to Shakespeare's recourse to the common source, Holinshed (*Shakespeare's History Plays* [London: Chatto, 1944], 315–318). As a novel coda to *Macbeth*'s topical associations with monarchy, Prince Charles played the title role in a school production at Gordonstoun in 1965.

The text of *The Tragedie of Macbeth* published in the 1623 Folio is the basis for all subsequent critical editions of the play; there are no editions that were produced during Shakespeare's lifetime. The brevity of *Macbeth*, particularly compared with Shakespeare's other contemporary tragedies, has been a frequent cause of critical concern. Anecdotal suggestions that James was said to prefer short plays might offer an intuitive explanation for the play's length. Pointed gestures of flattery for James, such as references to Banquo's descendants or the royal ability to cure The King's Evil (4.3.141–161), may remain in the printed text as relics of a court performance.

The Folio text appears to be based on a theatrical promptbook (the script originally used in the playhouse to guide the performance) because it is particularly unambiguous in detailing actors' exits and entrances and designating individual characters' speeches. There is also a printed quarto version of 1673 that adds a number of extra scenes featuring the witches, who were clearly the focus of great potential for spectacular extrapolation. Further settings for the witches appear in the adaptation produced during the 1660s by William Davenant and published in 1674 (see "Production History," below).

There have been many attempts to reconstruct exactly what happened to the text between the 1606 productions, in which Shakespeare had a hand, and the 1623 Folio. It was first suggested in the late eighteenth century that certain sections of *Macbeth* may have been written by Thomas Middleton at some point following Shakespeare's retirement or death. Full texts of the songs referred to after 3.5.33 ("Come away, come away . . .") and 4.1.43 ("Black spirits . . .") are found in Middleton's *The Witch*, and it is now commonly accepted that both scenes in their entirety are most likely not by Shakespeare. It seems that *Macbeth* was made more spectacular through the addition of Middleton's songs and that these settings were employed in each case to provide an accompaniment to Hecate's elaborate departure from the stage by means of some form of theatrical machinery or primitive special effect that would make her appear to fly. The play may have been revised to use more elaborate stage effects that became available in indoor theaters such as Blackfriars. Assignments of authorship in the extant version of *Macbeth* are complicated by the fact that Middleton may well have drawn upon Shakespeare's unrevised play for his own dramatic composition.

A further perceived obstacle to establishing the integrity of the Shakespearean text has been the scene with the Porter at Macbeth's gate (2.3.1–34), as the drunken comedy generates a change of pace from the preceding murder scene. Samuel Taylor Coleridge dismissed the Porter's scene as being "written for the mob by some other hand, perhaps with Shakespeare's consent" (quoted in *Macbeth: A Casebook*, ed. John Wain [London: Macmillan, 1968], 84), though the pertinence and congruity of the language and imagery to this scene's overall hellish tone have been conclusively set out in Kenneth Muir's introduction to the Arden edition of *Macbeth* ([London: Routledge, 1951; rev. ed. 1984], xxv–xxxii).

Editorial policy regarding scene division in act 5 is by no means uniform. The early modern convention of defining scenes is that a scene ends when the stage completely empties of actors. In act 5 of *Macbeth* there is an interlinked series of exits and entrances as characters meet, fight, flee, or die. Such a structure does not affect a theatrical performance, but in the printed text each time the stage empties momentarily a new scene can be identified. This is the editorial practice used in the Oxford and Norton editions of Shakespeare (recording eleven scenes to the Folio's seven). The "Plot Summary," above, follows the Riverside edition (Boston: Houghton Mifflin, 1997).

## SOURCES FOR THE PLAY

Shakespeare's Macbeth is based on a real historical figure who ruled Scotland from A.D. 1040 to 1057 and is mentioned in the *Anglo-Saxon Chronicle* for the year 1053 in reference to his struggles against the English Earl Siward. Shakespeare's principal source for the events of *Macbeth* was the volume of Holinshed's *Chronicles* dealing with the history of Scotland. *Macbeth* stands as a further demonstration both of Shakespeare's familiarity with Holinshed and of the sophistication with which he adapts his sources. Shakespeare's play draws upon Holinshed's account of Macbeth's rise to power, his killing of Duncan, his resort to the supernatural for prophecy, and the final march of Birnam Wood to Dunsinane. Shakespeare combines these details with Holinshed's earlier account of how King Duff (who reigned from 952 to 967) was secretly murdered by Donwald and his wife while residing in their household. The linking of these regicide stories may have been suggested to Shakespeare by the fact that both Macbeth and Donwald are urged on by ambitious wives. Shakespeare also employs an episode dealing with Duff's son King Kenneth III's murdering his own nephew, and this may be the basis for the depiction of Macbeth's guilty conscience and the voice that cries, "Sleep no more!" (2.2.38). Shakespeare may have had direct access to several of Holinshed's sources, such as Boece's *Scotorum historiae* (translated into Scots in 1531 by John Bellenden) and George Buchanan's *Rerum Scoticarum historia* (1582). *Macbeth* reveals many techniques of source manipulation that Shakespeare employs in the English histories, including the compression of chronology (Macbeth ruled successfully for ten years between killing Duncan and Banquo) and the alteration of individual figures' ages and roles to suit the overall narrative structure.

One can also trace sources for significant themes and images in *Macbeth*. Shakespeare's depiction of witches as ugly, malicious hags is far closer to the representations of witchcraft found in contemporary demonological treatises, such as James's *Daemonologie* and Reginald Scot's *Discoverie of Witchcraft* (1584), than to the less sinister description of the three "weird sisters" in Holinshed as enchantresses. Scot actually sought to dispel existing stereotypes of those identified as witches, though his detailed account of the errors propounded by his "witch-monger" contemporaries made his text a superlative source for early modern representations and perceptions of the supernatural, including Shakespeare's presentation of fairies. Shakespeare could also have drawn upon James's own ideas about his divinely ordained constitutional role (and the abomination of regicide) set out in the king's treatises *The True Law of Free Monarchies* (1598) and *Basilikon Doron* (1599).

There are echoes in *Macbeth* of some of Shakespeare's earlier works, particularly those relating to tyrants: Macbeth's realization that his murder of Duncan has lost him all the ease that should accompany old age (5.3.22–26) recalls a similar moment of contemplation by Tarquin in *The Rape of Lucrece* (Bradbrook, pp. 22–24). A general affinity in character construction and dramatic structure between *Macbeth* and the English histories can also be observed. Both tetralogies (*1, 2, 3 Henry VI* and *Richard III*; *Richard II*, *1, 2 Henry IV*, and *Henry V*) deal with usurpation and an interrogation of competing claims of might versus right, and critics have long noted particular similarities between *Macbeth* and *Richard III*. Like *Richard III*, *Macbeth* evinces the influence of Senecan tragedy (available in English translation from 1580) through its use of violence, its inclusion of supernatural forces, and its interest in critiquing tyranny and absolutism. In Shakespeare's characterization of Lady Macbeth, for example, there are clear echoes of Seneca's *Medea* and of similar Medea-like figures found in contemporary neo-Stoic closet drama, such as Fulke Greville's *Mustapha* (ca. 1594–1596) and *Alaham* (ca. 1599).

The extent of Shakespeare's use of Christian and scriptural allusions in *Macbeth* is often overlooked by modern students of the play, but Jane H. Jack identifies a continued reference throughout to passages and images from the Bible; she compares, for example, Lady Macbeth's incrimination of the sleeping grooms (2.2.51–53) to Jezebel's plan to falsely accuse Naboth in I Kings 21:8–14 ("*Macbeth*, King James, and the Bible," *English Literary History* 22 [1955]: 173–193). Glynne Wickham explained the Porter's jesting by comparing him to similar comic gatekeeper figures in medieval mystery plays representing Christ's Harrowing of Hell ("Hell Castle and its Door-Keeper," in Muir and Edwards, eds., pp. 39–45). By leading his audience to recall the porter of Hell's gate, Shakespeare compounds the infernal image of Macbeth's castle into which Macduff—eventual liberator of Scotland—enters. Pursuing this direction of source-analysis Chris R. Hassel Jr. examines *Macbeth*'s debt to medieval Herod plays, in particular the similar attempts in each at a slaughter of the innocent to prevent the fulfillment of prophecies ("'No boasting like a fool?': Macbeth and Herod," *Studies in Philology* 98 [2001]: 205–224).

## STRUCTURE AND PLOTTING

After *The Comedy of Errors* and *The Tempest*, *Macbeth* is the third-shortest of Shakespeare's plays and marked out from the other great tragedies and Roman plays by the absence of a subplot. The focus of the plot-narrative remains fixed on the title character's murderous rise and violent fall. Even when not on the stage Macbeth is the center of attention throughout: during the witches' planning concerning his destiny; during the report of his struggle with the rebel Macdonwald; as Lady Macbeth reads of her husband's predicted fortunes; during the choric episodes in 2.4 and 3.6 where Scottish nobles lament their country's fate; and in the scenes between the apparitions' prophecies and the siege of Dunsinane. Macbeth is verbally ever-present and the play's principal motive force, dictating the actions and thoughts of all the other characters. The story begins slowly with information being given to Macbeth by the witches and then contemplated during the remainder of act 1. Following Duncan's murder the play's pace quickens as Macbeth seeks to consolidate his position through removing Banquo and Macduff. Macduff mentions Macbeth's coronation in 2.4.31–32, but then Shakespeare quickly deviates from his sources in order to structure Macbeth's reign from the outset as a series of challenges to the crown, both perceived and actual. The watershed in Macbeth's reign comes in 3.6, where Lennox and another Lord begin to voice fears concerning the truth about Duncan and Banquo's deaths and there is a first mention of resistance to the "tyrant" king. Thereafter, action centers on the growing opposition to Macbeth, though critics have often noted the change of pace produced by the scene set in England, where Malcolm tests Macduff (4.3). Ponderous as it may seem to some, this episode serves an important function in setting out the credentials of these characters, who heretofore have remained undeveloped though vital for the play's denouement. Both have fled from Macbeth but must return to act as convincing heroes. The final act moves with even greater dramatic economy. Any form of extended invitation to empathize with Macbeth through exposure of the character's interiority is now wholly replaced by a series of battlefield encounters and terse verbal exchanges culminating in the final fight between Macduff and Macbeth. With the tyrant deposed and Scotland liberated, the play comes to a close just over forty lines after Macbeth is slain.

*Macbeth* follows the same essential structure as *Richard III* in that it presents a bloody rise to power, fateful reign, and inevitable overthrow of tyranny. As such, Tillyard compares *Macbeth* to the providential paradigm he identifies in the English histories: the criminal acts of a villain are punished and the ruling monarch celebrated (*Shakespeare's History Plays*, pp. 315–318). Order is restored by the figure from outside the kingdom, as in *Hamlet* with Fortinbras. Such a wholly pro-James view of *Macbeth*'s shape and theme has been challenged by those critics who see the play as offering a far more equivocal statement on conceptions of monarchy and natural order.

The pattern of the play's structure can also be examined in several other ways. The first might be described as witch-oriented: that is to say, all of the play's events derive from the working through and realization of the two sets of equivocal prophecies given in 1.3 and 4.1. The second pattern is murder-oriented, and it can be argued that it is the unnatural crime of killing Duncan that initiates all of the bloody events that follow; as Macbeth says, "Things bad begun, make strong themselves by ill" (3.2.55), that is, one evil act is often consolidated by another. Tragedies structured upon a character's attempts to exact revenge for the murder of a family member or lover became increasingly popular on the Jacobean stage during the period in which *Macbeth* was produced. Although Shakespeare presented more orthodox examples of revenge tragedy in *Titus Andronicus* and *Hamlet*, *Macbeth* does include several embedded revenge trajectories within the plot. Macbeth employs the Murderers by contriving a wrong done to them by Banquo that they should now redress (3.1.77–89), and Malcolm urges Macduff to take revenge on Macbeth for killing his family (4.3.228–229; see also 5.2.3–5). In his dying breath Banquo calls to his son to avenge his murder (3.3.17–18); and although Fleance never appears again in the play, Banquo is certainly vindicated by the "show of eight kings" and the prophecy of the future greatness of his line, which includes James I.

## MAIN CHARACTERS

Characterization in the play is essentially Macbeth-centered. Shakespeare manipulates his sources to stress both the brutal and reflective nature of the titular character, to fashion Duncan as the pious victim, to develop characters that either encourage or condemn the play's central murder, and to present figures that will seem worthy enough finally to destroy Macbeth and restore order to Scotland. There remains a trace of the morality play structure in Shakespeare's characterization as we find a central character torn between the influence of good and evil forces.

### Macbeth

Emrys Jones argues that, faced with turning the chronicle history of Macbeth into tragic plot narrative, Shakespeare used his earlier construction of Richard of Gloucester's villainous career as a model (*Scenic Form in Shakespeare* [Oxford: Clarendon, 1971], 200–202). However, while there are similarities in the plays' structures, and in the way that both protagonists cross the line that distinguishes warrior from murderer, characterization of Macbeth is made more complex by the alternation between descriptions and reports of his brutal offstage acts, and scenes that show soliloquies and exchanges revealing his doubts, fears, and anxieties. The play presents Macbeth's gradual descent into the role of murderer and villain and his recognition that his praiseworthy warrior qualities might be easily and productively used for his own personal gain. The first we hear of Macbeth is in the Sergeant's report of the rebel Macdonwald's violent dispatch (1.2.7–23). "Disdaining" his seeming ill fortune in battle (that is, the fact that he is outnumbered, 1.2.17), Macbeth nevertheless wins, disembowels Macdonwald, and places his head on the battlements. Shakespeare alters his source, where the rebel's carcass is simply found amongst the slain, to stress Macbeth's heroism. Complexity is added to Macbeth's character by Lady Macbeth's comment that he is "too full o' th' milk of human kindness" to kill Duncan (1.5.17). We learn at the same time that Macbeth is ambitious but also quite weak when forced to work on his own initiative or outside of the predetermined obligations of his place within a hierarchical society. Macbeth is thus perhaps particularly susceptible to the suggestions of those figures placed outside of such hierarchical obligations (Lady Macbeth, the witches). As mentioned above, Shakespeare uses the history of Kenneth III in order to create the sense that Macbeth is clearly troubled by his conscience following Duncan's murder (for example, 2.2.32–40). There is perhaps even a measure of sympathy evoked in the scene where Duncan nominates his son Malcolm, as Prince of Cumberland, heir to the throne (1.4.37–39). As David Norbrook writes, "presumably the implication is that he could have nominated someone else, that the system is not one of pure primogeniture" ("*Macbeth* and the Politics of Historiography," in *Politics of Discourse: The Literature and History of Seventeenth-Century England*, ed. Kevin Sharpe and Steven Zwicker [Berkeley: U of California P, 1987], 94). Frustration at being overlooked for such a promotion might feasibly be construed as motive for further grievance and a fertile area of contention for Lady Macbeth to develop.

The important thing to note is that Macbeth's character changes during the course of this short play, and it is this alteration that heightens both the audience's engagement with the central character and the sense of tragedy generated by that character's moments of vulnerability and contemplation. If Macbeth were presented as an unthinking murderer from the outset, there would be little perceptible struggle between good and evil; the central protagonist would be no more engaging than the nameless individuals who murder Banquo. Yet Shakespeare records Macbeth's descent into evil through a series of soliloquies and asides in which access is momentarily granted to a form of conscience and interiority. Such a process of reflection on murder begins with Macbeth's brief consideration of what must be done to realize the "swelling act / Of the imperial theme" (1.3.128–129), continues in 1.7.1–28 ("If it were done, when 'tis done, then 'twere well / It were done quickly"), and reaches a climax in the dagger scene (2.1), at the end of which he is resolved to kill Duncan. Shakespeare had already created the character of a thoughtful, potentially admirable assassin with the figure of Brutus in *Julius Caesar*, although there the murder was stimulated by public motives and republican idealism, whereas Macbeth is driven purely by ideas of personal gain.

As Macbeth continues on his murderous path, the audience witnesses no remorse or vacillation but instead hears speeches in which he registers doubts and fears for his own position, as in 3.1.47–71 concerning Banquo. Following Banquo's murder, Macbeth's character is largely presented at something of a distance, either distracted by the vision of Banquo's ghost or simply described as a brutal offstage presence, no longer thinking or worrying, only acting. In act 5 Macbeth finally becomes aware of how much he has changed, how through his actions he has forfeited all of the comforts and security that old age should bring. Awareness of loss generates a sense of tragedy here, as does Macbeth's all too late realization of "th' equivocation of the fiend / That lies like truth" (5.5.42–43), though he still feels no trace of guilt. But there remains something admirable about the re-appearance of Macbeth the warrior, and there is a circularity to the play in the way he finally places trust in his sword and armor (as he did in the recounted battle with Macdonwald) rather than in the false protection afforded by prophecies. The instinctive attraction toward the resolve of the defeated villain has been compared by some to that engendered at the beginning of John Milton's *Paradise Lost* in the presentation of Satan. Shakespeare does, however, provide a final, visual indication of how far the central character has changed since the beginning of the play when Macduff enters bearing Macbeth's head, unavoidably suggesting a parity with the fate of the rebel Macdonwald (1.2.23). The rebel-killer Macbeth is himself now defeated, his role supplanted by Macduff.

## Lady Macbeth

Lady Macbeth plays a vital role in transforming her husband from hero to villain and serves to realize and reify Macbeth's "[v]aulting ambition" (1.7.27). At least initially, Shakespeare presents Macbeth as a thoughtful figure who remains troubled by the "horrible imaginings" of regicide (1.3.138). Lady Macbeth, however, is the force that acts upon her husband's moments of coy speculation on murder (such as 1.3.127–142 and 1.4.48–53) and turns contemplation into action. Without Lady Macbeth the witches might simply be three innocuous old ladies encountered on the heath. From her first appearance in 1.5 one is struck by her complete lack of any apparent doubt or moral hesitation; she reads of the witches' prophecy and immediately knows what must be done to capitalize upon the sovereign destiny seemingly ordained by "fate and metaphysical aid" (1.5.29). It is this kind of single-minded purpose that prompted Sigmund Freud's psychoanalytic reading of Lady Macbeth. Freud argued that the change in Lady Macbeth's character perceptible after Duncan's murder might be seen as a form of disillusionment and mental collapse following the realization of an extreme objective (excerpted in Wain, ed., pp. 131–138). Even more striking is Lady Macbeth's readiness to renounce any form of contemporary stereotype of female identity—and its associated traditional attributes of weakness, compassion, and reserve—in order to facilitate the murderous course of action. Like Shakespeare's earlier depictions of "unnatural" or monstrous female figures, such as Margaret of Anjou in the first tetralogy or Tamora in *Titus Andronicus*, Lady Macbeth figuratively unsexes herself in order to operate effectively within the male warrior culture of the play. She plays upon her husband's warrior identity as she attempts to strengthen Macbeth's resolve by equating masculinity with the capacity to commit murder (Janet Adelman, "'Born of Woman': Fantasies of Maternal Power in *Macbeth*," in *Cannibals, Witches, and Divorce: Estranging the Renaissance*, ed. Marjorie Garber [Baltimore: Johns Hopkins UP, 1987], 93), taunting him that "When you durst do it, then you were a man"

(1.7.49). In her professed willingness to dash out the brains of a child to demonstrate her commitment to the murderous cause, Lady Macbeth attempts to prove she is more of a man than Macbeth himself (1.7.54–58). Like male Shakespearean villains, such as Iago or Richard of Gloucester, Lady Macbeth is evidently successful in her ability to argue and persuade, using the image (reminiscent of Claudius's poisoning Hamlet's father) of pouring her "spirits" in Macbeth's ear to describe her rhetorical skill (1.5.26). Her implication of the grooms demonstrates her powers of scheming. It is somewhat surprising then that a single moment of remorse (mentioned in 2.2.12–13) prevents Lady Macbeth from killing Duncan herself.

The unnatural, androgynous gender performance of Lady Macbeth has invited many commentators to compare her to the "perverted femininity" of the witches and identify a continuity or collusion between the witches' and Lady Macbeth's powers of temptation (Stallybrass, pp. 196–200). Lady Macbeth is certainly willing to accept the implications of the witches' reported prophecy without any sense of suspicion, and her first words to Macbeth in the play (1.5.54–55) directly echo the witches' greeting two scenes earlier (1.3.48–50). Similarly, Malcolm concludes the play with a final reference to Macbeth's "fiend-like" queen (5.9.35). As Adelman suggests, Lady Macbeth is more frightening than the witches as she transfers all of the primitive, violent "otherness" associated with witchcraft into a more domestic, tangible space (Adelman, pp. 100–101).

Once Macbeth's murderous momentum has been gained, Lady Macbeth's function is largely fulfilled and her resolve begins to crack. Like her husband, Lady Macbeth changes during the play. She voices doubts in 3.2.4–7 concerning the security of the Macbeths' position, but this is selfish fear for personal safety, not the articulation of moral conscience. However, following the banqueting scene (3.4) Lady Macbeth appears far less able to dictate the course of her and her husband's actions, and she is then absent from the stage for a whole act before re-emerging sleep-walking in 5.1. Like Banquo's ghost she is now a reminder of the initial crime, and her ranting before the Doctor and Gentlewoman serves to expose the culpability of the Macbeths in the murders of the play and to justify the removal of the tyrant that begins in the following scene. Report of Lady Macbeth's death compounds the sense of loss evoked in the final act; as if to guide the audience's reactions, Macbeth uses the occasion, not to express grief at this particular loss, but to meditate on mortality and the meaninglessness of existence (5.5.19–28).

## Duncan

Duncan I reigned from 1034 to 1040 and, as James Calderwood states, for Holinshed he was simply "one of a series of eleventh-century Scottish kings who were slain by successors" (*If It Were Done: "Macbeth" and Tragic Action* [Amherst: U of Massachusetts P, 1986], 82). Shakespeare, however, characterizes Duncan as the embodiment of pious, just kingship in order to stress the enormity of the crime of regicide when he is murdered. Shakespeare creates little depth of character or psychology for Duncan, defining him more in terms of his constitutional and dramatic functions, that is, he is a king whose murder forms the play's central action. Duncan's language in 1.2 characterizes him as a courtly, genteel figure who is certainly most demonstrative in his reward of loyal service, making Macbeth Thane of Cawdor (1.2.63–65) and sending him a token of gratitude for his hospitality (2.1.12–17).

Sympathy for Duncan is evoked by deliberate emphasis placed upon the king's age in Lady Macbeth's description of him sleeping (2.2.12–13) and her rhetorical question, "Yet who would have thought the old man to have had so much blood in him?" (5.1.39–40). There is also a naive innocence to his exchange with Banquo concerning the "pleasant" atmosphere of Macbeth's castle (1.6.1–10). Emphasis of Duncan's positive qualities further provides an explanation for Macbeth's troubled conscience following the murder. Shakespeare highlights the infernal nature of regicide by changing his sources so that, rather than simply being slain by Macbeth on the battlefield (as in Holinshed), Duncan is murdered covertly in a domestic, private location. The initial secrecy surrounding Duncan's murder characterizes the act as criminal rather than military. The fact that we never get to see the murder or the corpse and that Macduff cannot describe the murder-scene (2.3.64–65) is a vital part of Shakespeare's commentary on the metaphysical nature of kingship, as he constructs regicide as a horror so great as to defy physical and verbal representation.

### The Witches

The presentation of the witches as aged crones with facial hair evokes the stereotypical image of figures that Shakespeare's audience could have found in contemporary witchcraft literature (including James's *Daemonologie*). The witches are characterized as an inversion of normative codes of gender identity and domestic function. Their "beards" (1.3.46) suggest a form of androgyny, and the cauldron scene and litany of monstrous ingredients (4.1.1–38) "draws attention to a sphere of feminine power separate from sexuality but equally as threatening to men" (Diane Purkiss, *The Witch in History: Early Modern and Twentieth-Century Representations* [London: Routledge, 1996], 212). Banquets are an important symbol of security and community in *Macbeth*, but this representation is inverted or polluted by Hecate and the witches' demonic entertainment in the cauldron scene. Nevertheless, Shakespeare's portrayal of the witches is not entirely sinister; they offer great opportunities for comedy and spectacle, as is seen in early stagings and adaptations.

*Macbeth* is not a play about witchcraft per se or a story based on a contemporary witch trial, and Shakespeare certainly does not incorporate every characteristic found in early modern beliefs about witches. The witches are part of a greater examination of the role of metaphysical powers within Jacobean conceptions of kingship, but it is an interrogative process that eschews providing complete, unequivocal answers. Shakespeare fosters a deliberate ambiguity regarding both the nature and role of the witches. Banquo's remark at the first encounter initiates the interpretative debate: "What are these / So wither'd and so wild in their attire, / That look not like th' inhabitants o' th' earth, / And yet are on't?" (1.3.39–42). Are the witches a form of demonic threat directly guiding Macbeth to pursue his murderous trajectory? Or do they merely reveal details of the future, like the classical Fates? They are referred to in the Folio only as the "weyward" sisters, though this is commonly seen as a compositor's error for the word "weird" (1.3.32), meaning one connected with fate or destiny. The witches might also be seen to represent an externalization of Macbeth's own ambition, since he is ultimately guided by what he wants to hear from them, a selective interpretation of their riddles. Just as the first half of *Hamlet* centers on examining the veracity of King Hamlet's ghost, so *Macbeth* plays upon the witches' ambiguity to interrogate the efficacy of supernatural agency. The interrogation of the supernatural initiated by the witches has been taken up by Terry Eagleton, who attempts to stress the witches' positive role and lauds them as the heroines of *Macbeth* for exposing "a reverence for hierarchical social order for what it is, as the pious self-deception of a society based in routine oppression and incessant warfare" (*William Shakespeare* [Oxford: Blackwell, 1986], 2). Through forcing an audience to engage in speculation and interpretation of the metaphysical, the witches destabilize the integrity of all forms of myths and beliefs within *Macbeth*, particularly those associated with the perceived inviolability of royal power.

## Banquo

In Holinshed, Banquo is a willing accomplice in Duncan's murder; but Shakespeare deliberately deviates from his source so as to ameliorate Banquo's character and offer a compliment to his professed descendent, James. Shakespeare omits any reference to Banquo's culpability and plays up his noble, Christian, and rational qualities. Banquo's initial response following the witches' disappearance is to propose a physiological explanation for what occurred: "have we eaten on the insane root / That takes the reason prisoner?" (1.3.84–85). When Rosse reveals that the witches spoke the truth about Macbeth's becoming Thane of Cawdor, Banquo immediately distances himself from the prophecy, ascribing it to devilish "instruments of darkness" contrived to lead them into damnation (1.3.124).

Banquo's innocence heightens the tragedy when he is murdered, and his character offers a commentary on Macbeth's descent into evil by demonstrating the path of virtuous restraint that could have been chosen following the prophecy. He also functions as another obstacle that Macbeth must negotiate following Duncan's murder, both in practical terms, due to the threat Banquo presents to Macbeth's rule (expressed in 3.1.47–71), and because he becomes a reminder of Macbeth's guilty conscience, as seen in the banqueting scene (3.4), an episode of Shakespeare's own invention. There are several points, however, where Shakespeare's characterization of Banquo leaves room for doubts and suspicions. Banquo is naturally curious regarding his own destiny following the prophetic greeting to Macbeth (1.3.52–61); and in the scene immediately before Duncan's murder he promises to keep his "bosom franchis'd and allegiance clear" (2.1.28), an equivocal statement that may be construed as offering fealty as much to Macbeth as to the king. An audience who knew the Macbeth story from Holinshed might remain sensitive to suggestions that Banquo may still play the villain. Even in his musing upon the prophecies' fulfillment (3.1.1–10) Banquo does not initially condemn Macbeth but wants to see whether the witches' prediction for his own decscendants proves true, which it ultimately does, though he never lives to see it. Banquo perhaps represents the dilemma of those forced to choose between rebellious action and passive inaction or acquiescence when faced with a culture of increasing violence and fear.

## Macduff

Two other characters that find themselves, at various times, placed in a position similar to that of Banquo are Macduff and Malcolm. From his first appearance Macduff serves to undermine the efficacy of Macbeth's reliance upon prophecies and metaphysical aid. Macduff's arrival at the castle in 2.3 threatens to catch the Macbeths red-handed (literally), and the Harrowing of Hell allusion evoked in the Porter's scene already casts Macduff into the role of harbinger of divine justice. Forced to flee and sacrifice his family to Macbeth's tyranny, Macduff demonstrates his bravery and loyalty in the long dialogue with Malcolm in 4.3, a scene that functions to exonerate Macduff of accusations of cowardice for leaving his family by placing the onus on his sense of responsibility for his country's fate; witness his frequent references and apostrophes to Scotland in the scene. From this point onward Macduff pursues personal vengeance upon Macbeth, but this quest is placed within the greater context of his seeking national liberation. Macduff is clearly marked out as the chosen means of removing the tyranny, and whatever metaphysical forces have encouraged Macbeth in his murderous career also ultimately contrive to employ Macduff. It is Macduff's seemingly unnatural birth that forces Macbeth to rely once more on brute strength in the final combat.

### Malcolm

Malcolm is lightly developed. After the revelation of Duncan's murder he has a brief exchange with his brother Donalbain (who never appears again after this point) concerning the need to escape (2.3.135–146) and then only features in accusatory reports until the scene in England with Macduff. It is here that Shakespeare provides the most information on Malcolm through the testing of Macduff, in which he reveals his skills of political tactics and diplomacy and displays a youthful deference to his more experienced potential allies: "What I am truly / Is thine and my poor country's to command" (4.3.131–132). Malcolm also represents the restoration of law and order to Scotland, as is expressed in his final speech with its promise to rule "by the grace of Grace" (5.9.38).

### Other Characters

Distributed around the central protagonists are a number of lesser characters whose dramatic function is to comment upon the culture of horror and violence that dominates the world of the play. The Porter's dark comedy not only serves to characterize the infernal nature of Macbeth's castle but also heightens the tension in anticipation of the inevitable discovery of Duncan's murder. The Porter is the Clown figure of *Macbeth* and was probably originally played by the King's Men's principal comic actor, Robert Armin. Such "low" characters frequently employed topical allusions as the basis for their comedy, and the Porter manages to bridge the worlds of the story and the audience through his references to contemporary events and concepts, such as equivocation. Neither Rosse nor Lennox is developed in any way, but both provide contextual information and choric commentary on the declining state of Scotland in the scene with the Old Man (2.4.1–20), the conversation with the Lord following Banquo's murder (3.6), and the exchange with Lady Macduff concerning her husband's flight (4.2.14–26). Lady Macduff herself serves an important role in offering a demonstration of Macbeth's savagery in his ruthless slaughter of the innocents. The murder of her son compounds the sense of pathos here. Shakespeare frequently uses the motif of infanticide to heighten the tragic ef-

fect, manipulating historical characters' ages to make them appear as younger, innocent victims, as with the Earl of Rutland in *3 Henry VI* and Arthur in *King John*.

## DEVICES AND TECHNIQUES

*Macbeth* was composed during what is commonly considered to be the creative
height of Shakespeare's career, by which point the playwright had fully developed
a wide range of dramatic techniques of characterization, versification, and imagery
with which he was able to turn the chronicle narrative of Macbeth into a taut, powerful tragedy. The play presents a multiplicity of appeals to the ear, eye, and imagination. Plays in the early modern theaters were performed in daylight, and the
audience had to rely on Shakespeare's language and poetry to evoke the sense of
altered time and place, both in simple exchanges such as that between Banquo and
Fleance at the start of act 2 ("How goes the night, boy?" 2.1.1), and in more extended
schemes of imagery and reference. Nearly two-thirds of *Macbeth* is set at night, and
Shakespeare propounds the horror of regicide and tyranny through imagery associated with darkness: Lady Macbeth calls upon the night itself to veil the terrible
act of killing Duncan (1.5.50–54); Macbeth evokes a similar tenebrous tone as he
imagines "night's black agents" rousing to do ill (3.2.53); and the witches themselves
are called "secret, black, and midnight hags" (4.1.48). Macbeth's castle is represented
as a form of hell in the Porter's scene, and Macbeth himself characterized in similar diabolic terms (5.8.3). The murders of Duncan and Banquo take place during
the secrecy of night. Indeed, Shakespeare presents Macbeth's whole reign as a noc-
turnal period in which freedom and order are asleep. Another scheme used to characterize the debilitated state of Scotland is that of a corrupted or sick body. As seen
in the conversation between Macduff and Malcolm, Shakespeare may have been influenced by Buchanan's frequent recourse to the body-politic analogy (see 4.3.31
and 39–41).

The theme of blood also provides an important "matrix" for the language of
*Macbeth* and had a particular resonance for Shakespeare during his preparatory
reading (Frank Kermode, *Shakespeare's Language* [Harmondsworth, Eng.: Penguin,
2000], 215). There are fourteen references to blood in *Macbeth*; these are complemented by a further half-dozen sanguineous images and metaphors. Images associated with blood largely fall into two groups. The first relates to violence, viscera,
and bloody acts, as in the bleeding Sergeant's report of Macbeth's "bloody execution" of his duty (1.2.7–42), Macbeth's vision of the bloody dagger (2.1.46), and the
description of Duncan's "silver skin lac'd with his golden blood" (2.3.112). The second group relates to the metonym of blood used to refer to lineage and family relationships. Macbeth, for example, informs Duncan's sons that "the fountain of
your blood / Is stopp'd" (2.3.98–99), and he is preoccupied for the remainder of the
play with the blood relations of Banquo and Macduff. The two categories of blood-
image frequently unite in the play as blood is spilt by Macbeth to remove rival blood
relations and heirs. *Macbeth* shows both the hack-and-slash, positivist means of
gaining the crown by spilling blood and the biological means of succession achieved
through continuity of bloodlines.

William Blissett identifies a sequence of imagery related to the latter path but
centered on sterility and fertility; he demonstrates the significance of binary oppo-

sites in the play's imagery ("'The Secret'st Man of Blood': A Study of Dramatic Irony in *Macbeth*," *Shakespeare Quarterly* 10 [1959]: 397–408). Caroline Spurgeon examines the prevalence of imagery relating to clothing and armor that Shakespeare employs in the play to suggest that "Macbeth's new honours sit ill upon him, like a loose and badly fitting garment, belonging to someone else" (*Shakespeare's Imagery and What It Tells Us* [Cambridge: Cambridge UP, 1935], 325); as Angus says of Macbeth: "Now does he feel his title / Hang loose about him, like a giant's robe / Upon a dwarfish thief" (5.2.20–22). In *The Well-Wrought Urn* (1947) Cleanth Brooks develops Spurgeon's findings to highlight the significance of clothing and nakedness in *Macbeth*, and in particular he traces the image of the "naked newborn babe" (1.7.21) to yoke together schemes relating to blood, fecundity, and lineage into a broader symbolic pattern ([rpt. London: Methuen, 1968], 25–39).

Whereas nowadays one refers to "seeing" a play in performance, early modern audiences—as the word suggests—commonly referred to going to "hear" a play, as Theseus does in *A Midsummer Night's Dream* (5.1.81). A playwright could expect that at least a sizable proportion of playgoers would be particularly attuned to the linguistic and rhetorical aspects of his work. To those with a sensitive ear, Shakespeare generates a grim gallows humor in puns, such as Lady Macbeth's promise to "gild" the faces of the sleeping grooms, "For it must seem their guilt" (2.2.53–54). This image is picked up in the reference to Duncan's "golden blood" in 2.3.112. The witches in the cauldron scene promise to cheer up Macbeth's "sprites" (that is, spirits, 4.1.127) with a ghostly dance to appease his angry response to the "show of eight kings" that culminates in Banquo's spirit (stage direction after 4.1.111).

There is also a rich vein of dramatic irony in lines uttered by characters ignorant of where the play's violent actions will lead: Duncan refers to Macbeth as a "peerless kinsman" (1.4.58), though as M. M. Mahood observes, Macbeth's desire to be literally without peers or equals leads him to Duncan's murder (*Shakespeare's Wordplay* [London: Methuen, 1957], 44); and Macbeth's request for Banquo's "presence" at the banquet (3.1.15) is honored to all intents and purposes despite the fact that he has had Banquo killed that evening. Punning allusions to the Gunpowder Plot and Garnet's ideas of equivocation are found in the Porter's scene. *Macbeth* as a whole centers on the signification of the witches' and apparitions' equivocal prophecies and the perceived correct interpretations of statements that can be taken as both literal and figurative. Thus Macbeth anticipates that Birnam Wood must literally move to Dunsinane, and he is consequently undone by the action of Birnam Wood's figuratively being borne to Dunsinane by Malcolm's soldiers.

While the majority of the lines in *Macbeth* are in blank verse (unrhymed iambic pentameter), Shakespeare deviates from this meter for dramatic reasons. Several episodes are written in prose to characterize the speaking individuals or subject matter as socially inferior, often for purposes of demotic comedy, as in the Porter's scene. *Macbeth* also demonstrates how Shakespeare employs prose to note a shift in register, as when Lady Macbeth reads the letter (1.5.1–14) and when she reveals her mental disintegration in the sleepwalking scene. Shakespeare also uses rhyming couplets to mark out the speech of the supernatural characters (the witches, Hecate, the apparitions) in all of the scenes in which they appear. Couplets are employed both in conversation between characters (for example, 1.1; 3.5) and in the incantations and interpolated songs (4.1.1–47), as if to evoke the form of a spell or charm through highlighting the significance of verbal formulae as the means through which magic is enacted. Rhyming couplets were actually one of the "hallmarks" of Jacobean stagings of witches, and one finds them used in *The Masque of Queens* and *The Witch* (Purkiss, p. 210). This may also be the reason that Macbeth himself is often given speeches featuring rhyming couplets, particularly when he contemplates evil deeds, for example, in 3.2.52–55 and 4.1.94–101.

The witches' dance and spectacular exits exemplify the play's use of stunning visual effects, and there are several key moments that focus on an important figure or stage property that appeals to the eyes of the audience and certain select characters. It is only the audience and Macbeth who can see Banquo's ghost when he takes up the royal seat at the banquet table (stage direction at 3.4.36). His presence not only confirms the reality of metaphysical forces in the play but also implicitly aligns the audience's perspective with that of the guilt-ridden Macbeth. The apparitions in the cauldron scene again offer great potential for spectacle and assume forms in which they—like the prophecies uttered—are both mysterious and disturbing (a bloody child, a crowned child bearing a tree). The movement of Birnam Wood, while rationally explained for the audience simply as Malcolm's forces employing camouflage, is a vital visual cue for Macbeth: the report of this phenomenon prompts him to begin to doubt "th' equivocation of the fiend" (5.5.42). There is also the dagger that appears to Macbeth alone (though sometimes represented visually in modern productions), the presence of which invites speculation for Macbeth and the audience (as did the witches) concerning the relationship between visions of the supernatural and the violent realization of ambition (2.1.33–61).

The dagger scene also demonstrates the great appeal in *Macbeth* to the imagination and how Shakespeare makes the audience conscious of what they do *not* get to see through elaborate report of offstage actions, also a common feature of classical tragedy (D. J. Palmer, " 'A new Gorgon': Visual Effects in *Macbeth*," in Brown, ed., pp. 54–69). The audience never sees inside the murdered Duncan's bedchamber but is led to imagine the grisly scene evoked by descriptions from Lennox and Macbeth (2.3.101–105, 111–116). A similarly horrific image is created in the following scene in Rosse and the Old Man's report of Duncan's horses eating each other (2.4.14–20). Shakespeare can certainly create graphic scenes of onstage violence, such as the blinding of Gloucester in *King Lear*, but the employment of offstage report in *Macbeth* intensifies the culture of fear and secrecy and generates what in moviemaking would be termed "psychological horror," where the audience is left to imagine the worst.

## THEMES AND MEANINGS

Earlier generations of critics committed to seeing *Macbeth* primarily as a study of character and humanity tended to place great emphasis on the theme of evil. *Macbeth* thus presents one man's descent into evil, a fall from greatness into loss comparable to medieval conceptions of tragedy. Like medieval morality drama, or its sixteenth-century distillates (such as Christopher Marlowe's *Dr. Faustus*), *Macbeth* shows the tragedy of a character's personal ambition that leads to a series of wrong choices and concludes with the justice of that character's punishment. Throughout the play there is an evident dichotomy between the forces of good and evil and a number of inversions of what G. Wilson Knight called "life-themes," themes associated with life, health, and courage, such as warrior-honor, sleeping and feasting, and ideas of natural generation (*The Imperial Theme* [rpt. London: Methuen, 1951], 125). The focus on evil also informs the dominant schemes of imagery and language identified above, such as those relating to darkness and blood. *Macbeth* can be seen as an anatomization of evil that explores the nature of evil forces (the witches) and of those who become evil (Macbeth), as well as those placed somewhere in between (Lady Macbeth). Many have observed that *Macbeth* is an intense study in the concept of fear, as Shakespeare examines the wider effect of evil on a society and nation (Lily B. Campbell, *Shakespeare's Tragic Heroes* [rpt. London: Methuen, 1961], 208).

More recent criticism has moved away from the study of universals and abstract concepts in Shakespearean tragedy in order to view the plays as sites of speculative inquiry into the nature of positivist ideologies and institutions. Kingship is a major governing theme in *Macbeth*, and the historical context of issues and events closely relating to Jacobean politics (see "Publication History," above) has a great impact on Shakespeare's use of source, dramatic technique, and theme. Succession to the crown—whether by election, primogeniture, or force—is a central preoccupation in *Macbeth* and becomes a murderous obsession for the title character. The importance of lineage informs repeated reference in *Macbeth* not only to blood but also to time (mentioned forty-four times), with characters continually looking ahead to the fulfillment of prophecies or the inheritance of power (Kermode, p. 213). *Macbeth* continues the interrogation of kingship seen in Shakespeare's English history plays and questions in particular the metaphysical authority upon which the legitimacy of Jacobean monarchy rests. In *Richard II* Shakespeare had already explored the concept of the divine right of kings, the idea that the king sat at the top of a natural order of being that was entirely ordained by God, to whom the monarch was solely responsible. James himself in his treatises on monarchy asserted that the king had absolute, unimpeachable powers, and it was his son Charles I's inveterate pursuit of absolutist power that led to the English Civil War in the mid-seventeenth century. The report of King Edward's curing of "The King's Evil" offers a complimentary allusion to the play's royal audience concerning traditions associated with the mystical nature of sovereignty (4.3.141–159). Macduff's report of Duncan's murder reflects the sacral conception of kingship: "Most sacrilegious murther hath broke ope / The Lord's anointed temple, and stole thence / The life o' th' building" (2.3.67–69). These lines also characterize the act of regicide not simply as the death of an important individual but as a violent injury to the divinely ordained natural order itself. The unnatural act of regicide is reflected within *Macbeth* by the omens and "things strange" witnessed by Rosse and the Old Man in 2.4.1–20, as if all sense of natural order were now lost. Similar portents of assassination are reported in *Julius Caesar* (1.3.3–32). The reference to the falcon killed by the owl in *Macbeth*—a detail taken from Holinshed's account of omens concerning Duff's murder—presents a miniature allegory of Macbeth's own violation of established hierarchies (2.4.11–13). Attempts on King James's life both by Gowrie and the Gunpowder conspirators form an important thematic context for the play's initial production, as does James's use of witchcraft to elevate his own constitutional role within a perceived struggle with the forces of evil.

Like the episode in *2 Henry VI* concerning the Duchess of Gloucester and the witch Margaret Jordin (1.4), *Macbeth* offers an example of the transgressive powers associated with political prophecies in the early modern period, particularly regarding how prophecy closely relates to alternative, subversive means of obtaining the crown. Throughout the reigns of Elizabeth and James statutes prohibited the casting of prophecies relating to the monarch. Whereas Macbeth's growing reliance upon the diabolic agents of "fate and metaphysical aid" (1.5.29) set him in opposition to the divinely ordained Good King, it also leads modern critics such as Eagleton and Norbrook to examine the relationship between competing forms of metaphysical authority and sanction, and to consider exactly what distinguishes the qualities required for successful rule from those practiced by a tyrant. *Macbeth* raises potentially subversive questions about absolutism as it explores the conditions deemed appropriate for the legitimate deposition of a monarch.

## CRITICAL CONTROVERSIES

Some of the earliest critical commentaries on *Macbeth* were concerned with the play's text. In consultation with Samuel Johnson the actor David Garrick sought to re-establish the status of the Folio version, which had been supplanted on the popular stage for more than forty years by William Davenant's heavily edited adaptation, and to present *Macbeth* as Shakespeare wrote it. Garrick defended his "recovered" text in a pamphlet published in 1744, and Johnson himself wrote a series of observations on *Macbeth* in which he contextualized Jacobean credulity in witchcraft. Garrick and Johnson's responses to *Macbeth* exemplify eighteenth-century preoccupations with character types and reductive moral lessons in Shakespeare.

Later, at the turn of the eighteenth century, critics were still closely influenced by the play in production. Commentary upon particular actors' interpretations of Macbeth and Lady Macbeth led to an ever-increasing interest in psychological readings of the play. Walter Whitier's 1794 *Specimen of a Commentary on Shakespeare* traces recurrent patterns of imagery in characters' speech in order to investigate the minds of both the characters and playwright; it anticipates the preoccupations of Romantic critical readings of *Macbeth*, particularly Samuel Taylor Coleridge's observations on characters' motives and imagination and Thomas De Quincey's 1823 essay "On the Knocking on the Gate in *Macbeth*" (excerpted in Wain, ed., pp. 63–93). Nineteenth-century critical inclinations to view *Macbeth* as a detailed study of the characters of the two leading protagonists inform A. C. Bradley's highly influential *Shakespearean Tragedy* (1904), in which he analyzes the characters of *Macbeth* as if they were real people and consciously eschews issues of style, diction, and versification ([rpt. London: Macmillan, 1985]).

L. C. Knights attacked Bradley's mode of character-criticism in his 1933 essay "How Many Children Had Lady Macbeth" (rpt. in Knights, *Explorations* [London: Chatto, 1946], 1–39). *Macbeth* became an important testing ground for "New Critical" approaches centered more on examination of the words on the page than on character or Shakespearean psychology. This is the direction taken in many studies of *Macbeth* written during the 1930s and 1940s that focus on tracing patterns of language and imagery (including those by Spurgeon and Brooks, discussed above in "Devices and Techniques") to suggest how the play functions as a coherent whole. Along similar lines G. Wilson Knight identified thematic schemes associated with life and death in *Macbeth*, though in many studies of this kind there is a tendency toward schematization and finding patterns for their own sake. The same can be said of works concerning the extent to which *Macbeth* can be seen as an overtly

Christian tragedy: Roy Walker's *The Time Is Free* (London: Dakers, 1949) identifies an elaborate schema of medieval Christian doctrine within the play's dramatic structure, and G. R. Elliott attempts to reduce all of Macbeth's decision making to a series of struggles with (and ultimately against) grace (*Dramatic Providence in "Macbeth"* [Oxford: Oxford UP, 1958]). In *The Business of Criticism* Helen Gardner uses Brooks's reading of *Macbeth* to criticize the way New Critical constructions of associative patterns in Shakespeare ignore the possibilities for interpretative ambiguity on the playwright's part in favor of discovering a key for accessing exactly what Shakespeare intends in his use of any given image ([Oxford: Clarendon P, 1959], 52–61). More post-structuralist readings of *Macbeth* argue that equivocation, ambiguity, and the struggle to interpret language and images correctly are actually a constitutive part of the play as a whole (Stephen Booth, *"King Lear," "Macbeth," Indefinition, and Tragedy* [New Haven: Yale UP, 1983], 89).

Character analysis of *Macbeth*, albeit of far greater sophistication than Bradley's, remains a major area of critical controversy and forms the basis of studies on gender and sexuality in the play. The extent to which Macbeth suffers a crisis of masculinity is a frequent topic of criticism: Coppélia Kahn's psychoanalytic critique sees Macbeth suffering from an incomplete sense of manhood due to his dependence on a woman to goad him on (*Man's Estate: Masculine Identity in Shakespeare* [Berkeley: U of California P, 1981], 155). Using a now unfashionably polarized conception of gender identity, Marilyn French sees the play as the necessary victory of the brutal, evil, masculine world of slaughter over feminine virtues of compassion and kindness (*Shakespeare's Division of Experience* [London: Cape, 1982], 241–251), and Adelman similarly identifies Macbeth's struggle to destroy the feminine principle within and female bodies without as a representation of "primitive fears about male identity and autonomy" (Adelman, p. 90).

Johnson's attempts to discuss *Macbeth* in relation to the context of Jacobean beliefs and practices are essentially a form of "old" historicist criticism, but he is by no means the only critic engaged in locating the play in relation to the politics of early modern theater and the theatricality of contemporary politics. In *The Royal Play of Macbeth* (New York: Macmillan, 1950) Henry N. Paul followed Tillyard's line in viewing *Macbeth* as an extended advocacy of Jacobean order and orthodoxy, identifying a wealth of topical allusions and arguing that the play is wholly complimentary to the king. However, Michael Hawkins refutes Paul's claims, arguing that *Macbeth* is far more ambiguous and equivocal in its praise of Jacobean preoccupations ("History, Politics and *Macbeth*," in Brown, ed., pp. 155–188). The latter line is taken up in Norbrook's essay (cited above) and by Alan Sinfield in *Faultlines: Cultural Materialism and the Politics of Dissident Reading* ([Oxford: Clarendon, 1992], 95–108); both critics discuss how *Macbeth* actually raises questions about the limitations of monarchical power and functioned as a site for potential controversy when it was first produced. Arthur Kinney offers a more nuanced study of the play's topicality in *Lies Like Truth: Shakespeare's "Macbeth" and the Cultural Moment* (Detroit: Wayne State UP, 2001).

## PRODUCTION HISTORY

The only account of a performance of *Macbeth* staged during Shakespeare's lifetime is that recorded by Simon Forman in 1611. This raises more questions than it solves regarding the play's early production, however, as Forman's description of what he saw is selective in focus and supplemented by his knowledge of the Macbeth story (and illustrations) in Holinshed. It is also impossible to gauge from Forman's account the role that elements of spectacle played within the production at this point. The whole issue of the potential for spectacular elaboration in staging the supernatural characters in *Macbeth* has long been a concern during the play's production history. After the theaters reopened following the Restoration in 1660, William Davenant presented a revised version of *Macbeth* in 1664 full of operatic spectacle with new songs and dances for the witches, and elaborate mechanisms to make them appear to fly. Davenant also drastically altered the text, omitting the Porter's scene, playing up Lady Macduff's role as a counterpoint to Lady Macbeth, and paring down scenes and characters deemed extraneous.

Davenant's more operatic *Macbeth* occupied the stage for more than eighty years until Garrick's 1744 version initiated a return to the language and structure of the Folio. Garrick's version still retained the singing and dancing witches and replaced Macbeth's offstage death with an onstage dying confession explaining his motives. Garrick's Macbeth (played from 1744 to 1768) was an exercise in the kind of emotional intensity and studied understanding of character that might now be termed "method acting" and presented the tragedy of an individual led into evil by the urging of his wife, played by Hannah Pritchard. Later in the eighteenth century, the model of Pritchard's most active Lady Macbeth was developed further by Sarah Siddons, who played the part from 1785 to 1819 opposite her brother, theater-manager and director Philip Kemble. While the Kemble-Siddons productions continued to emphasize the spectacular (including the addition of a chorus of fifty dancing witches), there was still great appeal to characters' psychology, and Kemble had Banquo's ghost appear to Macbeth's imagination only. The Garrick and Kemble productions were unequivocal in presenting Lady Macbeth as the primary agent for Macbeth's ambitious trajectory and tragic fall, and as a consequence the witches in both productions are played for comedy and spectacle and shorn of any instigating responsibility for the tragedy. Giuseppi Verdi's opera *Macbeth* (first performed 1847, revised 1865) largely adopts a similar approach, though it also looked back to Davenant's version in its polarization of the Macbeths and Macduffs as respective embodiments of evil and good.

However, nineteenth-century productions increasingly shift the presentation of blame away from Lady Macbeth and instead treat Macbeth as a willing criminal (aided by a supportive, more feminine wife), who is led into realizing his evil desires by the more overtly demonic witches. The most successful exponent of this approach was William Charles Macready, whose Macbeth dominated the mid-nineteenth-century stage. Later Victorian productions continued to feminize Lady Macbeth and demonize the witches. With the later exception of Herbert Beerbohm Tree's characteristically imaginative and visually engaging 1911 production, around the turn of the century there is an attendant decline in the resort to spectacular elaboration.

Glen Byam Shaw's 1955 production at the Memorial Theatre, Stratford-upon-Avon, starring Laurence Olivier and Vivien Leigh, continued to evoke the nineteenth-century vogue for a weaker, more feminine Lady Macbeth. This was complemented by Olivier's brooding, acquiescent descent into evil that culminated in a demanding final duel with Macduff. In 1974–1975 Trevor Nunn directed Nicol

Williamson and Jane Lapotaire in a sexually charged, energetic production in Stratford and London, though Nunn was far more successful two years later in a stripped-down production at the Other Place, Stratford, starring Ian McKellen and Judi Dench. The stage was marked out by a twenty-foot chalk circle surrounded by packing crates on which the cast sat when not within the playing space, and while he created a deliberate anti-realistic *mise-en-scène*, Nunn foregrounded metaphysical and religious aspects, heightening the sense of the witches' agency and subtly casting the lead characters as victims. Nunn's McKellen-Dench *Macbeth* was taped and televised in 1979, and a version of the Williamson-Lapotaire production directed by Jack Gold was recorded for the British Broadcasting Company's Shakespeare series in 1982. More recent stagings continue to exploit the play's potential for both character-based exposition and spectacular entertainment. Mark Rylance's 1995 *Macbeth* at the Greenwich Theatre, London, received widespread praise for its intense, claustrophobic mood and gained a certain notoriety for its presentation of the sleepwalking scene that culminates with the diminutive Jane Horrocks's Lady Macbeth urinating on the stage at the height of her madness. The 2001 season at Shakespeare's Globe, London, saw Tim Carroll's rather minimalist production featuring a tuxedo-clad cast, jazz score, and rhumba-style cauldron scene, set alongside Welcome Msomi's *Umbatha: The Zulu Macbeth*. In 2002 at the Albery Theatre, London, Edward Hall directed Sean Bean and Samantha Bond in a modern-dress production that stressed the martial aspects of Macbeth's character, implicitly evoking Bean's earlier warrior roles as Boromir in *The Fellowship of the Ring* movie (2001) and Richard Sharpe in the television dramatization of the Bernard Cornwell novels.

The twentieth century saw many innovative adaptations of *Macbeth*, including Orson Welles's 1936 "Voodoo" *Macbeth* (Lafayette Theatre, New York), a heavily cut version set in the Caribbean that played up the supernatural spectacle and emphasized the influence of witchcraft on Macbeth. Akira Kurosawa's 1957 film *Throne of Blood* is an ambitious recasting of the Macbeth story set within feudal Japan—evoking a parity with the militaristic society of medieval Scotland—that sees the Macbeth-figure Washizu urged by his wife Asaji to murder Tsuzuki. The film powerfully combines the subtle gestures reminiscent of Noh theater with the broad sweep of feudal epic; one finds a similar translation of *Macbeth* into medieval Japan in Yukio Ninagawa's stage production performed at the Edinburgh Festival in 1985. Sponsored by Playboy Productions and featuring naked witches and a nude, sleepwalking Lady Macbeth, Roman Polanski's 1971 film *The Tragedy of Macbeth* (aka *Macbeth*) was widely criticized for its violent scenes and amplification of sex. However, the script, co-authored by Kenneth Tynan, offers a creative exploration of violence in society and evokes a pervasive culture of self-interest through elaborating the ambitions of minor characters, such as Rosse and Donalbain. In a similar fashion, criminal and gangster culture is employed in the movie adaptations *Joe Macbeth* (1955) and *Men of Respect* (1990) to comment upon the violence of Macbeth's world. *Macbeth* has influenced many other works of popular culture, including those by several leading modern fantasists. J.R.R. Tolkien felt compelled to invent the Ents (tree-men) in *The Lord of the Rings*, as he explained to W. H. Auden, due to his "bitter disappointment and disgust from schooldays with the shabby use made in Shakespeare of the coming of 'Great Birnam Wood to high Dunsinane hill'" (quoted in *J.R.R. Tolkien: A Biography*, Humphrey Carpenter [London: Allen

Jon Finch as Macbeth and Francesca Annis as Lady Macbeth in Roman Polanski's 1971 film *The Tragedy of Macbeth* (aka *Macbeth*). Courtesy of Photofest.

and Unwin, 1977], 27–28). Terry Pratchett's 1989 novel *Wyrd Sisters* offers a brilliant parody of the play and its characters, particularly the witches, and one even finds a band called "The Weird Sisters" entertaining the young witches and wizards in J. K. Rowling's *Harry Potter and the Goblet of Fire* (2000).

## EXPLICATION OF KEY PASSAGES

**1.5.38–54. "The raven himself is hoarse . . . To cry, 'Hold, hold!'"** Prior to these lines Lady Macbeth has read Macbeth's letter reporting the witches' prophecy, and she immediately plans to nurture her husband's ambition to enable him to obtain the promised "golden round" (1.5.28). Her speech at this point echoes Richard of Gloucester's soliloquy in *3 Henry VI*, 3.2.124–195, in which he works out the murderous path that must be cut through the "thorny wood" (l. 174) of impediments lying between him and the crown. However, unlike Richard, Lady Macbeth is resolved from the outset regarding what must be done; there is no argument with herself projected here regarding Duncan's murder. It is not a question of if but when it must happen. Throughout the scene she speaks with full awareness of the qualities needed to perform the deed; and when news comes of Duncan's imminent arrival, capacity can finally combine with occasion. Lady Macbeth's response to the Messenger's report is a key point in the play because it hastens the movement toward an externalization and realization of the Macbeths' ambitious, murderous imaginings.

The passage begins with a touch of gallows humor as Lady Macbeth imagines that the raven—whose cry was a traditional omen of death—has cried itself hoarse with betokening Duncan's fate at Macbeth's castle; such is Lady Macbeth's murderous resolve that even the apparatus of metaphysical portents are strained. Lady Macbeth then begins her invocation and conjuration of demonic forces, the repetition of imperative "Come" suggesting a ritual process of figurative transformation. She calls upon the spirits of evil (and it is never entirely clear whether these are within her mind or external to her) to change her body so that she can commit the murder, specifically to "unsex" her (1.5.41) and remove any trace of feminine attributes of remorse or compassion. The reference to thickening her blood to stop up access to the seat of remorse can be interpreted as a call to eradicate the "compunctious" stirrings of her heart or conscience (1.5.45), but there is also an effacement of her reproductive and maternal functions. Thickening of blood could refer to the cessation of menstruation and monthly "visitings of nature" (ibid.), and thus Lady Macbeth now wholly embraces the positivist, violent route to the crown rather than the natural path of biological succession. Reginald Scot suggested that the "stopping up" of blood within menopausal women might actually cause the vain beliefs that one could interact with diabolic forces (*The Discoverie of Witchcraft*, ed. B. Nicholson [London, 1886; rpt. Wakefield: E. P. Publishing, 1973], 42). The second invocation ("Come to my woman's breasts, / And take my milk for gall," 1.5.47–48) further extirpates her maternal function as she calls on invisible demonic forces ("sightless substances," 1.5.49) to replace her milk—something associated earlier with human kindness (1.5.17)—with bitter, poisonous gall. Adelman suggests that this is a call for the spirits to suckle upon her milk as gall, evoking contemporary beliefs that witches suckled demonic familiars and so further associating Lady Macbeth with the weird sisters (Adelman, p. 98). Lady Macbeth's unsexing conjuration performs a dehumanizing function as it offers a verbal formula for transforming oneself into a killer.

The final invocation calls for night itself to veil the acts that must be done so that her "keen knife" (a punning allusion to the blade's sharpness and her own eagerness, 1.5.52) will not be restrained by her conscience activated by the sight of wounding Duncan. Almost as predicted, the sight of the dormant king stays her hand (2.1.12–13). As Macbeth enters following this speech, Lady Macbeth reveals that she has already moved figuratively into the future to a point where her fantasies must be realized, where contemplation turns to action.

**1.7.1–28. "If it were done, . . . And falls on th' other—[.]"** The opening stage direction describing music from "Hoboys" and various "servants with dishes" crossing the stage indicates that Macbeth's speech is a moment of reflection stolen during the feasting of Duncan. The passage as a whole is the most extended so far of Macbeth's points of hesitation and vacillation concerning the plan to murder Duncan, his uncertainty perhaps reflected in the awkward syntax of the opening lines: "If it were done, when 'tis done, then 'twere well / It were done quickly." Repetition of "done" here (and similar repetition of "deed" in the passage) emphasizes the central theme of Macbeth's thoughts: doing the murderous deed. The first seven lines entertain a scenario where the murder can be done quickly as a singular act without further consequences. If this were possible then Macbeth would certainly risk judgment in the hereafter. However, Macbeth immediately undercuts such resolve with his realization that there may still be temporal repercussions; blood will beget blood. Such justice turns the deed into the proverbial "poison'd chalice" (a harmful object or act that appears innocuous, 1.7.11), an observation that certainly proves true in the play thereafter.

The reference to "chalice" then activates a new direction of thought (and doubt) concerning Macbeth's responsibilities as Duncan's kinsman, subject, and host. The first two obligations should be enough to stay anyone's hand, but it is the violation of good hospitality that heightens the villainy of the ultimate crime; the preceding scene functioned to underline the importance of the guest-host relationship between Duncan and the Macbeths. Macbeth further argues himself out of committing murder by recounting Duncan's positive qualities: indeed, lines 16–25 offer the play's best description both of the king's virtues and why his death would (and will) be universally condemned. This passage explains why the murder will weigh so heavily on Macbeth's conscience as it heightens sympathy for Duncan and simultaneously emphasizes Macbeth's soon-to-be-broken obligations. Macbeth concludes the passage by admitting that though he possesses "vaulting ambition" he has no "spur" to drive him on to action (1.7.27, 25), and the reference brings a series of equestrian metaphors in the passage ("trammel" [3], "jump" [7], "horsed" [22]) to a rather anticlimactic end. However, following Macbeth's initial speech, and almost as if summoned by his closing statement, Lady Macbeth enters. It is clear that she must function as the necessary "spur." This passage is vital in serving as the first part of a dialogue during which Lady Macbeth spurs on her husband by playing upon his sense of masculinity and her own renouncement of encumbering femininity enacted in the passage discussed above. By the close of the scene Lady Macbeth's dehumanized rhetoric of masculinity defeats Macbeth's lingering appeals to humanity.

**2.1.33–64. "Is this a dagger . . . to heaven or to hell."** Immediately before this passage an air of anticipation is created as Banquo converses with Fleance about an uneasiness that he feels that night and reveals to Macbeth that his mind still wrestles with the implications of the witches' prophecy. Once Banquo and Fleance leave, Macbeth's imagination once more turns to murder, though he is now far more resolved than in 1.7.1–28; in a play that hinges on the transition between fantasies of power and their realization this passage is the moment where Macbeth's murderous intentions, symbolized in the form of an imagined dagger, are turned into actions, as shown in line 41 where he draws his own (real) dagger. As with the appearance of the witches or Banquo's ghost, the reported vision of the dagger initiates an interrogation of the boundaries between physical and metaphysical, "sensible" and imaginary. Lines 33–49 show Macbeth slowly interpreting the dagger as a signifier of his own murderous trajectory and resignedly accepting that although "There's no such thing" (2.1.47), it is his imagination that "informs" (gives shape to, 2.1.48) the dagger before him.

Macbeth's attention then turns from the dagger to the context in which murder must take place, and the passage continues to draw upon the play's dominant images of darkness and blood. Lines 49–56 create an intensely sinister tone through allusions to death, nightmares, and witchcraft, together with a personification of murder itself stalking its prey like the Roman king Tarquin (whose rape of Lucrece forms the subject of one of Shakespeare's poems). Reference to Tarquin's strides in line 55 are picked up in the following line as Macbeth calls upon the earth not to betray his own murderous steps, and there is a lingering trace of hesitation here as he fears his own footsteps might (like Lady Macbeth's feared sight of the wound she must inflict) diminish the present sense of "horror" necessary for him to commit the crime (2.1.59).

Just as Macbeth's reasoning curtails his speculation on the dagger in lines 47–49, so clarity and resolve return in line 60 as he realizes that as long as he only speaks of threatened deeds Duncan remains alive. The bell's tolling rouses Macbeth to action. His simple line, "I go, and it is done" (2.1.62) presents a blunt encapsulation of the dehumanized, unthinking figure that Macbeth has become. True to his word, when Macbeth next appears he has done the deed. Macbeth's dagger speech is the last moment where we see Macbeth's troubled conscience; all further glimpses of the character's interiority presented in the play reveal merely a selfish fear of discovery or general despair at life itself.

**5.5.17–28. "She should have died hereafter; . . . Signifying nothing."** These lines constitute Macbeth's response to hearing the cry of women and news from Seyton that Lady Macbeth is dead. They are a significant demonstration of how lacking in compassion or emotion Macbeth has become by the close of the play. Whereas once Macbeth looked to his wife for guidance and encouragement, and described her in his letter as "my dearest partner of greatness" (1.5.11), his lines here are a fatalistic meditation on the meaninglessness of life far more than they are an expression of loss and mourning: contemplation of Lady Macbeth does not extend beyond the first two lines of the passage. The first line itself—"She should have died hereafter" (5.5.17)—is ambiguous, since it could be interpreted as an observation either that she should have died at a time more suitable for mourning or, more dismissively, that she would have died sooner or later anyway. Either reading reveals Macbeth's engagement with time here, though the latter is specifically in keeping with the idea of transience that occupies Macbeth's thoughts for the rest of the passage. This soliloquy is important because it represents the culmination of Macbeth's reflections on time and on the difficulty of trying to place time or temporality within a structure of meaning. Macbeth had earlier recognized that because of his tyrannous reign his old age would lack "honor, love, obedience, troops of friends" (5.3.25). Throughout the play characters are always looking ahead to future events: to Duncan's murder, to the prophecies' fulfillment, to Birnam Wood's coming to Dunsinane, to the liberation of Scotland. It is the future that makes the present meaningful for the play's central characters, and it is in the future that the equivocal prophecies are expected to be reified.

However, in this passage Macbeth finally recognizes the folly of such a teleological world-view. The repetition of the word "tomorrow" in line 19 suggests the ponderousness and triviality of life, which creeps ever onward toward "dusty death" (5.5.23). Reference to illumination provided by the hopes and aspirations of the past ("all our yesterdays," 5.5.22) is taken up in the next four lines as Macbeth first compares life to the short burning of a candle and then, shifting the metaphor using the doubleness of "shadow" (an early modern term for actor, as in *A Midsummer Night's Dream*, 5.1.423), compares life to the brief time that a player "struts and frets his hour upon the stage" before being heard no more (5.5.25). Life's transience is characterized using the metaphor of Jaques' well-known lines from *As You Like It* (2.7.139): "All the world's a stage." Such a metaphor had added resonance in the early modern theater, where actors were given only the lines for their assigned characters, together with catchwords indicating where they should enter. They would rarely hear a play's complete text until a full rehearsal or performance in which those words would be placed within a temporal structure of meaning. Macbeth finally admits that life exists only for the here and now of its "performance." It is simply words, "a tale / Told by an idiot" (5.5.26–27)—with a possible doleful pun here on told/tolled—that signifies nothing.

In the lines immediately following this passage, Macbeth learns that Birnam Wood appears to be marching on Dunsinane and that any hopes of future security offered by the prophecies are founded merely on the deceitful "equivocation of the fiend" (5.5.42). Following this scene Macbeth lives only for the present and places his trust in the temporal powers afforded by sword and armor.

## Annotated Bibliography

Aitchinson, Nick. *Macbeth, Man and Myth*. Stroud: Sutton, 1999. Entertaining, informative examination of the real Macbeth.

Brown, John Russell, ed. *Focus on "Macbeth."* London: Routledge, 1982. Essay collection; includes material by Michael Hawkins, D. J. Palmer, and Peter Stallybrass.

Calderwood, James L. *If It Were Done: "Macbeth" and Tragic Action*. Amherst: U of Massachusetts P, 1986. Views *Macbeth* alongside *Hamlet* and examines the role of action and violence in Shakespeare's conception of tragedy.

Kinney, Arthur. *Lies Like Truth: Shakespeare's "Macbeth" and the Cultural Moment*. Detroit: Wayne State UP, 2001. An examination of *Macbeth* in its immediate context of performance.

Muir, Kenneth, and Philip Edwards, eds. *Aspects of "Macbeth."* Cambridge: Cambridge UP, 1977. Essay collection; includes essays by M. C. Bradbrook and Glynne Wickham on sources.

Norbrook, David. "*Macbeth* and the Politics of Historiography." In *Politics of Discourse: The Literature and History of Seventeenth-Century England*. Ed. Kevin Sharpe and Steven Zwicker. Berkeley: U of California P, 1987. 78–116. Sophisticated discussion of Shakespeare's sources revealing that Holinshed's *Chronicles* was already controversial by the time Shakespeare used the work as the basis for his narrative.

Purkiss, Diane. *The Witch in History: Early Modern and Twentieth-Century Representations*. London: Routledge, 1996. Examines the wider historical and literary context of Renaissance witchcraft, including discussion of Elizabethan and Jacobean witch plays.

Rosenberg, Marvin. *The Masks of "Macbeth."* Berkeley: U of California P, 1978. Monumental study on staging *Macbeth*. Useful for reference.

Sinfield, Alan, ed. *Macbeth*. London: Macmillan, 1992. Essay collection closely engaging with modern literary theory; includes material by Terry Eagleton, Marilyn French, and Coppélia Kahn.

Wain, John, ed. *"Macbeth": A Casebook*. London: Macmillan, 1968. Essay collection; includes material by Samuel Taylor Coleridge, A. C. Bradley, Sigmund Freud, Caroline Spurgeon, and Cleanth Brooks.

# *Antony and Cleopatra*

## Harold Branam

### PLOT SUMMARY

**1.1.** The play begins in Egypt, where Antony's friends Demetrius and Philo are discussing how Antony dotes on Cleopatra. The once-great Roman triumvir, one of three joint rulers of the Roman Empire, has been completely unmanned by Egypt's queen, who keeps him under her spell. Philo says that Antony's "captain's heart" has "become the bellows and fan / To cool a gipsy's lust" (1.1.6, 9–10). Antony, the "triple pillar of the world," has been "transform'd / Into a strumpet's fool" (1.1.12–13).

The two middle-aged lovers, Antony and Cleopatra, accompanied by her train of ladies and eunuchs fanning her, enter to prove Philo correct. It quickly becomes clear that the accomplished Cleopatra is able to play with Antony at will. While she teases him about how much he loves her, a messenger from Rome enters. Cleopatra taunts Antony that his wife Fulvia is angry or the young Octavius Caesar, another of the triumvirs, is sending him orders. Her taunt causes Antony to blush and say, "Let Rome in Tiber melt, and the wide arch / Of the rang'd empire fall!" (1.1.33–34). He refuses to hear the messenger and instead proclaims that the lovers should continue with their night of "pleasure" and "sport" (1.1.47).

**1.2.** Still at Cleopatra's court, her ladies are joking with a soothsayer, who makes predictions about their looks and their love lives, though the double-edged nature of his predictions introduces an ominous note that goes unnoticed amid all the frivolity. Cleopatra enters, looking for Antony and complaining, "He was dispos'd to mirth, but on the sudden / A Roman thought hath strook him" (1.2.82–83). When he appears, she huffily leaves with her train.

Once he is alone, Antony finally listens to the messengers from Rome, who are appearing with alarming rapidity. The first messenger tells Antony that his wife Fulvia is brewing civil wars against his brother and against Caesar, that a Parthian force is invading Antony's Asian territories, and that Antony's reputation is suffering in Rome. The second messenger makes Antony realize that "[t]hese strong Egyptian fetters I must break, / Or lose myself in dotage" (1.2.116–117). The third messenger informs Antony that Fulvia is dead. The messengers also bring news that Sextus Pompeius has taken control of the seas and threatens war against the triumvirs. Antony finally realizes that he must leave Egypt and return to Rome. He announces his decision to Domitius Enobarbus, another friend, who defends Cleopatra as a passionate, loving woman and warns that she will be devastated.

**1.3.** As the scene begins, Cleopatra is instructing her ladies on how to manage men by acting contrary to their moods and wishes. When Antony enters, Cleopatra gives another demonstration of her talents. She detects that he has some good news from Rome, complains that she has no power over him, upbraids him for being false to Fulvia, and sees a warning for herself in his treachery to his wife. When he tells her that he is leaving and that Fulvia is dead, her suspicions seem to be confirmed, and her histrionics take on some heartfelt reality. Amid tears and mutual protestations of love, they say farewell.

**1.4.** In Rome, Octavius Caesar and Lepidus, the third triumvir, are discussing Antony's dotage and negligence. The situation grows worse when messengers enter with news that Sextus Pompeius (called Pompey for short) is dominating the open seas, and pirates are raiding Italy's shores. Caesar and Lepidus decide to gather their forces to meet these threats. As for Antony, Caesar says, "Let his shames quickly / Drive him to Rome" (1.4.72–73).

**1.5.** In Egypt Cleopatra laments Antony's absence. Melodramatically she wants to drink mandragora, an opiate. She says she envies Antony's horse for bearing his weight and fondly remembers how he used to call her " 'my serpent of old Nile' " (1.5.25). She rates Antony as the best of the Romans, including Julius Caesar and Cneius Pompey, with whom she has had affairs. When she receives a message from Antony offering to give her the kingdoms of the East, she resolves to send him a letter every day that he is away.

**2.1.** Pompey is conferring with his lieutenants, Menecrates and Menas. Pompey seems uncertain about the anticipated battle, pinning his hopes on Antony's staying in Egypt. These hopes are dashed when a messenger brings news that Antony is expected in Rome. But Menas thinks that Antony and Caesar might not mend their differences, created when Fulvia and Antony's brother warred against Caesar.

**2.2.** Antony and Caesar are working out their differences in a meeting of the triumvirs and their followers. The scene begins with Lepidus urging everyone to speak softly, but, after an initial greeting between Antony and Caesar, the talk is anything but soft. They immediately raise the issue of the wars against Caesar that Fulvia and Antony's brother waged. Antony denies any part in them and apologizes for not coming to Caesar's aid "when poisoned hours bound me up / From mine own knowledge" (2.2.90–91). Apparently Antony thinks that drunkenness and dotage are excuses. Caesar sees little chance of avoiding their personality clash but hopes some bond will hold the two men together. At this point Agrippa, one of Caesar's followers, proposes a marriage between Antony and Octavia, Caesar's sister. After a brief discussion, the marriage is agreed upon, Antony and Caesar shake hands, and the triumvirs go off to prepare for Pompey. Enobarbus, Agrippa, and Maecenas, another of Caesar's men, are left onstage. Enobarbus now describes his first mesmerizing sight of Cleopatra sitting in her barge and Antony's encounter with her. He believes that Antony will never leave her.

**2.3.** As the scene opens, a meeting of Antony, Caesar, and Octavia, who apparently has agreed to the marriage, is concluding. After Caesar and Octavia leave, the

Egyptian soothsayer enters, urges Anthony to return to Egypt, and warns him that Caesar's luck is much better than his. When the soothsayer exits, Antony acknowledges the truth of his words and decides, "I will to Egypt; / And though I make this marriage for my peace, / I' th' East my pleasure lies" (2.3.39–41). To keep the East quiet, he sends a lieutenant, Ventidius, to put down the invading Parthians.

**2.4.** Lepidus, Agrippa, and Maecenas are all leaving for battle with Pompey, satisfied that peace has been made between Antony and Caesar.

**2.5.** In Egypt Cleopatra impatiently suffers Antony's absence. None of her usual pastimes, such as music, billiards, or fishing, please her, and she has to be satisfied with remembering their good times in the past, such as when she outdrank Antony, causing him to fall into bed, where she put her clothes on him and took his sword. Cleopatra's lascivious imagery continues when a messenger from Italy arrives and she says, "Ram thou thy fruitful tidings in mine ears, / That long time have been barren" (2.5.24–25). The messenger stretches out his message, and Cleopatra prolongs it, paying the messenger for good news—that Antony is not dead but well and friends with Caesar. But then the messenger has to tell her that Antony has married Octavia—for which he is paid another way: The hysterical Cleopatra beats him, bribes him to retract his words, and, when he will not, draws a knife on him. When he flees, Cleopatra has him brought back, made to repeat his awful news several times, and then instructed to report on Octavia's features. Finally she has to be led to her room.

**2.6.** Near Misenum a parley occurs between the Roman triumvirs and Pompey in an attempt to settle matters peacefully before going to battle. Pompey has some grudges against Antony, who took the home of Pompey's father in one instance and in another failed to thank Pompey for protecting Antony's mother. But in the tense present situation Pompey accepts the written terms of the triumvirs, who give him Sicily and Sardinia in exchange for ridding the sea of pirates and sending wheat to Rome. Peace is made, and the opposing leaders exit for a celebratory feast aboard Pompey's galley. Enobarbus and Menas are left onstage, with Menas upset that Pompey has accepted peace and that Antony and Caesar are firmly knit by Antony's marriage to Octavia. Enobarbus predicts that the marriage will be the cause of a rift between Antony and Caesar because Antony will leave Octavia to return to Cleopatra.

**2.7.** Aboard Pompey's boat the leaders' celebration of the peace degenerates comically into a wild drunken party. The scene satirizes the behavior of great men, especially in Lepidus, who "bears the third part of the world" (2.7.90) but has to be carried off intoxicated. But the scene also plays up the strong contrasts among the leaders. Menas urges Pompey to slaughter his opponents while he has the chance, but Pompey refuses. Lepidus is obviously the least significant of the triumvirs, while the partying Antony, showing the influence of his Egyptian experiences, urges the puritanical Caesar to "[b]e a child o' the time" (2.7.100). After the men hold hands and sing a song to Bacchus, god of wine, Caesar breaks up the party by saying "the wild disguise hath almost / Antick'd [made fools of] us all" (2.7.124–125) and leaving the boat.

**3.1.** Ventidius appears briefly with his soldiers after repelling the Parthians from Antony's Asian territories.

**3.2.** The Romans say good-bye after the party aboard Pompey's boat. Enobarbus and Agrippa note how the lesser triumvir Lepidus, now suffering a hangover, is caught between the greater triumvirs Antony and Caesar. Antony and Octavia leave for Athens, with Octavia in tears. Caesar, near tears, stresses the importance of Antony and Octavia's relationship, and Antony reassures Caesar: "You shall not find, / Though you be therein curious [inquisitive], the least cause / For what you seem to fear" (3.2.34–36).

**3.3.** In Egypt the messenger returns to Cleopatra with news that her rival Octavia is "dull of tongue, and dwarfish" and moves like "[a] statue" (3.3.16, 21). These and other unattractive features of Octavia reassure Cleopatra and her ladies.

**3.4.** Some time has elapsed since the party aboard Pompey's boat. In Athens Antony complains to Octavia about her brother's threatening moves: Caesar has renewed the war with Pompey, has read his generous will to the Roman public, and praises Antony coldly. Antony grants her request to return to Rome by herself in an effort to mend the peace, but meantime he will also prepare for possible war with Caesar.

**3.5.** Enobarbus and Eros discuss even worse news: After Caesar and Lepidus defeated and killed Pompey, Caesar removed Lepidus from power, accused him of treason, and condemned him to die.

**3.6.** In Rome Caesar is complaining about Antony's threatening moves: Antony has returned to Egypt, made Cleopatra and their sons rulers of Egypt and Asian provinces, and sent news to Caesar demanding part of the spoils from the recent actions against Pompey and Lepidus. Octavia, on her peacemaking mission, arrives in time to hear all this and to learn that Antony has cast her off for Cleopatra. The stage is thus set for war between the remaining triumvirs, Antony and Caesar.

**3.7.** The opposing forces prepare to fight the crucial sea battle offshore of Actium. Cleopatra and Antony debate with their followers, Enobarbus and Canidius, over tactics. Cleopatra will lead her ships in battle alongside Antony's, but Enobarbus disapproves, saying her presence will only distract Antony from his leadership duties. Enobarbus also disapproves of fighting Caesar at sea, where Antony lacks the advantage that his forces have on land.

**3.8.** Caesar instructs his leaders to hold back land forces and fight first by sea.

**3.9.** Antony places his land forces on a hillside where they can watch the sea battle.

**3.10.** Enobarbus and Scarus run onstage and, horrified, recount what they saw from land: In the midst of the sea battle, even though they might have been winning, Cleopatra led her ships in a sudden retreat, and, seeing her flee, Antony led his ships in flight after hers. Canidius then rushes in and reports that, seeing their sea forces fly, the land forces also broke and ran or surrendered without a fight.

**3.11.** Back in Alexandria after the battle, Antony is trying to deal with his shame. He urges his loyal followers to leave him and make a separate peace with Caesar, and he is so distraught that at first he does not see or hear Cleopatra and her ladies enter. When she gets his attention, he reproaches Cleopatra for leading him into flight and making it necessary for him now to negotiate humbly with the young Caesar. But finally he forgives her with a kiss and calls for wine and food.

**3.12.** At his army's encampment in Egypt, Caesar receives Antony's old schoolmaster, whom Antony has made his ambassador. Caesar refuses Antony's requests that he be allowed to retire and live a private life in Egypt or Athens; instead, Caesar sends back word for Cleopatra to exile or kill Antony. Caesar then dispatches his own slick ambassador, Thidias, to win over Cleopatra and observe Antony.

**3.13.** Enobarbus, talking with Cleopatra and her ladies, blames the doting Antony rather than Cleopatra for their defeat. Antony enters, listening to the report of his schoolmaster-ambassador, and sends back to Caesar a challenge to personal combat, which in an aside Enobarbus scoffs at as a foolish gesture. Antony and his ambassador exit, and Thidias, the ambassador from Caesar, enters. The subtle Thidias tells Cleopatra that Caesar knows Antony compelled Cleopatra's love (a suggestion that Cleopatra accepts: "Mine honor was not yielded, / But conquer'd merely" [3.13.61–62]) and desires for her to desert Antony and come under his protection. Cleopatra accepts the offer, saying "I kiss his conqu'ring hand" (3.13.75) and offering her own hand for the ambassador to kiss.

At this point Antony reenters and is enraged at the sight, has Thidias led off to be whipped, and throws up Cleopatra's whorelike past to her, recalling when she was a "morsel" and a "fragment" for other great Romans, "besides what hotter hours, / Unregist'red in vulgar fame, you have / Luxuriously pick'd out . . ." (3.13.116, 117, 118–120). He sends the whipped ambassador back to Caesar, saying Caesar can in return "whip, or hang, or torture" (3.13.150) Hipparchus, a bondman who deserted Antony for Caesar. Cleopatra then swears her love for Antony, who is "satisfied" (3.13.167) and makes plans to battle Caesar again: "Our force by land / Hath nobly held; our sever'd navy too / Have knit again" (3.13.169–171). Cleopatra hails Antony's renewed spirit, and Antony calls for wine to flow again in celebration. Everyone goes off to party except Enobarbus, who decides it is time to desert Antony.

**4.1.** Caesar receives Antony's challenge to personal combat, laughs scornfully at it, and is urged by his lieutenant Maecenas to attack the opposing forces while Antony's judgment is clouded by anger. Caesar decides to put deserters from Antony in the front ranks of the attack on him.

**4.2.** Antony praises and says a final good-bye to his servants, causing them to break into tears and Cleopatra and Enobarbus to wonder at these omens.

**4.3.** Another omen of defeat occurs when some of Antony's soldiers hear strange music all around announcing the departure of the god Hercules, Antony's guardian spirit.

**4.4.** The next morning Antony arises early, dons his armor with the help of Eros and Cleopatra, and, in an expansive mood, proudly announces his warlike intentions. He says good-bye to Cleopatra with a brisk "soldier's kiss" (4.4.30).

**4.5.** Antony learns that Enobarbus has gone over to Caesar's side, wishes him well, and has his former friend's treasure delivered to him.

**4.6.** Caesar dispatches Agrippa to begin the battle and declares, "The time of universal peace is near" (4.6.5). Enobarbus, now one of Caesar's party, is left alone onstage to note Caesar's cold behavior toward turncoats and regret his decision. When news arrives of Antony's generosity to him, Enobarbus declares himself "alone the villain of the earth" (4.6.29) and resolves to "go seek / Some ditch wherein to die" (4.6.36–37).

**4.7.** The first day of battle concludes, with Agrippa and his men retreating. Caesar is hard pressed. Antony, the wounded Scarus, and Eros enter the stage in triumph.

**4.8.** The victory celebration continues, with Antony, Scarus, and others marching into Alexandria and being received by the rejoicing Cleopatra. Antony gets Cleopatra to let Scarus kiss her hand, and she also rewards him with a gold suit of armor. Antony calls on the trumpets and drums to sound out.

**4.9.** Two sentries that night witness the end of Enobarbus, who dies repenting his disloyalty and praising Antony as "[n]obler than my revolt is infamous" (4.9.19).

**4.10.** The next morning Caesar's forces prepare for battle at sea. Again Antony places his land forces on hillsides where he and they can watch the sea battle.

**4.11.** Again Caesar instructs his land forces to hold back.

**4.12.** Antony witnesses the disastrous sea battle: His ships desert and join Caesar's. Shouting "All is lost!" (4.12.9), Antony urges his land forces to flee, blames Cleopatra's treachery for the defeat, and threatens to kill her in revenge: "Triple-turn'd whore! 'tis thou / Hast sold me to this novice, and my heart / Makes only wars on thee" (4.12.13–15). Cleopatra enters, hears his threats, and flees. Summoning up the dying rage of his guardian spirit Hercules, Antony declares, "The witch shall die" (4.12.47).

**4.13.** Cleopatra hides in her tomb and sends word to Antony that she has killed herself.

**4.14.** Antony receives the message that Cleopatra is dead. He suddenly forgets his desire to kill her and, overcome by sorrow, rushes to join her in death. He asks Eros, who accompanies him, to stab him, but instead Eros stabs and kills himself. Antony then stabs himself but does not die immediately. Diomedes, Cleopatra's servant, enters to prevent Antony from killing himself, since Cleopatra had on second thought feared this reaction from Antony, but Diomedes is too late. The dying Antony instructs his guards to carry him to Cleopatra.

**4.15.** The guards and Cleopatra's ladies lift Antony to the top of Cleopatra's tomb with her, where he dies in her arms, content that he has lived a great life and "do now not basely die" (4.15.55) lorded over by Caesar. After swooning, Cleopatra wakes with a resolution to follow his example: "Let's do't after the high Roman fashion, / And make death proud to take us" (4.15.87–88).

**5.1.** Decretas, one of Antony's men, enters Caesar's camp with Antony's bloody sword and news of Antony's death. Caesar and his generals pause to acknowledge Antony's greatness and to lament his death. A messenger from Cleopatra enters, asking for Caesar's instructions to her. Caesar sends the messenger back with reassurances, then sends Proculeius to prevent Cleopatra from doing herself harm and escaping his triumphal march through Rome.

**5.2.** Proculeius enters Cleopatra's tomb and gives his reassurances of Caesar's good will, but then Roman soldiers enter and capture her and her ladies. Cleopatra draws a dagger to kill herself, but the weapon is taken away. She vows to kill herself anyway by starving or other means rather than be a part of Caesar's triumphal march or "be chastis'd with the sober eye / Of dull Octavia" (5.2.54–55).

The Romans leave Cleopatra guarded by Dolabella, an officer who is attracted to her and on whom she uses her wiles. She praises Antony as a colossus and wishes that she "might see / But such another man!" (5.2.77–78). Dolabella admits that Caesar means to include her in his triumphal march. Caesar and his officers then enter, and Caesar also promises that she will be treated well but warns that her lack of cooperation might jeopardize her children. Cleopatra makes a show of her submission, kneeling to Caesar and presenting him with a list of her valuables. But her treasurer, Seleucus, says she is holding back half her goods. When Caesar and his men leave, Cleopatra makes plans with her ladies to prevent themselves from being part of the Roman show, where she expects to be parodied by balladeers and comedians and to "see / Some squeaking Cleopatra boy my greatness / I' th' posture of a whore" (5.2.219–221).

Cleopatra's plans are carried out. A clown (rustic) from the countryside enters bringing her a basket of figs, in which are hidden asps, whose venom is deadly. Dressed in her finest, Cleopatra kisses her ladies good-bye, and Iras falls dead. Seeing with what ease life leaves, Cleopatra applies the asps to her breast and arm and, with a few last words, dies. As the guard rushes in and raises an alarm, Charmian applies an asp to herself and also dies. Caesar and his men enter to find all the women dead. Caesar praises the women's noble courage and directs that Cleopatra be buried beside Antony in the same tomb. Instead of marching the two lovers through Rome in his triumphal procession, Caesar orders the Roman army out of respect to attend their solemn funeral.

## PUBLICATION HISTORY

The conjectural date of *Antony and Cleopatra* is 1606–1607, based on an entry of the play's script in the Stationers' Register for May 20, 1608, and on evidence that Shakespeare's play influenced Samuel Daniel's revision of his tragedy *Cleopatra*, published in 1607. This date puts *Antony and Cleopatra* near the last stage of Shakespeare's career, after he had completed his great history plays, comedies, and most recently his tragedies. He had probably also completed his sonnets, which were likely written over a span of time beginning in the early 1590s and were published in 1609. Shakespeare was thus at the height of his poetic powers when he wrote *Antony and Cleopatra*, a judgment borne out when one reads or hears the play's rich verse. The play was first published in the First Folio (1623); this version and subsequent editions supply the definitive text.

*Antony and Cleopatra* marks Shakespeare's return to the Roman history dramatized in *Julius Caesar* (1599) and picks up where that play leaves off, depicting the civil wars that continued off and on for some ten years and bringing Roman history to the consolidation of the Roman Empire in 30 B.C. and the threshold of the peaceful and glorious Augustan Age (named after the play's character Octavius Caesar, later called Caesar Augustus). *Antony and Cleopatra* is the first of several later Shakespearean plays set in Greek or Roman times (*Coriolanus, Pericles, Cymbeline*). The reason for Shakespeare's return to Greek and Roman subjects is unknown, but sources were easily available to him, including Thomas North's classic English translation of Plutarch's *Lives of the Noble Grecians and Romans* (1579, plus a 1603 edition), which Shakespeare used repeatedly.

The most important point to make about the historical background of *Antony and Cleopatra* is obvious but has been overlooked by some critics. Since Latin and Latin writers were the main subjects studied in school and since Roman history was popular, Shakespeare could assume some knowledge of Roman history in his audience, particularly of the legendary figures in his play. He was able to make use of this knowledge much as the Greek dramatists made use of well-known myths. He did not have to bring the battles and other big events onstage; they constituted a historical background that he could assume with only token representation. He could also make use of dramatic irony and foreshadowing. These help deepen a sense of tragic inevitability in the history depicted.

Assuming his audience had some knowledge of the historical background in *Antony and Cleopatra* also enabled Shakespeare to focus more on character and historical meaning. Shakespeare was part of the Renaissance, which viewed the ancient world as its model, with great civilizations to learn from and emulate. Besides finding the lives of the Greeks and Romans fascinating in themselves, the Renaissance, like Plutarch, looked to them as moral examples, for better or worse. One studied the lives of the Greeks and Romans for the way they exemplified civic duty, courage, military achievement, and other virtues—or else their opposites. One also noted how the lives of great individuals impinged on and affected the outcomes of history. Finally, one noted patterns of events and historical parallels between one's own time and the ancient world.

For Shakespeare's audience, the events dramatized in *Antony and Cleopatra* offered a significant historical parallel. The consolidation of the Roman Empire at the end of the play parallels the unofficial unification of England and Scotland in the reign of James I, which began in 1603 (the union did not become official until more than a hundred years later). No one was quite sure how the unification would work or what to make of the new king after the long reign of Elizabeth I. But there were the examples of the civil wars in *Antony and Cleopatra* to show what could happen if the unification did not work. In contrast, there was the peaceful and glorious Augustan Age to illustrate what could happen if the unification succeeded. Shakespeare was not above flattering James I, who would inaugurate the new Augustan Age, as this parallel implies. After all, James thought much the same way about himself. In an Augustan vein he had also appointed Shakespeare's acting company as the King's Men almost immediately after his accession, and during the plague year of 1603 when the theaters were closed they often entertained him with private performances. Happily, the new king showed some of the pleasure-loving qualities of Antony, which might balance the sternness of Caesar required to inaugurate an Augustan Age. James also saw himself as a peacemaker at home and abroad, just like Augustus, who had inaugurated the pax romana (roman peace).

*Antony and Cleopatra* could also reflect even more of the playwright's personal history. The character of Cleopatra bears a strong resemblance to the Dark Lady of the sonnets: She is swarthy, sluttish, inconsistent, manipulative, and intoxicating. Her power over Antony resembles the Dark Lady's power over Shakespeare's persona in the sonnets. Like Antony, Shakespeare's persona in the sonnets suffers from dotage, declining powers, middle-age crisis, and guilt. He, like Antony, is committing adultery (though the wronged wives are absent, forgotten about, and get no say in the matter). Despite much ongoing controversy, it has never been proven that the situation depicted in the sonnets is factual or that the Dark Lady ever existed, but the portraits of these two memorable women who strongly resemble each other suggest that Shakespeare based them not just on historical research and imagination but rather on personal experience.

## SOURCES FOR THE PLAY

The main source for *Antony and Cleopatra* is Thomas North's translation of Plutarch's *Lives of the Noble Grecians and Romans* (1579, and probably also the 1603 edition). Another source is Appian's *Civil Wars* (translated by W. B., 1578). Other available sources that Shakespeare might have consulted include Samuel Daniel's original version of his play *Cleopatra* (1594, 1599) and Lucius Apuleius's *The Golden Ass* (translated 1566).

Shakespeare found North's translation of Plutarch extremely helpful, paying tribute to the quality of its language and details by making extensive use of them. Here, for example, is North's description of Cleopatra sitting in her barge:

> the poop whereof was gold, the sails of purple, and the oars of silver, which kept stroke in rowing after the sound of the music of flutes, hautboys, citherns, and viols. . . . And now for the person of herself, she was laid under a pavilion of cloth of gold of tissue, apparelled and attired like the goddess Venus commonly drawn in picture; and hard by her, on either hand of her, fair boys apparelled as painters do set forth god Cupid, with little fans in their hands.

Here is how Shakespeare has his character Enobarbus describe the same scene:

> The barge she sat in, like a burnish'd throne,
> Burnt on the water. The poop was beaten gold,
> Purple the sails, and so perfumed that
> The winds were love-sick with them; the oars were silver,
> Which to the tune of flutes kept stroke, and made
> The water which they beat to follow faster,
> As amorous of their strokes. For her own person,
> It beggar'd all description: she did lie
> In her pavilion—cloth of gold, of tissue—
> O'er-picturing [bettering] that Venus where we see
> The fancy outwork nature. On each side her
> Stood pretty dimpled boys, like smiling Cupids,
> With divers-color'd fans, whose wind did seem
> To glow the delicate cheeks which they did cool,
> And what they undid did. (2.2.191–205)

Although making heavy use of his source, Shakespeare also shows here how he added and deleted details and subtly changed the language to transform it into great poetry that communicates Cleopatra's heated sensuality.

Similarly, Shakespeare closely followed the story told in his source but made large omissions for the sake of dramatic compression and introduced major changes in characterization. For example, Shakespeare omits a whole stretch of years during which Antony and Octavia were married and had children. He also compresses the time between the battles of Actium and Alexandria and between the deaths of Antony and Cleopatra. The Parthian campaigns, covered extensively by Plutarch, get only a brief scene in Shakespeare. Shakespeare also created or developed a number of characters, most notably Cleopatra's ladies and Enobarbus. Enobarbus is an especially important character because he seems to be the playwright's invented spokesman, praising Cleopatra and Antony and balancing the chorus of disapproval that other characters in the play voice. Finally, consistent with the notion that Enobarbus is his spokesman, Shakespeare, without hiding their flaws, portrays Cleopatra and Antony much more sympathetically than does Plutarch. Plutarch paints Antony as constitutionally weak, prone to drink and dissipation, and easily deceived; he sees Cleopatra as the worst thing that could happen to Antony, taking advantage of his nature to bewitch and enslave him. Thus in

Plutarch the loving pair are bad examples, but in Shakespeare they are only too human.

For the Egyptian background in the play, Shakespeare might have been indebted to Apuleius's *The Golden Ass*, a novel about initiation into the mysteries of the Egyptian goddess Isis that includes some voluptuous scenes. Isis is mentioned lightly several times in the play: Cleopatra's ladies jestingly pray to her (1.2.64–74), and Cleopatra swears by her (1.5.70). But references to the goddess also contribute to a pattern of Egyptian imagery in the play. Isis was associated with the earth, the moon, and fertility. These associations link her to the river Nile, whose floods nourish the crops and whose mud is said to breed serpents and crocodiles (2.7.26–27), and to Cleopatra, who appears ceremonially dressed "[i]n th' abiliments of the goddess Isis" (3.6.17). This pattern of imagery suggests the fertility of Cleopatra and Egypt and, in the last act, evokes an aura of ritual death symbolizing Egyptian rebirth and immortality.

## STRUCTURE AND PLOTTING

It was once typical for critics to condemn what they saw as the loose structure and plotting of *Antony and Cleopatra*. For example, A. C. Bradley thought the play was the most poorly constructed of all Shakespeare's tragedies (*Shakespearean Tragedy* [New York: St. Martin's P, 1904; New York: Meridian Books, 1955], 205). The older critics were referring to such features of the play as its large gaps in time, its numerous short scenes that jump around the Mediterranean (especially in acts 3 and 4), its unattached Parthian scene, and its split catastrophe (with Antony dying in act 4 and Cleopatra in act 5). Certainly the play violates the neoclassical unities of time (twenty-four-hour time limit), place (one setting), and action (single), which were artificial and rarely observed anyway, particularly in Shakespeare's time. But more recently critics have found unity in the play's thematic opposition of Rome and Egypt, which governs the alternation of character and scene as the plot develops. Furthermore, if one keeps in mind that *Antony and Cleopatra* dramatizes a historical action of epic proportions, one can even argue that the play is a masterpiece of construction. Through the tightness and efficiency of the play's structure, Shakespeare keeps many of the events offstage and focuses instead on his main characters onstage.

Like an epic, the play begins in medias res. Antony has already met, courted, and come under the spell of Cleopatra. He luxuriates and languishes in her Circe-like court, neglecting his duties, but messengers arrive to start the play's action and Antony's internal conflict, caught between Egypt and Rome. The play then switches to Rome to introduce Octavius Caesar and the Roman perspective. By beginning in medias res, Shakespeare immediately reveals the full impact of Cleopatra on Antony, sets up the play's thematic opposition, and begins the action to resolve it. Only in act 2 does Shakespeare backtrack and, through Enobarbus's famous account, tell about Antony and Cleopatra's first meeting and subsequent events.

Like the story of the lovers' first meeting, much of the play's action is covered offstage and secondhand, through messengers and eyewitnesses. Critics have marveled at the large number of messengers who fly in and out. The messengers are a useful plot device, enabling Shakespeare to impel the play's action. But he also makes them do double or even triple duty. The messengers lend a sense of urgency and importance to events in the vast empire. Part of the glue holding the empire together is the relationships of the main characters, who are scattered and have to resort to messengers to try to sustain their shifting and crumbling alliances. Reactions to the messengers are also used to delineate character, as when Antony refuses to hear the emissaries from Rome, when Cleopatra beats the messenger bringing bad news, and when Antony has the messenger from Caesar whipped.

Shakespeare uses eyewitnesses from Antony's side, including Antony himself, to recount the large-scale sea battles, again moving the action rapidly and avoiding the daunting problem of trying to stage the battles. The eyewitnesses pretend to stand on hillsides and watch, then rush onstage shouting, conveying in a few lines the awful alarm, rout, and import of the defeats. Similarly, Shakespeare does not dramatize the land battles, only the results, coming in at the end of the fighting with the Parthians and the first day's battle in Alexandria. Shakespeare seemingly was averse to filling the stage with battles, which would be noisy, distracting, and clumsily enacted, so he simply omitted them. He uses the same principle of omission for large segments of time—Antony's marriage to Octavia, the lengthy Parthian campaigns—that would distract from his main theme. The effect of seeing the brothers-in-law Antony and Caesar hugging good-bye in act 3, scene 2, and then falling out the next time Antony appears in scene 4 is abrupt but still another example of Shakespeare's economy in structuring.

A number of critics have pointed out the split catastrophe at the end of the play, and some have found it anticlimactic to kill off Antony in act 4, leaving act 5 for Cleopatra's death. But the two deaths are intimately related, in a way repeating *Romeo and Juliet*, with Antony stabbing himself because he thinks she is dead and Cleopatra killing herself because he is dead. One could just as well argue that the play's climax is merely prolonged (the original Folio text, anyway, does not have act and scene divisions after 1.1). Of course, the lovers also have another reason for killing themselves—they have been defeated and do not want to fall into Caesar's hands. Although they are defeated by Caesar, their deaths are, in a sense, the triumph of Egypt over Rome: Cleopatra has lured Antony back to Egypt, where he is buried with her, and she ends the play with her ritually satisfying Egyptian death.

With its structure, particularly its many short scenes, alternations of setting, and swift pace, *Antony and Cleopatra* seems made for Hollywood (other Hollywood elements are the parties, the battles, the death scenes, and the star characters). But, strictly speaking, *Antony and Cleopatra* does not need a film adaptation to be effective. The play was designed to be acted on Shakespeare's bare stage, and it seems equally well designed for technically advanced modern productions.

## MAIN CHARACTERS

One of the glories of *Antony and Cleopatra*, besides its poetry, is its characters. The two title characters are among Shakespeare's most complex, with Cleopatra a candidate for his greatest female portrait. The other main figures, Caesar and Enobarbus, are also notable achievements of characterization. Some lesser characters, such as Lepidus, Octavia, Pompey, and Dollabella, are given memorable touches. Even some of the messengers, the soothsayer, Cleopatra's ladies, and the country clown who brings the asps stand out. Besides creating this rich lineup of characters,

Shakespeare shows his outstanding dramatic skills by making use of commentators, confidants, character foils, and symbolic or representative characters.

### Enobarbus

Shakespeare seems to have developed the character of Enobarbus primarily to act as a commentator and confidant. As a commentator, Enobarbus is almost a one-man chorus (which was sometimes used on the Renaissance stage, as in *Romeo and Juliet*, *Henry V*, and *Pericles*). His observations are spicy, plainspoken, and humorous, providing a sense of reality. He thinks Antony should intimidate the young Caesar by not shaving and by speaking over Caesar's head "as loud as Mars" (2.2.5–8), but Enobarbus himself is not intimidated by any of the play's major figures, whom he looks upon as merely human. He refuses to swap flattery with Pompey, makes jokes about the drunken Lepidus, and answers Antony's reprimand for speaking up by replying, "That truth should be silent I had almost forgot" (2.2.108), and by describing himself as "your considerate stone" (2.2.110). It is hard not to see Enobarbus as the voice of Shakespeare.

Most importantly, Enobarbus balances the negative commentary about Antony and Cleopatra from other characters and from each other. He is a friend and confidant of both Antony and Cleopatra and, while understanding their faults, still appreciates their depth and generosity. Enobarbus delivers the long description of Cleopatra in her barge as well as other flattering remarks about her, such as "Age cannot wither her, nor custom stale / Her infinite variety" (2.2.234–235). When Antony blames her for the defeat at Actium, Enobarbus points out that Antony did not have to turn and follow her. But Enobarbus also sticks by Antony for much of the play, showing through his loyalty that Antony is a worthy friend and leader, mistakes and failings notwithstanding. Finally, Shakespeare uses Enobarbus's desertion of Antony and his prompt regret, despair, and death to underline Antony's nobility: Enobarbus's dying words are "O Antony, / Nobler than my revolt is infamous" (4.9.18–19). Enobarbus's death from heartbreak might seem excessive and sentimental by today's standards, but Shakespeare apparently liked it so much that he repeated it with variations, having Eros stab himself rather than his leader Antony and having two of Cleopatra's ladies/confidantes die with her.

Besides defending Cleopatra and Antony, Enobarbus also speaks up for the Egyptian way of life. Enobarbus enjoys the drinking, partying, and frivolity, and he urges Antony not to leave Cleopatra and return to Rome. Later Enobarbus is the informal master of ceremonies at the Roman generals' drunken party aboard Pompey's boat, leading them to "dance now the Egyptian bacchanals" (2.7.104) and directing the generals to join hands and sing a song to Bacchus. Although a fine soldier in the Roman mold himself, Enobarbus seems able to balance the Roman and Egyptian ways of life better than any of the other characters. As friend and confidant of Anthony, he is a strong influence on Antony to achieve the same balance.

Finally, Enobarbus is used to foreshadow events in the play through his predictions, for which he relies on understanding of character and rational analysis, in contrast to the superstitious foreshadowing that comes from the soothsayer. Enobarbus rightly predicts that Cleopatra will be anguished by Anthony's departure, but his most important predictions are that Antony will never give up Cleopatra and that Antony's marriage to Octavia, far from binding Antony and Octavius Caesar together, will be the eventual cause of their breakup when Antony leaves Octavia for Cleopatra. Later Enobarbus fearfully and correctly predicts the outcomes of the military decisions to let Cleopatra lead her forces in battle and to fight by sea. Only at the end does the analytical Enobarbus not make the right prediction: Seeing Antony's own descent into irrationality, Enobarbus decides to desert to the other side but fails to foresee the effects of his decision on himself.

### The "Commentators"

Besides making Enobarbus a commentator, Shakespeare has his characters talk about each other in the usual way people do. Such talk becomes a primary means to introduce different perspectives and thus indirectly develop the complexity of the main characters. An example is the play's opening, where Antony's friends Demetrius and Philo discuss how he has degenerated since falling for Cleopatra; after this conversation, they have no part in the play. Other examples are Caesar's disapproving comments about Antony in act 1, scene 4, and Cleopatra and her ladies' unfavorable evaluation of her rival, Octavia, in act 3, scene 3. If it were not for the way other characters, especially his rivals, praise Antony's military prowess and generalship, there would be little evidence for either, since the action of the play shows Antony committing one military blunder after another. Such praise helps build up Antony as a tragic hero by showing the extent of his fall. Similarly, the wide-ranging comments about Cleopatra characterize her variously as a slut, a great beauty, a woman to die for, or a human goddess, among other things (and some of these radically different comments come from the same man, Antony).

An interesting variation on such talk or gossip is public opinion. What might be called "vox populi" is mentioned frequently. Demetrius sadly notes that Antony's dotage "approves the common liar, who / Thus speaks of him at Rome" (1.1.60–61). Antony asks a messenger to "mince not the general tongue; / Name Cleopatra as she is call'd in Rome" (1.2.105–106). Antony asks Octavia to "[r]ead not my blemishes in the world's report" (2.3.5), and he later complains that Caesar courted public opinion by having his will "read . . . [t]o public ear" (3.4.4–5). Caesar again seeks to draw Roman public opinion to his side by circulating accounts of Antony's outrageous behavior in Egypt (3.6.21–25). While her own people seem to adore her, to the extent "that the holy priests / Bless her when she is riggish [that is, wanton]" (2.2.238–239), Cleopatra is deathly afraid of being dragged before Roman public opinion, which she feels will make her the target of parody. The references to public opinion are a reminder that the main characters are great political figures playing out their roles on the world stage, which adds another complicating dimension to their behavior: How much is their personal behavior influenced by their public roles?

### Lepidus and Pompey

Besides indirectly characterizing his main figures through commentary about them, Shakespeare also uses character contrasts or foils. The triumvirs are good examples. It is abundantly clear that Caesar and Antony are the strong men of the three, with Lepidus little more than a temporary peacemaker caught between them.

Drunk at the party, Lepidus is reduced to an object of comedy, and later Caesar easily disposes of him when it is convenient. A more formidable character who contrasts with Caesar and Antony is Pompey, threatening dominance of the seas. But in person Pompey comes across mainly as a complainer who calculates his chances, hesitates at crucial moments, and lacks the stomach for a good fight. Again, Caesar later disposes of him too, weeding out his competitors one by one and gaining experience to take on the main one, Antony.

## Caesar

The contrast between Caesar and Antony helps to characterize both and is central to the play's action and theme. Militarily, the young Caesar seems no match for the hardened and experienced Antony, but Caesar makes up in patience and shrewdness for his youth and limited battlefield experience. A cold, calculating politician, he bides his time, pits his opponents against each other, courts the Roman public, and takes advantage of Antony's mistakes and weaknesses. Caesar stands up to Antony in their personal confrontations, but he is careful to mend relations and remain allies with Antony long enough to eliminate Pompey and Lepidus and to consolidate his position at Rome. To maintain the alliance, he willingly sacrifices his beloved sister Octavia by marrying her to the known reprobate Antony. Later he just as willingly uses Antony's abandonment of Octavia as the final excuse for war, thereby getting double duty out of her. Caesar is not one to let personal considerations or feelings interfere with his steady pursuit of power, while Antony, "kiss[ing] away / Kingdoms and provinces" (3.10.7–8), is just the reverse.

Despite his cold and calculating nature, Caesar projects a personal image that, on the surface, is vastly superior to Antony's and likely to appeal to his fellow Romans. While Antony is wallowing in Egyptian sensuality and dotage, Caesar is the epitome of Roman sobriety and discipline. As unswerving in his personal behavior as he is in his pursuit of power, Caesar holds firm even when other Romans weaken and succumb. He is generally scornful of Antony and Cleopatra and seems one of the few Romans immune to her charms. Most revealing are his puritanical reactions to the party aboard Pompey's boat, where the other Romans relax their morals. Caesar considers drinking wine "monstrous labor when I wash my brain / And it grow fouler" (2.7.99–100), and he "had rather fast from all, four days, / Than drink so much in one" (2.7.102–103). At the end of the party, which he breaks up, he fears that "the wild disguise hath almost / Antick'd us all" (2.7.124–125). His aversion to these "Egyptian bacchanals" (2.7.104) marks Caesar as a prime representative of the Roman way.

## Octavia

Caesar's female counterpart is his sister, Octavia. Octavia appears in only a few scenes but is onstage long enough to be seen as dutiful and disciplined. Caesar calls her a "piece of virtue" (3.2.28), and Maecenas describes her as having "beauty, wisdom, modesty" (2.2.240). Octavia seems all that a staid, upright Roman would want in a wife. Without complaint, she does as she is expected, willingly marrying Antony and leaving with him for Athens. Apparently Antony has no complaints against her either, since she appears to be a good, dutiful wife to him. But Antony stays with her only as long as is convenient and, when the peace starts breaking down, sends her back to her brother in Rome, ostensibly on another peacemaking mission. Before she reaches Rome, Antony returns to Egypt and Cleopatra, and Caesar must comfort Octavia by telling her to tough it out like a Roman. Poor, patient Octavia is left as a "wronged," "abus'd," and pitied woman (3.6.65, 86, 92).

Antony's treatment of Octavia does not speak well for him, but their marriage was only a peace arrangement from the beginning, with Antony plainly saying in a soliloquy that "though I make this marriage for my peace, / I' th' East my pleasure lies" (2.3.40–41). The contrast between Octavia and Cleopatra is another means Shakespeare uses to set off and exalt Cleopatra's attractions. Though a fine woman, Octavia is no match for Cleopatra, the woman of "infinite variety" (2.2.235). Their differences are comically drawn out by the messenger whom Cleopatra pays to spy on Octavia. The messenger reports that Octavia is shorter than Cleopatra and "low-voic'd" (3.3.13), from which Cleopatra concludes that she is "dull of tongue, and dwarfish" (3.3.16). But the report gets worse: In her "motion" Octavia is more "[a] statue, than a breather" (3.3.19, 21), and she is a widow, thirtyish, round-faced, brown-haired, with a low forehead (3.3.27–34). Cleopatra scornfully triumphs, "This creature's no such thing" (3.3.41). Elsewhere Enobarbus sums up Octavia as "of a holy, cold, and still conversation [demeanor]" (2.6.122–123) and predicts that Antony "will to his Egyptian dish again" (2.6.126).

## Cleopatra

What man would not prefer a hot dish to a cold one? Again and again Cleopatra is described through food imagery, especially in connection with the Roman men who enjoy her. For example, Pompey uses a food metaphor to taunt Antony about Cleopatra's earlier lovers: "your fine Egyptian cookery / Shall have the fame. I have heard that Julius Caesar / Grew fat with feasting there" (2.6.63–65). Even Cleopatra calls herself a "morsel for a monarch" (1.5.31) when she refers to her affair with the great Roman. But the food imagery is mostly used by men and suggests a man's point of view. The food imagery emphasizes Cleopatra's physical attractions, her sensuality, and the pleasures she gives, but it also belittles her power by implying that men can enjoy her and move on. In fact, things work just the other way around: her physical attractions and sensuality are so powerful that she acts like a drug on men. As Enobarbus notes, "Other women cloy / The appetites they feed, but she makes hungry / Where most she satisfies" (2.2.235–237). The great Julius grows fat with his feasting, and the brave Antony sinks into voluptuousness, dotage, and ineffectuality. Antony might seem to love and leave her, but the main point of the play is that he returns.

Cleopatra's power over men is demonstrated by her brief encounter with Dolabella in act 5, when Cleopatra has been captured by the Romans. Dolabella, assigned to guard her, asks if she has heard of him. Obviously he has heard of her and is already enamored. Cleopatra does not know him or his reputation but immediately recognizes the situation: another man has fallen under her spell. She uses her wiles—praising the dead Antony as a colossus and wishing there were "such another man" (5.2.78)—to get Dolabella to find out Caesar's plans for her. Dolabella promptly fulfills her "command," which his "love makes religion to obey" (5.2.198–199).

As her encounter with Dolabella also shows, Cleopatra is fully aware of her power over men and does not hesitate to use it. But, since she had a husband and a succession of lovers who left her with a house full of children, one can hardly call her a man-hater. She does not use her power over men maliciously or for its own sake; rather, it flows incidentally from her experience and her nature, which seems to be defined mostly by her sensuality and lust for life. This same essence explains the complexities of her otherwise fickle character and why other people forgive her promiscuity, her inconsistency, her cowardice, her changeableness, her constant playacting. None of these are admirable qualities and might characterize her as totally amoral. But these same qualities make her interesting and unpredictable, and they might also be explained as necessary for her self-preservation and enjoyment of life. It is significant that Cleopatra carries a knife and draws it twice in the play; this woman is ready to defend herself in a mean, cruel world. Similarly, she is ready to adapt to changing circumstances, even to kill herself, in order to preserve her own nature. Some people might see her life as tragic, but others might see it as exciting, eventful, full, and fulfilling.

Symbolically, just as Caesar and Octavia represent the Roman attitude, Cleopatra is associated with the feminine, the East, and the exotic—the Egyptian way of life. For the Romans, the Egyptian outlook remains largely a mystery and indeed incorporates the mysterious, the inconsistent, and the irrational, particularly in the worship of Isis. The Romans joke about Egyptian behavior but also see it as immoral and decadent, thus tempting and dangerous. Subconsciously for the Romans, the Egyptian way of life seems to represent a part of themselves that they must repress, control, deny, and constantly guard against slipping into.

## Antony

What most of the Romans hold against Antony is that he is guilty of slipping (or plummeting) into the Egyptian mode. He had always shown erratic tendencies in that direction, and Cleopatra pulls him overboard to drown in the Egyptian abyss, as the Romans see it. At the same time, however, the Romans seem to envy Antony for his affair with Cleopatra and his wallowing in sensuality: Antony experiences what they would probably like—but will never have the opportunity or nerve—to experience. For that reason, they condemn him even more strongly and see his fall as tragic. In this view, often expressed in the play, Antony is a once-great man who succumbs to his tragic faults of dissolution and concupiscence. This interpretation of Antony is Plutarch's and can legitimately be argued by Aristotelian critics, but it seems too neat and simplistic.

Rather than falling into the Egyptian style of life, Antony deliberately chooses it, at least the second time around. He does fall for Cleopatra at their first meeting, as Enobarbus tells it, and he seems to be hooked ever after like the fish she catches. But as Enobarbus also says, a man would not have a wife "of a holy, cold, and still conversation [like Octavia] . . . that himself is not so; which is Mark Antony" (2.6.122–126). Instead, "Antony will use his affection where it is" (2.6.130). If it seems unfair to Octavia to marry her to a man like Antony, it is just as unfair to him to be bound to Octavia when Cleopatra loves him with such passion. Antony is Cleopatra's "man of men" (1.5.72), over whom she flies into a jealous rage, draws her knife, and faints when she hears he is married to Octavia. Cleopatra faithfully waits for him, sure he will return to her, and he does. The two are soul mates. Symbolically, Antony's return to Cleopatra is his choice of the Egyptian way of life as more true to his nature.

## DEVICES AND TECHNIQUES

Some of the devices and techniques that Shakespeare used in *Antony and Cleopatra* have been discussed in the sections on structure and plotting and on characters. For example, Shakespeare compressed the action by structuring the play almost cinematically, through such devices and techniques as beginning in medias res, using messengers and eyewitnesses, and creating numerous short scenes. In addition, he filled in background and developed characters indirectly by relying on commentators and character foils. But in a play as rich and complex as *Antony and Cleopatra*, Shakespeare also used many stylistic, rhetorical, and poetic devices and techniques. Among the most prominent of these are dramatic irony, hyperbole, paradox, foreshadowing, mythological allusions, and patterns of imagery.

Dramatic irony permeates the play. Some shorter instances emerge from the party of great men aboard Pompey's boat, Cleopatra's jealous comparison of Octavia to herself, and Octavia's peacemaking mission. At Pompey's party the great men, after joking about and showing their ignorance of Egypt, celebrate an Egyptian bacchanal and degenerate into drunkenness. Comparing Octavia's humble charms to her own, Cleopatra comes out feeling much better, though Octavia is the one who has Antony. The situation is reversed when Octavia returns to Rome on her peacemaking mission, only to learn that Antony has abandoned her for Cleopatra. But most of the dramatic irony is bigger and more sweeping: the precipitous decline of the much-admired Antony into dotage and defeat; the warlike preparations and heated negotiations that lead to tenuous peace, which eventually unravels; the marriage of Antony and Octavia that is meant to keep the peace but becomes a further occasion for war; the decisions by Antony, the superior strategist, to fight at sea when he is better prepared to fight by land (and his resulting defeats); Antony's challenge of Caesar to personal combat; and Caesar's disappointing victory at the end, when he is deprived of his prize captives and instead they are honored.

Other frequently used devices that contribute to the play's rich complexity are hyperbole and paradox. Not surprisingly, for the "drama queen" Cleopatra the typical mode of expression involves hyperbole and paradox, which seem essential to her personality and charm. She exaggerates her emotions, as when she cannot enjoy her usual pastimes and wants to take poison because Antony is absent or when she beats and draws a knife on the messenger with bad news. She expresses her love for Antony through hyperbole, comparing him to "[t]he demi-Atlas of this earth" (1.5.23) and later to the Colossus (5.2.82). Sometimes her hyperbole verges over into paradox, as when she tells Antony that "my becomings kill me when they do not / Eye well to you" (1.3.96–97) or when, at the end, she calls the biting asp "my baby at my breast, / That sucks the nurse asleep" (5.2.309–310).

Other characters use paradox to describe Cleopatra, who seems a bundle of charming contradictions. To Antony, she is a woman whose every emotion, word, and action attracts, "Whom every thing becomes—to chide, to laugh, / To weep" (1.1.49–50). Enobarbus describes her in even more extravagant paradoxes, ending with the statement that "vildest [vilest] things / Become themselves in her" (2.2.237–238). All of these paradoxes help to characterize Cleopatra as a woman of "infinite variety" (2.2.235) and appeal. They might also help explain why Antony would throw everything to the wind for her and why, after thinking she has betrayed him, calling her "'[t]riple-turn'd whore" (4.12.13), and vowing, "The witch shall die" (4.12.47), he goes back to loving her.

These devices and techniques (besides the actions and characters) tend to make *Antony and Cleopatra* an immensely complicated play. Other devices and techniques help bring order to the complexity and make it more understandable. Among these is foreshadowing, the more irrational twin to the rational predictions that Enobarbus and other characters make. Much of the foreshadowing involves the soothsayer, who appears earlier in the play and functions somewhat like the witches in *Macbeth*. He introduces an ominous note into the play, helping to remind the audience that this is a tragedy.

The soothsayer first appears amid the frivolity of Cleopatra's court, where he tells the fortunes of Cleopatra's ladies, not entirely to their liking. He tells them that their fortunes are the same and that their lives so far have been better than what is to come, foreshadowing their deaths with Cleopatra's at the end. The soothsayer then accompanies Antony to Rome—for no apparent reason except to issue some serious forebodings. In Rome he warns Antony to return to Egypt and to beware of Caesar, "whose fortunes shall rise higher" (2.3.16) and who "at any game . . . [has] that natural luck, / He beats thee 'gainst the odds" (2.3.26–28). These predictions foreshadow the battles and outcome of the civil war between Antony and Caesar, allow Antony to remain the better man of the two, but yet make room for destiny (and history) to run its course. The predictions also emphasize the fact that Antony's star is sinking. It finally does sink, but not before some more bad omens on the eve of the last battles near Alexandria, when Antony says a drunken farewell to his tearful servants and even his guardian spirit, the god Hercules, abandons him.

Mythological allusions, like the one to Hercules, also help guide understanding of the play. Antony and Cleopatra are paralleled with Mars/Venus and Aeneas/Dido, other great lovers who were warlike and beautiful, respectively, but whose illicit love ended in tragedy. But the most important parallels are to Hercules, the legendary Greek hero famed for his physical strength, and to Isis, Egyptian goddess associated with the earth, the moon, and fertility. Shakespeare also seems to allude to the historical Antony, who thought he was descended from Hercules and even dressed like him. Unfortunately, Hercules was also known for his angry rages, and the last item of clothing he wore was the poisoned shirt of Nessus that his wife gave him. These details suggest broad parallels to, and perhaps an ironic comment on, Antony's fate in the play. Similarly, Cleopatra dresses like Isis and evokes many of the same associations as the goddess. All of the mythological allusions help build the impression that Antony and Cleopatra are likewise legendary, larger than life, and somehow transcend it.

Still other guides to understanding the play are sets or patterns of imagery, which help to interpret actions, characters, and themes. This mode of literary interpretation, advocated and practiced by the Shakespearean critic G. Wilson Knight, seems to work well for *Antony and Cleopatra*, a play rich in poetic imagery. In fact, the imagery suggests an underlying symbolic unity to the play in a progression from dissolution through death and decay to rebirth. The most significant images here are the images of destruction and dissolution, images of vileness, and images of the Nile.

The images of destruction and dissolution almost forecast the tragedy and certainly go along with it. At the beginning of the play, rather than hear the messengers from Rome, Antony rashly shouts, "Let Rome in Tiber melt, and the wide arch / Of the rang'd empire fall!" (1.1.33–34). This image is so good that Shakespeare later gives a variation to Cleopatra: "Melt Egypt into Nile! and kindly creatures / Turn all to serpents!" (2.5.77–78). After their defeat at Actium, one of Antony's men casually observes, "we have kiss'd away / Kingdoms and provinces" (3.10.7–8). Besides calling attention to the unfolding tragedy, these images, whether violent or offhand, support the play's theme of the world well lost for love. The theme and its supporting imagery are reminders that Antony and Cleopatra are passionate lovers such as the world has rarely seen. True, they suffer tragedy as a direct consequence of their passionate natures, but their love paradoxically transcends tragedy for the same reason.

The images of vileness work in much the same way. Right after Antony's rash exclamation mentioned above, he adds, "Kingdoms are clay; our dungy earth alike / Feeds beast as man" (1.1.35–36). This image expressing contempt for earthly life is echoed by Cleopatra's assertion at the end that in death one "never palates more the dung" (5.2.7), an image so disgusting that some editors have emended it. Cleopatra is also the source of other disgusting images: Before she will let herself be dragged through Rome, she had rather her corpse be thrown into an Egyptian ditch or "rather on Nilus' mud / Lay me stark-nak'd, and let the water-flies / Blow me into abhorring!" (5.2.58–60). These images of dung, decay, and death, mostly coming from Cleopatra, are consistent with her preparation of her own tomb and the manner of her death. The images also recall Enobarbus's paradoxical statement that "vildest [vilest, basest] things / Become themselves in her" (2.2.237–238).

The images of the Nile likewise combine vileness with rebirth. If dung, decay, and death are disgusting, they also form the basis of new life. As the annual flooding of the Nile "ebbs, the seedsman / Upon the slime and ooze scatters his grain, / And shortly comes to harvest" (2.7.21–23). According to Lepidus, the Nile's flooding even produces animal life: "Your serpent of Egypt is bred now of your mud by the operation of your sun" (2.7.26–27). Antony calls Cleopatra " 'my serpent of old Nile' " (1.5.25); Cleopatra uses the serpents of the Nile for her death, and her image of lying naked and fly-blown in the Nile mud mimics seed being sown. These references and others (such as her dressing like Isis) connect Cleopatra to the Nile imagery and rebirth, even if only in the spirit of the asp that feeds like a baby at her breast and crawls off, leaving its trail of slime.

Taken together, these patterns of imagery suggest a mystical interrelationship between life and death. Such an interrelationship was featured in ancient Egyptian religion, which got its cues from the annual cycle of the Nile and led to the practice of mummification and the building of the pyramids. Belief in the religion would explain why Cleopatra could embrace death as easily and enthusiastically as she did life.

## THEMES AND MEANINGS

The events, character contrasts, and cultural references all set up a bipolar conflict in *Antony and Cleopatra* between Rome and Egypt and the ways of life that they represent. The working out of this conflict is the play's overall main theme. But the main theme also embraces a number of others, some of them fairly major. These include such subjects as the interplay of public and private identity, the nature of mature love, the conflict between youth and age, and the changeover from an old to a new order.

The play's examination of public versus private identity has been noted by various critics who point out that the main characters are public figures inclined toward theatricality. They are all playing a public role in an unfortunate conjunction of politics and the stage that Shakespeare depicts and that still plagues politicians. Sometimes their identity seems to consist only of their public persona, either because nothing else in them ever developed or because all else was consumed or repressed by their public role. Young Octavius Caesar, perhaps tugged by ambition or a sense of destiny, is such a figure. He is an extremely efficient would-be emperor, but still one feels a little sorry for him. His sister, Octavia, in playing the role of the dutiful official wife, is similar. They exemplify the Roman way, which does not allow much deviation from one's public role. Mark Antony, however, is conflicted. He tries, even in dotage and defeat, to continue playing his public role of the big general. When he is in his cups or otherwise lapses, he is said not to be "himself" (a revealing term referring to his public identity), but he obviously departs from "himself" in his love of pleasure, strong drink, and Cleopatra. As a result, he dies having lived a full life.

Cleopatra's life is richer still. She has a husband, several lovers, a houseful of children, and still lives as a queen admired by her subjects and the world. Her secret seems to be a seamless public and private identity. Although her behavior is theatrical to the extreme, she is still true to her passionate nature, whether in public or in private. Part of her secret also seems to be cultural and religious. It is significant that Egypt has a female leader in a time when male leadership was the norm, especially in Rome, where women were expected to be like Octavia. Egypt is also a more ancient civilization than Rome. Finally, the Egyptian religion, based on the annual fertility cycle of the Nile, embodies these ancient, female principles. Cleopatra is the ideal leader for Egypt, an exotic land more relaxed and accepting than Rome. She has no need to separate her public and private identities in a kingdom where even "the holy priests / Bless her when she is riggish [wanton]" (2.2.238–239).

Another theme of *Antony and Cleopatra* is the nature of mature love, balancing Shakespeare's treatment of young love in *Romeo and Juliet*. By the time Antony and Cleopatra meet, both are middle-aged and have extensive track records. One might wonder how two such great ones, important world figures, could ever come together. Possibly they are impressed by each other's reputation, or maybe they feel like trophies that each has earned. Such an interpretation is suggested by Harold Bloom, who feels that their relationship is based on "mutual fascination" and lust (*Shakespeare: The Invention of the Human* [New York: Riverhead Books, 1998], 548–549). Sexual indulgence is certainly important for these two sensualists, but if they are mutually fascinated, it seems to be less by reputation than by each other's volatile, unpredictable personality. Cleopatra even teaches unpredictability as a principle of love to her ladies.

Because sex and volatile personalities enter so much into Antony and Cleopatra's relationship, it has some of the dish-throwing nature of love as described by D. H. Lawrence. Perhaps mature love has to be of this nature, since it brings with it so much baggage, including the history of prior relationships and other commitments to the world. Cleopatra loves Antony while he is married to Fulvia and, despite her jealous rage at first, takes him back after he has married Octavia. Similarly, Antony brings up Cleopatra's prior lovers only when he is mad. These other relationships seem to have little effect on their own except to make them more experienced lovers. Nor does it seem to matter to their love that Antony and Cleopatra have children from prior relationships and suffer a long separation. Their relationship also survives its own setbacks, including Cleopatra's cowardice in the first sea battle, her suspected treachery in the second, and Antony's threats to kill her. Still they keep returning to each other and even follow each other into death. One might argue that they could love each other amid such circumstances only because they were mature.

Maturity does not come off quite so well in the conflict between youth and age, a theme developed through the rivalry of Caesar and Antony. As discussed earlier in the section on characters, Antony has the advantage over Caesar of greater military experience and prowess, but he seems to fritter it away. It is as if Antony is tired of keeping up his public role and would be happy to retire to Athens or Alexandria—a request that he eventually makes to Caesar. Antony, apparently superstitious, is also intimidated by the soothsayer's pronouncement that young Caesar has all the luck. In reality, Caesar has only youth on his side, plus Antony's self-destructive tendencies, so it is a safe bet that he will win out if he survives long enough. But young Caesar is also cunning, careful, and patient—traits not often associated with youth, but perhaps developed in him because of his early prominence and his intelligence—making him a superb politician. Ironically, in a youthful pattern of pulling down one's heroes, Caesar maintains respect for Antony, maybe even a little awe, at the same time he is working to defeat and destroy him.

Caesar might understand that Antony is a better man than he is, at least as judged by an earlier heroic age that valued courage and fighting skills more than intelligence and political skills. The challenge to personal combat that Antony makes is a typical gesture of the earlier age, but Caesar scoffs at the challenge as a relic of the fields of ancient Troy. No mythological comparisons are made to Caesar in the play, as they are to the flamboyant Antony. Instead, Caesar is a more scaled-down leader, more like a forerunner of Machiavelli's prince. Caesar inaugurates an age of universal peace, definitely a plus, but it is an age of peace maintained by military power, bureaucracy, and politics, not an age of adventure and heroic figures.

Some of the older time lives on, however, in Egypt, land of the Nile and the pyramids where Antony and Cleopatra are buried. Again ironically, in the culture clash between Egypt and Rome, Rome wins militarily, but the Egyptian way of life seems much richer than the Roman. In their superior way, the Romans deal with Egypt by joking about it, especially its queen. But in doing so they show both their ignorance and their fear. They reduce Egyptian life to crude stereotypes yet at the same time seem attracted to it, as shown by Antony's conversion and by the Egyptian bacchanal aboard Pompey's boat. In other words, their jokes are a defense mechanism. The Egyptian way of life—laid-back, sensual, pleasure-loving—represents a side of themselves that the Romans have repressed. Secretly they are attracted to it but, like Caesar, are afraid of the consequences of letting go. After all, they see the awful example of Antony, a great general who fell into doting on the lustful Egyptian queen, as a warning to them.

Although Shakespeare had to be true to history in showing Caesar the winner, the play, as the title indicates, belongs to Antony and Cleopatra. They are much more attractive characters than Caesar, suggesting that the Roman order he brings is a dreary diminishment, a falling off in the world. The triumphant but empty Roman order is also represented by the abandoned Octavia. Antony makes a statement about the respective ways of life by deliberately choosing Egypt over Rome. But the fullest statement about the Egyptian way of life is given to Cleopatra in the last act, where Caesar is the victor but Cleopatra dominates. She had rather be dead than in Rome, and she chooses a ritual death that celebrates the continuity of life and death according to the Egyptian scheme of things. The Roman victory is a historical fact, but through its religious beliefs the Egyptian way of life transcends history.

Cleopatra declares that she is "fire and air; my other elements / I give to baser life" (5.2.289–290). Octavius has triumphed by sea and land, but these are the baser elements, earth and water. Antony and Cleopatra retain the higher and purer elements of air and fire. In a final irony, at the end of the play Antony and Caesar still divide the world between them. In life Antony enjoyed the more lively and exotic half of the empire. In death he retains the more desirable half of those elements that make up the world.

*Antony and Cleopatra* resembles Shakespeare's English history plays, which show that victory goes to the more skillful politician, not to the better man. Richard II is theatrical and poetic, but he is no match for the politically savvy Bullingbrook, who gains Richard's crown. Hotspur is more honorable than Henry IV, but Hotspur's temper alienates his potential allies and leads to his destruction. Shakespeare understands what leads to success, but he also presents the old order with sympathy and gives it a charm lacking in the efficient new world that triumphs.

## CRITICAL CONTROVERSIES

The section on structure and plotting dealt in context with a couple of critical controversies arising from *Antony and Cleopatra*: the feeling of some older critics that the play is poorly structured and what Anne Barton describes as the play's "divided catastrophe." A related controversy is whether *Antony and Cleopatra*, despite its memorable poetry and characters, ranks in quality with Shakespeare's other great tragedies: *Hamlet*, *Othello*, *King Lear*, and *Macbeth*. Judgment in these and other controversies seems to depend on one's expectations and interpretations of the play and its characters. For instance, does Cleopatra love Antony, or is she just using him? As Janet Adelman points out in *The Common Liar: An Essay on "Antony and Cleopatra,"* possibly the finest commentary on the play, the main critical controversies result from the play's multiple perspectives, which make it extremely difficult to interpret.

Adelman goes on to explain that *Antony and Cleopatra* dramatizes world-shaking events but portrays the world shakers mostly from without, in the manner world leaders are usually seen. Unlike Shakespeare's other great tragedies, where the main characters frequently speak their minds in soliloquies, *Antony and Cleopatra* has only a few brief soliloquies by the main characters. Astonishingly, the two lovers are seen together by themselves, without a crowd around, again only briefly, and then Antony is threatening to kill her. The protagonists change their minds, behave in contradictory ways, and are often putting on an act. So Antony and Cleopatra cannot be known from inside the way one knows other characters in the tragedies, even the villains Claudius, Iago, Edmund, and Macbeth. Instead, one must interpret their feelings and motives based on what they say, what they do, and what others say about them, which includes opinions ranging from one extreme to another.

From Adelman's argument, it seems clear that *Antony and Cleopatra* operates differently from the other great tragedies and must be judged differently. The other great tragedies gain unity by concentrating on one main character, with whom audience members and readers are encouraged to identify. The other great tragedies engage the emotions, while *Antony and Cleopatra* engages the intellect. In the other great tragedies, Shakespeare nudges audiences along with dramatic overkill—ghosts, witches, villains proclaiming their villainy—as if he is afraid the audiences will not get the point (his pushy concern shows even more when one reads the plays). But in *Antony and Cleopatra*, except for help from Enobarbus and the last act, the audience is on its own, challenged to interpret what the play means, as in real life.

An example of this challenge is the question of whether Cleopatra loves Antony or is just using him. As Adelman notes, the question itself is an affront to romantic expectations. People like to believe in true love, but many of the world's great love stories end up with one of the lovers being untrue, and in real life lovers often remain strangers to one another or are unfaithful. Certainly the evidence is against Cleopatra. She has already used two other Roman generals before she gets to Antony. In the opinion of the Romans (including Antony at one or two points), she is a whore. She or her navy also deserts Antony in the sea battles, and it remains possible that she sold him out in both instances. She certainly tries to make a deal with Caesar's envoys after Antony's defeat. But the evidence against Cleopatra can be interpreted in other ways that, while not excusing her, leave open the question of whether she loves Antony. Even in defeat, she rejects outright Caesar's demand that she kill or exile Antony, and she lovingly follows him in death.

Few characters have benefited as much as Cleopatra has from changing cultural attitudes about sexuality. Before this change, audiences, readers, and critics alike tended to agree with the Romans that she is nothing more than a whore, but the sexual revolution has made her behavior seem far less scandalous. In addition, Cleopatra and the play as a whole are now viewed much more favorably because of such recent critical movements as deconstruction, feminism, post-colonialism, and reader response theory. Some critics in these schools see Cleopatra not just as sexy but as an independent woman politically adept at handling her Roman conquerors with the only means available to her. More controversially, Cleopatra is also seen as embodying the archetypal female, a creature superior to man in her acceptance of both life and death. A good example of recent critical judgment of *Antony and Cleopatra* appears in Harold Bloom's *Shakespeare: The Invention of the Human*, where Bloom considers Cleopatra Shakespeare's greatest female character and ranks the play as one of Shakespeare's five great tragedies.

## PRODUCTION HISTORY

Little or nothing is known about *Antony and Cleopatra*'s production history during Shakespeare's time, except that the women's parts, including Cleopatra, would have been played by boys. It is assumed that the play was first acted in 1606–1607 at the Globe and became a part of the repertoire of Shakespeare's company. After

Shakespeare's time, the play as he wrote it disappeared from the stage for over two centuries. The Restoration period, when women began playing female roles, preferred its own versions of the Antony/Cleopatra story, notably John Dryden's heroic play *All for Love* (1677), which proudly observed the neoclassic unities. Shakespeare's *Antony and Cleopatra* was produced once during the eighteenth century and frequently during the nineteenth century, but using scripts that were cut, bowdlerized, and mutilated practically beyond recognition (sometimes conflated with Dryden's play). Otherwise, the play was generally considered too difficult to stage and the part of Cleopatra too difficult or too immoral for a self-respecting actress to portray effectively. Only in the twentieth century was *Antony and Cleopatra* revived in a form faithful to Shakespeare's text, with leading actresses vying to play the part of Cleopatra in numerous stage productions as well as movie and television versions.

Richard Madelaine, editor of *Antony and Cleopatra* in the Shakespeare in Production Series (Cambridge: Cambridge UP, 1998), argues that "sociological and cultural factors" partly account for the play's "strange stage history" ("Introduction," p. 1). He speculates that boys on the Renaissance stage possibly had an easier time acting Cleopatra than actresses have since then. For most of the play's stage history, actresses playing Cleopatra have been caught in a double bind: if they fully displayed her eroticism, they risked being labeled as immoral, but if they were not sexy enough, they were judged as disappointing. Since Cleopatra was also exotic, the Anglo-Saxon world felt for a long time that foreign actresses might be best for the part. As late as 1953, British drama critic Kenneth Tynan thought that "the great sluts of world drama, from Clytemnestra to Anna Christie, have always puzzled our girls; and an English Cleopatra is a contradiction in terms" (quoted in Madelaine, p. 95). In one of the strangest cultural twists, British actresses playing Cleopatra were, until recently, usually red-headed or wore red wigs.

During the eighteenth and nineteenth centuries, pictorial production values also dominated the English stage. It was an age for scene painters, set designers, costumers, and curtain drops at the end of every scene. Spectacle rather than fine words and acting wooed the audiences. These production values militated strongly against Shakespeare's *Antony and Cleopatra*, and productions of the play were theatrical and sometimes financial disasters. The pauses for noisy scene changes were maybe even worse than modern television commercials, and the script was cut and changed drastically to emphasize exotic spectacle, sometimes with music, dancers, and a supporting cast of hundreds. A few productions even tried to bring Cleopatra's barge and the battle scenes onstage. Despite these conditions, one or two productions stood out—most importantly, David Garrick's 1759 Drury Lane production reviving the play, though in a cut and revised version, and Samuel Phelps's 1849 Sadler's Wells production starring Isabella Glyn, the first great Cleopatra.

Only in the twentieth century did authentic productions of Shakespeare's *Antony and Cleopatra* make a comeback. Some productions continued to cut the script, but others staged the play in full, and in general there was more respect for Shakespeare's text. Financial stringency during the world wars and Great Depression left theaters with less funding for spectacle (which could now be depicted more easily in movies), and an atmosphere of experimentation encouraged a return to the bare stage and continuous staging of Shakespeare's time. Experimentation also led to productions using modern dress, to point up the relevance of the play to modern power politics.

Richard Burton as Marc Antony and Elizabeth Taylor as Cleopatra in a scene from Joseph L. Mankiewicz's 1963 film *Cleopatra*. © Bettmann/Corbis.

In productions still emphasizing pictorial elements, these became more manageable as a result of technical developments in lighting and movable stages.

Keen interest in race, gender, and post-colonialism made *Antony and Cleopatra* an especially popular play during the last two or three decades of the twentieth century. Some productions cast black actors and actresses, especially as Egyptians, and the play was sometimes interpreted as a study of colonialism and resistance to it. The play also became a vehicle for the study of sexual politics, especially after actress Janet Suzman gave Cleopatra a strong feminist slant in a 1972 Stratford Memorial production (which became the basis for a television version broadcast on ABC in 1975). Since then, other actresses have followed suit. Feminist interpretations culminated in a 1989 British production, titled *Cleopatra and Antony*, that revised the play to make Cleopatra the protagonist (and might signal another round of bowdlerism). These contemporary interests have also led to performances of *Antony and Cleopatra* in translation, most famously Peter Zadek's 1994 Brechtian production in German.

The role of Cleopatra, once shunned, is now much sought after. In the last half of the twentieth century Cleopatra was played by such distinguished English and American actresses as Peggy Ashcroft, Katharine Hepburn, Vanessa Redgrave, Glenda Jackson, Helen Mirren, Diana Rigg, and Judi Dench. Their performances, especially Peggy Ashcroft's, all helped revive Shakespeare's play. But the actress perhaps most identified with Cleopatra is Elizabeth Taylor, who played the role in the popular 1963 Hollywood movie titled *Cleopatra*. Taylor had little trouble convincing audiences that she was sexy enough for the role, since at the time she was having her sensational affair with married actor Richard Burton, who played Antony in the movie.

## EXPLICATION OF KEY PASSAGES

**2.2.190–239. "I will tell you . . . when she is riggish."** Often quoted (as earlier) to show how closely Shakespeare followed the words of his source, this passage is also key to understanding Cleopatra and Antony's doting upon her. Enobarbus is telling Agrippa about the couple's first meeting, Cleopatra's stunning appearance, and its effect on Antony. In the scene described by Enobarbus, Cleopatra definitely exhibits her talent for grand productions. She makes a striking entrance, lounging back in her golden barge that has purple, perfumed sails. She is dressed as Venus, the boys fanning her are little Cupids, and the gentlewomen with her are made up as mermaids. The townspeople rush to the wharfs to gape at the sight, leaving Antony alone on his throne in the marketplace. When Cleopatra invites him to supper, Antony is similarly stricken. Enobarbus goes on to describe Cleopatra as a woman whose many attractions are enhanced even by her faults. After his description, the bad press that Cleopatra has been receiving from the Romans, including Antony, is blunted. Cleopatra is clearly an extraordinary woman worth a man's troubles.

The passage's verse, fitted to the subject, is unusually sensuous, demonstrating why the poetry in *Antony and Cleopatra* is so often praised. Shakespeare starts the passage with a simile tied together with alliteration: "The barge she sat in, like a burnished throne, / Burnt on the water" (2.2.191–192). The alliteration and metrical substitution at the beginning of the second line hit on the word *burnt* and emphasize the paradoxical image of burning on the water and the elemental forces evoked by this woman. More alliteration, another initial metrical substitution, and further play with the elements continue in the following lines: "The poop was beaten gold, / Purple the sails, and so perfumed that / The winds were love-sick with them" (2.2.192–194). These opening lines grab one's attention as irresistibly as Cleopatra and propel one through an astounding buildup of images, assertions, and paradoxes. What Shakespeare is able to do here with a few subtle changes to his source defines a poet.

Although the passage fills in background events, its underlying message is about love. The winds are "love-sick" (2.2.194), the water is "amorous" (2.2.197), Cleopatra is "[o]'er-picturing that Venus where we see / The fancy outwork nature" (2.2.200–201), and the little Cupids fanning her both heat and cool her, echoing the image of burning on the water. These images and later paradoxes also recall the conventional Petrarchan conceits and oxymorons used in sonnets, but here raised to a highly sophisticated level. However, other levels are at work in the passage, including the images associating love with food: Accepting Cleopatra's invitation to supper, Antony "for his ordinary [meal] pays his heart / For what his eyes eat only" (2.2.225–226). Then there is Agrippa's crude encomium to Cleopatra: "Royal wench! / She made great Caesar lay his sword to bed; / He ploughed her, and she cropp'd" (2.2.226–228). Agrippa's manner here is typical of the way the Romans talk about the Egyptians, as the following key passage demonstrates.

**2.7.16–126. "Thus do they, . . . your hand."** This key passage also has multiple effects. After making peace, the Romans are partying aboard Pompey's ship. There is a great deal of irony in that none of these men can trust each other. Only shortly before, they were bringing serious charges against each other and were ready to go to war. After the party, they will go their separate ways, clash in various civil conflicts, and be eliminated by Caesar one by one. Even during the party, Menas tries to persuade Pompey to take advantage of the situation and slay his enemy guests. Pompey replies that it would have been commendable for Menas to carry out the assassination plan, but now that he knows about it, Pompey's honor prevents him from approving it. Pompey's laughable splitting of hairs about honor recalls the old adage that there is no honor among thieves (which Enobarbus and Menas had earlier called each other [2.6.92–93]).

The passage also satirizes great men and the notion of power more directly. The main figure of fun is the drunken Lepidus, weak sister of the triumvirs. Antony the cosmopolite mocks Lepidus's drunkenness and ignorance about matters Egyptian:

*Lepidus*: What manner o' thing is your crocodile?

*Antony*: It is shap'd, sir, like itself, and it is as broad as it has breadth. It is just so high as it is, and moves with its own organs. It lives by that which nourisheth it, and the elements once out of it, it transmigrates.

*Lepidus*: What color is it of?

*Antony*: Of its own color too. (2.7.41–47)

Enobarbus and Menas also crack jokes at Lepidus's expense. Enobarbus describes an attendant who carries off Lepidus as "a strong fellow" because he "bears the third part of the world" (2.7.88–90). Menas replies, "The third part then is drunk. Would it were all, / That it might go on wheels!" (2.7.92–93). Menas's wish forecasts what comes next: After laughing at Lepidus, the other men proceed to get almost as drunk as he is. In their drunken revelry, they present an image of political power that is funny and scary at the same time: Is the fate of the world in such hands?

Just as Lepidus's drunkenness images that of the others, so does his ignorance of matters Egyptian. Even Antony, the expert, seems to have mainly superficial knowledge; for him, the Nile floods, the breeding of serpents from the mud, the pyramids, and the transmigration of souls are only exotic curiosities, not part of a religious belief system. Like the other Romans, Antony jokes about Egyptian life, only more expertly. The Romans' jokes reflect their ignorance and casual assumption of superiority. At the same time, as indicated earlier, their jokes are also a defense mechanism. As the key passage shows, the Romans are secretly attracted to "Egyptian bacchanals" (2.7.104). Terrified by the attraction, Caesar is almost panicked about resisting Egyptian "levity" if Roman gravity is to be preserved (2.7.120–121).

**5.2.243–319. "Hast thou the pretty worm . . . and then play—[.]"** This key passage is Cleopatra's death scene, the play's climax. *Antony and Cleopatra* is noted for being a tragedy that has substantial comic and satiric elements. This admixture occurs even here when a clown, "a rural fellow" (5.2.233), brings the basket of asps that will kill Cleopatra. The clown is a jolly, talkative sort who plays with indirection. For example, he uses antonyms—*immortal, honest,* and *fallible*—for what he really means, and he calls the asp a "worm," giving it both sexual and mortal innuendos. Some of his statements are similar: He says that "those that do die of it [the asp's bite] do seldom or never recover" (5.2.247–248), and twice he wishes Cleopatra "joy of the worm" (5.2.260, 279). Probably the clown is trying to talk Cleopatra out of doing what she intends, certainly warning her repeatedly about the asp's potency. His speaking in riddles also suggests the existential uncertainty that prevails throughout the play.

At the same time, the clown's tone and statements introduce theological considerations that carry over into Cleopatra's death. The clown is an Egyptian figure of death who jokes about it because death is also a rebirth. As a countryman, he is directly connected to the annual cycle of regeneration in the soil, and so is the basket of asps that he brings. It is this cycle that Cleopatra returns to when she has "[i]mmortal longings" (5.2.281) to join Antony and mock Caesar. As Iras shows by dying first, "[t]he stroke of death is as a lover's pinch, / which hurts, and is desir'd" (5.2.295–296). In this spirit Cleopatra applies the asps to her breast and arm and dies. Charmian sums up the event: "Now boast thee, death, in thy possession lies / A lass unparallel'd" (5.2.315–316).

## Annotated Bibliography

Adelman, Janet. *The Common Liar: An Essay on "Antony and Cleopatra."* New Haven: Yale UP, 1973. Arguing that *Antony and Cleopatra* incorporates a variety of dramatic perspectives that require audience members and readers to make their own judgments, Adelman has contributed most to a contemporary understanding of the play.

Bloom, Harold. *Shakespeare: The Invention of the Human.* New York: Riverhead Books, 1998. Steeped in Shakespearean criticism, including the latest, but holding his own common-sense views, Bloom provides the most readable recent overview of Shakespeare's work. He includes *Antony and Cleopatra* among Shakespeare's five great tragedies and considers Cleopatra Shakespeare's greatest female character, whose complex eroticism previews modern love.

Drakakis, John, ed. *Antony and Cleopatra.* Basingstoke: Macmillan, 1994. Reflecting recent critical theories, this anthology of criticism collects a range of postmodern views on the play, addressing such issues as gender, race, genre, history, and politics. It includes an excerpt from Janet Adelman's book (listed above).

Madelaine, Richard, ed. *Antony and Cleopatra.* By William Shakespeare. Cambridge: Cambridge UP, 1998. Madelaine's 138-page introduction focuses on the stage history of the play. He also gives a chronological list of productions and a full bibliography; the play's text is accompanied by extensive production notes on how various scenes, passages, and lines have been played.

Rose, Mark, ed. *Twentieth Century Interpretations of "Antony and Cleopatra."* Englewood Cliffs, NJ: Prentice-Hall, 1977. An anthology of pre-1980 criticism of the play, this collection includes an excerpt from Janet Adelman's book (listed above) and Maynard Mack's influential essay "*Antony and Cleopatra*: The Stillness and the Dance" plus the editor's introduction arguing that *Antony and Cleopatra* is a transitional work between Shakespeare's major tragedies and his later romances.

# *Coriolanus*

## Andrew Macdonald

### PLOT SUMMARY

**1.1.** Mutinous citizens range the streets of Rome, complaining that Caius Martius Coriolanus is their chief enemy, a patrician who is happy to see them starve in this period of famine. Menenius Agrippa, a patrician and a friend of Coriolanus, tries to divert their wrath, arguing that the shortage of corn is the fault of the gods, not the aristocratic classes withholding food to raise prices. Menenius counters plebeian complaints with a famous analogy: the different parts of the body, the legs, eyes, and so on, once rebelled against the stomach, arguing that it did no work but received all the benefit of the other body parts' struggle for food. The belly answered that it served as the storehouse and "shop" (1.1.133) of the body, sending all of value to the other parts and retaining only the chaff. It is exactly the same with the Roman patricians, according to Menenius's parable: the complaining citizens are no more than minor body parts, while the aristocrats are the storehouse and central part of Rome.

Coriolanus enters in the middle of the scene and immediately insults the plebeians, calling them "curs" (1.1.168), "hares" (1.1.171), and "geese" (1.1.172). "Hang 'em!" (1.1.190) is his answer to protests about hunger, telling Menenius that his sword would solve the problem. He is particularly aggrieved because the plebeians have been awarded five tribunes to represent them, and Coriolanus thinks that this concession will simply provoke further demands. A group of senators enters with the news that, led by the warlike Tullus Aufidius, the Volsces, a rival tribe, are threatening Rome. Coriolanus is enlisted, willingly, to take charge of the defense of the city. The scene ends with Sicinius Velutus and Junius Brutus, two of the new tribunes, scheming about how this war can be turned to their advantage.

**1.2.** Tullus Aufidius and the senators of Corioles, the main city of the Volsces, discuss attacking Rome. Tullus looks forward to confronting his old antagonist Coriolanus.

**1.3.** Volumnia, Coriolanus's mother, boasts to Virgilia, Coriolanus's wife, that she sent her son off to war when he was only a boy, to make him a man. Virgilia, who

dislikes the harsh Roman principles that honor war above all else, refuses to accompany her friend Valeria and Volumnia on a walk out-of-doors since she wishes
dutifully to await Coriolanus's return home. Valeria, a friend of the family, reports
that Virgilia's son takes after his father, in anger tearing apart a butterfly.

**1.4.** Coriolanus, in an excess of warlike fury, alone chases the retreating Volsces
into their city, where the gates close on him. Given up for dead, he escapes, bleeding.

**1.5–7.** In a series of quick scenes we see Coriolanus's bravery, which rises to blood
lust; he repeats, "Come I too late?" for battle (1.6.24, 26), upset that he may have
missed some conflict.

**1.8.** Coriolanus fights Aufidius, and we see that they are two of a kind, furious
warriors with huge egos.

**1.9.** Coriolanus has won the battle but refuses to accept the spoils that are legitimately his, and he seems disposed to minimize his achievement: "You shout me
forth / In acclamations hyperbolical, / As if I lov'd my little should be dieted / In
praises sauc'd with lies" (1.9.50–53). He is not fighting for profit; he simply loves
war and battle, and cares little for praise. However, he is awarded the name Coriolanus in honor of his triumph at Corioles (previously, he has been identified by
his given name, Caius Martius). Tellingly, Coriolanus wants to help a poor man of
Corioles who gave him aid earlier, but he cannot remember his name.

**1.10.** In the camp of the Volsces, Aufidius, frustrated by being defeated by Coriolanus in five encounters, promises to destroy Coriolanus by fair means or foul, a
prediction that creates tension throughout the rest of the play.

**2.1.** In Rome Menenius and the two tribunes, Sicinius and Brutus, discuss Coriolanus. Both tribunes claim that Coriolanus is overly proud and arrogant. Menenius
gives the patrician side, but to little avail. Volumnia, Virgilia, and Valeria join Menenius with news that Coriolanus is on his way home. Virgilia hopes that he has not
been wounded, but Coriolanus's mother retorts, "There will be large cicatrices [scars]
to show the people, when he shall stand for his place" (2.1.146–148). That is, his scars
will provide visible proof of his character and will convince the masses of the city that
he has served them well and consequently deserves public office. The scene shifts back
to Sicinius and Brutus, who plot about how to prevent Coriolanus from being selected consul. They think he will be too unbending and proud to show his wounds
suffered in the defense of Rome, as was the custom for candidates for consul.

**2.2.** Two officers discuss Coriolanus's inability to practice moderation: he will
not flatter the public, so he goes to the other extreme and "seeks their hate" (2.2.18).
After Cominius praises him before the senators and tribunes, recounting his first
battle at age sixteen and his seventeen battles since, the Senate votes to make him
consul, but Coriolanus balks at showing his wounds: "As if I had receiv'd them for
the hire / Of their breath [to buy the public's approval] only!" (2.2.149–150). He
does not want anyone to think that he acted as he did in the hope of rewards.

**2.3.** Some citizens remember Coriolanus's intractability about the shortage of
corn and his insults, calling them the "many-headed multitude" (2.3.16–17), like the
monster Hydra. Though reminded by Menenius that the worthiest of candidates
have shown their wounds and demonstrated humility, Coriolanus still resists. He is
surly and churlish in asking for votes, and one citizen points out he has not "lov'd
the common people" (2.3.93), to which Coriolanus counters that his love is not
common. In spite of his attitudes, Coriolanus is chosen consul. However, Brutus
and Sicinius urge the crowd to revoke their approval.

**3.1.** Tullus Aufidius is again up in arms. Like Coriolanus, he has cursed his own followers: Tullus has contempt for the Volsces for so easily giving up Corioles. He and Coriolanus are well matched, and ache to fight again. Coriolanus also cannot control his contempt for ordinary Romans, calling them "children," "a herd," and "minnows" (3.1.30, 33, 89) despite Menenius's attempts to establish amity. Coriolanus is choleric, upbraiding the citizen "rabble" (3.1.136) for cowardice in war and greed for the distribution of free corn: plebeian "crows" will "peck at the eagles" (3.1.139) of the Senate, the patricians.

Brutus and Sicinius argue that Coriolanus deserves death for these treasonous sentiments: he should be hurled from the Tarpeian cliff, as were all offenders against the state. Coriolanus fights off his plebeian attackers, who would carry out the sentence on the spot, but feels no remorse for his intemperance, which provoked the attack. Menenius is correct when he says that Coriolanus says exactly what he thinks, without softening his criticism or considering the consequences of his statements, "His heart's his mouth; / What his breast forges, that his tongue must vent" (3.1.256–257).

**3.2.** Even Volumnia concedes Coriolanus is "too absolute" (3.2.39) and urges him to speak in a conciliatory way to the plebeians, even if doing so goes against his grain. He finally agrees to act "mildly" (3.2.145).

**3.3.** Coriolanus attempts to put his new resolution into practice. But the tribunes have conspired to incense him by calling him a traitor, and he responds just as they have expected. He erupts: "The fires i' th' lowest hell fold in the people! / Call me their traitor, thou injurious tribune!" (3.3.68–69). Sicinius proposes his banishment as an enemy of the people, and Coriolanus retorts that he banishes the plebeians in turn. He is then banished from Rome.

**4.1.** Coriolanus leaves Rome stoically, "alone, / Like to a lonely dragon" (4.1.29–30).

**4.2.** Volumnia confronts the tribunes Sicinius and Brutus, calling their followers "Cats," without the skill or ability to judge Coriolanus's worth any more than she can interpret the secret mysteries of heaven (4.2.34–36).

**4.3.** A Roman, Nicanor, and a Volsce, Adrian, discuss the shaky state of Rome now that Coriolanus, Rome's military protector, has been banished and conflict is brewing between plebeians and patricians.

**4.4.** Coriolanus seeks out Tullus Aufidius in the city of Antium, musing on the irony that he has made widows of many of the citizens and is now putting himself at the mercy of his great enemy.

**4.5.** Coriolanus is confronted by Tullus's servants in a comic interlude before he meets his old foe and offers his services against Rome, saying he will give up his throat to be cut if he is not wanted. Aufidius greets him warmly, however, proclaiming "more dances my rapt heart / Than when I first my wedded mistress saw / Bestride my threshold" (4.5.116–118). He offers Coriolanus half his forces to revenge himself on Rome. Coriolanus is honored by Tullus and other Volsces at a banquet.

**4.6.** The setting returns to Rome, where the news is that the Volsces are now attacking, and Coriolanus heads one half of the force. Menenius speaks for the patricians, blaming the tribunes for banishing Coriolanus and provoking his revenge. The cowardly citizens deny responsibility for the banishment.

**4.7.** The act ends with Aufidius admitting jealousy of Coriolanus to his lieutenant, for Coriolanus has typically been haughty and domineering even in his exile. Aufidius remarks that "our virtues / Lie in th' interpretation of the time" (4.7.49–50), meaning that what is a fault in one situation could be seen as a virtue in another, depending on the context and the interpreters of the act. He declares that Coriolanus's reckoning will come at Aufidius's hands after Rome has been conquered.

**5.1.** Cominius complains that Coriolanus has rejected his appeals for mercy for Rome; Coriolanus is distant and unmoved by the potential slaughter of his old friends and family. Menenius, the master politician, resolves to catch Coriolanus in a positive mood after he has eaten a good meal.

**5.2.** Menenius tests his theory that food will be the route to Coriolanus's heart but is initially rejected cruelly by Coriolanus's guard: Coriolanus, he says, wants nothing to do with former Roman intimates. When the general himself comes on the scene, accompanied by Tullus Aufidius, Menenius weeps, but to no avail, and is sent packing.

**5.3.** Coriolanus admits his pain at rejecting Menenius. Virgilia, Volumnia, Valeria, and Coriolanus's young son appear, dressed in mourning. They represent all the bonds of Nature to Coriolanus, as distinct from his personal promises to Tullus and the Volsces to remain unmoved by his Roman past: "I'll never / Be such a gosling to obey instinct, but stand / As if a man were author of himself, / And knew no other kin" (5.3.34–37). With these lines Coriolanus expresses the classic sentiments of the Renaissance overreacher, the character whose pride and arrogance, like Marlowe's Dr. Faustus, lead him to believe he can define himself and his own destiny. The appeals of Coriolanus's womenfolk move his emotions, but initially he wills himself to stay his course; even Volumnia's call for a compromise does not at first change his mind, although his wife, mother, and son literally beg on their knees. He turns his back, in silence. But then Coriolanus softens and agrees to Volumnia's compromise, to seek a peace. Ominously, an aside from Aufidius shows he plans his own revenge on Coriolanus.

**5.4–5.** Menenius despairs over the imminent destruction of Rome. The fickle citizens of Rome are ready to lynch their tribunes, whom they blame for expelling Coriolanus, ignoring their own role in doing so. When the news of the compromise reaches them, they celebrate at the end of scene 4 and in scene 5.

**5.6.** Tullus Aufidius plots to regain his ascendancy, which he claims Coriolanus has taken away, seducing Tullus's followers and then making peace "[a]t a few drops of women's rheum" (5.6.45), the tears of Virgilia and Volumnia. Tullus and his coconspirator complain of the loss of booty (since Rome will not be sacked) and are jealous of Coriolanus's new glory.

The Lords of the Volsces are swayed by Tullus, convinced that by showing mercy Coriolanus has broken faith with them. When confronted with the accusations, Coriolanus flies into a fury at Tullus's words "traitor" and "boy" (5.6.86, 100), terms chosen to provoke Coriolanus into a rage. Coriolanus retorts that "like an eagle in a dove-cote, I / Flutter'd your Volscians in Corioles. / Alone I did it. 'Boy!' " (5.6.114–116), rubbing in his earlier slaughter of the Volscian population, doves to his eagle. Like the Roman rabble who expelled him, the Volsces turn into a mob when provoked by Tullus's rhetoric, calling for Coriolanus's death; only a couple of lords call for restraint. Tullus and his conspirators kill Coriolanus, and Tullus stands triumphantly on his body, the winner at last. His enemy gone, Tullus then admits to sorrow.

## PUBLICATION HISTORY

The play probably dates from 1607 or 1608, for the stylistics of *Coriolanus* suggest a date late in Shakespeare's canon, as do some internal references. For example, the January 1608 fires built on the frozen Thames may provide the reference for "coal of fire upon the ice" (1.1.173), and some of the descriptions of the masses seem to allude to 1607 grain riots and disturbances in the Midlands. Besides, the play draws on Camden's *Remains* (1605) for the fable of the belly (1.1.96ff), and so the play must have come after that publication. Some critics detect an allusion in 3.1.95–97 to Hugh Middleton's 1609 project to bring water into London, an enterprise certainly talked about in 1607 or 1608.

The story is set in the streets and homes of early republican Rome, and in the towns of the Volsces tribe, Corioles and Antium. Although there was plenty of bread, the patricians refused to distribute it to the common people, so there were hunger riots and class conflicts, as citizens railed against the upper classes. In general, the historical situation pits patricians and plebeians against each other to decide who would control Rome, with military interference by the Volsces complicating the political conflict. As already noted, similar rioting was occurring in England at the time. In 1598 there had been unrest in Stratford over the hoarding of grain, and Shakespeare at the time had eighty bushels stored in his barns at New Place. According to Park Honan, a Stratford weaver said he hoped to see the hoarders "hanged on gibbets at their own doors" (*Shakespeare: A Life* [Oxford: Oxford UP, 1998], 241).

The issue of civil war was never far from the mind of Englishmen; memory of the fifteenth-century Wars of the Roses had not faded. James I's blatant claim to rule by divine right was already raising controversy, and even early in his reign he was demonstrating less skill than his predecessor, Elizabeth, in reconciling England's various religious, social, and political factions.

*Coriolanus* was one of sixteen plays registered by Edward Blount and Isaac Jaggard on November 8, 1623, before publishing the 1623 Folio edition. The First Folio text of Shakespeare's plays contains the only surviving version of *Coriolanus*. It was the second play in the Tragedy section. All later printings derive from that source. The Folio edition includes only acts; Nicholas Rowe in his 1709 edition added scene divisions, and nineteenth-century editor Alexander Dyce set up the present act-scene arrangement as a whole.

The Folio edition probably was printed from Shakespeare's own draft, or foul papers: that is, an early script of the play. This edition includes one or two bookkeeper notations. Stage directions match stage action; generally, entrances and exits are marked. However, problems occurred from the compositors' difficulty in reading Shakespeare's handwriting: for example, confusing his word "one" with "on" or "shoot" with "shout." There is also some mislineation in the verse, maybe because Shakespeare had not yet finished working out all his verse or perhaps because of compositorial manipulation due to the print limitations on copy width.

## SOURCES FOR THE PLAY

Shakespeare follows Sir Thomas North's version of Plutarch's *Life of Coriolanus*, sometimes very closely, using North's language at times but changing emphasis, tone, and balance by his selection, arrangement, omission, and addition of details. Basically, Shakespeare's attitude toward the characters and their politics is different from Plutarch's more sentimental views: the Roman writer found in the story lessons in political restraint and patriotism. Shakespeare follows Plutarch's order of events; he includes most of the same characters, though he modifies them a great deal. Some speeches even closely follow Plutarch's; for example, the speech in which Coriolanus offers his services to Aufidius (4.5.65ff) and Volumnia's plea with her son to spare Rome (5.3.94ff). Yet, Plutarch's Coriolanus is "churlish and uncivil, and altogether unfit for a man's conversation," and Shakespeare's interpretation of the significance of events is quite different from Plutarch's. The Roman ladies talking about the young Martius is Shakespeare's unique creation. Shakespeare makes Volumnia fiercer than Plutarch does. Shakespeare also draws on Camden's *Remains* (1605), which contained a more detailed version of the fable of the belly and the body members than that of Plutarch or Livy.

## STRUCTURE AND PLOTTING

The play's structure emphasizes Coriolanus's failure to learn from experience. In 1.1 the initial attack on Coriolanus goes unheeded; in 3.1–3 the tribunes, Brutus and Sicinius, lead the Roman plebeian revolt and accuse Coriolanus of being a traitor, a key word often repeated throughout the play. They consider his death, then decide on banishment. In 5.6 Aufidius leads a Corioli mob, again accusing Coriolanus of being a traitor. Coriolanus never can control his rage, and finally Aufidius demands and gets his death.

As in most Shakespearean plays, the structure builds on foils, characters who parallel each other; our understanding of one sheds light on the other, and sets of foils together provide the audience with different facets of a central idea. For example, Aufidius is a foil to Coriolanus. Both are fearless warriors fighting for the State, but their motives and methods differ. Aufidius is after personal glory, is filled with hatred for his enemy, is untouched by a sense of honor and aristocratic ideals; he uses any means, fair or foul, duplicity and treachery to attain his ends. He is the ignoble level to which Coriolanus could sink if he became political and yielded to the mob. Ironically, Coriolanus is blind to Audifius's nature and believes they share the same values; because he mistrusts the integrity of everyone except aristocrats, whom he mistakenly assumes are always honorable and valiant, he embraces his darkest enemy as his most beloved friend.

A Chorus is another structuring device. This role is assumed by Menenius, who comments on the action, directs the sentiments of the audience, makes clear the positions of both Coriolanus and his adversaries, points out the pride and corruption of the tribunes, and expresses the destructive effects of politicians catering to and manipulating the affections of the masses. These expository functions go far beyond his role in the plot of the play.

Finally, the pattern of the "tragic hero," the rise and fall of a great man, structures the play. Aristotle says a tragic hero is basically a good man with a serious fault, or "tragic flaw," that causes him to fall from a position of power and prestige. He cannot be directly blamed for the fault because it is simply a part of his nature; but he can be blamed for his blindness to this flaw and for behavior that allows it to rage uncontrolled. Ironically, Coriolanus's virtues are also his vices, and his rise to power contains the seeds for his fall. Act 1 explores the superhuman bravery of Coriolanus that merits reward. Act 2 shows him rewarded for his service by being chosen as consul. At the end of act 3 he is been banished from Rome for speaking his mind too freely. Act 4 sees him successfully leading an army against Rome, only to be slaughtered by his enemies at the end of act 5. This structural pattern of the rise and fall of a great man is one common to Shakespeare's time and is certainly dramatic in any age. It is varied here to some degree in that the rise seems to end in act 3, only to continue upward again in act 4. However, his banishment from Rome in act 3 is the beginning of the end for him: when he turns his military might against his own people, friends and relatives, he has already begun the decline from greatness.

## MAIN CHARACTERS

### Coriolanus

Coriolanus is an extreme of one trait. Coriolanus's honesty, his compelling need to express the truth as he sees it, overwhelms caution, common sense, being politic, being kind—being completely human, in other words. Coriolanus is a one-note character, useful to his fellow Romans as a warrior but dangerous when his martial skills are not required. His honesty becomes bluntness and a refusal to acknowledge the point of view of others; he becomes isolated, a kind of monster, unable to control himself in human society.

Coriolanus seems well aware of his temper, but he stubbornly refuses to curb his tongue, even when all his friends urge him to do so. He seems to indulge his out-of-control behavior and even to enjoy it. Coriolanus is an ambiguous hero in an ambiguous play. For the modern reader, his anti-democratic tirades smack uncomfortably of fascism. He believes that all but the aristocrats are mindless, treacherous, dangerous children who claim adult status while indulging the desires of the moment. Modern readers/viewers should not be too bothered by all this, since this view of the "masses" was conventional Elizabethan political science, which Shakespeare quite naturally reflects. Democratic rule had never existed in English society, and it is unreasonable to expect Shakespeare to have democratic sympathies. Also, much of the action has some historical basis, at least as reported by Plutarch, Shakespeare's source.

Most unsettling for the audience is Coriolanus's double nature, the ties between his extreme virtue and his extreme vice, which happen to be the same quality. Coriolanus's nature makes him the perfect soldier, but an execrable politician; his leadership in war is unquestionable, but, unfortunately for him, he must be judged by the citizenry. His inability to lower himself to tolerate this level of pandering for approval is Coriolanus's tragic flaw, the fixed nature of which can be appreciated by comparing the parallel scenes in which the Romans and the Volsces accuse him of treason. He has learned nothing from being banished and reacts again with excessive anger. He is aware of his shortcoming, but he simply cannot bring himself to do what others tell him he must, as opposed to what his instincts tell him is right and true. It is this clear-sightedness about himself that perhaps also makes Coriolanus different from purely Aristotelian tragic heroes, and that perhaps also makes him a true Renaissance hero—a man who reaches for perfection and attains a purity that makes him unfit for a flawed world, defined by the compromises of such politicians as Menenius.

Coriolanus is a firm adherent of the medieval and Renaissance idea of a world order called the Chain of Being, a view that everyone and everything has its proper place and order in a hierarchy from low to high. Each class has its function and place, and the aristocracy must force the ignorant and fickle masses to do what is best for the state. The aristocracy is at the top of the human social and political hierarchy and must control the masses for the good of all. Thus, to Coriolanus's way of thinking, catering to the masses is dangerous to the state, a reversal of the proper order. The ideal for politics is a military model of rank, with those best fitted for command at the top. It is not enough to say that Coriolanus is an authoritarian. He clearly thinks that rights are earned and that a military orientation should be the model for civilian order.

## Volumnia

Volumnia, Coriolanus's fierce mother, is also aristocratic and proud. Extremely patriotic, she values honor and nobility and abhors cowards. For her the noblest form of death is to fall battling for one's country, and death is always preferable to dishonor. She is stoic, and when necessary, heartless. For her, manhood means toughness, military prowess, and loyalty—values she instills in Coriolanus, whom she pushes into war at an early age. In the hierarchy of family life, Volumnia wields authority. In 1.3 the discussion between Volumnia and Virgilia shows the Roman character, as the women speak starkly and realistically about battles and bloodshed, even as they sew. Volumnia is a real Roman matron, bloody and tough, a warrior at heart. She declares that "The breasts of Hecuba, / When she did suckle Hector, look'd not lovelier / Than Hector's forehead when it spit forth blood / At Grecian sword" (1.3.40–43). She is responsible for Coriolanus's nobility and for his unbending nature, for she teaches him a soldier's values and fails to temper them with policy and diplomacy. Only his love for her can sway Coriolanus from obstinately pursuing what he thinks is right. Volumnia is a valiant woman, but, like her son, at times almost inhuman in her stoicism and her adherence to warrior values. Her pleas for patriotism, honor, and history save Rome, just as her training of her son almost destroys it. She is responsible for her son's going into politics though he is unsuited for the role of politician. An overbearing mother, she is much to blame for her son's failings.

## Virgilia

Volumnia intimidates Virgilia, Coriolanus's wife, and so Virgilia is usually silent onstage. She is modest, patient, meek, and retiring, and hence takes second place to Coriolanus's domineering mother in his life. She seems the outsider in this family because she alone has, or shows, fear. When Volumnia proudly envisions Coriolanus's bloody brow, Virgilia replies, "His bloody brow? O Jupiter, no blood!" (1.3.38). Virgilia hopes that Coriolanus will not fight Aufidius; Volumnia eagerly imagines their encounter. Her son by Coriolanus is a miniature version of his father, with the same fierce martial spirit: he prefers swords and drums to schoolbooks and rips a butterfly to pieces in his rage.

## Aufidius

Tullus Aufidius, general of the Volscians, serves as a foil to Coriolanus, both fearless warriors fighting for the state but with differing motives and methods. Whereas Coriolanus shuns glory, Aufidius seeks it. He uses any means, fair or foul, even duplicity and treachery, as when he finally dispatches Coriolanus. Aufidius acts exactly like the Roman tribunes. While Shakespeare shows that the masses can be manipulated by crafty politicians, he also demonstrates that leaders, whatever their birth, can be deceitful and treacherous. In general *Coriolanus* can hardly be said to portray the aristocracy favorably, however idealistic its title character may be.

## Menenius

Menenius, a wise Roman patrician, respected for his wit, his ability to talk to patricians and plebeians alike, and his sense of justice, is like a chorus. He points out the pride and corruption of the tribunes as well as the destructive effects of politicians catering to and manipulating the affections of the masses. Unlike Coriolanus, he knows how to deal with people and sometimes acts as a sort of liaison between Coriolanus and the citizens. He demonstrates the values of moderation, but also their limitation. He cannot prevent the tribunes from inciting the mob, and he cannot restrain Coriolanus. Nor can he save Rome. His plea to Coriolanus in 5.2 goes unheeded, and he anticipates the city's destruction at the hands of Coriolanus.

## Brutus and Sicinius

The tribunes Brutus and Sicinius, thirsty for power, are as contemptuous of the people as is Coriolanus. In private, they agree with the patricians' slanderous characterization of the people as "beasts" (2.16), senseless masses with stinking garlic breath (2.1.236). Their images are especially nasty when they are watching the public reaction to Coriolanus's return: their constituency is summed up by the "prattling nurse" who ignores her baby to watch the spectacle of Coriolanus's entrance (2.1.206) and the other women of the town who behave vulgarly before their godlike hero (2.1.205–221). Brutus and Sicinius incite the mob to do their will and act for their personal benefit rather than for the good of the public. Their blatant plans to manipulate the mob and their confidence in their chances of success show how easily they think the people can be swayed: "Doubt not / The commoners, for whom we stand, but they / Upon their ancient malice will forget / With the least cause these his new honors" (2.1.226–229). Brutus and Sicinius are ambitious individuals whom Menenius describes as "herdsmen of the beastly plebeians" (2.1.95). They act to help make Coriolanus unpopular with the citizens and to get him thrown out of Rome.

## Titus Lartius and Cominius

Minor characters include Titus Lartius, a Roman general who serves with Coriolanus against the Volscians and admires Coriolanus for his military prowess and his soldiering. Cominius, another Roman general, also supports Coriolanus, speaking on his behalf before the Senate and reporting his acts of bravery. It is Cominius who gives Caius Martius the name Coriolanus to honor his victory. These characters serve to reinforce the image of Coriolanus as a noble figure.

### The Patricians and the Plebeians

The patricians and the plebeians are themselves mass groups significant to the plot. Menenius represents the former while Sicinius and Brutus stand in for the latter, but the social classes form a general identity as the play progresses, just as Shakespeare makes us imagine armies by having a few soldiers run onto the stage shouting about what is happening in battle. The patricians share Coriolanus's contempt for the masses but fear their power. The plebeians instigate conflicts, threaten riots, and judge leaders. Mocked and denigrated by the aristocratic patricians, their favor is nonetheless necessary for any leader to survive. Neither group comes off well, although the patricians have the better lines and are at least not mob-like.

## DEVICES AND TECHNIQUES

Shakespeare's devices and techniques are those he uses in all his plays: foils, or contrasts, to reveal different facets of a concept or character; a few soliloquies and many public speeches to test the true nature of a character; figurative language to make complex concepts visual; dramatic irony; and appeals to the imaginations of his audience to people his stage with the masses and armies a stage cannot contain.

*Coriolanus* makes extensive use of foils, playing off Coriolanus and his mother Volumnia as both similar in their warlike attitudes but different because of gender and social role; Volumnia and Virgilia, the martial Roman matron against the stereotypically feminine wife; Coriolanus and Menenius, the man of action against the consummate politician; Menenius the patrician against Sicinius and Brutus, the heavy-handed plebeian politicians; and finally, the two warriors, Coriolanus the Roman and Tullus Aufidius the Volscian. Each of these pairs of foils adds different facets to Coriolanus's character, showing him set off against opposites or characters whose similarities throw Coriolanus's attributes into relief. For example, Coriolanus and his mother seem very much alike in their complete commitment to warrior values, but Volumnia moderates her position at the end of the play: Coriolanus intends to sack Rome and suppress all his merciful impulses, while Volumnia begs for a compromise. Whether the cause of this difference is gender, age, or her social role as a mother and Roman matron is never established, but that is the point of foils, to highlight character by comparison and contrast.

Volumnia and Virgilia are similarly set off and contrasted. They are a domestic pair of opposites, with the martial strength of the former showing one possible extreme of Roman female behavior, while Virgilia depicts a Roman wife who is timid, fearful of violence, and totally committed to husband and child.

Menenius bends in every direction, dramatizing for us how furiously unbending is Coriolanus. Both seek Rome's best interest, and they pretty much agree on where that interest lies (military strength; patrician rule). However, they differ as to means, Coriolanus favoring the soldier's aggressive, forthright approach, while Menenius exhibits the politician's tact. Sicinius and Brutus are socially and intellectually lower versions of Menenius, barely controlling their mob-like constituency and operating at an even baser level of self-interest than the patrician. Finally, Cori-olanus and Tullus Aufidius are a magnificently matched pair, nearly equal in bat-tle after battle until the Volscian resorts to treachery at the end of act 5. However, Aufidius, like the tribunes, seeks personal glory, even at the expense of his people. He lacks the code of honor that guides (and destroys) Coriolanus. Through the use of foils Shakespeare connects Roman history with human psychology, making his characters meaningful to readers and viewers centuries later.

The language of the play is also significant in conveying theme and relevance. Coriolanus has only one soliloquy, and apart from a few brief asides, the exposi-tion is entirely public, spoken only to other characters or in social and political sit-uations. Cominius's speech to the citizens in 2.2.82–122, for example, promotes Coriolanus as consul, a speech very recognizable in modern political terms as a form of promotional rhetoric. Other speeches, by Menenius, Volumnia, and Cori-olanus himself, are also expositions of political or philosophical positions, some-times intended as persuasive, sometimes (especially in the case of Coriolanus) explosions of angry denunciation about issues of social class, politics, or charac-ter. The people are the many-headed hydra or "the beast / With many heads" (4.1.1–2).

Shakespeare also uses imagery to convey his message. Menenius's use of the belly comparison (1.1.96–146) discussed above is actually a true extended analogy, but numerous shorter metaphors also characterize and define. Coriolanus is repeatedly called a "dragon" (see, for instance, 4.1.30), not simply to show the fierceness of his war-making but also to emphasize his isolation from human society, his singular status as an anomaly of nature. Thus, Menenius tells the tribune Sicinius, "This Martius [Coriolanus] is grown from man to dragon: he has wings, he's more than a creeping thing" (5.4.12–14). Another of Menenius's images from his address to the plebeian mob is "[Y]ou may as well / Strike at the heaven with your staves as lift them / Against the Roman state" (1.1.67–69)—an analogy that captures the futility of rebelling against the republic, which, like the planets and stars, proceeds in its course indifferent to the concerns of mere mortals. Images of ice and cold define Virgilia, while Coriolanus is hot and fiery. Strong emotions are expressed in cou-plets, like those that end 4.7, Aufidius's plan of action:

> One fire drives out one fire; one nail, one nail;
> Rights by rights fouler, strengths by strengths do fail.
> Come, let's away. When, Caius, Rome is thine,
> Thou art poor'st of all; then shortly art thou mine. (ll. 54–57)

Here, the imagery of Coriolanus and Rome as two fires whose strengths, when brought together, will destroy each other, is one Shakespeare has used to good ef-fect before, as in *The Taming of the Shrew* when Petruchio tells Baptista, "And where two raging fires meet together, / They do consume the thing that feeds their fury" (2.1.132–133).

Dramatic irony runs throughout the play: the irony of a great military hero being a mother's boy, the irony of Coriolanus wanting to be consul but not wanting to pay the political price, the irony of the egalitarian plebeians nevertheless needing their aristocratic defenders—all these contradictions lead to a sense of modernity and even modern dramatic irony in Coriolanus. Coriolanus is a tragedy about wanting it both ways and refusing to compromise or accept less than all that is desired. The Jacobean court in London had a darker, less optimistic view than the magnificent Elizabethan one that preceded it, and this harsher vision of human nature perhaps informs the play.

Finally, Shakespeare makes good use of a stage technique necessary in all history plays: small groups of actors run on and off the stage to represent the clash of thousands in battle. Action is reported rather than depicted, allowing the imagination to fill the tiny Shakespearean stage with compelling images of war.

## THEMES AND MEANINGS

*Coriolanus*, Shakespeare's last Roman play, also represents a new, darker phase of Shakespeare's career, one possibly reflecting the gloomier vision of the Jacobean court. The play, however, is also startling in its modernity, touching a number of twentieth- and twenty-first-century concerns. It is set apart from many of the works that preceded it. There are no noble kings in the egalitarian society of Rome, no clowns and jesters spending chunks of stage time on silly jokes, no songs or dances, no decent great men marred by a clear tragic flaw we can empathize with, no Horatio promising Hamlet he will tell the tragic story after the hero's death. The sudden, shocking assassination of Coriolanus offers no hope for the future. In a number of ways, Rome's landscape looks oddly like parts of our own: a powerful, accomplished society torn between social classes, the ordinary people easily distracted by the scandal of the moment and appeals to identity politics, demagogues who stir the passions of the many against scapegoats, guns-or-butter arguments pitting military safety against social welfare. In a way this similarity is not surprising: Rome had much more in common with modern nation states than did the small European monarchies of Shakespeare's early tragedies.

Perhaps the most fundamentally modern issue in *Coriolanus* is the proper role of the exceptional person in an egalitarian society. It has often been remarked that modern democracies set their rulers on impossibly high pedestals and then tear them down. Coriolanus is just such a figure, raised up when needed and then, because of his own unbending nature, torn down. The Renaissance looked upon its great figures with fear and fascination, both in literature (Christopher Marlowe's Doctor Faustus and Tamberlaine, Milton's Satan) and real life (Sir Francis Drake, Sir Walter Raleigh, Queen Elizabeth, Galileo). These overreachers grasped the new freedoms and knowledge of the Renaissance, felt liberated from medieval constraint, and generally accomplished wonders, but in doing so shook the foundations of their society, which valued their contributions but feared dramatic change and usually destroyed the superachiever. Raleigh was executed, his accomplishments notwithstanding. Galileo was silenced by the Inquisition.

*Coriolanus* looks forward to the problem of the will to power, the Nietzschean *übermensch*, or superman figure, running free in society. From Napoleon to Hitler, from Stalin to Mao, modern society has been terrorized by these evil geniuses, who turn on their comrades and own people with brutal ferocity. The heroic male warrior in his purest untamed form has practical uses for guarding the city, but what is to be done with him during peacetime? Critic John Holloway has called Coriolanus a typical "scapegoat figure," a disturbing influence in the society to be symbolically driven out to restore peace (cited in Arthur Eastman, *A Short History of*

*Shakespearean Criticism* [New York: Random House, 1968], 369). Exile seems a good compromise to the tribunes, but this sentence backfires when Coriolanus, his ego bruised by rejection, embraces Rome's worst enemy. Whether he represents the overreacher or the masculine principle out of control or some combination, a warrior such as Coriolanus cannot easily be pushed into the desert permanently like a biblical scapegoat. Figures like Coriolanus are part of society itself, to be endured or dealt with. Whether we agree with the majority of critics that *Coriolanus* is a play about such politics of control or see it as Swinburne did, as a play that focuses on the private, domestic history of an over-sized hero (*A Study of Shakespeare* [London: Chatto and Windus, 1880]), the problem is one for our time, not just for Shakespeare's.

A second modern theme is the role of nurture over nature. Coriolanus has clearly been shaped by his mother's upbringing in Roman warrior values; he is to a large degree a creature of his past and his setting. Few other Shakespearean heroes have their natures so linked to environment. The key to understanding Coriolanus lies in his childhood with Volumnia and his early patrician environment, a link between upbringing and behavior that is a cliché of modern psychology, both popular and academic. Linked to this emphasis on nurture is a gender issue with modern resonances: Coriolanus has been instilled with the most rigid warrior values since his first battle at the age of sixteen. True, a woman, Volumnia his mother, has been his tutor, but Shakespeare still puts the question before us: how damaging is the aggressive male principle distilled to its essence—damaging to society and damaging to the male himself? How much, too, is Coriolanus bound by gender and societal expectations whereby no show of weakness or deep emotion can be admitted? In a fascinatingly modern way Shakespeare looks at Coriolanus's nature as peculiarly male, rather than as simply natural for a great warrior. Bound up in Coriolanus's male identity is also the question of pride. His pride stems from his special skills and his heroic stature, but it keeps him from being an effective political leader and nearly prevents his yielding to the pleas of his family not to punish Rome. Volumnia, a stalwart Roman matron, is fiercely "masculine" in her martial virtues, and has proudly raised Coriolanus in this model of manhood. We understand through Virgilia, who is more conventionally "feminine" and deplores her husband's violent ways and his influence on their own son, a toddler going the destructive way of his father, that Volumnia's sentiments are no more natural than are Coriolanus's, for Virgilia is Volumnia's mirror image. How do two people of similar class and background turn out so different in their gender identities? Nowhere else in Shakespeare's works are gender questions confronted so directly and so seriously. These issues are as modern as the twenty-first century, a staple of current feminist analysis.

Another troubling modern theme that also bedeviled Shakespeare's Renaissance is the fear of mob rule. Actual revolution would face England at home and in America and France, but not until generations after the first performance of *Coriolanus*. Fear of mob rule, however, dated back hundreds of years in British history and runs through *Coriolanus*, which balances the equally abhorrent prospects of rule by an uncontrolled general always teetering on the edge of fury, and policy made on the streets by self-serving tribunes and their rabble-like followers. The whims of the "many-headed multitude" (2.3.16–17) are opposed by aristocratic disdain, patricians like Coriolanus who have no time for legitimate public concerns, such as the famine. *Coriolanus* exemplifies a common modernist dilemma, a lack of belief in monarchy and aristocracy and nervousness about the alternative, the tyranny of the "democratic" mob. The U.S. Constitution provides checks and balances to address these tensions, yet the choice between direct rule by the populace (as with special propositions to be voted on) as opposed to representative republican governance (the U.S. Electoral College is an example) remains controversial and divisive. Just as in Shakespeare's Rome, the passions of the moment can still swing public policy from one extreme to its opposite, and well-organized interest groups can easily trump both the general will and the common good. *Coriolanus* speaks loudly to us here.

In addition to these central themes, the play introduces many other concerns. There is the question of reputation, its power and its fleeting nature; the appraisal and standards of worth, whether based on military triumphs or civic contributions; and the distinction between words and deeds, an issue that relates to Shakespeare's ongoing interest in questions of appearance versus reality. Shakespeare is also considering questions of friendship and loyalty. Whom can one trust? Does the fact that two people fight on the same side make them automatic friends? Or can people be friends for a moment of common interest when in fact their values are totally antithetical? This concern relates to questions of rivalry as summed up in the relationship of Aufidius and Coriolanus. The gender roles and expectations in this play raise questions of proprieties and of the limitations placed on women. Virgilia is a model of passive acceptance associated with traditional female roles, but Volumnia stretches the boundaries of what it means to be a woman (or Roman woman) and shares masculine values with her son and grandson. Another recurring Shakespearean theme is that of fortune and fate, the degree to which human beings create their own fate or have fate thrust upon them: Is Coriolanus doomed no matter what choices he makes or actions he takes? The conflict between the patricians and the plebeians is central to this play. It is clearly a class conflict between the haves and the have nots, and it raises questions about why revolutions occur. But in some ways it involves a more significant conflict, that between the past way of doing things and progress toward other ways. The patricians stand for tradition, the past, the established ways and means of conducting the business of the state. The plebeians seek change and what they imagine is progress. Coriolanus is out of date, a holdover from the past who cannot find his place in a shift toward new governmental, social, and economic patterns and therefore a man who is doomed. In contrast, Menenius understands both positions and, standing in the middle, tries to support the best of the past and interpret it to those who will bring in the changes that will make up the future. *Coriolanus* thus speaks to us about ambition, social class, gender roles, and democracy as few other works of its time can. Shakespeare's tragic canon illuminates human nature as no other dramatist has, but with this play we are also given insight into the problems of the modern age that was just beginning.

## CRITICAL CONTROVERSIES

Early critics complained of a violation of tone in *Coriolanus*, such as when, for instance, Menenius, a senator of Rome, fails to measure up to the ideal of his office, and instead plays the buffoon. Modern critics recognize as a Shakespearean forte his ability to show realistically the differences between public and private speech. Menenius knows his audience, and Shakespeare is not bound by the classical requirements of decorum. Another early objection was the play's violation of the neoclassical unities of time, place, and action. Unlike most Greco-Roman tragedies, *Coriolanus* ranges over time and space and addresses various concerns, including the plebeians' political demands, military threats to Rome, and the famine. By the end of the eighteenth century, these concerns no longer influenced judgments of drama.

Throughout the history of critical investigation of the play the nature of Shakespeare's language has been in question, with one group asserting that it is unimaginative and others finding interesting and complicated patterns of diction in the play. David Lucking's "'The Price of One Fair Word': Negotiating Names in *Coriolanus*" (see bibliography below), Carol M. Sicherman's "*Coriolanus*: The Failure of Words" (*English Literary History* 39 [1972]: 189–207), and James Calderwood's "*Coriolanus*: Wordless Meanings and Meaningless Words" (*Studies in English Literature* 6 [1966]: 211–224) all focus on Coriolanus's limited rhetorical powers and trace his political failure to his inability to manipulate language. In contrast, G. Thomas Tanselle and Florence W. Dunbar in the *Shakespeare Quarterly* article "Legal Language in *Coriolanus*" (13.2 [Spring 1962]: 231–238) assert the complexity of language in this play, focusing in particular on the leitmotif of legal terminology used effectively. Caroline Spurgeon in *Shakespeare's Imagery and What It Tells Us* (Cambridge: Cambridge UP, 1935) explores the links between images of the body and disease and Shakespeare's theme, while J. C. Maxwell and Wolfgang Clemen in *The Development of Shakespeare's Imagery* (Cambridge, MA: Harvard UP, 1951) discuss the play's use of animal imagery, and G. Wilson Knight in *The Imperial Theme* (London, Oxford UP, 1931) sees metallic and mechanical imagery working together to make for unexpected and powerful links between characters and ideas.

Nineteenth-century author Algernon Charles Swinburne found the play a private, domestic, work rather than a public or historical tragedy—the story of a son's tragedy. This conflict between the play as a psychological study versus the play as an historical analysis persists in modern criticism (see Arthur Eastman, *A Short History of Shakespearean Criticism* [New York: Random House, 1968], 153). Wyndam Lewis called Coriolanus the coldest of all Shakespeare's heroes, one who never escaped his schoolboy notions of privilege and social distinction, a "machine of unintelligent pride" (Eastman, p. 233). He finds Coriolanus speaking frequently like a god, when, in fact, he is a conventional military hero, the product and ornament of a strong aristocratic system (ibid., p. 244). The question of the true nature of Coriolanus continues to be explored in critical articles. Does he embody the failings of the military mind and the need for citizens to keep tight controls on military leaders? Is he a pre-Freudian study of the effects of an overbearing mother? Is he a truly tragic hero, or is he villainous in deeds in spite of his sense of right? The nature of Coriolanus, of masculinity as defined by Coriolanus and his mother, and the military mind are at the center of many debates about this play.

Since the Renaissance, both Shakespeare's play and Plutarch's original story have served the political ends of various factions, mainly European. In some ways the work has served as a political Rorschach test, with groups having dramatically divergent philosophies finding in it grist for their mills. In fifteen-century Milan, long before Shakespeare wrote, city residents staged a Coriolan pageant to inspire civic support for a campaign against the Venetians. Fifteen different interpretations of the story were in print between 1625 and 1821.

A 1930s German translation of the play was taught in a textbook edition that introduced Coriolanus as a prime example of "valor and heroism . . . as Adolf Hitler in our day wishes to lead our beloved German fatherland" (Royal Shakespeare Company,

The Michigan Residence, The Plays, Coriolanus, www.umich.edu/pres/rsc/plays/corio lanus/onstage.html). After World War II, American troops banned the play in occupied Germany. In 1953, after what he called "two idiotic wars," Bertolt Brecht adapted *Coriolanus* for the German stage. His adaptation downplays Coriolanus's valor. That same year, Günter Grass's play *The Plebeians Rehearse the Uprising* echoed Brecht's efforts to produce *Coriolanus* amid the political upheaval in East Berlin. Ironically, a controversial 1935 Russian production at the Moscow Maly Theatre provided a Marxist take on *Coriolanus*, advertising the play as a "drama of individualism" showing "a superman who [has] detached himself from the people and betrayed them" (www.umich.edu/pres/rsc/plays/coriolanus/onstage.html). In other words, Coriolanus is either about the virtues of the *übermensch*, the larger than life military hero who is superior to other beings, or it is about the vices of the individualistic overachiever, who fails to fit in with his community of ordinary citizens and therefore must be purged for the good of society. These distinctly different stage interpretations of this play sum up in a nutshell the ongoing critical debate.

*Coriolanus* has been the heated subject of critical commentary and debate by critics and scholars from every point on the political compass, left and right and middle-of-the-roaders. It has been read as Shakespeare's conservative defense of autocratic rule, and as his liberal approval of democratic principles, communist economics, and revolutionary uprisings against oppressive dictatorships. It has been taken as a warning about the horrors of war, especially civil war, and the indifference of the military mind to civilian suffering. It has been read as a class conscious exploration of the tensions between upper-class and lower-class, and as a cynical study of the personal motives that drive most politicians and make their public selves quite different from their private realities. The debate over Shakespeare's political attitudes behind the public façade required to keep his head and stay in business will continue as long as his history plays and Roman tragedies are read and viewed. It is quite likely, in consequence, that modern American readers will see in Coriolanus a model for military heroes in wars abroad or a warning against trusting too much in a military establishment headed by out-of-control "Coriolanuses." As mentioned above, the play seems to serve as a psychological ink blot test, allowing readers and viewers the opportunity of projecting their most closely held political values into Shakespearean drama. Article titles reveal the directions of the debate: Bryan Reynolds's " 'What Is the City but the People?' Transversal Performance and Radical Politics in Shakespeare's *Coriolanus* and Brecht's *Coriolan*," in *Performing Transversally: Reimagining Shakespeare and the Critical Future* (New York: Palgrave Macmillan, 2003, 85–110); Paul Menzer's "Crowd Control: The Corporate Body on the Renaissance Stage," a 2002 dissertation for the University of Virginia; Alex Garganigo's "*Coriolanus*, the Union Controversy, and Access to the Royal Person," *Studies in English Literature, 1500–1900* (42.2 [Spring 2002]: 335–359); Paul Cefalu, " 'The End of Absolutism': Shakespeare's *Coriolanus* and the Consensual Nature of the Early Modern State," in *Renaissance Forum: An Electronic Journal of Early Modern Literary and Historical Studies* (2000: 4; http://search.epnet.com/direct.asp?an=2000060692&db=mzh); R. B. Parker's "Cori-Ollie-Anus-: Shakespeare's Last Tragedy and American Politics in 1988," *Shakespeare: Text and Theater: Essays in Honor of Jay L. Halio*, ed. Lois Potter (Newark: U of Delaware P, 1999, 194–208); and Francis Barker's "Nationalism, Nomadism, and Belonging in Europe: *Coriolanus*," in *Shakespeare and National*

*Culture*, ed. John Joughin and John Drakakis (Manchester, Eng.: Manchester UP, 1997, 233–265).

For further discussion of the critical controversy, see Bruce King's *"Coriolanus": The Critical Debate* (cited in the bibliography) and Lee Bliss's "What Hath a Quarter-Century of *Coriolanus* Criticism Wrought?" in *The Shakespearean International Yearbook*, vol. 2, "Where Are We Now in Shakespearean Studies?" ed. W. R. Elton and John M. Mucciolo (Aldershot, Eng.: Ashgate, 2002, 63–75).

## PRODUCTION HISTORY

*Coriolanus* was perhaps Shakespeare's first play to be performed at the private Blackfriars Theatre, which the King's Men began using in 1609. Shakespeare's chief tragedian, the forty-year-old Richard Burbage, probably played the lead. A Drury Lane playbill dated January 12, 1669, listed it as "formerly acted at the Blackfriars."

Nahum Tate produced a grisly political adaptation of the play at Drury Lane in 1682, entitling it *Coriolanus, The Ingratitude of a Commonwealth*. Its gory act 5 consisted of a succession of horrors of Tate's invention. Another Drury Lane adaptation, John Dennis's *The Invader of his Country, or the Fatal Resentment* (1719), was driven off the stage after only three performances. It had reduced the entire first act to one scene and sought to "improve" Shakespeare in other ways, particularly to make the play adhere more to the unities of time, place, and action by much cutting and pasting, to terrible effect. Dennis also made Coriolanus seem like the Stuart Pretender to the English throne, who had prompted an ill-fated attempt to wrest the crown from the Hanoverian George I in 1715. George C. D. Odell calls this play one of the most boring productions of *Coriolanus* ever (*Shakespeare from Betterton to Irving*, 2 vols. [New York: Charles Scribner's Sons, 1920], 1: 241). James Thomson's January 1749 blank-verse dramatization of *Coriolanus*, produced at Covent Garden, has very little to do with Shakespeare's play. It is Thomson's own creation, a unified, stately, rhetorical tragedy that explores the historical figure in ways Shakespeare did not imagine. Volumnia, the mother of Coriolanus, and Virgilia have only one scene as supplicants in the fifth act, though this scene does follow the spirit of Shakespeare's depiction of the women. The play begins with Coriolanus's coming to the Volscian camp and ends with a long harangue on the virtues and vices of Coriolanus. It was never acted again after its first season. In 1754 David Garrick revived Shakespeare's play for eight performances. Thomas Sheridan tampered with the play for a December 1754 production, omitting the first act, except for the scene with Veturia and Volumnia (Thomson's names for the characters), and mixing Thomson's recreation with bits and pieces from Shakespeare (Mrs. Pritchard played Volumnia).

Bell's 1773 printing of Shakespeare's play was from a Drury Lane prompt-book, an actor's version of the Thomson-Sheridan-Shakespeare mix. John Philip Kemble's 1789 version of the play followed the Drury Lane model, with additions from poet John Dryden. It was basically Shakespeare's version until act 3, after which it was cut heavily and reworked with bits from past productions (particularly inserts by Thomson) to emphasize the jealousy between Coriolanus and Aufidius. Volumnia draws her dagger and rants, threatening dire acts. Kemble was Coriolanus, a role he continued to play, usually with his sister, Mrs. Siddons, as Volumnia, until 1817. His performance was the first of many celebrated Coriolanuses. A sequence of

Ian McKellen as Caius Martius Coriolanus in Shakespeare's *Coriolanus* at the Olivier Theatre in the National Theatre, December 7, 1984. © Getty Images.

nineteenth- and early twentieth-century performances followed, with varying degrees of success, featuring the famous actors Edmund Kean, William Macready, Samuel Phelps, and Henry Irving. The American star Edwin Forrest, best known for his brawny portrayals of an American Indian chief, played the battle-scarred Coriolanus in the 1850s.

The Henry Irving 1901 Lyceum revival of *Coriolanus* was a Victorian spectacle of staging and pageantry, with what a *Times* critic described as, "tier after tier of white-robed senators seated in concentric semi-circles round the altar," rising as one to welcome Coriolanus with joyous shouts (Odell, 2: 456). Anthony Quayle, Alec Guinness, Richard Burton, Nicol Williamson, and Alan Howard have all played Coriolanus. Laurence Olivier performed Coriolanus in 1938 and again in 1959. In the final scene of the 1959 production, impaled by a half-dozen spears, he fell backward off a promontory some twelve feet above the stage and dangled there upside down, held by the ankles. This was a politically inspired image of Mussolini, whose corpse Italian partisans hung upside-down on a meat hook. Traditionally, what was called the Spy Scene (4.4) has been omitted from most productions.

Shakespeare provides some specific directions for performance in *Coriolanus*; for example, Coriolanus's listening to Volumnia's plea for Rome and watching her kneel and rise is followed by the instructions "He holds her by the hand, silent" (5.3), clearly a significant gesture that Shakespeare did not want left out. However, such production details seem irrelevant when the play takes on a life of its own and in the staging comes to stand for far more than what Shakespeare ever imagined. For example, the Riverside edition of Shakespeare's works (Boston: Houghton Mifflin, 1997) notes a famous Paris performance of *Coriolanus*, produced between World War I and World War II; ironically both Communists and Fascists rioted over the play because they construed it as propaganda against their respective causes (1442).

Mark Rose in *Shakespearean Design* (Cambridge, MA: Harvard UP, 1972) points out that Shakespeare's directions often produce a stage meaning missing from the words of the text. For example, after crowded scenes, the tribunes stay behind, drawing closely together, a visual act that marks their mutual dependence, which as individuals they do not admit. In 4.4 Coriolanus, banished from Rome, appears, according to Shakespeare's directions, "in mean apparel, disguis'd and muffled," a startling change from his patrician garb, one that captures his humiliation and shame more than do the words in his soliloquy. The power of the final scene likewise comes as much from the characters encircling the stage as from the protagonists.

## EXPLICATION OF KEY PASSAGES

**1.1.124–146. "I will tell you . . . but the bran."** Menenius's parable of the revolt by the parts of the body against the stomach is significant far beyond being a clever putdown of the plebeians (one of whom he calls "the big toe" [1.1.155], the lowest in the mob). The passage illustrates a key Renaissance concept. According to the Great Chain of Being, the explanatory model that underpinned the political philosophy of the time, different elements of the world and society exist in parallel analogical layers, each repeating the pattern of its neighboring "links" up and down the Chain of Being. Just as God is the Father to humanity, so the king is father to his country, and the ordinary father the absolute ruler of his household. Each repeated link reinforces the validity of the others; the world is seen as an orderly series of correspondences, similar by analogy rather than because of the laws of science.

The belly analogy is thus much more than a cute, clever metaphor. Just as each body part has its function, so each social class has its place, and any attempt to change that relationship, by electing tribunes, for example, violates the very laws of nature, evident even in the human body. Whether Shakespeare shared these beliefs is impossible to say. Coriolanus the character has many faults and excesses, but there is nothing in the play to suggest that Shakespeare supported the plebeians. Rather, the stomach analogy can be taken as a correction of Coriolanus as well as of his enemies: Coriolanus is overstepping his bounds just as they are, allowing his anger and emotions to usurp his proper role in society as a patrician leader.

**1.3.1–37. "I pray you . . . lose his hire."** Several scenes help define Coriolanus's nature. Volumnia's discussion of her maternal bonds as she talks with Virgilia and Valeria in 1.3 shows her to be the consummate Roman patrician matron: "I had rather had eleven [sons] die nobly for their country than one voluptuously surfeit out of action" (1.3.24–25). Virgilia's more conventional sentiments do not faze Volumnia at all; we can compare Volumnia to the famous Spartan mothers who told their sons to come home carried dead on their shields rather than empty-handed without them (fleeing soldiers threw away their shields to allow easier escape). For Volumnia, as for the Spartans, duty to country and tribe take precedence over any family feeling or personal connection. In fact, apart from his clear feelings for Volumnia and some warm speeches directed to Virgilia and of course his love for his son, Coriolanus lives up to the image of the dragon, alone in his den, a beast with which he is frequently associated throughout the play (for example, 4.1.30, 5.4.13). A great irony is that one of the warmest responses to Coriolanus comes from his old enemy, when Tullus Aufidius claims he is as happy to see him as he was to greet his bride on his wedding night (see 4.1.116–118). (The equation of battle and sex also recurs, suggesting that for these warriors, war substitutes for warmer domestic pleasures.) Taken together, these scenes suggest to a modern reader that Coriolanus has been emotionally stunted, valued, even by his mother, only for what he can provide to the state of Rome and made monstrous as a result. He has had few human connections, and is thus unable to form new ones with the citizenry, whom he regards as selfish and grasping, in complete violation of the value system with which he has been brought up.

**3.3.120–135. "You common cry . . . There is a world elsewhere."** This short speech is a capsule summary of Coriolanus's dramatic problem, his tragic flaw if we see him as an Aristotelean tragic hero. His choleric humor is so out of control that he lashes out at his plebeian tormentors, leaving no door open for a possible return to Rome. He calls the plebeians a "common cry of curs" (3.3.120), mongrel dogs in a ravening pack. Coriolanus thus reduces them to less than human. (Menenius and the tribunes have applied similar terms to the plebeians, but only when the plebeians were not listening.) His description of how he hates the plebeians' breath "As reek a' th' rotten fens" (l. 121) suggests not only a foul odor but also disease-inducing vapors. He is saying, in other words, "You make me sick." He goes on to state sarcastically that he values the love of the commoners as much as he does dead, unburied bodies, which, again, "corrupt my air," that is, breed illness (l. 123). His "I banish you!" (l. 123), besides being an empty threat that he lacks the power to enforce, seems petulant, the rejection of one who has been rejected. Aufidius's description of Coriolanus as "thou boy of tears!" (5.6.91) is not totally off the mark. Coriolanus also appears here as a hypocrite, since he was just soliciting the approval of the plebeians he now criticizes.

In the rest of this speech he condemns the plebeians to constant terror of their potential enemies until they are reduced to slaves by some weak enemy whom they no longer can defeat. In his final lines he literally and figuratively turns his back on his native city. His anger means more to him than his city, so that the charge of treason that Sicinius levels at him (3.3.66) appears to be not totally fatuous.

**4.5.101–135. "O Martius, Martius! . . . for Rome itself."** Aufidius here greets Coriolanus with effusive warmth, moving the plot along by making credible Coriolanus's quick acceptance by his old enemies the Volsces and the two warriors' proposed joint assault on Rome. Just as importantly, the speech highlights the martial values that drive both men. Aufidius's language is overtly sexual ("Let me twine / Mine arms about that body" [4.5.106–107]; "but that I see thee here, / Thou noble thing, more dances my rapt heart / Than when I first my wedded mistress saw / Bestride my threshold" [4.5.115–118]). Combat was a conventional metaphor for the sparring between men and women, as when a man "lays siege" to a woman. Here the imagery is ironically reversed, with the metaphor of love applied to the two warriors. For these men war has replaced love. Using imagery that again supplants love with war, Aufidius says that he has dreamt of fighting Coriolanus: "We have been down together in my sleep, / Unbuckling helms, fisting each other's throat" (4.5.124–125). One sees, too, that Aufidius is so given over to military life that he can speak of even the most intimate of relationships only in military terms.

Aufidius's speech also indicates that the alliance with Coriolanus is hardly secure: Aufidius has kept count of the times he has been beaten by Coriolanus (twelve) and has dreamt of more combats. Yet the bonds of war have linked the two men. Aufidius seems, and may in fact be, truly angry with Rome for banishing so valiant a fighter.

**4.7.28–57. "All places yields . . . art thou mine."** Just two scenes after greeting Coriolanus enthusiastically, Aufidius now reveals his true evaluation of his erstwhile foe and current ally and predicts what will happen after the anticipated victory over Rome. In the conflict itself Coriolanus will be like "the aspray to the fish" (4.7.34). According to Renaissance lore, fish yielded themselves to the osprey without a fight, acknowledging the bird's superiority. Aufidius recognizes that Coriolanus is flawed, and those flaws, pride, poor judgment, inflexibility, led to his banishment. Aufidius understands that "our virtues / Lie in th' interpretation of the time" (4.7.49–50). The qualities that earn praise in war will appear less admirable in peace. As a commentary on relativism, the notion that there is no permanent truth, only shifting interpretations relative to circumstance, Aufidius's observation is astonishingly modern. He goes on to say that "[P]ower, unto itself most commendable, / Hath not a tomb so evident as a chair / T'extol what it hath done" (4.7.51–53). That is, no achievement, however worthy of praise, will enjoy permanent recognition. Rather, it must rely on what the person in the seat of power says. Tombs have permanent tenants and stand for a long time. Chairs get new occupants and are themselves movable. Whereas Coriolanus believes that heroism is always admirable and so rejects relativism, Aufidius shows himself the modern man and the shrewd politician. Coriolanus cannot be "other than one thing" (4.7.42). Such constancy may appear to be admirable, but it is hardly the road to success in a world subject to flux. Aufidius concludes that just as one fire drives out another or one nail expels another, so one reputation replaces another, one hero supplants another in the popular mind. All is subject to time, chance, and mutability. To emphasize this point, Aufidius says that after Coriolanus becomes a hero by conquering Rome, Aufidius will supplant Coriolanus.

**5.6.70–115. "Hail, lords! . . . Alone I did it. 'Boy'!"** The final scene of the play picks up two themes introduced earlier: Coriolanus's attitude toward the commoners expressed in 3.3.120–135, and his sensitivity to charges of treason (3.1.163–170; 3.3.67–74). Coriolanus earlier had spoken of the infectious breath of the commoners. Now he returns triumphant, "No more infected with my country's love / than when I parted hence" (5.6.71–72), as if patriotism for Rome were a disease he has cleverly avoided. Indeed, Coriolanus regards love of any kind as a disease to be shunned because it represents weakness. The depth of Coriolanus's hatred for Rome can be measured by this image. His betrayal of homeland is no longer a breach of faith but an escape from the plague.

Coriolanus goes on to brag of the spoils he has won from Rome and the shameful peace treaty he has forced his former home to accept. But Coriolanus did yield to his mother's plea so far as not to destroy Rome. Aufidius, knowing how sensitive Coriolanus is about his honor, goads him by calling him a traitor for concluding peace "For certain drops of salt" (5.6.92). The reference is to the tears of Volumnia, though Aufidius may hint at bribery: salt was given as part of the Roman soldier's ration and lies at the root of the word "salary." Aufidius calls Coriolanus "Martius" and "Caius Martius" (5.6.86, 87), as one would address a boy. He denies the hero the name of Coriolanus. To cap the insult, Aufidius calls him "thou boy of tears!" (5.6.91). Aufidius is thus playing on the qualities he noted in Coriolanus in 4.7.29–57, and he gets precisely the reaction he had expected. Coriolanus addresses the Volsces with the same asperity he did the Romans in 3.3.120–135. He reminds his listeners that he "Flutter'd your Volscians in Corioles" (5.6.115) like an eagle in a dovecote. He is the noble, powerful bird, not a child.

What he says is true, but his words are hardly likely to gain him supporters among the doves he has fluttered. The people rush to kill him, remembering, "He kill'd my son!—My daughter!—He killed my cousin Marcus!—He killed my father!" (5.6.121–122). He thus dies as he has lived, intemperate, anger-driven, violent to the point of self-destruction, proud, heroic. Aufidius's plan, outlined at the end of 4.7, has succeeded, but as the play concludes even Aufidius acknowledges his enemy's nobility.

## Annotated Bibliography

Barton, Anne. "*Julius Caesar* and *Coriolanus*: Shakespeare's Roman War of Words." In *Shakespeare's Craft: Eight Lectures*. Ed. Philip H. Highfill Jr. Carbondale: Southern Illinois UP, 1972. 24–47. In a world dependent on verbal rhetorical persuasion, Coriolanus's distrust of language and his personal use of language without regard to audience response alienate and isolate him.

Coote, Stephen. *William Shakespeare, "Coriolanus."* New York: Penguin, 1992. This is a close investigation of the play and a good guide to help students start thinking about the tragedy.

Crowley, Richard C. "*Coriolanus* and the Epic Genre." In *Shakespeare's Late Plays: Essays in Honor of Charles Crow*. Ed. Richard Tobias and Paul Zolbrod. Columbus: Ohio UP, 1974. 114–130. *Coriolanus* merges tragedy and epic to explore the conflict between mercy and honor.

Datta, Pradip K. "The Paradox of Greatness and the Limits of Pragmatism in Shakespeare's *Coriolanus*." *CLA Journal* 38 (September 1994): 97–108. Datta criticizes the character of Coriolanus, explores his paradoxes and inner conflicts, considers the significance of his having no full-length soliloquy, and demonstrates the limitations of pragmatism in a warlike setting.

Givan, Christopher. "Shakespeare's *Coriolanus*: The Premature Epitaph and the Butterfly." *Shakespeare Studies* 12 (1979): 143–159. Givan considers Coriolanus's identity as revealed through his relationship to the Roman mob; asks why Coriolanus hates the mob; and explores the reasons for his self-destructive character.

Huffman, Clifford Chalmers. *"Coriolanus" in Context*. Lewisburg, PA: Bucknell UP, 1971. Huffman goes against the critical grain to argue that the Elizabethan political image of the Chain of Being that forbade rebellion and promoted order did not apply to Shakespeare's Roman plays, which in fact approved just rebellion. The "mixed government" of republican Rome created a very different context from that of the English history plays and the tragedies, where rebellion could be equated to domestic politics.

Hunt, M. "'Violent'st' Complementarity: The Double Warriors of *Coriolanus*." *Studies in English Literature* (Rice) 31 (Spring 1991): 309–316. Hunt believes the principle of complementarity illuminates the relationship between the warriors Coriolanus and Aufidius. She explores their self-destructive dialectical love/hate relationship, relates it to that of Othello and Iago, and makes clear the erotic overtones of Aufidius's welcoming speech.

King, Bruce. *"Coriolanus": The Critics Debate*. Atlantic Highlands, NJ: Humanities International P, 1989. King, as his title confirms, surveys and comments on the critical debate surrounding this play.

Lucking, David. "'The Price of One Fair Word': Negotiating Names in *Coriolanus*." *Early Modern Literary Studies* 2.1 (1996): 4.1–22. URL: http://purl.oclc.org/emls/02-1/luckshak.html. Lucking examines the critical argument that *Coriolanus* could be read "as a drama about names and naming, about who is empowered to name and on what basis, about what a name designates, and about the relation between names and identity" (p. 1). He finds the character Coriolanus deliberately disregarding the practical realities of language use that at times require ambiguity and subtlety. Instead, he speaks his mind, even when his ideas are insulting. He thereby keeps the political focus on himself. The paradox of self-identity is that the codes through which Coriolanus separates himself from his community derive from that community, as do the definitions of selfhood.

McAlindon, T. "*Coriolanus*: An Essentialist Tragedy." *Review of English Studies* 44 (November 1993): 502–520. *Coriolanus* is a political tragedy of class conflict and manipulation of power in a realistic, historically specific society.

McKenzie, Stanley D. "'Unshout the Noise That Banish'd Martius': Structural Paradox and Dissembling in *Coriolanus*." *Shakespeare Studies: An Annual Gathering of Research, Criticism, and Reviews* 18 (1986): 189–204. Amid chaotic reversals, betrayals, and paradoxes, where only the adaptable survive, the unchanging consistency of Coriolanus dooms him.

Miller, Shannon. "Topicality and Subversion in William Shakespeare's *Coriolanus*." *Studies in English Literature, 1500–1900* 32.2 (Spring 1992): 287–310. *Coriolanus*'s intricate structure of topical references draws direct parallels with James I and with early seventeenth-century issues of authority and monarchy, the conflicts and contradictions of Shakespeare's age.

Rackin, Phyllis. "*Coriolanus*: Shakespeare's Anatomy of 'Virtus.'" *Modern Language Studies* 13.2 (Spring 1983): 168–179. *Coriolanus* warns of the narrow, exclusive inadequacy of the Roman ideal. The hero's Roman virtues ironically are the vices that doom him.

Wheeler, David, ed. *"Coriolanus": Critical Essays*. New York: Garland, 1995. Wheeler provides a thorough production chronology, accompanied by major reviews and photos of the most representative *Coriolanus* productions in Britain and the United States. He includes critical commentary from the seventeenth century to the present, together with influential critical analyses. A critical introduction and three original essays on the play complete the volume.

# Timon of Athens

## Robert Appelbaum

### PLOT SUMMARY

**1.1.** A Poet, a Painter, a Merchant, and a Jeweler gather in Athens near the home of Lord Timon, a wealthy aristocrat. The Poet has written a book of verse he wants to dedicate to Timon, in return for a token of the latter's patronage—that is, money. The Painter has painted a portrait he wishes to sell to the wealthy Lord. The Jeweler has a gem for sale. How much are the commodities worth? How much will the generous Timon agree to give? The Poet and the Painter both play a game of false modesty, while also vaunting their abilities and the goods they have produced. The Jeweler is sure of the gem's value, but anxious about getting paid for it. The Poet, however hypocritically, has actually written a cautionary allegory about a person like Timon. In the allegory the goddess Fortune rewards the Timon figure, whom other men then clamor to follow. But soon Fortune changes her mind, and when Timon's luck changes, the others do nothing to help him.

Timon enters, followed by a messenger and various servants. The messenger reports that Timon's friend Ventidius has been thrown into jail for debt and needs Timon's help. Timon agrees to pay Ventidius's debts in full, and to help him recover financially. An Old Athenian appears on stage. He complains that his daughter is being courted by one of Timon's servants, Lucilius, who is socially and financially unworthy of her. Rather than forbid his servant to see the girl again, as the old man expects, Timon determines to elevate Lucilius and provide him with as much money as the old man's daughter is worth. In short order he then promises to reward the Poet and the Painter for their labors and also expresses his interest in buying the Jeweler's gem at an inflated price.

Apemantus, a cynic, comes along. He insults all around him, including Timon, accusing them of being fools, knaves, and liars. A young aristocrat, Alcibiades, appears on the scene along with a large retinue. Timon invites Alcibiades, Apemantus, and others in to feast with him.

**1.2.** A banquet at the home of Timon. Ventidius is there to express his gratitude and return the money Timon paid for him. Timon refuses the money. "You mistake my love," Timon says. "I gave it freely ever, and there's none / Can truly say he gives if he receives" (1.2.9–11). Timon and Apemantus argue about generosity and affection and the goodness of human nature. Apemantus thinks that all men are venal, ready to flatter one another with friendship when it suits their interest, and ready to kill one another when murder suits them instead. Apemantus scorns Timon, Timon's food, and above all Timon's so-called friends. Timon will have none of Apemantus's cynicism. He asserts, "We are born to do benefits" (1.2.101–102) and brings himself to tears at the thought of the friendships his generosity creates. He continues receiving and dispensing gifts.

"What will this come to?" Timon's steward, Flavius, worries (1.2.191). (The steward was responsible for managing a household, including its finances.) Timon in fact is running out of money but neglects his affairs. "His promises fly so beyond his state / That what he speaks is all in debt: he owes / For ev'ry word" (1.2.197–199). Timon even tries to exert his generosity on behalf of Apemantus. "Now Apemantus, if thou wert not sullen," he says, "I would be good to thee." "I'll [have] nothing," Apemantus replies. If Apemantus, too, were obliged to Timon, "there would be none left to rail upon thee, and then thou wouldst sin the faster" (1.2.236–240).

**2.1.** A Senator presses a servant, Caphis, to collect money that Timon owes him.

**2.2.** Caphis and the servants of other Lords (also identified as "usurers") approach Timon to collect debts that are past due. Timon, not understanding what is happening, goes off to confer with his exasperated steward. Apemantus and a Fool come by and swap insults with the money collectors. As Flavius and Timon return, the others exit. Flavius and Timon discuss the deterioration of Timon's financial situation. The steward claims that the problem was a long time coming, but Timon wouldn't listen when he tried to warn his master. Timon kept spending money on his friends. Now it is too late. Timon has no cash, and his lands have all been mortgaged or forfeited. As Flavius weeps in frustration, Timon forms a plan. "I am wealthy in my friends," he says (2.2.184). He orders three of his servants to go request loans from them. He sends the steward to ask for money from Ventidius, who has recently inherited a sizable estate.

**3.1.** Timon's servant Flaminius visits Lord Lucullus to request a loan. Lucullus claims that he has often chided Timon for his lavish lifestyle and dismisses Flaminius's request, saying, "[T]his is no time to lend money, especially upon bare friendship without security" (3.1.41–43).

**3.2.** Lord Lucius, visited by a man named Hostilius and a pair of strangers, is told that Lucullus denied Timon a loan, and Lucius expresses indignation. He would never have done such a thing, he claims. Then Timon's servant Servilius comes in to borrow money. Lucius sends him away, claiming that he has nothing to give. Hostilius and the strangers are indignant. This is the way of the world, says one stranger. "[A]nd just of the same piece / Is every flatterer's sport" (3.2.64–65).

**3.3.** A third servant visits the Lord Sempronius. Told that Lucullus, Lucius, and Ventidius have all turned Timon down, Sempronius replies that he is insulted that Timon has come to him last. He sends the servant away empty-handed: "Who bates mine honor shall not know my coin" (3.3.26).

**3.4.** A group of money collectors, some of them servants of men whom Timon had greatly benefited, converge on Timon's home. The steward briefly appears to tell the money collectors off and assure them that there is no money in the household left to collect. Timon himself comes out "in a rage" (s.d. after 3.4.78). First he inveighs against his creditors. "Cut my heart in sums. . . . Tell out my blood. . . . Tear me, take me, and the gods fall upon you!" (3.4.92–99). Then he reappears with the steward, still in a rage but saying he will throw one more grand feast for "the rascals" (3.4.112).

**3.5.** Timon's friend Alcibiades—possibly Timon's only true friend—pleads before a tribunal of Senators on behalf of a man never identified. The man has killed his opponent in a duel. Alcibiades pleads for mercy and praises the man's valor and sense of honor. The Senators take exception to Alcibiades arguments. As Alcibiades continues to seek ways to extenuate the man's guilt and lessen his punishment, a Senator responds: "We are for law, he dies, urge it no more" (3.5.85). When Alcibiades persists, the Senators condemn Alcibiades to exile.

**3.6.** Another banquet at Timon's house. The guests seem to think that Timon was only fooling when he claimed to be poor and asked for loans from his friends. As they sit down to the banquet Timon offers a surprising prayer to the gods on the theme of generosity and gratitude that quickly turns to bitterness and curses. He concludes, "For these my present friends, as they are to me nothing, so in nothing bless them, and to nothing are they welcome. Uncover, dogs, and lap!" (3.6.82–85). The dishes are uncovered; they are full of nothing but warm water. The banquet ends in a riot, as Timon throws the water in the faces of his guests, curses them, and drives them out.

**4.1.** Outside the walls of Athens, in another mock prayer Timon hurls curses at the town and all its people: "Plagues incident to men, / Your potent and infectious fevers heap / On Athens, ripe for stroke!" (4.1.21–23). He then determines to live alone in the woods, away from detestable mankind.

**4.2.** Back at Timon's home, his servants mourn their master's turn of fortune. They do not respond as employees about to lose their jobs; they mourn for Timon, not for themselves. Flavius offers to pay the servants what he can out of his own savings and says to them all, "Let's yet be fellows" (4.2.25). He resolves to find Timon and continue to serve him.

**4.3.** Timon in the woods is still cursing mankind. "All's obliquy," he says (probably meaning: all is "obliquity," that is, immorality). "There's nothing level in our cursed natures / But direct villainy. Therefore be abhorr'd / All feasts, societies, throngs of men!" (4.3.18–21). He proposes to feed himself on nothing but roots, but as he begins digging he finds gold, something he now despises.

Timon's friend Alcibiades enters, marching through the woods with an army and accompanied by a pair of prostitutes, Timandra and Phyrnia. Alcibiades had been away, in exile, during Timon's troubles, but now comes to make war on his native city, Athens. He offers to help Timon with money, but Timon refuses, and offers Alcibiades his own newly discovered gold instead. He gives the prostitutes money while inveighing against them, and against Alcibiades too.

After Alcibiades and the two women leave, Timon keeps digging and finally finds a root to eat. At that moment Apemantus arrives. Apemantus has come because he has heard that Timon is imitating his cynicism. He tells Timon to return to Athens and get back into the good graces of his old friends—by way of flattery, of course. "Do not," he says, "assume my likeness" (4.3.218). The two argue at length. Apemantus claims that Timon is a cynic only by chance, and only superficially. Timon claims that being a cynic is easy for someone like Apemantus, who never had any luck in life; if Apemantus had been successful, he wouldn't have been a cynic. "But myself," Timon says, "Who had the world as my confectionary, / . . . I to bear this, That never knew but better, is some burthen" (4.3.259–267). Apemantus tries to be kind to Timon, but Timon refuses his attentions. They swap insults and Apemantus departs.

Bandits then come by. Timon insults them, but says that in being thieves they are no different from anyone or anything else. He gives the bandits money, and enjoins them to go out and steal more from Athens, which is a land of thieves. But Timon's actions instead persuade them to reform their ways and lead honest lives.

When the bandits leave, Flavius comes by. At the sight of Timon in his present state, Flavius is moved to tears. He asks to serve Timon again. Timon is moved to remark that here at last is an honest man. He gives Flavius some gold and wishes him well, but also wishes that Flavius use his money to do ill.

**5.1.** The Poet and the Painter, having heard that Timon is giving away gold, come to visit the recluse. He sends them away with nothing. Flavius and two Senators of Athens enter. The Senators tell Timon that the city needs him back to help fend off the army of Alcibiades. They promise that the city is ready to "blot out what wrongs" he has suffered (5.1.153). Timon sends them away, saying that if any Athenians wish to avoid affliction, they are welcome to a tree in Timon's woods on which they may hang themselves.

**5.2–3.** As Alcibiades makes war on Athens, a soldier finds a grave and a grave marker that says "Timon is dead" (5.3.3). Unable to decipher the inscription on the tomb, he makes a wax impression to bring to his captain.

**5.4.** Alcibiades and his army appear before the walls of Athens. Senators on the walls sue for peace, making various excuses for the behavior of the city toward Alcibiades and Timon. Alcibiades accepts their terms, which give Alcibiades full satisfaction for his grievances; he enters the town as a conqueror. A soldier enters to announce the death of Timon and reads the epitaph that was inscribed on the tomb:

> Here lies a wretched corse, of wretched soul bereft;
> Seek not my name: a plague consume you, wicked caitiffs left!
> Here lie I, Timon, who, alive, all living men did hate;
> Pass by and curse thy fill, but pass and stay not here thy gait. (5.4.70–74)

## PUBLICATION HISTORY

*Timon of Athens* was first printed in the First Folio of Shakespeare's works in 1623. It was included among the tragedies, between *Romeo and Juliet* and *Julius Caesar*. That space had originally been intended for *Troilus and Cressida*. A problem with that play's copyright delayed its inclusion, so *Timon* was inserted in its stead. Because *Timon* is considerably shorter than *Troilus* (eventually included in the First Folio between the Histories and Tragedies), there is a gap in the pagination between *Timon* (ending on page 99) and *Julius Caesar* (beginning on page 109).

Because of certain features of the text, such as the fact that its stage directions are unusually ample and clear, it is likely that it was prepared from an authorial working draft, that is, from Shakespeare's foul papers. However, given certain inconsistencies in style and dramatic development, it is sometimes thought either that Shakespeare was not the sole author of the play, his contemporary Thomas Middleton usually being supposed the second author, or that the play as received by the printers was incomplete. There is no record of any performances of the play in Shakespeare's lifetime, and there are no references to contemporary events in the play that would help determine its date of composition. Because of its affinities with certain other plays in theme or language, it is usually placed after *King Lear* and among the last tragedies, along with *Coriolanus*, but some editors date it before *King Lear*, closer in time of composition to the similarly pessimistic *Troilus and Cressida*.

As is often the case, the historical background of *Timon* is many-layered. Three layers in particular are worth mentioning. The first is the period of the historical Timon, a notorious "misanthrope" or man-hater who lived in Athens at the time of the Peloponnesian War (430–404 B.C.). A contemporary and friend of the equally notorious Alcibiades, Timon is said to have been a prominent aristocrat of the late fifth century B.C., who, as a result of the ingratitude of his friends, turned into a bitter cynic and went to live in solitude, keeping company with no one except Alcibiades and the town clown Apemantus. Both Plato and Aristophanes mention Timon, Aristophanes having written a comedy now lost of which Timon was the subject. Plato also includes a famous scene in his dialogue *The Symposium* in which the historical Alcibiades appears; Alcibiades praises his beloved Socrates as the one man who could make him feel ashamed of himself.

Shakespeare does not fully exploit this historical background; he does not fully develop the cause of Alcibiades's troubles with the Athenians, or even examine the meaning of the great events underlying the story of Alcibiades and Timon. For the most part he keeps the focus on Timon's misanthropy as if it were something apart from the political controversies of the day, leading at least one critic, A. D. Nuttall, to suggest that *Timon* is in that respect an "ahistorical" play. At the very least, however, the background of the Peloponnesian War must be in the minds of any members of an audience who have been educated in classical culture and history—such members as formed a large part of Shakespeare's original public—and the underdeveloped but important subplot concerning Alcibiades's conflict with Athenian government refers directly, if vaguely and inaccurately, to the politics of late fifth century B.C. Athens.

Apart from the historical Timon, there is a second layer of history, the legend of Timon as the very type of the misanthrope. It is worthwhile considering what such a figure could have meant to various peoples in various regions and eras up to Shakespeare's own. In classical culture the misanthrope would seem to have represented a rejection of all that classical humanism stood for. If, as the Greek philosopher Protagoras had put it, "Man is the measure of all things," then misanthropy represented a rejection not only of men but of the measure of life, the very standard by which the life of man was to be assessed. The idea is not innocent of absurdity, and the legend of Timon made it clear that Timon had personal and perhaps pathological motives for his misanthropy and that the moral posture of misanthropy, though intriguing, is not philosophically coherent. However, misanthropy could also be associated with the respectable philosophical movement known as cynicism, which first flourished in the fourth century B.C. at the hands of such famous spokesmen as Antisthenes, a disciple of Socrates, and above all Diogenes of Sinope. Cynics like Diogenes, of whom the play's Apemantus is a type, eschewed the comforts, the conventional morality, and the fictions upon which they thought Greek civilization was based. Diogenes was famous for having moved to

Athens and lived as a beggar and marketplace philosopher, attempting to call people to a more natural, ascetic, and honest way of life. The word "cynic" means "dog-like," perhaps in reference to the idea that cynics lived like dogs, in the street, begging for food, or perhaps marking the idea that cynics spent their time sniping at the heels of the citizenry, barking against the folly of mankind.

The philosophical attitude of cynicism was handed down to the humanists of the Renaissance, in a witty and malicious but perhaps unthreatening form, in the Greek writings of Lucian of Samosta (A.D. 120–ca. 180). Lucian wrote philosophical dialogues and tracts combining prose and verse in the form of what is now known as Menippean satire, in deference to a famous satirist named Menippus. His own writings are now lost, but a fictionalized Menippus appears as the hero of many of Lucian's writings. Lucian's Menippean satires had a direct impact on Renaissance humanism, inspiring such important works as Sir Thomas More's *Utopia* and Erasmus's *The Praise of Folly*. Shakespeare's *Timon of Athens* is the Bard's contribution to the genre. Among later contributions to Menippean satire on the theme of misanthropy are the rather tamer but greatly admired play by Molière, *The Misanthrope*, and Jonathan Swift's *Gulliver's Travels*.

The legend of Timon played a role in the culture of Elizabethan and Jacobean England, and the figure Timon appears in many writings of the English Renaissance. Given his story, Timon, interestingly enough, often appears in the context of discussions about commerce and usury, the lending out of money at interest. Many critics have thus discerned in Shakespeare's *Timon* a third layer of history, for the play is concerned with a conflict between an aristocrat, living by the ideals of traditional aristocratic hospitality, and the world of merchants and moneylenders, who operate according to an antithetical system of values. The practice of hospitality was central to the cultural, political, and social identity of the landed gentry. This hospitality included not only the patronage of the arts and sciences, as in Timon's financial support of the Poet and the Painter, but more importantly the playing of host to society at large. Lavish feasting and gift-giving, as Timon engages in it, was a practice by which members of the gentry marked their importance to society and communicated their power, economic and otherwise, over the natural and social resources of the country.

But even as the pressure to live lavishly pressed harder and harder on the landed gentry of the time, the economy of Shakespeare's day often militated against the aristocratic way of life. Money was being made in new ways: through trade, banking, and large-scale quasi-industrial activity, like glass-making. In this new world of commerce and money, traditional aristocratic affinities had only a limited role to play. Many aristocrats themselves joined in with the spirit of the times and set themselves up as successful businessmen; but the values defining and supporting the exalted social status of the aristocrat had little to do with the practice of modern commerce.

One register of the transition from a traditional landed economy, animated by values of aristocratic hospitality, to a moneyed, mercantile economy, animated by the profit motive, was found in changing attitudes toward usury and debt. Christianity and even a long-standing classical tradition, with its origins in Aristotle, were contemptuous of lending money at interest. And many a writer of the English Renaissance continued the tradition, fulminating against the practice, even though it was becoming more and more widespread, and crucial to economic growth. But by the time of the publication of Francis Bacon's *Essays* (1597–1625), we often hear sentiments like those expressed in that work: "Since there must be borrowing and lending, and men are so hard of heart as they will not lend freely, usury must be permitted" (*Francis Bacon, Oxford Authors*, ed. Brian Vickers [Oxford: Oxford UP, 1996], 421).

In Shakespeare's play, the historical and legendary figure of Timon of Athens stands in part for the uncompromising English aristocratic, who won't bend to the new rules and conventions, and thereby destroys himself. But the self-destruction of the wealthy gentleman could be explained not only as a failure to compromise with capitalism, but also as a misunderstanding or abuse of traditional aristocratic privilege. "Many times," wrote the Oxford scholar Robert Burton, "that word [hospitality] is mistaken, and under the name of bounty and hospitality is shrouded riot and prodigality; and that which is commendable in itself well used . . . hath become by his abuse the bane and utter ruin of many a noble family. For some men live like a rich glutton, consuming themselves and their substance by continual feasting and invitations" (Robert Burton, *Anatomy of Melancholy* [New York: New York Review of Books, 2001], 108). Some scholars have noted that among those gentry who flirted with ruin by devoting themselves to lavish hospitality, there was none more visible and familiar to Shakespeare than the new king of England, James I.

## SOURCES FOR THE PLAY

For information about Timon Shakespeare drew on brief accounts included in two of Plutarch's *Lives*, the "The Life of Marcus Antonius" and the "The Life of Alcibiades." The complete *Lives* had been translated into English by Sir Thomas North as *Lives of the Noble Grecians and Romanes* in 1579, and Shakespeare used the translation extensively for his other classical plays: *Julius Caesar, Antony and Cleopatra*, and *Coriolanus*. Shakespeare may have also used Lucian's dialogue "Timon the Misanthrope," which had recently been published in a French translation and which Shakespeare may even have studied in its Latin version while in school. A manuscript survives of a play known as *Timon*, a comedy that has been dated as early as 1601 and as late as 1611. It is possible that Shakespeare drew upon the play, but it is also possible that the *Timon* comedy drew upon a version of Shakespeare's *Timon of Athens*. Clearly Shakespeare's *Timon* enters into dialogue with the comedy and similar texts of the day. The "malcontent" was a common figure in early seventeenth century drama, and real cynics like Diogenes as well as Timon are sometimes discussed or even personified in the writing of the period.

## STRUCTURE AND PLOTTING

No play by Shakespeare is more schematic in its structure than *Timon of Athens*. The first half of the play shows Timon thriving as a philanthropist, a lover of men, performing kindnesses and bestowing gifts and grants to everyone he can. The climax of his generosity is represented in the course of a lavish banquet. He then suddenly finds himself deeply in debt, betrayed by his friends, and helpless. So he throws a second banquet, this one the opposite of the first, and he behaves as the opposite of a benefactor, throwing everyone out. In the second half of the play Timon appears wholly converted into a misanthrope, a hater of men. If he was once at the center of cultural life of Athens, he is now in self-imposed exile, living in the woods. People from the town pay him visits, and he rejects them all. Nothing much happens because no one can entice Timon out of his isolation and his contempt for humankind. Later, back in Athens, after his fellow exile Alcibiades has returned in triumph to the town, Timon's death is reported, and with his death an epitaph through which Timon excoriates mankind from beyond the grave.

This schematic structure is what the detractors of the play have most decried. Shakespeare's other plays are more organic. They exhibit a development of impulses and ideas, of personalities in process and events in motion, that moves the action along an arc from beginning to middle to end, where each part seems to fit with another, and resolution comes in a mode of tragic loss or comic recovery. In *King Lear*, for example, a play which otherwise has much in common with *Timon*, Lear's self-imposed exile, in response to the ingratitude of his family and friends, leads not only into madness but into insight, acknowledgment, and redemption. His sojourn into nature and his experience of the fragility of human dignity bring him into a condition where he can eventually rejoin the world of civilization, though only by being caught up in a plot of warfare that he himself let loose, and only therefore in a mode of tragic loss. Similarly, in the comedy of *As You Like It*, another play with which *Timon* resonates, an exile into the forest, in response again to the failures of civilization in the guise of the failures of kindness and gratefulness ("Blow, blow, thou winter wind, / Thou art not so unkind / As man's ingratitude" [2.7.174–176]), provides the means by which problems can be sorted out and adjustments made in human relationships, and its characters may happily return to civilization.

In *Timon of Athens* such common Shakespearean modes of development are thwarted. The play does not feel resolved in the end. The characters do not change and grow in the course of coming to terms with their problems. The plot does not develop in a way to resolve fundamental conflicts and disturbances in the world of the characters. In the second half of the play there is little dramatic conflict to speak of, and the work ends with neither a tragic nor a comic resolution. Timon is not even allowed to commit a tragic suicide at the end (although admittedly, the source material said nothing about a suicide, either). He simply dies: by what means we do not know. Even one of the more admired bits of stagecraft in the play, the sequence in act 3 where Timon's requests for money are turned down by four different characters, the last rejection being handled offstage, is schematic rather than fully worked out. One, two, three, and then four episodes in which beneficiaries of Timon's generosity show themselves to be self-seeking hypocrites and scoundrels all follow in order to prove a point that is as logical as it is dramatic: Timon's friends are contemptibly ungrateful, exactly worthy of the curses Timon will hurl upon them and the inhumane humanity he takes them to stand for.

Although it is hard to overcome the feeling that *Timon* suffers by comparison with other Shakespearean plays, which seem to be better constructed in terms of character and plot, the schematic form of the play may well be part of its message, and hence a part of its strength as a dramatic essay. To the extent that *Timon* is not only a play about a misanthrope but an exploration of the meaning of misanthropy, its schematic shape serves to underscore the crippling and paradoxical nature of the hatred of mankind: misanthropy in this play is something apart; it is something that makes people unable to participate in the usual course of human affairs; it cannot enter into the usual plots and twists of human drama. What looks schematic about the play may well be considered rather as an expression of the play's dialectic: its development of an argument that exposes the nature of misanthropy, its causes and implications, by way of a case study based on legend.

That argument is not only suggested by what is being called the dialectic of the drama's plot; it is also suggested by the symbolic terrain of the play. As Timon's generosity climaxes on the occasion of a feast, and his turn to misanthropy is climactically signaled by a second feast of water, smoke, and stones, so the story of Timon as a whole is largely structured by Timon's symbolic relation to food and feeding. His beneficiaries are said to have "tasted" him (1.1.274). Apemantus, by contrast, marks his refusal to go along with Timon's sponging followers by saying, "I eat not lords" (1.1.204). Timon's self-appointed role in society is that of a nurturer, both in the general sense of being someone who "nurtures" the welfare of others—their careers, needs, and ambitions—and in the specific, partly metaphoric and partly literal sense of being someone who feeds and thus "nourishes" everyone who comes to him. Even inanimate objects seem to have been fed, or rather feasted, by his bounty. When, in a rage, Timon thinks himself momentarily locked into his house, he refers to it as "The place which I have feasted" (3.4.82).

Later, when Timon is trying to live as a hermit in the woods, he seems to define his condition by insisting that he is someone who will now eschew feasts and live on roots (4.3.20–23). From great meals, where such meat-eating is practiced as that a hint of man-eating is never too far below the surface, to a fake meal where there is nothing to eat at all, and finally to solitary feeding in the woods where only root vegetables—such as wild turnips—are to be consumed, Timon's descent into misanthropy is figured as a change in Timon's relation to food and feeding. Significantly, even as Timon tries to live alone on roots he continues to find himself in significant, complex relations to food, feeding, and nurturing. Digging for his root, he finds gold—probably, someone's forgotten buried treasure—and is disappointed. "I cannot eat it," as he says to Alcibiades, when the latter offers him yet more (4.3.101). Still concerned to find a root to eat, instead of more gold, which he cannot eat, he exclaims, "That nature being sick of man's unkindness / Should yet be hungry!" (4.3.176–177). When he encounters Apemantus in the woods, Timon begins eating the root that he has finally discovered in the earth and exclaims, "That the whole life of Athens were in this! / Thus would I eat it" (4.3.281–282). Yet ironically, provided in the woods with nothing but a root to eat and a cache of gold he will not use to buy any commodities, Timon's relation to others is still a relation of giving: he remains a benefactor to Alcibiades, to Timandra, to Phrynia, to Flavius, and to the thieves, giving them un-nurturing gold.

As a kind of counterpoint to the structuring theme of feeding, Shakespeare also introduces a few other repeating figures and ideas. The imagery of dogs is perhaps the most notable. A cynic is a "dog." A dog in that sense is outwardly someone whose words are sniping and offensive and whose own condition is despicable. "Y'are a dog" says the Painter to Apemantus (1.1.200). But perhaps there is a dignity to the doghood of the cynics. Dogs in themselves in this play are mainly lowly, mangy, potentially dangerous creatures. "Grant I may never prove so fond / To trust . . . a dog that seems a-sleeping," says Apemantus in his mock prayer (1.2.64–67). But from a cynical or misanthropic perspective they are at least better than men. "For thy part," says Timon to Alcibiades when they meet in the woods, "I do wish thou wert a dog, / That I might love thee something" (4.3.55–56). However, dogs in Shakespeare are also commonly figures of fawning servility: thus, when Timon says at the second banquet, as noted above, "Uncover, dogs, and lap!" (3.6.85), he uses "dogs" in the sense of lowly, shameless, and unctuous creatures. The very way they drink (by lapping) suggests their lowliness; the fact that they would eat from a dish given to them (and placed on the ground) by someone else only confirms the point. The suggested image, that when given their dishes of food these noble guests are at least spiritually or symbolically wagging their tails with delight as they put their heads into their plates, only underscores how people can lack any hint of dignity. So throughout the play "dog" bears a diversity of meanings, some of them at opposite poles to one another: the dog as gadfly, the dog as a reproach to the pretentiousness of civility; the dog as a dangerous and mangy creature; the dog as an object of affection; the dog as a sign of shameless servility and flattery; the dog as an undignified tail-wagging bundle of appetites. Shakespeare is not making a comment on the nature of dogs; but, using a variety of received ideas about the nature of dogs (and the people who called themselves "cynics"), he colors the drama with what in music would be called a recurrent theme or leitmotiv, which both adds coherence to the dialogue and troubles its meaning. Nor is the dog imagery the only structuring element of this kind. There are others: "bounty," "kindness," nature, disease (plagues and venereal disease), whoredom.

## MAIN CHARACTERS

Just as the plot of *Timon* is the most schematic or dialectic to be found in Shakespeare's plays, so its characters, at least among the tragedies, may be the most one-dimensional or stereotypical: embodiments of ideas and moral tendencies rather than rounded individuals. Apemantus, Flavius, the Painter, the Poet, even Alcibiades (who in the source material is a very complex figure), not to mention the hypocritical Lords, the two prostitutes, and the thieves, all seem to represent types of people and behavior rather than full-fledged human beings. Apemantus is of course the cynic, with some affinities to other gadflies in Shakespeare, like Jaques in *As You Like It*, and the Fool in *Twelfth Night* or *King Lear*. Flavius is the good and faithful servant, with affinities to old Adam in *As You Like It* and Kent in *Lear*. The Painter and the Poet are sycophants and parasites: artists for hire. Alcibiades is the military man, obeying a code of honor for which violence is a prime resort. The others, similarly, are embodiments of specific ideological types and moral tendencies, and never deviate from the givens of their natures. To be sure, there are hidden dimensions to some of the characters. Beneath his sniping, Apemantus has a soft spot for Timon and is not incapable of kindness. When, in his final scene with Timon, he is caught up in trading insults once again, expressing contempt for his interlocutor, he is clearly goaded by Timon—and even more clearly loses the match of wits, perhaps because he is less motivated than Timon. Flavius is not just a loyal servant: he is loyal in the face of the many trials that Timon's behavior imposes upon him, and generous and kind to those below him in the social order, an advocate of fellowship. Alcibiades is likewise seen to be a true friend to Timon, motivated by both a sense of obligation and genuine affection. The Painter and the Poet, hypocritical sycophants though they are, are complex in their art. They intend to flatter their patrons at all costs, and yet their art is apparently subtle and spirited. The Poet's allegory of Fortune, contrived to flatter Timon and win his approval, is also cautionary: it is a moral tale that warns Timon about the danger he is courting. It is perhaps contrived in a spirit of spite as well. After all, in the Poet's allegory, the Timon figure, at first beloved by Fortune, eventually falls, suffering humiliation at the hands of the men he took to be his friends.

Timon is the obvious exception in this play. And yet Timon, too, may be interpreted as being one-dimensional. "The middle of humanity," Apemantus says of Timon, "thou never knewest, but the extremity of both ends. When thou wast in thy gilt and thy perfume, they mock'd thee for too much curiosity [that is, fastidiousness]; in thy rags thou know'st none, but art despis'd for the contrary" (4.3.300–304). An extremist, either too loving or too hateful, either too lavish or too sparing, Timon cannot act by degrees. He never knows what it means to behave prudently, cautiously, self-reflectively. He always embodies either too much generosity toward men or too much contempt. When prosperous he won't hear of anything negative, whether about the quality of men or the state of his finances. When poor, he won't hear anything positive.

There are, however, depths to Timon, only they are such depths as lead to singlemindedness. Timon was the stuff of legend, and a fitting subject of Shakespeare's art, precisely because of his all-or-nothing response to life. He is not content to be a kind or sociable person: he has to be everything to all people, asserting, "We are born to do benefits" (1.2.101–102) and finding in friendship a fraternal community of wealth: "O, what a precious comfort 'tis to have so many like brothers commanding one another's fortunes!" (1.2.103–105). Conversely, he will not stop at being angry at his erstwhile friends or bitter at his lot. He must be a misanthrope, hating all men for all time, and he must be contemptuous of the universe as well.

## DEVICES AND TECHNIQUES

*Timon* is the kind of play where it is almost impossible to talk about "devices" and "techniques" without really talking about structure and meaning. The clusters of images, metaphors, ideas, and linguistic forms that are woven through the drama are as much a part of what the drama says or argues as are character, plot, and theme. One of these image clusters concerns eating. Flavius the Steward responds to Timon's creditors by asking,

> Why then preferr'd [presented] you not your sums and bills
> When your false masters eat of my lord's meat?
> Then they could smile, and fawn upon his debts,
> And take down th' int'rest into their glutt'nous maws. (3.4.49–52)

By the time Flavius makes this remark we have heard about the eating of Timon's meat a number of times. We have seen some of Timon's presumed creditors at table with him. We have already been advised (by Apemantus's language) that there may be something inherently parasitical or even cannibalistic about "eating Lords," and we are made aware of the idea that feasting may be not only noble and handsome, as Timon thinks it is, but also somewhat disgusting. Flavius's insult is yet another moment in the ongoing discourse of eating and dependency that runs throughout the play. This particular moment in the discourse comes with a bang, but it comes with a bang we have been prepared for.

The argument Flavius is making includes the following chain of ideas: (1) your masters had a chance to ask for their money when they were the beneficiaries of Timon's hospitality; (2) in not doing so they betrayed their falseness; (3) they smiled and fawned while receiving his hospitality and dining at his feasts; (4) smiling and fawning, they disguised their gluttony, which is to say their selfishness. But that is not all. The argument also deliberately conflates "earning money" with "devouring food." And so it implies (5) that being given the opportunity of devouring food at no cost to oneself is equivalent to taking advantage of financial transactions for profit at someone else's expense (for example, by lending money at interest). It is such, at least, if one devours the food in a selfish spirit, and to excess, that is, gluttonously. Of course, the argument doesn't really work from a logical point of view. Taking food and taking interest are not equivalent. But the language develops a kind of dramatic pressure on the world of Timon. It might even be said to stoke a kind of dramatic conflict. If generosity is figured as a form of feeding others, and if operating in the world of finance is a form of taking care that one is fed, at least two kinds of conflict arise. One is between Timon the giver and his creditors the receivers. Since their transactions lack genuine reciprocity, their dealings with one another are unequal and unstable. Neither the giver nor the receivers can be entirely satisfied: Timon can never give the love he wants to give; the creditors can never get their money.

A second conflict, even worse, is metaphysical. The demand on Timon's side for pure giving and therefore pure receiving is met by a demand for prudent business dealings and therefore calculated giving and receiving. As neither demand can give way, a pressure is built up whose only release may well be an escape, as in Timon's flight into the woods and into an economy of hatred where giving is all but impossible except in an attempt not to advance but to undermine the welfare of the receivers.

Throughout *Timon of Athens* one encounters moments like this, where figures of speech turn into arguments with a faulty but inexorable logic, leading to irreconcilable conflict. The chief "device" or "technique" of this play is to enclose the characters and their audience in an imaginary and symbolic space from whose inherent conflicts there is no possible resolution and no satisfactory escape.

The Alcibiades subplot is not fully developed, but it does offer an alternative to Timon's misanthropy. Historically, Alcibiades was an Athenian general during the Peloponnesian War. When the Athenian Assembly turned on him, he defected to Sparta but then was reconciled with the Athenians (though he later again was rebuffed by Athens and went over to the Persians). In *Timon of Athens* he has reason to hate the Athenians, but after the city surrenders, he promises to "use the olive with my sword" (5.4.82). That is, he will not be vindictive. Earlier in act 5, when the Athenian Senators seek reconciliation with Timon, he tells them to hang themselves. Timon and Alcibiades thus become exemplars of excess and moderation, respectively.

## THEMES AND MEANINGS

The main themes of the play are clear: hospitality is in conflict with prudence; the desire for love and friendship is in conflict with the need of self-preservation and the hope for prosperity; the habits of the aristocracy are in conflict with the demands of a moneyed economy; the love of mankind may be just another side of the hatred of mankind; from a general hatred of mankind there may be no escape; gold may well be an enemy to mankind too. As feminist scholars have shown, the attitudes toward life that Timon displays both in his philanthropic and misanthropic modes may be founded in misogyny. In the first case, the philanthropist attempts to take the place of the woman as the nurturer of society. (Significantly, there are no women in the world of the first part of the play, except as Amazon dancers.) In the second case, the misanthrope denies that women have any place in the world except as whores. He maintains that "a dozen of them" out of twelve will "be—as they are" (3.6.78–79). As for the way of the world of men, it may well be an inhospitable place altogether, although it is built on fine sentiments. Certainly it would seem to have need of cynics, who refuse to buy into the pretensions of the world to higher ideals. A cynic is not the same thing as a misanthrope, though. The two use the same language, but for different purposes. Apemantus the cynic has a social function; like Shakespeare's fools, he rails against society in order to keep it honest. Timon the misanthrope has no social function at all.

Perhaps the meaning of the play depends on a response to the inherently illogical or irrational but persuasive figures of speech and emotions of the play. Perhaps Timon errs when he cries out for a community of friendship that includes shared wealth (1.2.102–103). But his vision has its appeal. His subsequent cynicism is equally one-sided, and yet it, too, has its logic:

> The sun's a thief, and with his great attraction
> Robs the vast sea; the moon's an arrant thief,
> And her pale fire she snatches from the sun;
> The sea's a thief, whose liquid surge resolves
> The moon into salt tears; the earth's a thief,
> That feeds and breeds by a composture stol'n
> From gen'ral excrement; each thing's a thief. (4.3.436–442)

Even if we acknowledge the appeal of figures and emotional outbursts, however, we have not fully come to terms with the meaning of the play. What, finally, does it mean to be confronted with a spectacle of misanthropy, which in the above example expands into a hatred of the universe? Where are we supposed to stand in relation to it? What does the existence of the imaginative possibility of cosmic misanthropy mean for us? Even the best of critics have yet to answer that question.

The play illustrates a conflict that Shakespeare often addresses in his work: that between an older, idealistic, aristocratic view of the world and an efficient, pragmatic new order. Timon initially believes that "We are born to do benefits" (1.2.101–102), that among friends wealth is held in common. He discovers that this lovely vision is false; only the cash nexus links people. For personal gain a Talbot (*1 Henry VI*), a Clarence (*Richard III*), an Edgar or Lear (*King Lear*) will be sacrificed without compunction. So here all those whom Timon has helped refuse to aid him. Long before Edmund Burke pronounced its epitaph, Shakespeare shows that the age of chivalry is dead.

## CRITICAL CONTROVERSIES

Critics have early on—indeed, at least as early as the Restoration—responded to what seems to be the failings of the play as a drama. "I have made it into a play," boasted the playwright Thomas Shadwell in 1678 on publishing his much revised version of the text (Thomas Shadwell, *The History of Timon of Athens, the Man-Hater* [London, 1678]) By the nineteenth century critics were urging that parts of the play could not have been written by Shakespeare, that some material included in the text must have been taken down in an incomplete form, or that Shakespeare himself never bothered to finish the work. Critics now agree that some parts of the play may well be by Thomas Middleton, a worthy playwright on his own account who frequently collaborated with other writers and whose language is often similar to the language of *Timon* in terms of its mechanics; many also now agree, however, that it is almost impossible to say precisely which parts are by Middleton. The speech cited above, for example, "The sun's a thief," contains a somewhat slogging chain of analogous metaphors, expressed in verse that scans irregularly, leading toward a weakly phrased generalization: "each thing's a thief."

Such a speech may seem to be unworthy of Shakespeare but just the kind of artifact one expects from a fine but lesser pen like Middleton's. But the failings of the speech may be deliberate, where the master poet has Timon unable to break past the mechanical figures and awkward rhythms of his obsessive anger. Critics also now agree that there are undeveloped parts of the play and loose ends in it. The Alcibiades subplot, for example, seems truncated. It is hard to see how the author of the related play *Coriolanus* could have failed to take the opportunity to explore the relationship between democracy and timocracy (the rule of honor) in *Timon*. At the first banquet hosted by Timon the masque of "Amazons" is brought onto the stage. It seems peculiar that the masque is not written out, as was (say) the magnificent wedding masque in *The Tempest*. But critics continue to disagree as to why such material is missing.

That the play is nonetheless powerful in its own right, even if it lacks the force of a more amply developed drama like *Lear*, or even *Coriolanus*, is now more or less taken for granted. However, critics debate in what that power consists, in how Shakespeare intended for audiences to respond to it, and what significance lies in the ideological and psychological conflicts of the play.

Critics do not often take Timon's misanthropy seriously. That is, they seldom regard it as anything but a symptom or product of something else. It is clear that, like the sources he seems to have drawn upon, Shakespeare takes pains to explain Timon's misanthropy, to show it as a consequence of frustration at the ingratitude of his friends. So critics have focused on examining the causes and contexts of that frustration, and largely read the play as a function of that. Thus there are critics who have read the play as a commentary on the rudeness of such times as would frustrate the genuinely noble impulses of a man like Timon. That reading of the play lent itself to the view that in *Timon* Shakespeare was precociously critiquing what would become the political economy of capitalism. In this interpretation, both the impulses toward aestheticism among mid-twentieth-century critics and the example of Karl Marx have been relevant. Aestheticism can find little but disappointment in the cultural effect of capitalist society. Marx saw capitalism as a destructive power that broke apart all the traditional bonds of society in favor of the impersonal bonds of capital itself, and much admired Timon's speeches about gold, "This yellow slave" (4.3.34), "thou sweet king-killer, and dear divorce / 'Twixt natural son and sire!" (4.3.381–382). If Timon is a noble man at heart ("Unwisely, not ignobly, have I given," Timon insists [2.2.174]), then it is the ignobleness of the times, devoted to capital symbolized by gold, that brings about his ruinous conversion to misanthropy.

But is Timon genuinely, or unambiguously noble in his behavior? Many critics, along with Apemantus, have seen Timon's devotion to hospitality as itself a pathological condition. Others, noting that it may be both pathological and appealing, have turned to psychology or history for explanations. Psychoanalytic criticism can find infantile wishes animating Timon's early behavior, and an equally infantile reaction emerging as a result of the frustration of his infantile demands. Feminist psychoanalytic criticism can add that these are infantile drives and reactions that are to be associated with masculinity, which must wrestle with an egoistic need to both merge with and destroy the maternal safeties of childhood. These drives can perhaps be found in particularly aggravated form in the age of Shakespeare, where family relations were being reinvented, confusing the structure of male identity, and where a king came to replace a queen at the center of power. This king found a need to play the role of nurse to his people and also found, increasingly, that he was personally driven by homosexual rather than heterosexual inclinations. But the main historical explanation behind Timon's frustration may lie more precisely in the problem of coming to terms with the new moneyed economy, which thwarted aristocratic needs even as it also encouraged aristocrats to undertake escalating expenditures. In that sense, a man like Timon could be frustrated not in opposition to the tendencies of his society but in his very attempts to live in agreement with them.

Still, what is missing is an attempt to assess what happens when we are confronted with the spectacle of Timon's misanthropy. Granted, we can fabricate explanations for why Timon became a misanthrope: the play encourages us to do so. But what are we to make of the experience of misanthropy and the challenges it wants to level against the ways of humankind? What are we to say or feel when Timon refers to "My long sickness / Of health and living" (5.1.186–187)? Is life, as he implies, ultimately a disease? Are we not, at the very least, required to respond to the idea that it is possible to think that it is? And when we find that to the very end Timon will not deviate from his hatred of men, including himself in the thing he hates, refusing all solace, all tenders of friendship and mitigation, are we not being asked to be shaken out of our complacencies, our easy verities? Does the play offer any reason to think that mankind ought instead to be loved? Does it provide any reason to want to avoid the extremes, and neither hate nor love mankind, but simply accept it, to adopt the "lukewarm" stance that Timon alludes to in the second banquet scene? Does it make us think that simply accepting mankind is an acceptable alternative? As a Menippean satire as well as a tragedy, *Timon of Athens* is unsettling.

## PRODUCTION HISTORY

There is no record of any performance of *Timon of Athens* during Shakespeare's lifetime. That does not mean that it was never performed, but no evidence of any stage tradition for the play exists prior to Shadwell's rewriting of the play as *The*

Timon (James Earl Jones, left), fallen from his noble position in Athens, is comforted by his servant Flavius (James Greene, right) in a scene from *Timon of Athens*, directed by Lloyd Richards. Yale Repertory Theatre, 1980. Courtesy of Photofest.

*History of Timon of Athens, the Man-Hater* (1678). Shadwell's adaptation, which among other things inserts a love interest and often included music, was successful on the stage for decades. It was further revised by other hands in the late eighteenth century. Something approaching Shakespeare's original text was finally produced on the London stage in 1816, where the famous tragedian Edmund Kean played the title role movingly and romantically, with grandeur and passion, calling attention to Timon's battle with despair. But it was not until the 1920s that the play was performed with the text as given in the First Folio. Since then, the play has been performed sporadically in theaters across the world: never the most popular of plays in performance, it has often proved to be among the most provocative.

*Timon of Athens* was among the first modern-dress performances of Shakespeare on the English stage (in Birmingham, in 1947), and it has since provided many opportunities for directors to explore the uses of tragic satire in an age when playwrights around the world were exploring tragically satirical and satirically tragic material. The plays of Brecht, Beckett, Sartre, and others have provided inspiration for treating the play as a darkly humorous or bitter encounter with the wages of injustice and alienation. Prominent directors like John Schlesinger (Royal Shakespeare Company [RSC], 1965) and Peter Brook (RSC, 1962; Paris, 1971) have tried their hand at it, often in a spirit of experimentation, and noted actors like Paul Scofield (RSC, 1965), Richard Pasco (Stratford-upon-Avon, 1980), and Michael Pennington (RSC, 1999) have played the title role. Trevor Nunn directed a modern-dress production at the Young Vic in 1971, with David Suchet in the title role. In that year Joseph Papp presented *Timon* at New York's Shakespeare Festival in Central park, with Sheppard Strudwick in the title role. Walter Kerr (*New York Times*, July 11, 1971) and Clive Barnes (ibid., July 2, 1971) expressed disappointment with the acting. Jazz great Duke Ellington wrote much admired music for it, originally performed in Stratford, Ontario, in 1963 and revived by the Royal Shakespeare Company in 1999. The modern tendency is not to romanticize the figure of Timon or worry too much about the Jacobean context of the play. It has been instead to make the play into a case study either of madness, of existential angst, or of disparities in a given society between action and intention, between words and deeds, and between human needs and the dehumanizing demands of commerce.

## EXPLICATION OF KEY PASSAGES

**1.2.88–108. "O, no doubt, . . . I drink to you."** One of the lords at Timon's banquet complains—insincerely, as we soon find out—that Timon has never given his friends a chance to reciprocate his gifts. Timon's response is to assure the lord that he has nothing to worry about. He seems to want to say that there will be opportunities for reciprocation, even if none has arisen so far. But the tenor of his argument is that between friends there is such a bond that the idea of reciprocity is inadequate. The proof of friendship that the lord fears he has been unable to make is unnecessary. Since I have already chosen you as my friends, Timon says, I do not need any proofs. Do you not "chiefly belong to my heart? I have told more of you to myself than you can with modesty speak in your own behalf" (1.2.92–94). Yet Timon goes on to assert that people always in fact need their friends, and even "have use" of them (1.2.98). If we do not need and use our friends, they are like musical instruments stored in their cases, and never played.

But what kind of use or need is he talking about? He goes on to express the idea that friends are like brothers who command one another's fortunes, but it seems to be the potential use of someone else's money and not the use itself that he treasures. And the thought, surprisingly, brings him to tears. Timon seems to be trying to work his way through a paradox. He believes that he is not trying to buy friendship by his gifts. The friendship comes first; gifts are only a natural expression of it. But by entering into an economy of gift-giving, friendship is what Timon sees himself experiencing. It is what he receives. Only friendship as Timon (and a long tradition behind him) understands it is never something received; it is only something given.

**4.1.1–41. "Let me look . . . Amen."** Several passages in the second half of the play show Timon emphatically contradicting the sentimental paradox of civil friendship that earlier brought him to tears, and progressing from anger at his particular circumstances to a generalized anger, and from spite against his friends to spite against first the Athenians, then all of humanity, and finally the universe itself. In 4.1 Timon finds himself outside the walls of Athens, hurling curses at the city and its people, wishing that whatever restraints there are among the people to keep them from debauchery, violence, and suffering should be let slip. "Piety, and fear, / Religion to the gods, peace, justice, truth, / Domestic awe," and so forth, are the things that keep humanity in a state of civilization, and in his anger they are the things that Timon wants to see "Decline" to their "confounding contraries" (4.1.15–20). For it is only what the people of Athens deserve, given their unkindness, and in response Timon can only pray to the gods that the Athenians may suffer a social collapse and that Timon's hatred for the Athenians "may grow / To the whole race of mankind" (4.1.39–40).

**4.3.1–48. "O blessed breeding sun, . . . out for earnest."** Timon calls upon the sun to act not as a creative force, a giver of light, heat, and life, but as infective agent, and bring about illness and unhappiness. Timon's curses soon slide into bitter observations about human nature: "There's nothing level in our cursed natures / But direct villainy" (4.3.19–20). Hence, he is determined to live alone, feeding on roots. When he discovers gold instead, he finds something at once inside nature (since gold occurs naturally as a mineral) and outside of it (since it is the significance humans attach to it that gives gold its value) that is only worthy of his contempt. In gold he finds an explanation for the depravity of human affairs. "This yellow slave / Will knit and break religions, bless th' accurs'd, / Make the hoar leprosy ador'd" (4.3.34–36). His anger mounts as he calls upon "damn'd earth, / Thou common whore of mankind" to yield gold in order to continue subverting society (4.3.42–43).

**4.3.416–448. "Your greatest want . . . Amen."** Timon is inspired by his encounter with the bandits (having been inspired earlier by Apemantus's inadequate cynicism, Alcibiades's inclination to warfare, and the prostitutes' trade in lust and venereal disease) to see the universe as a corrupt and venal organism. The ways of the bandits are only an example of how everything in the world exceeds what would seem to be its proper limits, grasps at things beyond its natural needs, and steals its livelihood from other creatures. When Timon asks why the bandits have to steal, since nature bears enough of its own to sustain the lives of men, the First Bandit declares, "We cannot live on grass, on berries, water, / As beasts and birds and fishes" (4.3.422–423). Human beings need more. But you thieves, Timon replies, cannot live "on the beasts themselves, the birds and fishes; / You must eat men" (4.3.424–425). One would think that there are alternatives: for example, if not living on berries, then living on the products of agriculture. But thievery rather than honest labor is for Timon at this point the very essence of the order of things. When Timon finally tells the Bandits, "Love not yourselves, away, / Rob one another. There's more gold. Cut throats, / All that you meet are thieves" (4.3.444–446), he has perhaps hit bottom, the nadir of his misanthropy. Theft is the opposite of gift-giving, the provision of bounty. Not only is murder, likewise, the opposite of the nourishing of men that the bounteous aristocrat is supposed to stand for; but murder by throat-cutting is a violent act that first of all attacks the gullet, the very vessel of nourishment that a bountiful patron is dedicated to provide.

### Annotated Bibliography

Adelman, Janet. "Making Defect Perfection: Imagining Male Bounty in *Timon of Athens* and *Antony and Cleopatra*." In *Suffocating Mothers: Fantasies of Maternal Origin in Shakespeare's Plays, "Hamlet" to "The Tempest."* New York: Routledge, 1992. 165–192. Shows how Timon's misanthropy often turns to misogyny. Contempt of the female, and a desire to replace the female with masculine bounty, is the prime source of Timon's hatred of men.

Bevington, David, and David L. Smith. "James I and *Timon of Athens*." *Comparative Drama* 33.1 (1999): 56–87. Argues that an important though not definitive parallel can be drawn between Timon and James I, James being "the most visible and influential practitioner of large-scale extravagance" in Shakespeare's England (57). The parallel shows how the fictional Timon never understood that his generosity was motivated by self-interest: his unspoken desire to buy influence, friendship, and status.

Fischer, Sandra K. "'Cut My Heart in Sums': Shakespeare's Economics and *Timon of Athens*." In *Money: Lure, Lore, and Literature*. Ed. John Louis DiGaetani. Westport, CT: Greenwood P, 1994. 187–195. A brief article explaining two competing systems of metaphor and idea on the subject of money and usury. It argues that Timon never learns the lesson about modern economic behavior and the claims of human bonds that was available for him to learn.

Jackson, Ken. "'One Wish' or the Possibility of the Impossible: Derrida, the Gift, and God in *Timon of Athens*." *Shakespeare Quarterly* 52.1 (2001): 34–66. A clear attempt to apply insights of deconstruction to the paradoxes of gift-giving and gift-refusing in the play, with a view toward modern Christian and Judaic existentialism.

Kahn, Coppélia. "'Magic of Bounty': *Timon of Athens*, Jacobean Patronage, and Maternal Power." *Shakespeare Quarterly* 38.1 (1987): 34–57. Couples psychoanalytic, feminist, and new historicist critical practices, focusing at once on deep fantasies of the maternal body and topical resonances in the play. Anticipates the article by Bevington and Smith (above) by looking at the extravagance of James I and examining the cultural meanings of gift-giving. Anticipates Adelman (also above) by seeing the gift culture of Timon (and James I) as an effort to co-opt the principle of female bounty and subsist on a "primitive identification with a powerful maternal woman" (54).

Klein, Karl, ed. *Timon of Athens*. Cambridge: Cambridge UP, 2001. Left incomplete at the time of the editor's death, the editorial apparatus is not without flaws, but it is still a useful critical edition of the play and contains invaluable material on authorship and stage history.

Nuttall, A. D. *Timon of Athens*. Boston: Twayne, 1989. Not really an introductory guide to the play, as the series title suggests. It is rather a brilliant scene-by-scene reading of the text emphasizing ambiguities, ironies, inconsistencies, and dead ends, and laying to rest many traditional interpretative controversies.